Old Testament Theology

Biblical Hermeneutics Rediscovered

The Series as the name suggests will focus on Biblical Hermeneutics, i.e., literary works concerned with methods of interpreting the Old and New Testaments of Bible via different stream of topics like Literature & Poetry, Indigenous Philosophizing, Ethical response towards Ecology, Health & Healing, Science & Technology, Feminist Theology, Sociological approach towards Human Rights, Law & Politics, Arts, History of Ideas, Ancient Civilizations, Cultural Contiguity, Religious Cosmologies & Mysticism, Appraisal of various Theologians, World Peace & Harmony, Global Capitalism, Network Marketing, Cybertheology, Population & Demographics, Epigraphic Studies, Contextualized Education, and many others. We welcome a Mss. on any topic/s mentioned, whether they are original works, scholarly monographs, collections of conference papers, revised dissertations, or translations of historical documents. Through the Series we, the Publishers, are striving to put forward published works that may help Institutions, Academic Bodies, Researchers, Scholars and the World at large in furthering their respective knowledge and understanding on the concerned subject. We welcome your comments on our efforts and further suggestions on how we can enshrine new ray of analysing & explaining the written Texts through our upcoming books.

Biblical Hermeneutics Rediscovered - 3

Old Testament Theology

History, Issues, and Perspectives

Kondasingu Jesurathnam

Christian World Imprints

Edition : 2022

Christian World Imprints
Christian Publishing & Books from India
A-71 Group, Wazirpur Industrial Area
Delhi-110052
cwidelhi2017@gmail.com
www.ChristianWorldImprints.com
Phone: +91 11 41526079

ISBN : 978-93-5148-151-5 (HB)
ISBN : 978-93-5148-152-2 (PB)

Printed in India.

Dedicated to the students of theology at various institutions I taught all over the world whose insights, comments and critical observations shaped the material in this work.

Prologue

Writing a text-book is both exciting as well as laborious in today's world where we see the revolution of communication media. No one will have time and interest to read big volumes of materials as patiently as it was done some decades ago. Yet the written documents and text-books like this sort will have their own worth and cannot be replaced with any other simple ways of communication. It is interesting to note that despite several negative tendencies to give less importance to the Old Testament in the Indian Christian theological and church context over against the New Testament, Old Testament has always been a popular part of the Holy Bible among the common people in India. In order to avoid a lot of misconception on the reception and use of the Old Testament in India it would be better for us to make a detailed study on the history of the discipline of the Old Testament Theology from the nineteenth and twentieth centuries of Christian era. In several church preaching sermons and other meetings and theological schools the Old Testament is taught only in relation to the New Testament. That shows how the Old Testament is made as a mere forerunner to what is described in the New Testament. This type of erroneous understanding of the Bible must be stopped. The main objective of this volume is to clarify and remove such a reductionistic view of the Old Testament. This volume fosters the idea that the Bible is one comprehensive whole of God's salvation history manifested and fulfilled in the faith communities from the times of the Old Testament (OT), New Testament (NT) and even today. Moreover, both the church and academia has the tendency to compartmentalize the issues and themes within different parts of the OT and the NT. Such fragmentation lacks an integrative approach to the reality of God's ways of working in the communities of faith.

In the light of the above discussion the present volume on Old Testament theology endeavours to present the material related to the subject matter as a comprehensive whole in order to see the entire Bible as single plan of God's salivific activity for God's people from ancient times till today. This does not mean that we are advocating for a monolithic ideas in all different trajectories of faith expressions in the Bible. Even when there are diverse views and opinions of the authors they all serve to communicate the liberative purpose of God's mighty deeds in this world and in the entire creation.

With the above plan the work is divided into four major sections: First section summarizes the historical antecedents of the discipline of the OT theology in the nineteenth and twentieth centuries. This section will enable the readers to clearly see where the OT theology stands today. Second section deals with some issues in the Old Testament that cannot be easily resolved and thus require a fresh approach in every epoch so that every interpretive community will have an opportunity to look and appropriate such issues in a meaningful way. Third section takes up the themes both in historical sequence and theological manner in an integrated way. This will enable the readers to see how the comprehensive approach of the biblical themes serve the purpose of understanding of God's dynamic liberative work in the lives of faith communities then and now. Fourth section probes in detail select themes of Old Testament by reflecting on them theologically and in relation to Indian contextual application concluding with the task of OT theology in the Indian context as on today.

Selected bibliographic entries are given at the end to enable the readers to probe further on the subject according to their choice and interest.

I trust and hope that this volume serves the purpose and goal mentioned in the above lines and wish the readers to have some grip in the subject matter under consideration.

I take this opportunity to thank several people before concluding this prologue section. Thanks to all my MTh students of Old Testament at the United Theological College, Bangalore with whom I interacted and had elaborate discussions over the last several years of my teaching. Thanks to the staff at UTC library for their help in getting the appropriate materials. Above all I thank my wife Beatrice Veena and son David Sunil for their understanding when I had to spend several hours at the study table before my computer in writing this material.

To God be the glory who by his wisdom teaches us everything that is beyond our comprehension and understanding and from whom I learn and cherish every second of my life.

Kondasingu Jesurathnam
March 2016

Contents

Introduction

The rise of Old Testament theology as a discipline distinct from the dogmatic theology did not occur until the eighteenth century A.D. Until that time, all theology was considered to be biblical, or the distinction between dogmatic theology and biblical theology was not really grasped and executed. The Bible was understood as the repository of the very truth that the theologians sought to delineate in a systematic manner. The Bible was thus seen as the basis for the theological enterprise and no tension was perceived between biblical faith and contemporary formulations as doctrines of the church. It was a long struggle in the history to argue and assert independence for the Old Testament Theology as a distinct discipline. We shall return to this issue later in the course of our discussion while talking about the other aspects of the history of the discipline.

One of the fundamental questions in our study is to talk about the definition of OT theology or what is OT theology? It is not an easy task to define what OT theology is. However, a preliminary attempt could be made in this regard as follows: OT theology is systematic presentation of various aspects of faith of the OT religion as they are reflected in the Old Testament. Some would even argue that OT theology does not merely stand in conformity with the Old Testament, but it is that theology described and contained in the Bible.

One of the difficult tasks for the scholars in the initial stages of Old Testament theology was to define the nature, function and scope of OT theology. For a long time the issues related to this was not resolved as they continue to debate until they settled for some consensus. We shall look at few proposals of the leading scholarly opinions in this regard.

Walther Eichrodt states that the task of OT theology is descriptive. By which he means that OT theology is supposed to present a coherent and systematic presentation of the Old Testament material. In other words Eichrodt is of the view that the task of OT theology is to "construct a complete picture of the Old Testament realm of belief."[1] By this Eichrodt wanted to suggest that the study

1 Walther Eichrodt, *Old Testament Theology*, Vol. 1, trans J. A. Baker (Philadelphia: The Westminster Press, 1960), p. 25.

of the Old Testament theology is scientific and systematic and also it is to be considered as historical discipline.

Quite apart from the above definition Gerhard von Rad[2] states that the task of OT theology is constructive, systematic, apologetic and normative. This view leads us to think that the Old Testament literature may be seen in the perspective of systematic and dogmatic theology. If we accept this view then the Old Testament theology is basically confessional and dogmatic.

Claus Westermann[3] is of the view that the task of OT theology is "summarizing and viewing together what the Old Testament as a whole in all its sections says about God."[4] By this Westermann reiterates similar descriptive approach earlier proposed by Eichrodt. Similar to Westermann, Walther Zimmerli states that "any OT theology has the task of presenting what the OT says about God as a coherent whole."[5]

The above discussion reveals that on the one hand OT theology serves as a bridge between the work of historical criticism (understanding the context) and the needs of contemporary theology and preaching. On the other hand OT theology is also concerned with biblical text and its contemporary relevance.

Another important question that the scholars always debated was the scope of OT theology. The question raised in this regard is: should OT theology include materials within the Old Testament canon or materials outside OT canon (Deutero-canonical material etc.)? Should OT theology include all the Old Testament in all its details or can it be developed with some fair representative coverage that will present the interest of a total OT theology? To address this issue we may point out by saying that the scope of OT theology may be restricted to the canonical books of Jewish collections because to include Apocryphal and Deutero-Canonical books would weaken the purpose of discussing the wholeness of OT theology. We must note at this point that the scope of OT theology should also involve us to go beyond the history of Israelite religion. This issue continues to surface in all the scholarly debate and we shall deal with this later in another section. We must be cautious to know that in OT theology we cannot take the individual texts and treat them as individual bricks or in other words we cannot be selective in dealing with the material of the Old Testament in OT theology. We need to look at the material in unity. In this way OT theology is distinct and has its own individuality as a distinct discipline quite apart from the New Testament, although at many places Old Testament points to the New Testament issues and theology in order to show a vibrant connection between the OT and NT.

2 Gerhard von Rad, *Old Testament Theology*, Vol. 1, trans D. M. G. Stalker (London: Oliver & Boyd, 1966), p. 28.

3 Claus Westermann, *Elements of Old Testament Theology* (Atlanta: John Knox Press, 1978), p. 22.

4 Ibid.

5 Walther Zimmerli, *Old Testament Theology in Outline* (Atlanta: John Knox Press, 1978), p. 21.

In the above light, we may argue that care should be taken that in doing OT theology we must consider it as an exegetical discipline on its own right and not an aid to construct systematic theology. In this line the plan of the present work could be seen as follows:

The first section of the present book deals with the issues and concerns related to the historical foundations of the discipline of the Old Testament theology beginning from 18th century CE both in the ecclesial and academic circles. The issues in this regard involve the very coining of the term "Biblical Theology" and other related trends associated with it. The trends like scholastic orthodoxy, pietism, rationalism, philosophy of Hegel, influence of conservatism and salvation history school, and history of religions school and so on the emergence and development of biblical theology will be dealt briefly in this section. All these issues should lead us to the point to see how the decline and revival of Old Testament theology took place during the early 20th century.

The second section takes up some continuing and debatable issues in relation to OT theology for a detailed discussion and reviews their present situation. Issues and debatable themes like canonization of the Old Testament, plurality of Old Testament theologies, history, tradition and story of the Old Testament, the possibility of a centre of the Old Testament, history of Israel and/or Old Testament theology, the relationship between the OT and the NT. By discussing on the above mentioned issues an attempt will be made to see how and where the current scholarship stands on the key theological issues not only in the Old Testament but also in the New Testament.

The third section of this book concentrates on some major theological topics from an integrative perspective and their relationship in the Indian context. Major themes in the Old Testament will be studied from the canonical, chronological, theological and thematic focus. Moreover all the themes may be connected integrally to the entire Bible so as to present an integrative perspective on the Bible. In this process ancient West Asian and Indian parallel traditions are used where and when possible. Historical and theological treatment on different legal codes in the Pentateuch is taken up for discussion with appropriate parallels from the Indian context particularly from the Indian legal system. Judges and Kings are taken from the Old Testament as models of leadership and see their relevance in the Indian context. Prophets in the Old Testament are taken as inspired leaders with charisma who guided and motivated the people of ancient Israel and their ministry may be taken as an example in the contemporary Indian context for a vibrant and tangible proof of prophetic ministry. The ministry of sages and apocalyptic thinkers in ancient Israel is looked in terms of their significance in the present Indian ecclesial and social context.

The fourth section of this book studies certain important themes in the Old Testament an integrated approach is taken. In this venture an attempt is made to articulate the main themes from a theological and contextual perspective.

Particular attention is given to the contemporary application of the themes from an Indian context.

Creation and ecological concerns in the Bible are discussed in detail along with the issue of creation versus science in relation to the origins of creation. Yahweh, the God of Old Testament in relation to the revelation in ancient Israel is seen in the light of God's self-disclosure in and through Jesus Christ and God's continuous acts of revelation in today's world. God of covenant, blessing and curse in the Old Testament is reflected in the light of present Indian situation. God's manifestation and God's dealing with Israelites is seen in and through the themes like: election, law, justice and righteousness.

God of the Old Testament dealt with the people in a more concrete manner by means of certain offices and institutions like: monarchy, prophecy. In the same manner the Kingship of God further affirms universal significance of God's love and sovereignty to God's people. At this juncture it must be noted that in and through the above mentioned institutions and offices God's manifestation of shalom is seen in a more concrete manner. The application of the concept of shalom found in the ancient society of Israel is certainly be related to the present world and Indian situation where there is chaos and lawlessness. Land as a gift and blessing from God is yet another manifestation of people's identity and solidarity with their God will certainly be a useful reflective theme in the light of the land problems faced by many communities in the world.

Cult and the presence of God in the ancient Israel along with its various manifestations like the Temple, sacrifice and priesthood is yet another visible and tangible sign of God's way of dealing with God's own people. This theme has gained so much of significance in the contemporary Indian situation as the people of Indian Christianity live in a multi-religious pluralistic context.

Living with much aspiration and hope was the way of life in ancient Israel and it was concretely manifested in all their eschatological moorings. People of Israel were not upset or torn down by their present predicament or suffering rather they always looked with hope which was unfolded in their eschatological horizons. Further to this idea of eschatology, throughout their history, Israelites looked towards their God as a savior. God's deeds are reflected and concretely manifested in and through God's salivific deeds at every point in the history. Even when the earthly figures and institutions failed this salvation plan of God the people continued look for the Messiah who would fulfill their aspirations and establish justice and righteousness on this earth. This idea of salvation and Messiah is certainly relevant and useful for many suffering communities in today's problem ridden world.

As was stated earlier the task of Old Testament theology is not only descriptive but also confessional and normative for the ongoing life of the church. This means that the hermeneutical task of the Bible is so significant that it is not only important to see how the Bible was read and interpreted by the ancient

Israel, but also how it is read and interpreted in today's world with different kinds of problems than the ancient societies faced. This means then there are two listenings of the Bible, the first listening which is Hebraic and Jewish listening and every new listening that follows the first listening in the subsequent generations as they try and interpret and appropriate the biblical message to their own struggles and sufferings. Thus, one may also see the possibility of plurality in the biblical interpretation. It is this plurality that offers a dynamic hermeneutical function of the Bible and it offers that function in a new and fresh ways even for us today in our contemporary situation. Thus, on the one hand the Bible is not easy read and on the other hand the biblical interpretation is fluid and dynamic making different communities get involved as it offers hope and optimism for all those who engage with it.

With the above frame of reference we shall now venture into our task of dealing with different topics in all the four sections of the book.

Chapter 1

Historical Foundations of the Discipline of the Old Testament Theology

1.1 Bible and its Interpretation in the Period of Luther's Reformation

The reason why we begin with our starting point of biblical interpretation and the theology is that the reformation is understood as a starting point to proclaim the evangelical message of the Bible and liberate the Bible from the clutches of doctrinal interpretation of the church. Moreover, what was present in the biblical interpretation until then was the whole baggage of medieval epistemological framework with which the biblical theology has grown.[6]

Martin Luther as a serious biblical interpreter wanted to radically shape the biblical interpretation in the light of what was not acceptable to him of his own day. What Luther wants to bring out is rightly summarized by Brueggemann:

> Luther asserted that the "evangelical substance" of biblical faith is not and cannot be contained the habituated, accustomed, and reductionist reading of church theology that made God simply an integral part of a church-administered system of salvation.[7]

What Luther wanted to affirm and courageously take a stand is that the Bible is a voice of revelation and that it should not be confused with any human attempt to categorize, domesticate and palatable. This means we must receive the Bible and interpret it in its odd form and without reductionism garnished by human attempt to embellish it. In effect what the reformation theology affirms

6 Walter Brueggemann, *Theology of the Old Testament: Testimony, Dispute, Advocacy* (Minneapolis: Fortress Press, 1997), p. 2.

7 Ibid.

is that to let the Bible speak in its own voice and terms rather than guided by the church doctrines and formulations. In this way one may see the reformation time was a period of interpretive emancipation for the Bible although this is only a beginning and a long way needs to be travelled to achieve this in practical terms.

1.2 Interpreting the Bible in the Period Before and After 18th Century AD by the Academia and the Church

What is the Bible was a basic question that was raised by the church and academia at the beginning of the 18th century prior to the discovery and use of the historical critical methodology. Prior to the invention of historical critical method and its application to the Bible in general and the Old Testament in particular, 'divine inspiration paradigm' was the traditional and conservative method that is followed. This method insists that one needs to interpret and view the "Bible spontaneously and experiencing one's life directly mirrored in its pages."[8] While this method may look like an exclusive approach, it is generally followed by majority in the ecclesial and academic circles. In general terms this approach to the biblical theology and interpretation operates on three uncritical assumptions.[9] First, the assumption that the Old Testament consists of a single genre that is, the 'salvation history' in all its parts. Although there are different sections within the OT it can be viewed as a unified whole through a continuous thread of 'salvation history'. Second, the Bible is divinely authored. The biblical writers directly conveyed God's message to the people. Through the inspiration of Holy Spirit the human authors directly received God's word in the form of the Bible. Thus, human creativity in authoring the books in the Bible has no role to play. In the view of R. Holladay who quotes "Sanhedrin 999" to substantiates the above view as follows: "He who says that Torah is from God or even if he says that the whole Torah is from God with the exception of this or that verse which was not from God but Moses spoke from his own mouth—that soul shall be rooted up."[10] Third, divine inspiration paradigm emphasizes upon the uniformity of divine revelation within the canon. This means then all the words are God's words and no human words can be found in the entire Bible. The readers are thus expected to seek divine will in all through the in different portions of the Bible. Obviously we can note that this view may lead to proof text approach in one's interpretation of the biblical passages as the

8 Roy A. Harrisville and Walter Sundberg, *The Bible in Modern Culture: Theology and Historical Critical Method from Spinoza to Kasemann* (Grand Rapids, MI: William B. Eerdmans Publishing Company, 1995), p. 11.

9 For more detailed discussion on these points see Daniel Jones Muthunayagom, "Contemporary Approaches to Old Testament Interpretation," in Indukuri John Mohan Razu (ed), *Interweaving Methodology and Praxis-exploring Disciplinary Options in Today's World* (Bangalore: BTESSC/SATHRI, 2007), pp. 172-173.

10 Carl R. Holladay, "Contemporary Methods in Reading the Bible," in Leander E. Keck, et al (ed), *The New Interpreter's Bible,* Vol. 1 (Nashville: Abingdon Press, 1994), p. 126.

texts are drawn indiscriminately from all different parts of the bible without any care for their contextual and historical background. This view also presupposes the idea that the role of human mediator has no value in communication the divine message contained in the Bible.

The obvious problems inherent in the above mentioned model of biblical interpretation can be pointed out as follows:

First of all, it undermines the importance of human agency in the process of revelation that God works in an effective manner through human agency in order to communicate God's will to the world. Second, divine inspiration paradigm leads one to interpret the Bible without any parameters and rules of interpretation that the texts are drawn indiscriminately from every part of the Bible regardless of their contextual and historical background. Third, bringing all the material of the Bible under the frame of salvation history is too simplistic and undermines the dynamic message of the Bible.

1.3 Biblical Theology and Scholastic Orthodoxy

Prior to the development of scholastic orthodoxy the problem of methodology in doing Old Testament Theology has already emerged in the middle of seventeenth century. The main concern at that time was how to do a theology of the Old Testament. But later in the post-reformation period scholastic school developed the idea to formulate a logically perfect and impregnable structure of Christian doctrine. Scholastic orthodoxy took up the sole authority of the Bible seriously in the context of conflicts between different religions of the world. They further claimed to retain the doctrinal structures of the reformers like Luther, Calvin, Zwingli and others. The primary affirmation of the scholastic orthodox school was *Sola fidae* and *Sola Scriptura*. By this they wanted to uphold the scriptures over against the traditions of the church. Brueggemann summarizes this position of scholastic orthodoxy as follows:

> The ongoing community of interpreters on the whole, found the Bible's "oddness" excessive, and did what it could to counter and reduce the oddness ... It is clear that the large notion of "Rule of Faith," a term used both for the Bible itself and for the church's confessional rules of interpretation, intends to hold together Bible and church interpretation, or perhaps even to cover over the tension that belongs to our work of scholarship in Old Testament theology.[11]

Thus, what the Scholastic Orthodoxy affirms is that which is in the Bible not that which is developed based on the traditions of the church. In this sense the whole biblical theology movement seems to have begun or so to say emerged as against the traditions or the doctrines of the church. However, the term

11 Brueggemann, *Theology of the Old Testament*, p. 5.

"Biblical Theology" had appeared only after hundred years later from the time of reformation.

The term "Biblical Theology" was coined by a scholastic orthodox protestant scholar Wolfgang Jacob Christmann in 1629, in his first work "Biblical Theology" which had a character of dogmatic theology and even at time turned down to be handmaid (subservient) to dogmatic theology. Moreover, this work supports the doctrines of the church, that is, it affirms that the function of biblical theology is to support the doctrines of the church. In order to enhance this process, a series of proof texts were collected from exegesis with a view to assert the point that the orthodox (church) doctrines are grounded in biblical texts. In view of this position, it was further felt by the proponents of Scholastic Orthodoxy the biblical texts ought to be arranged to suit dogmatics in the order of God, Man and Salvation.

At this stage Biblical theology functioned under two uncritical assumptions. First, religious ideas in the Bible are entirely uniform. Due to this there was a lack of awareness to historical development within the Bible. Therefore the biblical texts were indiscriminately drawn from all parts of the Bible without any consideration to their historical context. Second, it is assumed that the doctrines of the Bible are entirely identical with the doctrines of the church.

At this juncture two more important figures ought to be mentioned in the ongoing process of biblical theology debate in the light of Scholastic Orthodoxy. The first among the two are:

Francis Turretin (1632-1687). Turretin points out that the Bible is supernatural book; it is word of God in all its parts, everything in it is divine, including the words, phrases and even the vowel pointing. Thus, Turretin would like to extend the infallibility of scripture to all parts of the Bible. According to him there is no room for any idea of historical development or of progression in revelation. Moreover, the revelation in both the Old and New Testaments is considered to be identical.

The second figure was Sebastian Schmidt (1617-1696). In his two volume work on biblical theology entitled *A Biblical Collection of OT and NT text explicated in relation to the series of standard theological topics, collected texts that support protestant church dogma*. For Schmidt the basic presupposition was that the church dogmas represented a correct interpretation of Christian religion. Furthermore it is affirmed that the dogmas of the church was given approval by the word of God. This view further assumed that the Bible was uniformly authoritative. The basic problem with the proposal of Schmidt was that the role of the Bible was reduced to providing proofs for the truth of dogmas and thus passages were chosen from all sections of the Bible. For instance, Schmidt talks about the doctrine of trinity with the aid of the following biblical references: Gen 1:1-3; Exod 23:20; 33; Isa 6:8; 63:8-9. His method was very simple based on the definition and elucidation of the individual doctrines. Schmidt has done a detailed exposition of the text to show how they support the particular doctrine; in this was the order of the subject matter was done in the same was as systematic theology.

The above approach of exegeting the biblical texts was opposed due to the following reasons: a) it seems to be a proof text method instead of allowing the scriptures to speak to us, it only searches proof for what is already present in the form of dogmas; b) uniform revelation throughout the Bible is improbable. Picking up biblical references at random does not do justice to all religious ideas found in the Old Testament. Exegesis was wrongly done in this method because the meaning of certain ideas were forced into the text (Eisegesis); c) the method of arranging biblical text was superficial and naïve since it was not derived from the Bible but from doctrinal system.

Despite the above mentioned problems this approach was well taken due to the fact that it made a beginning into the long history of the development of Old Testament Theology.

1.4 Biblical Theology and Pietism

During 17th century A.D. Biblical Theology was influenced by Pietistic Movement of Germany. Pietists disregarded the philosophical sophistication of Scholastic Orthodoxy; instead they wanted to return to biblical simplicity and thus called for a new Biblical Theology. Back to the Bible was the policy of the German Pietism that made inroads into the development of biblical theology in the coming decades and centuries.

One of the founding fathers of Pietism and its influence on Biblical Theology was Philip Jacob Spener (1635-1705) opposed Protestant Scholastic Orthodoxy with Biblical Theology. In his famous publication namely *Pia Desideria.* Spener proposed and called for knowledge of all scriptures by the church members through preaching, private study and reading, discussion, interpretation on the biblical materials. Spener condemned the approach of Scholastic Orthodoxy, its theology and theological educators, because he feels that their approach lack proper orientation of the Bible. Thus, he proposes a *true biblical theology* in contrast to the Scholastic theology. In his opinion, Scholastic theology while presenting foundations of faith from scriptures "builds on it with so much wood, hay and stubble of human inquisitiveness that the gold can no longer be seen."[12] Thus, it becomes exceedingly difficult to grasp and find pleasure in the simplicity of Christ and his teaching. The other figures that were influenced by Pietism at this time include: Carl Haymann (1708), J. Deutschmann (1710) and J. C. Weldner (1722), all of them oppose orthodox systems of doctrine with "Biblical Theology."

Despite the proposals made by Spener and others Pietistic movement of biblical theology still functioned within the circles of orthodox theology. There

---

12 Philipp Jacob Spener, *Pia Desideria,* trans Theodore G. Tappert (Philadelphia: Fortress Press, 1964), p. 56.

was no real change in the structure and presentation of the material from the systematic theology. In essence, the Pietistic theology continued to take the proof text approach to the biblical exegesis. However, the major contribution of biblical theology in this pietistic movement is that it opened up a way for biblical theology to be an independent discipline, from being subservient to dogmatic theology. From here on the rationalists pickup further and developed biblical theology in distinct lines.

1.5 Biblical Theology and Rationalism

During eighteenth century German theology was influenced by rationalism which is the combination of Enlightenment and Romanticism. The period of European Enlightenment as a German intellectual movement in the second half of the eighteenth century was associated with some figures like Herder, Lessing, and Immanuel Kant. The Enlightenment in a comprehensive sense as a European movement whose origin can be traced back at least to the mid-seventeenth century. In this sense the period of Enlightenment has become virtually synonymous with 'the Age of Reason.' Foundations were laid during this period for the historical critical study of the Bible that this trend has become dominant in the German universities for the later centuries to come.[13]

In the above mentioned period the idea of supernatural was looked at skeptically. The infallibility of the Bible was questioned. Reason became the final authority; the Bible was viewed as a document like any other document. In the words of Paul Achtemeier this is made clear:

> Scripture therefore must be seen as a collection of materials written by fallible men who reflected the culture out of which they came and for which they were writing. Accordingly, Scripture itself is best described as a mixture of the word of God with the erring words of its human authors.[14]

The historical critical method, particularly, literary criticism on the Pentateuch emerged during this period. Pioneer in this venture was Johann Salmo Semler (1728-1791). His discussion on the text was different from that of orthodox treatment in exegesis, but not in organization and form. Various treatments of biblical religion appeared during this time in the form of biblical theologies; however, they are more or less resulted in producing what was considered to be the theology contained in the Bible.

---

13 Francis Watson, "Enlightenment," in R. J. Coggins and J. L. Houlden, eds. *Dictionary of Biblical Interpretation* (London: SCM Press, 1990), pp. 191-194.

14 Paul J. Achtemeier, *The Interpretation of Scripture: Problems and Proposals* (Philadelphia: Westminster Press, 1980), pp. 43-44.

Another key figure in this line of thinking was Carl Haymann in 1708 in his writing *Biblische Theologie* gave a pointed expression to the growing conviction that church dogma and the concepts of the Bible were not always identical and that there should be separate account of dogmatics and biblical foundation produced with some independence from dogmatic systems.

It was Johann Philpp Gabler (1753-1826) took up various issues for the first time in a more systematic manner already addressed by his predecessors, especially Gotthilf Traugott Zachariä (1729-1777) to whom he is highly indebted. Zachariä in his work entitled: *Biblische Theologie Oder Untersuchung des biblischen Grundes der vornehmsten theologischen Lehren* 1771-75[15] has already addressed important concerns in relation to the question of independence of biblical theology from that of dogmatic theology. He addresses five issues in this regard: first, the obscurity of sacred scriptures at many places; second, tendency of the interpreters to read their own ideas and views into the scripture; third, the method of interpretation of the texts which is enslaved by dogmatics; fourth, the simplicity of theology is fully confused and mixed with the subtlety and stringency of dogmatic theology; and fifth, the negligence of the distinction between religion and theology.

Gabler picked up the above points proposed by Zachariä and developed them further along distinct lines to work out a clear distinction between biblical theology and dogmatic theology and also to show how they are related to each other. Gabler believed that much of the confusion in the Christian world of his own day was due improper use of the Bible and the failure of the Christians to distinguish between dogmatic theology and the simple historical religion of the Bible. In his inaugural address at the University of Altdorf, March 30, 1787 he delivered a lecture in this regard entitled as: *Die iuso discrimine theologiae biblicae et dogmaticae regundisque recte utriusque finibus* ("On the correct distinction between biblical and dogmatic theology and the proper determination of the goals of each."). On this account Gabler is often called as the father of biblical theology.

For Gabler dogmatic theology bears a didactic character, whereas biblical theology is historical in character, wherein its object is set forth what biblical writings say about God. Therefore, Gabler proposed the first task accordingly is to collect carefully the sacred views, which require a historical-critical approach, since these sacred writings do not contain the opinion of one person or of the same age, or of one and the same religion. Gabler's inductive, historical and descriptive approach to biblical theology is based on three essential methodological considerations: First, inspiration of the Bible is not to be considered in this whole biblical theology debate because "the Spirit of God most emphatically did not destroy in every holy man his own ability to understand and the measure of natural

15 For some details on G. T. Zachariä's argument see Gerhard F. Hasel, *Old Testament Theology: Basic Issues in the Current Debate* (Grand Rapids, MI: William B. Eerdmans Publishing Company, 1991), pp. 14-15. Fourth Edition.

insight into things."[16] What matters is not the divine inspiration and authority, but what the biblical writers thought about the Bible. Second, Biblical theology has the task of gathering "carefully assembled from Holy Writ, suitably arranged, properly related to general concepts, and carefully compared with one another."[17] This task can be accomplished by means of historical-critical method with the support of literary criticism, historical criticism and philosophical criticism. Third, Biblical theology as a historical discipline is obliged to "distinguish between the several periods of the old and new religion."[18] The main task here is to investigate which ideas are of importance for Christian doctrine, namely which one are relevant for today and which one have no validity for our time.

Based on the above framework Gabler set forth clearly the task of historical-critical theology as follows: "we must distinguish between the several periods of old and new religion as well as between several authors and finally between the several forms of speech, that each one uses dependent on time and place, be it the historical, didactic of the poetic genius."[19] This task is carried out in two steps: first, a careful exegesis and proper interpretation of the text, which requires careful and exact linguistic and philosophical work with the text; second, a careful comparison of ideas and the views of the biblical authors and the suitable arrangement of the true opinions of the biblical authors and a comprehensive presentation of the total religion of the Bible. This means then collecting and classifying the ideas of each of these authors and periods, using the ideas actually expressed in the scriptures; When they are not clearly expressed, through a comparison of the passages, the interpreter arranges them in his/her own way. Gabler called the result of this work as *true biblical theology*. Then a true biblical theology according to Gabler has a purely descriptive task, as Gabler writes: "a true and accurate description of the religion (religious ideas) of the bible in its various periods and contexts in a systematic and historical presentation."[20]

Gabler proposes next step as the investigation of the usefulness of these views which had been collected and arranged and related to general concepts for dogmatics. It meant a systematic presentation of God's eternal truths or the unchanging ideas found in the Bible which are valid for all times. Here, the main task is to investigate which ideas are of importance in the permanent form of Christian doctrine and constantly compare it to us and which was spoken only for the people of given age or were intended for a given form of instruction. Gabler noted that for doing this several factors are to be considered as follows: first, not all biblical writers stand on the same level; second, many ideas expressed in the

16 J. P. Gabler, *Kleine Theologische Schriften, II*, p. 186, cited in Gerhard F. Hasel, *Old Testament Theology: Basic Issues in the Current Debate,* p. 16.

17 Ibid.

18 Ibid.

19 Ibid.

20 Ibid.

biblical material were intended by God for only a limited historical time; third, much of the Bible must be seen as the authors' attempt to understand rather than the expression of timeless truths; fourth, universal ideas and notions are a mere reflection of pure doctrine than particular idea. Gabler called the result of this work of a systematic presentation of the eternal truths found in the Bible as *Pure biblical theology*.

Critique on Gabler's proposals: It was not the intention of Gabler to produce a full and detailed volume on Biblical theology and thus some inherent problems can be noted in his approach. Gabler has not fully clarified the division and distinction between a true biblical theology and a pure biblical theology or the process of distinguishing the particular from the universal or the historical from the trans-historical or the divine from the human etc. Nor does he demonstrate the separation of moving from a true biblical theology to a pure biblical theology. On the whole Gabler assigned the biblical theology a descriptive, objective and historical task. According to him, the biblical theology describes what the biblical writers believe without raising the question of relevance of values etc. On the other hand dogmatic theology is didactic in character; its object is to deal with and evaluate dogmatic matters of doctrines with the aid of philosophy in the context of theologians. The dogmatic theologians make use of the pure biblical theology and produces dogmatic systems which bear a didactic character. With this proposition distinction between biblical and dogmatic theology was made sharply and biblical theology became an independent discipline. On the whole Gabler assigned normative character for dogmatic theology and descriptive task for biblical theology. This is a real problem in the proposal of Gabler. Question can be raised to say that is biblical theology is also not normative? Can it only be reduced to a descriptive status? Of course, Gabler has not developed and produced a detailed and substantial work in these lines. But the basic ideas proposed by Gabler remained a basic ground for the further task of Old Testament theology which asks the fundamental question: whether Old Testament Theology is normative or descriptive?

One other person who contributed to the discussion of biblical theology under the auspices of rationalism is George Lorenz Bauer (1755-1806). He developed further biblical theology debate following the lines of Gabler. Bauer was the first one to separate biblical theology into Old Testament and New Testament theologies. His main purpose was to outline the religious ideas of Old Testament and distinguish between various periods and sources with sensitiveness to historical context. On the basis of this idea Bauer made the following divisions: theology and anthropology which was in the conventional lines with appendices on angles and demons. In the first section of theology he dealt with the doctrine of God and the divine relationship to humanity with two appendices (angles and demons). The problem in this kind of arrangement is that can Old Testament theology follow the order of dogmatic theology in the arrangement of its material?

Can we systematically organize the material of the entire Old Testament if we follow certain method of arrangement? If we follow some systematic division is it possible to include all the material as it is visible in Bauer's treatment, especially in his appendices. Can we not leave some material in the process our treatment of the entire Old Testament? Thus, Bauer was criticized for not offering really a historical treatment of Israelite religion. However, Bauer tried to answer this criticism subsequently by publishing a supplement to Old Testament Theology in which he dealt with the history of Israelite religion rather inadequately. However, this was the very first attempt to give an historical account of Israelite religion. Also Bauer was the first one to make a distinction between Old Testament Theology and history of Israelite religion. In OT theology he treated material systematically and in the history of Israelite religion he treated material genetically and chronologically.

1.6 Biblical Theology and Hegelians

The influence of Hegel (1771-1831), especially the triadic theory was seen in the 19th century in the process of the development of biblical theology. According to Hegel's theory the process of reflection is seen as a continuous movement leading from one idea that is, thesis to opposite that is, antithesis and hence a higher union of both that is, synthesis; and a newly gained insight became another thesis to be superseded by another synthesis and so on. The ultimate ground for this logic is to be discovered in human experience itself. According to Hegel the first stage in the development of religions is the natural religion in which God is viewed as the natural subject, second in the role of spiritual individuality where God is viewed as the spiritual individual, third stage is the absolute religion (like that of (Christianity) where God is absolute spirit.

On the basis of the above ideas of Hegel an attempt was made to write a biblical theology by Johann Karl Wilhelm Vatke (1806-1882), who published his work in 1835 entitled: *The Religion of the Old Testament presented according to the canonical books*. From the point of view of methodology Vatke rejected the idea that biblical theology and dogmatic theology is normative. He said that biblical theology should adopt a standpoint to evaluate the truth of the Old Testament and this standpoint was provided by Hegelian philosophy. He departed from the traditional order of arranging materials of the Old Testament Theology in the order of God, man and salvation; instead he arranged the material in a purely historical framework. Following the Hegelian triadic principle he grouped the Old Testament material under three periods: a) pre-prophetic period, according to Vatke it is the lower stage; b) prophetic period which is higher than the first stage; c) post-prophetic period, higher in this order of three. For Vatke this scheme represents the evolution of religion from a lower to a higher level. Vatke's treatment of history of Israel was very valuable. He was the first one to date P material in the post-prophetic period, till then it was dated in the pre-prophetic period. Later Julius Wellhausen also appreciated the contribution made by Vatke for the study of history of Israelite religion. But, on the whole Vatke's treatment of Israelite religion was somewhat obscure because of his preoccupation with the Hegelian speculations. From his work two statements pertaining to Old Testament theology may be noted:

First, concerning the nature of biblical theology: "the fundamental idea of biblical theology as a science is determined by its purpose which is to present the living movement of the main elements of biblical religion, namely its general concept, its subjective and historical appearance, and its idea." Second, concerning his formulation of the fundamental idea of Old Testament religion: "God is defined as pure subjectivity which, as unlimited power, is distinguished from everything particular but which, as absolute wisdom and holiness, nevertheless includes within itself and the particular in a simple, yet concrete identity." As mentioned above in 1835, Vatke's work as mentioned above is justified by himself as follows:

> The all important is hence to assume from the very outset a standpoint which itself, by virtue of its concepts, has the utmost generality. It must not, therefore, be derived from any particular point of view. This higher objectivity can be engendered only by philosophy, as the science of science; for philosophy abolishes the limitations of every individual science and every particular viewpoint, turning them into the fluid moment of a higher Whole, truth itself, and thus, in this very way, in the contemplation of history gathers together the Spirit's different forms of appearance into the idea of Spirit itself.[21]

Following Vatke his student Bruno Bauer (1809-1882) in the year 1838 published a work entitled *The Religion of the Old Testament in the Historical Development of its Principles*, argued that Old Testament Theology cannot be written in Hegelian framework. He raises the question whether biblical theology should accept the historical value and not normative value as proposed by Gabler. Bauer arranges his materials in the order of historical development but is not content with his description but wanted to find its value such as what is of religious value as Hegel intended? This is evidenced in his definition of OT theology: "the fundamental idea of our science (OT theology) ... may be defined as the presentation of self-consciousness of the absolute spirit in its free, historically mediated development. Its content is the historical movement in which the notion of revelation is carried to completion in a living idea. The method of our science

21 Wilhelm Vatke, *Die Religion des Alten Testaments nach dem kanonischen Büchern entwickelt* (*The Religion of the Old Testament Developed According to the Canonical Books)* (Berlin: G. Bethge, 1835), p. 16.

(OT theology) is to reproduce ... this movement of the notion in its historical expressions."[22]

On the whole we may conclude that apart from the contribution to the reconstitution of the development of Israelite religion, the contribution of Hegelians to OT theology as such was rather insignificant.

1.7 Biblical Theology and the Conservatives

To Hegelian's influence on Biblical theology, conservatives reacted. Instead they produced their own biblical theology between 1840 and 1860. Some of the earlier scholars who come under the conservative thought are J. C. F. Stendel (1840), Heinrich Ewald (1803-1875) Gustav Friedrich Oehler (1812-1872). These conservative scholars after Gabler affirmed the basic objective historical character of the discipline of OT theology. They combined the critical approach with a view of divine revelation which means sensitivity to history and Christian faith. OT theology was thus approached from the point of view of Christian faith.

One among the above mentioned figure Gustav Friedrich Oehler needs some elaborate discussion at this point. His book was published posthumously based on his lectures in 1870-71. He was influenced by the work of Johann Christian Konrad von Hofmann. He describes his work as follows:

> What is here unfolded is one great divine economy of salvation—*unum continuum systema*, as Bengel puts it—an organism of divine deeds and testimonies, which, beginning in Genesis with the act of creation, advances progressively to its completion in the person and work of Christ, and will find its close in the new heaven and earth predicted in the Apocalypse, and only in the context of this whole can details be rightly estimated ... Now, to introduce men and women to be organically historical knowledge of the Old Testament is the very business of the discipline to which these lectures are to be developed.[23]

Oehler reacted both against Marcionite brand introduced by F. Schleiermacher with the depreciation of the OT and the uniformity of OT and NT. He agrees for separate OT and NT theologies, but is of the view that OT theology can only function within the larger canonical context. He writes: OT theology is a "historical science which is based upon grammatical-historical exegesis whose task it is to reproduce the content of the Biblical writings according to the rules of language under consideration of the historical circumstances

22 Bruno Bauer, *Die Religion des AT in der geschichtlichen Entwicklung threr Principien,* 2 Vols. (Berlin: 1938) cited in Gerhard F. Hasel, *Old Testament Theology: Basic Issues in the Current Debate,* p. 19.

23 Gustav Friedrich Oehler, *Theology of the Old Testament,* trans. E. D. Smith and S. Taylor (Edinburgh: T & T Clark, 1874-93), p. 2.

during which the writings originated and the individual conditions of the sacred writers."[24] Oehler's treatment was considered as outmoded as he wants to treat the material of the Old Testament genetically (chronologically).

The work of Johann Christian Konrad von Hofmann (1810-1877) is significant at this juncture to discuss briefly. He produced a work entitled: *Weissagung und Erfüllung in Alten und Neuen Testamennte* in 1841-44 (Promise and fulfillment in the Old and New Testaments) was the first one to approach OT theology from the point of view of *heilsgeschichte (salvation history)*. In this way he viewed OT history a prophecy, which means that of a history which within itself contains the seat of fulfillment history, which is directed by God and it is arena of God's revelation; so the history is God's revelation. His view of *heilsgeschichte* brought to the forefront the view that OT history is not a non-theological framework into which religious ideas are brought in, but rather historical development as the arena of God's revelation is to be found and history is thought to be independent. In other words, history is non-theological container of religious ideas; but Hofmann is of the view that historical development itself has theological value which makes history is revelation. Hofmann's ideas gave rise to a complex question of how one views history within the framework of OT theology.

Hofmann is also of the view that the Bible is the linear record of linear saving history in which the active Lord of history is the triune God whose purpose is to redeem humankind. Hofmann's ideas on the salvation history and its importance in OT theology are summarized by Hasel as follows:

> Since Jesus Christ is the primordial goal of the world to which salvation history is aims and from which it receives its meaning, the OT contains salvation-historical proclamation. This an OT theology has to expound. Each book of the Bible is assigned its logical place in the scheme of salvation history. The Bible is not to be regarded primarily as a collection of proof-texts or a repository of doctrine but a witness to God's activity in history which will not be fully completed until the eschatological consummation. The influence of the "salvation-history school" on the development of both OT and NT theology has been considerable and is felt in the present day, though with a great variation and in new forms.[25]

On the whole it is to be summarized the "salvation history school" of the nineteenth century represented by Hofmann and others is based on three principles: first, the history of the people of God as expressed in the Word; second,

---

24 Gustav Friedrich Oehler, *Theology of the Old Testament,* trans. E. D. Smith and S. Taylor (Edinburgh: T & T Clark, 1874-93), p. 66.

25 Gerhard F. Hasel, *Old Testament Theology*, p. 22.

the idea of the inspiration of the Bible; and third, the preliminary result of the history between God and human beings in Jesus Christ.[26]

1.8 Biblical Theology and the School of Religionsgeschichte (History of Religions)

With the publication of Julius Wellhausen's prolegomena to the History of Israel a new phase of biblical theology developed, which marked a demise of the discipline of OT theology, which is replaced by the history of Israelite religion. As was noted earlier, Vatke used the history of Israelite religion for the presentation of religious values rejecting the systematic arrangement. G. L. Bauer on the other hand treated history of Israelite religion as a supplement. Conservatives combined both stands; consequently there was no clarity in the relationship between these two approaches.

This confusion was settled to a great extent with the appearance of Wellhausen's prolegomena to the history of Israel. Wellhausen pointed out the possibility of writing a critical scientific history of Israelite religion is confirmed to the general principles of the development of religions. It appeared as though only the scientific dealing with religious ideas was possible through history of Israelite religion. Wellhausen's prolegomena in 1878 marked the beginning of a new age for the demise of OT theology and prosperity of history of Israelite religion. R. C. Dentan comments on this development:

> It was now possible to for the first time to write a history of Israel's religion which not only appeared to be justified by a proper understanding of the sources, but also accorded with the intellectual temper of an age which had been taught by Hegel and Darwin to regard the principle of evolution as the magic key to unlock all the secrets of history.[27]

Subsequent to this development several treatments on history of Israelite religion began to appear extensively (writings by O. E. Oesterely, T. H. Robinson and others). For over a four decades or so OT theology was eclipsed by the influence of Religionsgeschichte. Hasel summarizes this situation rightly as follows:

> The full-fledged historicism of the "history of religions" approach had led to the final destruction of the unity of the OT, which was reduced to a collection of materials from detached periods and consisted simply of Israelite reflections of as many different pagan religions.

26 Gerhard F. Hasel, *Old Testament Theology*, p. 22.

27 Robert C. Dentan, *Preface to Old Testament Theology* (New York: Seabury Press, 1963), pp. 50-51.

> This approach had a particularly destructive influence both on OT theology and on the understanding of the OT in every other aspect.[28]

In continuation with the same idea on the decline of OT theology, Walther Eichrodt comments that "the essential inner coherence of the Old and New Testaments was reduced, so to speak, to a thin thread of historical connection and a causal sequence between the two, with the result that an external causality—not even susceptible in every case of secure demonstration—was substituted for a homogeneity that was real because it rested on the similar content of their experience of life."[29]

Even though history of Israelite religion dominated the scene, OT theology has not died out completely. For instance, Hermann Schultz in the year 1896 has produced a work entitled: *Theology of the Old Testament.* But this was the last work to be produced during this century. Schultz pointed out that OT theology is not incompatible with history of Israelite religion, but this was the only voice and there was no one to support it at this point of time. In 1904 A. B. Davidson has produced OT theology, but a purely edited work. Davidson is of the view that the OT does not have a theology but religion; for him OT is history of Israelite religion. Therefore he intended to arrange material in chronological order, but later the editor of his book (after his death) arranged the material in traditional systematic order. At this time in general history of Israel took over OT theology as a scientific discipline. Those who argued in support of the history of Israelite religion didn't say that it is impossible to write OT theology or it is completely incompatible with history of Israelite religion, but they only felt that history of Israelite religion could achieve better than what OT theology could not achieve.

1.9 Revival of Old Testament Theology During Early Twentieth Century

Following the first world war, theological climate changed an it became favorable to biblical theology. Revival in biblical theology was made possible due to the revival in general theological field following the world war. The disaster of war shattered the optimism of the liberalism in the 19th century and people's complacency. Three factors were in operation on this: first, was the general loss of faith in evolutionary naturalism that was dominant in the attempts to explain the history of Israelite religion in the framework of Religionsgeschichte; second, there was a reaction against the mid-nineteenth century conviction that historical truth can be achieved by a pure scientific objectivity; third, the trend of continental theology went back to reformation and its advocacy towards biblical studies as being profoundly relevant to modern theological problems.[30] As a result church was compelled to rethink about biblical truths and this change was marked by

28 Gerhard F. Hasel, *Old Testament Theology*, p. 22.

29 Walther Eichrodt, *Old Testament Theology* Vol. 1, p. 30.

30 Robert C. Dentan, *Preface to Old Testament Theology*, p. 61.

the production of Karl Barth's commentary on the book of Romans in 1918. This opened up a new era in the whole theological thinking and the beginning was made to the neo-orthodox school of theology. Those who belonged to this school began to demand something more than mere history of Israelite religion. They wanted more light on the theological dimension than historical dimension. Therefore, OT scholars began to pay their attention once again to the study of OT theology. In addition to this, there is a general trend within the narrow field of OT studies itself. Some specific developments took place in this awakening: first, the discovery of West Asian religions like Babylon, Ugarit etc has made a tremendous impact on the material of the Old Testament; second, the increasing trend in the phenomenology of religion, psychology, anthropology have become influential in the study of the Old Testament. These influences for instance, are reflected in the works of Sigmund Mowinckel's studies on *Psalms* (six volumes) in 1921, Johann Pedersen's *Israel: its life and Culture* (1926-28). But the problem with this kind of studies is that one cannot evaluate religions just by abstracting the ideas from other religions; instead religious ideas must be studies within the matrix of its particular cultural and social setting. It was inadequate to evaluate the Israelite religion using one or other formula like ethical monotheism, covenant etc. Moreover, the evolutionary approach followed by The Religionsgeschichte school to deal with history of Israelite religion was not appreciated from many quarters. This new climate stimulated the study of OT theology and it moved to the forefront of OT studies once again.

The first proper work after the war was the work of E. König's *Theologie des Alten Testaments* (1922). Although this work is not fully significant reading the sign of the times it made some impact in the revival of OT theology. König insisted that the characteristic phenomena of Hebrew religion, such as prophecy, cannot be explained merely by genetic and chronological and even by psychological methods, rather it should be considered as a product of actual disclosure from beyond what we find in the text itself. However, König has failed to translate his proposal in his organization of the material of the OT and he simply follows old dogmatic method.[31] However, König's proposal is valid at this time as he also insists not on "spiritual exegesis" which was the trend of his time, but emphasizes on the validity of historical-grammatical principles of the text. There is a tendency in his work still to move towards the explanation of the text on the basis of the history of Israelite religion.

The real beginning of the revival of OT theology was marked by an article written by C. Steuernagel in 1935 entitled: *Alttestamentliche Theologie und alttstamentliche Religionsgeschichte* (*OT theology and Religious history of the Old Testament*)[32]. This article was considered to be important to assert the autonomy and independence of OT theology alongside the history of Israelite religion.

31 Robert C. Dentan, *Preface to Old Testament Theology*, p. 62.

32 Appeared in *ZAW* 41, pp. 266-273.

Steuernagel tried to define the relationship between two disciplines through a description of respective limitations. OT theology is limited in various respects through its method. It deals its method according to topics; this method does not allow a presentation of the development of OT religion *entoto* (in totality). It also cannot bring out special and distinctive character and the significance of a given period of OT religion; likewise the method of OT theology cannot present the factors which are effective in the development of biblical religion and their actual effects. The method of OT theology will not only fail in all tasks which presently are regarded as the main task of the historian, but also forces the material into a system which is alien to it. However, Steuernagel says that this need not be necessarily the case always. According to him this system can very well lead to a system which conforms to the matter and which grows out of its development.

Just as OT theology has its limitations the discipline of history of Israelite religion also has its limitations from the point of view of religion. In general a purely historical presentation of the Old Testament is not sufficient since the study of religion tries to grasp the nature of religion as such by means of comparing with other religions; hence with the study of religion in general systematic presentation of single religion is needed.

According to Steuernagel from the point of view of theological science, a purely religious historical approach to the OT also appears to be insufficient, since the study of OT is a sub-discipline of theology; the other theological sub-disciplines expect that the OT scholars present their materials not only historically but also systematically in a systematic survey. In this context the question of systematic presentation of the OT material arises; nevertheless, Steuernagel emphasizes that the outline for OT theology must emerge from the material itself and must not be taken from dogmatic system. According to him Old Testament studies has two fold task: first, to investigate into the totality of the development of the Israelite religion and into the factors which are effective in it into its laws and aims. This we can do only in the form of s religious history of the Old Testament; second, we also have to follow all lines of special and single development and that we can do only in the form of systematic surveys or monographic treaties in the discipline of OT theology. According to Steuernagel both disciplines have same objective namely the religion of ancient Israel and both disciplines have the same method namely the historical method.

The work of Steuernagel followed another important article written by Otto Eissfeldt entitled: *Israelitischjüdische Religionsgeschichte und alttstamentliche Theologie* (*The History of Israelite and Jewish religion and OT theology*)[33] in which Eissfeldt pointed towards a tension existing between history and revelation, faith and knowledge; he considered this as the contemporary problem of theology. Eissfeldt also felt that history is not able to make any ultimate announcement; therefore the tension according to him leads to the question whether we can

33 Appeared in *ZAW* 44 (1926), pp. 1-12.

understand the religion of the OT as historical phenomena and whether we can present the OT material as we present other religions of antiquity. The main question was whether we can understand a history of Israelite and Jewish religions or should we understand the religion of OT as a religion which is the true religion and God's revelation and which consequently has to be presented as OT theology. From the point of view of historian (or student of religion) the questions will be answered in this way that: "the religion of OT has to be investigated into the same methods which are used by the historical science: philological and historical critical study of the sources, and presentation of theistic content based on an interpretation which emerges out of a personal sensitivity and sympathetic understanding."

According to Eissfeldt, the historical approach avoids question concerning truth and any valuation of the phenomena. On the other hand, the theological and ecclesiastical approach which is based on the understanding that the nature of the OT religion cannot be grasped through the use of historical method only. Faith alone is able to grasp the nature and religion of the Old Testament. According to this understanding the New Testament determines what is essential in the Old Testament. In Eissfeldt's judgment, this would however deprive the religious historical approach to the OT and its religion of their independence. On the other hand, he also criticizes the attempt to make theological approach a mere appendix to the historical approach. Eissfeldt summarized the development of this approach as follows: "the historical theoretical satire into the OT will never be able to go beyond the relative and imminent and on the other hand faith which is deeply affected by the absolute and transcendent is not an instrument which would understand the OT as a historical phenomenon."

Eissfeldt emphasizes that history of Israelite religion and theological approaches must not be mixed. According to him based on these two approaches OT belong to two different levels and represents two different activities of our mind. Both approaches must have their unlimited independence and we must bear in mind the tension that exists between them. The OT has been shaped by faith and hence it is faith which provides the object for knowledge and knowledge can help faith and it can enrich faith or relieve it from burdens such as elements of OT which are subnormal or which have national Israelite significance only. According to Eissfeldt the confusion between historical and theological approach is pathos. If one takes faith as an example as was done by the protestant church, in order to view history, the historical reality will be distorted, the historical knowledge and even the purity of faith will be adulterated as it was done in the case of Orthodoxy and pietism as two polar opposite examples.

Historical approach of the 19th century on the other hand was in danger of forgetting revelation and focusing on the history alone. According to Eissfeldt we must avoid both these mistakes but at the same time we must use both the approaches for the history of Israelite Jewish religion as well as for OT theology.

History of Israelite religion as a historical science is confined to the historical methods and excludes the question concerning the truth. Its nature is purely descriptive. As a historical science it must be pursued in independence from the religion and faith of the scholar or historian. Theology of the OT is however different in that it presents what has become the word of God to a scholar and his religious community. Even OT theology is of scholarly nature, it will have the character of the testimony. OT theology is the description of the revelation which faith discovers in the OT and therefore it can't have the form of historical presentation but must be systematic according to topics. According to Eissfeldt the historical and theological approach can be united only in so far as one and the same person can use both approaches. It is purely a confessional discipline. It's object of knowledge is rather the revelation of timeless truths contained in the OT and by definition, it includes evaluated judgments all the time. It acquires the knowledge of these timeless truths through the exercise of faith, so there is no harmony with the other disciplines where the truth could be persuaded. Only a shade of faith confession can do a common OT theology, so there are different OT theologies just like different religious confessions. Also no pronouncement can be made as to the validity since it is purely a matter of faith. Eissfeldt's view on the nature of OT theology is then is that, it is a theological, dogmatic, normative and confessional approach that perceives its object which is the revelation of timeless truth, through the faculty of faith. Eissfeldt was concerned with the issue of relation between history of Israelite religion and OT theology.

The above trend set by Eissfeldt was important for the future discussion on the methodology of OT theology. His solution suggested in this regard was to draw a line between the two (history of Israelite religion and OT theology) and attribute one to the field of knowledge and other to the field of faith. The problem with this kind of proposal made by Eissfeldt is that it violently divorced OT theology from history of Israelite religion. Eissfeldt's concern was with the timeless and historical. This overlooks the fact that, the OT itself claims that it was in the course of historical developments that God reveals. The OT theology necessarily involves history. Thus, Eissfeldt's line of demarcation is over simplified. However, his view was influential to some extent in the subsequent discussions and the development of the discipline of OT theology in the coming decades.

The revival of the OT theology continued what we may call the "golden age" from the year 1930 onwards. Significant works on OT theology were published by E. Sellin (1933) and L. Köhler (1936) both these works follow the dogmatic pattern of God-Man-Salvation. Walther Eichrodt (1933-39) produced a monumental work on OT theology with covenant as a central focus followed by W. Visher in 1934 published a work entitles as *The Witness of the OT to Christ*. Following this several works on OT theology appeared: H. Wheeler Robinson *Inspiration and Revelation in the OT* in 1946, O. Procksch (1949), O. J. Baab (1949), G. E. Wright (1952, 1970), Th. C. Vriezen (1949), P. van Imschoot

(1954), G. von Rad (1957, 1960), J. B. Payne (1962), A. Deissler (1972), G. Fohrer (1972), W. Zimmerli (1972), and T. L. McKenzie (1974). We shall use and discuss some of these works at appropriate place below during the course of our discussion on other topics.

Chapter 2

Old Testament Theology in the Light of Few Continuing and Debatable Issues

2.1 The Problem of Canonization of the Old Testament

The problem of canonization is not an easy issue to be resolved within the parameters of this work. What is intended here is a brief presentation of the issues connected with the theme and a possible solutions are proposed at the end for our continuing and open-ended debate on the issue. The question of canon as a central focus of OT theology was also taken up by some OT theologians in late 1970s and years that followed until the turn of the century. Notable among them was Brevard S. Childs who proposed what is called new biblical theology and has used what is called canonical criticism to talk about the final form of the text that is the canonical text given to us. The relationship between canon and OT theology is significant for our discussion since the process and the nature of canonization is both historical as well as theological problem. While we can talk about the formation of the Hebrew Scriptures as a historical process, the canon which is considered as an important step that gave status to the sacred scriptures and these scriptures eventually became a norm for the life and community of faith. For the believing community the canon has become the word of God that is both inspired and authoritative.

Terminology for Canon and its Definition: The Greek word *kanon* is derived from a Semitic root which means pole, reed, staff and straight. In the New Testament it came to mean as rule or standard or measuring stick.[34] Based on the above terminological meaning the word canon came to be used with twofold meaning in the later Christian tradition: first, it means and remains as

34 James A. Sanders, "Canon," in *Anchor Bible Dictionary*, Vol. 1. A-C (New York: Doubleday, 1992), p. 837.

the norm for the church through the centuries; second, it means the list of sacred writings from the Old and the New Testaments.[35] In the early church traditions and literature the word canon came to be used to refer to the biblical law as well as scripture, Holy scripture, the scared books etc. In general the word canon was generally used to mean the collection of sacred writings normative for faith and teaching.

Contribution of the OT theologians to the understanding of Canon: Various scholars of the Old Testament contributed to the understanding of canon in their own proposals made in relation to canon. We shall consider few important ones in this regard:

a) Ronald E. Clements: Clements is of the view that the function of Old Testament theology is to elucidate the role and authority of the OT in those religions which use it as a sacred canon and regard it as a part of its heritage, like Judaism, Christianity and Islam. Clements talks about the canonical context as a main subject matter in his discussion on OT theology. For him OT theology is: the received text and its canonical form of the literature represents "the norm" in the sense that it represents the way in which the OT was read and understood in the Jewish and early Christian communities. There are several levels of growth, of a tradition and the final canonical form is the one that came to be called as the Old Testament. So Clements calls the process of canon as "freezing of traditions." The first step of the canon was the writing down of the law (the book of Deuteronomy) which changed Israelites from a religion of cult to a religion of the book. And later writings like prophets was nothing else but preaching to call for repentance and return to torah. Thus, the formation of canon Pentateuch first and prophetic literature bring out significant theological themes of the OT that is, Torah. Therefore the process by which he OT has got canonical status is basically the process in which Torah was written down.
b) Claus Westermann: For Westermann OT is a history book and it is more than history alone, since it includes God's saving acts, God's blessings, God's judgments and human response towards these acts of God. Westermann in his structural model for describing the task of OT theology talks about the tripartite division of the Hebrew canon into torah, prophets and writings. For him these three divisions of the Hebrew Bible is the basis of OT theology. Torah as history which describes interaction between God and humankind, Prophets reveals the word of God which includes prophecy, laws and oral pronouncements, while Writings are the human response to God's action as praise,

35 Julio Trebolle, "Canon of the Old Testament," in *The New Interpreter's Dictionary of the Bible,* Vol 1. A-C (Nashville: Abingdon Press, 2006), p. 548.

thanksgiving and laments. Westermann also points out that within OT canon one can see at the original authors or redactors who might have had different understanding of God and his dealing and their understanding of God might have influenced by their socio-economic and political context.

Though Westermann starts from the tripartite division of the OT canon for an OT theology, yet later on he finds a common link between OT and NT. He states: "proclamation of God as saviour links the Old and New Testaments even though salvation here and there may mean something different." Furthermore Westermann comments that, "what the Old Testament says about God does not come to an end with the historical books of the Old Testament and what the New Testament says about God does not just begin with the birth of Jesus." Further Westermann states, "God's history with his people cannot be separated in the Old and New Testament from the history of humanity and the world."[36]

c) Walter C. Kaiser: Kaiser proposes a methodology for biblical theology by stating that the biblical theology draws the very structure of approach from the historic progression of the text and its theological seclusion and conclusions from those found in the canonical focus. Thereby it argues in part with the historical and sequential emphasis of the diachronic type of OT theology and the normative reemphasis of the structural type. And Kaiser claims that his method is more than merely synthesize or eclectically accept a new combination of what has been here to fore set of antithetical methods. It deliberately attempts to drive its theology from the exegetical insights of canonical sections.[37]

d) Brevard S. Childs: For Childs Old Testament theology is essentially a Christian discipline or Christian theological canon. For Childs the canonical study of the OT is to be distinguished from the traditio-historical approach in the way in which it evaluates the history of the text's formation. By assuming the normative status of the final form of the text the canonical approach evokes the strongest opposition from the side of traditio-historical criticism for which the heart of the exegetical task is the recovery of the depth dimension. James Barr observes that the basic conviction of Childs seems to be that one must not take up a hermeneutical base extrinsic to the text.

Concerning the relationship between the OT and the NT in the context of the canon Childs is of the view that "the two testaments retain their separate

36 See Claus Westermann's work on *Elements of Old Testament Theology*.

37 Walter C. Kaiser, *Toward an Old Testament Theology* (Grand Rapids, MI: William B. Eerdmans Publishing Company, 1978).

identity as Old and New, yet, on the other hand, the two testaments cannot be separated, as if the new no longer needed the old. There is a reciprocal movement of reading the NT confession of Jesus Christ in the light of the OT, and reading of the OT in the light of the NT." Childs firmly states that "the OT within the context of the canon is not a witness to a primitive level of faith, nor does it need to be Christianized within its historical context, it is a witness of Jesus Christ."[38]

In the canonical approach of the OT Childs proposes that the object of theological reflection is the canonical writings of the OT, that is, the Hebrew scripture which are received tradition of Israel—the 'canon'—the 'final form'. The materials for theological reflection are not the events or experiences behind the text, or apart from the construal in scripture by the community of faith and practice. Thus, the "discipline of OT theology derives from theological reflection on a received body of scripture whose formation was the result of lengthy history of development" that is, from pre-exilic period to the Hellenistic era. "Central to its history was a hermeneutical activity which continued to shape the material theologically in order to render it accessible to future generation of believers. Canonization proper, which was the final stage in the process established the scope of authoritative literature."[39]

Childs' canonical method is demonstrated in the way in which he applied it to the biblical text. For instance Childs' exegesis of Psalm 8 is very interesting. The original meaning of Psalm 8 is understood as the psalm reads: A hymn in praise of God who makes human beings lord over the creation, there is harmonious relationship between creator and creation, and within creation humanity knows God. In the next stage Childs picks up several citations of the psalm in the NT and dwells particularly on Hebrews 2:5-9, which develops Christological references for it. Jesus is the one 'made for a little while lower than the angles but, crowned with glory and honour' because of his suffering he then is exalted by God to become a representative for all people. Having outlines these two biblical texts, Childs then relates the two meanings. Theologically, the content of the psalmist's faith the glory of man, but the Christian writer says Jesus as the key to the doctrine of man.

The psalm is then seen in the context of Genesis 1 - 3 in which the focus is on the creation of human beings, and also in the light of the book of Romans with its extended discussion of the redemption of man's fallen nature. The final portion of the exposition is devoted to do "hearing" using as a background of another view of human situation in the book of Job and Ecclesiastes 3:11 which are in the tone of Psalm 8. Childs says that the NT writer of the Hebrews was grappling with sides of the question "what is man" and has seen the answer in Jesus Christ. Thus, for Childs, this Christological interpretation is legitimate. Thus, the canonical

38 Fore more details see Brevard S. Childs, *Old Testament Theology in a Canonical Context* (Philadelphia: Fortress Press, 1986).

39 Ibid.

way of reading the psalm integrates it into a general Christian view of man which is derived not from this or that text in isolation, but from the general drift of scripture read as a unified task.

While it is interesting to note the important approach taken by Childs, Bonnie Kittel[40] notes the following features: first, here the 'original meaning' and the canonical shape being identical, the tension in later explorations using the canonical approach is absent here; second, canonical approach requires setting the OT text against the material of NT that reutilize the material or that are similar to it; third, the Christological approach is employed to appropriate the message of the text—which is a precritical mode of interpretation; fourth, in order to "hear" both voices Childs is forced to hypothesize a stance for the writer of Hebrews that places than he appears to be from the plain sense of the NT text. This seems to be rather a convoluted way of bringing biblical texts together to suit one view point.

Old Testament as Scripture and the understanding of Canon: The early Christian church inherited Jewish Scriptures along with its understanding of canon. It was a general assumption that the biblical books were authoritative in the life of the church, even though the extent of the canon and the nature of authority continued to be debated. The early Church continued to adapt the list even while the process of the list of books continued to be debated over several years. The initial list of Old Testament canonical books was only set at the council of Hippo (393) and Carthage (397 and 497). All the books that had been accepted in the council were officially canonized and accepted many other books to be authoritative.[41]

The impact of Protestant Renaissance and Reformation on the development of canon was immense. The canon was seen as the product of the faith and tradition of the communities in Protestantism.[42] The Protestant reformers sought to free the Bible from the dominance of ecclesiastical tradition by emphasizing the pre-eminence of the word over tradition. Other reformers also sought the unity of scripture by holding together the historical and theological dimensions of the text, its literal and spiritual meanings. The Calivinistic reformers, for instance wanted to uphold the scriptures as against the traditions of the church which claimed their role in the formation of the Bible.[43]

In the sixteenth century a sharp polarity developed between the Protestant insistence in the sole authority of the Bible and the Roman Catholic claim of

40 Bonnie Kittel, "Reviews of Brevard S. Childs," *Introduction to the Old Testament as Scripture* with a response by B. S. Childs," *JSOT* 16 (1980), pp. 1-60.

41 John H. Hayes and Fredrick C. Prussner, *Old Testament Theology: Its History and Development* (Atlanta: John Knox Press, 1985), pp. 268-271.

42 Ibid., p. 269.

43 Brevard S. Childs, *Introduction to the Old Testament as Scripture* (London: SCM Press, 1979), pp. 43-45.

ecclesial authority. The reformers argued that the Bible was authoritative, not because the Church made it so, but because of the word of God which it contained. The Roman Catholic theologians however argued that the Church had been the human medium through which the Spirit of God had given the Scripture a concrete form and thus tradition could not be placed on par with the word of God. By mid nineteenth century the widespread recognition and acceptance of the historical criticism had played an important role in the dogmatic positions held both by Protestants and Catholics on the Bible.[44]

Canon and Criticism: As noted above B. S. Childs had proposed what is popularly called "canonical criticism" The contents of the final canonical form of the text are given a special significance. Childs sets the task of the analysis of the final form of the Hebrew Bible as descriptive one. This analysis focuses its attention on the final form of the biblical text, what is called canonical text. It also treats the literature in its own integrity and concerns to study the feature of this peculiar set of religious texts in relation to their usage within the historical community of ancient Israel. This final form of scripture lies in the peculiar relationship between text and people of God which is constitutive of the canon and reflects a history of encounter between God and Israel.[45] For Childs the canon is a medium through which this peculiar relationship between God and Israel is described and thus it reflects in the canonical text. Therefore the final form of the text must be given importance in the formation of canon.

As was noted earlier Childs' proposal has some inherent problems. James Barr argues that canonical criticism proposed by Childs has its own limitation and there is no single final form. Barr argues that if canon is taken as the final boundary for doing biblical theology, the factors such as the apocryphal literature, other non-biblical intertestamental literature, the Qumran scrolls, and other materials seem to be excluded from any real functional role. Without recourse to matters that lie behind or outside of the text the New Testament and many texts cannot be fully understood.[46]

The Relationship Between OT Theology and Canon: The relationship between OT theology and canon is undeniable as we have been presenting in this essay. In order to further probe the issues in this regard we shall make the following comments and observations:

a) Textual fluidity: One of the most interesting aspects of intrabiblical intertextuality is the fluidity of citation and allusion. Exact quotations are rare such as the verbatim citation of Micah 3:12 in Jeremiah 26:18;

44 Brevard S. Childs, *Introduction to the Old Testament as Scripture* (London: SCM Press, 1979), p. 80.

45 Ibid., pp. 70-75.

46 James Barr, *The Problem of Biblical Theology* cited in John H. Hayes and Fredrick C. Prussner, *Old Testament Theology*, pp. 271-273.

attribution is also rare within the Jewish canon (outside the historical books where even so it is not common until Chronicles) such as the mention of Jeremiah's prophecy in Ezra 1:1. But fluid references to earlier traditions are many, and these include reference to the authoritative traditions known from the biblical stories relating the great episodes in the Hexateuch as well as in the Davidic traditions. When they are alluded to or cited for the most part it was done for the authoritative value in them recognizable by the believing community for which the new speech or text was being composed.

b) Adaptability and Stability: Adaptability is a major characteristic feature of the very concept of canon. Throughout the period of canonical process in antiquity up to stabilization of text and canon, and even to a limited extent beyond it down today, a canon is marked by its malleability, citations and allusions throughout the literature of early Judaism including the New Testament exhibit the relative adaptability of authoritative texts and traditions. All situations find their own suitable texts from the canon. This characteristic feature makes the canon stable to a great extent.

c) The function of the canon as a norm: There are different theological orientations within the canonical documents (Jewish, Hellenistic, Apocalyptic Christianity, Catholic Christianity). In this regard, it is to be noted that canon reflects various strands mentioned above right from its inception in the early church. Some scholars also propose "canon within canon", that is, a principle or a center which is taken as the essential and controlling element within the larger canon, and which may serve as an interpretive element of the whole. Since, the canon is pluralistic in practice, the effort to define it a uniform and coherent norm would seem to be contrary even to the intentions of the early church, which canonized no single theological position but a range of theological viewpoints.

d) The hermeneutical value of the canon: as was stated earlier with Childs and other scholars there has been a growing interest in the relevance of the canon for theological exegesis resulted in what is called "canonical criticism." Two main forms of this enterprise can be noted on this point: first, the theological interpretation of scripture is properly attentive to the canon when it takes as its basis the "final canonical form" of a given text, as distinct from sources that can be identified behind the text or as distinct from an original form of the text, and interprets that text in terms of its "full canonical context," as distinct from an original historical context. Thus, the literary and theological context furnished by the canon itself is made the touchstone of interpretation; second, another form of canonical criticism attends not to the final form of a text or its intracanonical relationships, but to the canonical process exhibited within the texts, that is, the hermeneutical dynamics by which authoritative (preliterary) traditions were not only stabilized in writing, but were subsequently and repeatedly revised and adapted, reformulated and rewritten, so as to make them freshly relevant to the changing circumstances and needs of the religious community.

e) Canon and inspiration: it has been noted that "inspired" and "canonical" are not synonymous in their detailed probe as it appears to be at the surface level. On the contrary, many in Judaism and Christianity are said to have been "inspired by God," yet their writings are not in any community's canon whether or not these can be called Scripture is disputed. In any case the concept of inspiration is a broader one than that of canon. Understanding canon as having been guided by the Spirit through all its stages of formation permits it to continue functioning for a believing community as paradigm of how the Reality called "God" impacted the vision and thinking of ancestors in the faith and how it may continue to do so in the present.[47]

f) Integral link between OT theology and OT canon: B. S. Childs is right in suggesting the idea that one should do OT theology on the basis of the book of the canonical form rather than on the basis of historical and redaction critical hypothesis.[48] This means that the subject matter for the OT theology is the very canonical writings of the Old Testament not the events or experiences behind the text. But this proposal of Childs is not very tenable because of the fact that both the text and what happened behind the text as a result of which we were given the present canonical text cannot be separated and if it is done it will only result in shallow understanding of the text.

g) OT theology and canon within canon: OT theology does not consider reading the scriptures in the light of creeds, the rule of faith, the Church's theological tradition and exegetical tradition. OT theology cannot do justice to the reading of the OT books if it is based on the creeds and rule of faith established by the Church. For instance, OT theology treats the first part of the canon of the Hebrew Bible as significant in their own right. OT theology does not reevaluate and reinterpret its

47 For more information and discussion on the points a-d see the sources: Harry Y. Gamble, "Canon: New Testament," in *The Anchor Bible Dictionary*, Vol. 1. A-C (New York: Doubleday, 1992), Julio Trebolle, "Canon of the Old Testament," *The New Interpreter's Dictionary of the Bible*, Vol. 1. A-C, eds. Katherine Doob Sakenfeld, et. al (Nashville: Abingdon Press, 2006), pp. 548-563; Moshe Halbertal, *The People of the Book: Canon, Meaning, and Authority* (Cambridge: Harvard University Press, 1997); James A. Sanders, "Canon," *Anchor Bible Dictionary*, Vol. 1. A-C (New York: Doubleday, 1992), pp. 837-852.

48 B. S. Childs, *Old Testament Theology in a Canonical Context* (London: SCM Press, 1985), p. 6.

significant insights in the light of the way they are used in the New Testament, The New Testament's use of the OT texts has no necessary significance for what OT theology does with these texts.[49]

h) OT theology strikes balance in giving importance to OT and NT canons: at the same time OT theology does not undermine the canonical value of NT for its theologizing process. In this regard Rendtorff is right in suggesting "that the Hebrew Bible is itself a theological book. That means then the Bible does not only become theological through interpretation by a later-elaborated theology, be it rabbinic or Christian; rather, it is possible and necessary to find the theological ideas and messages of the biblical texts themselves."[50] Therefore, the confluence of various traditions and the combination of OT and NT canons are to be considered for an effective OT theological articulation in the light of its canonical theology.

On the basis of the foregoing discussion on the integral link between OT theology and the issues related to canonization we now make the following concluding evaluatory remarks in order to talk about the dynamic relationship exist between the issue of canonization and OT theology. First, the relationship between OT theology and canon talks about the community behind the process of canonization. This community may have existed apart from the 'original' authors or even the redactors. Second, this relationship talks about the dynamic unity exists between the OT and NT and one cannot replace another. Third, Christological stance is necessary part of the canonization that unites both the testaments in a dynamic way. Fourth, canon thus becomes not only a historical norm, but also an existential reality of every new generation who may seek to find the new meaning of the biblical text. Fifth, one should recognize the plurality of the canons that each community in the early period of the Christian church made it viable option for their own community norm. This plurality within the very canon itself and its formation in the subsequent periods of history must be respected. On the basis of the above observations we conclude that the issue of OT theology and its dynamic relationship with the question of canonization is an ongoing, continuing and debatable issue.

2.2 The Plurality of Old Testament Theologies

For some OT theologians the task of OT theology is to address and deal with the issue of the plurality of theologies within the OT theology; not only they seemingly are independent but at the same time coexisting with one another. While this plurality could be a welcoming sign for a creative presentation of the Old Testament material, it leads to other set of problems leading to disunity and

49 J. L. Mays, *Psalms* (Louisville: Westminster John Knox Press, 1994), pp. 154-155.

50 Rolf Rendtorff, *Canon and Theology* (Minneapolis: Fortress Press, 1993), pp. 40-41.

atomization in the very presentation of the OT materials as some would think.[51] For a long time it has not been recognized that there exists the plurality in doing the Old Testament Theology and the hegemony of some so called dominant theologies continued. For that matter the hegemony of dogmatic theology continued several centuries from which the Old Testament theology was redeemed. Now that OT theology itself has become hegemonic and it is the time to point out its inherent problems and the breaking of such hegemonic and monopolizing forces had to be urgently addressed so that OT theology can be liberated and become liberative force for the future biblical interpretation. Knierim insisted that the Old Testament's "plurality of theologies" requires a systematic and careful analysis, "or we will not know how to read the Old Testament theologically."[52] Further Knierim supposes that this criteria of reading OT with theological plurality must come from the Old Testament itself and not from the dogmatic theology as it happened before. Additionally Knierim suggests that the theme of "Yahweh's universal dominion in justice and righteousness" could become a criterion for talking about the plurality in the OT theology. This is not only a central theme for OT theology but a criterion by which all themes and theologies are measured and evaluated.[53]

Contribution of OT theologians for the interpretation of plurality in OT theology: It would be appropriate at this point to talk about various OT theologians who have contributed and enriched our understanding of plurality of Old Testament theologies and its debate.

a) Ben C. Ollenburger: According to Ollenburger the theological problem of the Old Testament's pluralism comes even to more focus when we look at it from the point of view of theological substance. Even though the OT presents itself towards unity under the theme Yahweh as a monotheistic claim, we need to question such a claim at the universal level. We need to ask the question where is pluralism present in the idea of monotheistic claims on Yahweh? Ollenburger suggests that our main task is the examination of the correspondence or relationship of the Old Testament's theologies themselves. We need to bring to the forefront the issue of the substantive or semantic structure of OT's pluralism, and its theological identity and validity. For Ollenburger this is the task of the OT theology because it reflects the OT's central problem. For such an examination, we need the proper criteria. These criteria have to be drawn from within the Old Testament itself. Their discernment and

51 For a detailed discussion on this issue read Rolf P. Knierim, *The Task of Old Testament Theology: Substance, Method, and Cases* (Grand Rapids, MI: William B. Eerdmans Publishing Company, 1995), pp. 1-6.

52 Ibid., p. 29.

53 Ibid., p. 49.

definition is the task of the methodology of or the prolegomena to OT theology.[54]

b) Rolf Knierim: As was stated earlier in the introduction of this essay Knierim is of the view that the plurality in the OT theology has to be carefully analyzed and studied. First of all Knierim opines that the Old Testament must be viewed as a whole and for this holistic dimension plurality can serve as an enriching phenomenon. This is further illustrated by Knierim with the help of tradition history and canon.

The tradition history in the ancient Israel is a type of pluralistic reality, generated the plurality of Yahweh theologies. But it is not clear how these plural theologies are interrelated to one another. According to Knierim this question has not been resolved till today. As long as the plurality of theologies in the tradition history did not become clear the problem remains and continues. However, one should not forget the fact that the tradition itself in the OT is developed in a pluralistic way[55]

The canon has addressed and finalized the above stated problem in that "the process of canonization, authoritative theological traditions from many generations and diverse settings were condensed into close juxtaposition on the same synchronic level. In the canon, they have come together face to face—so to say—to conference, and their canonic situation, if it means anything, authoritatively demands the clarification of their relationship."[56] Thus, Knierim is of the view that various theological positions in the Old Testament are substantively or semantically in agreement, if they are in relation to one another and how that relationship exists can become a key issue to be addressed because they coexist in the canon.[57]

Knierim further exemplifies his two points by raising few important questions: "I wonder what would have happened in Jerusalem around 612 BCE had an encounter taken place between the Deuteronomic theologians, the Jehovist, the priestly temple theologians, sages, and Jeremiah, Zephaniah, Nahum and Habakkuk; or a hundred years later, around 515 BCE, how a theological encounter would have looked with all of those just mentioned present, but now also with the addition of Ezekiel and his school, the deuteronomistic school, Deutero and

54 Ben C. Ollenburger, *The Flowering of Old Testament Theology* (Indiana: Eisenbrauns, 1992), pp. 472-473.

55 Rolf P. Knierim, *The Task of Old Testament Theology*, pp. 3-4.

56 Ibid., p. 4.

57 Ibid.

Trito-Isaiah and their disciples, and Haggai and Zechariah as well. Unfortunately, we are only left with their juxtaposition in the canon but not with any discussion about their relationship, neither their own discussion by those who juxtaposed them canonically."[58]

Knierim is of the view that even though all theologies in the Old Testament are united in affirming Yahweh as one and only God, yet their explanation of this affirmation vary or differ. These varying or differing explanations of the oneness or exclusivity of Yahweh reach to the heart of the theological problem of the Old Testament, especially as they coexist in the canon.[59] Thus, in effect what Knierim is suggesting is that we cannot take the existence of plurality in the OT at the face value even when the canon placed such pluralism as a possible one.

c) Erhard Gerstenberger: Gerstenberger objects those approaches, particularly the canonical approaches to OT theology that seeks to construct a coherent and unitary theology from the Old Testament that is binding for modern believers thus treating the final form of the Old Testament as both the object of interpretations and the authoritative subject from which modern interpreters should receive religious orientation and instruction. Gerstenberger objects that there is no one uniform coherent canon and that the preliminary stages of the literature prior to the completion of the individual books may not be discarded or ignored when investigating the theologies in the Old Testament.[60] For Gerstenberger the word "plural" is important in the context it refers to the faith of ancient Israel in its contemporary environment and in everyday life. In other words, the diversity of time conditioned experiences of faith, statements and systems (or ideas about God) current in the different social groups throughout the history of Israel witnessed to in the Old Testament. Although OT underwent a long history of development, we cannot solely rely on the written documents of the Old Testament as the object of study, but must also make use of archaeological finds and consult the ancient West Asian context and neighbouring cultures and religions into which the faith of Israel was embedded. In other words, Gerstenberger is of the view that ancient Israelite faith underwent several changes and in a pluralistic context of other influences from West Asian background it always functioned in ways that suits its religious and social environment. For

58 Rolf P. Knierim, *The Task of Old Testament Theology*, p. 5.

59 Ibid., p. 6.

60 Erhard Gerstenberger, *Theologies in the Old Testament* (Minneapolis: Fortress Press, 2002), pp. 13-14.

instance, Gerstenberger states the following to further clarify his claim as follows:

> 'Yahweh is one and only one' and reserved for Israel (Deut 6:4). Of course it is right that in their historical situation people in Israel should and may have worshipped the God who was exclusively real to them because he was near to them and cared for them. But we cannot conclude either from the exclamation or from the theological explanations of Deutero-Isaiah that Yahweh had an objective uniqueness which was equally clear to all other groups and which they accepted as binding. In a concrete way, the exclusiveness of Yahweh remains the hope and expectation of limited communities who are fond of transferring their claim to others. It is not an objective fact that can be verified, from which we may simply present in our theology. There were often monolatrous and indeed monotheistic claims in the history of ancient Near East ... such claims cannot conceal the fact that in principle any belief in God is limited to a particular group and that equally fundamentally in many Old Testament texts there is an almost unlimited openness to the neighbouring ancient Near Eastern cultures and religions.[61]

In the light of the above discussion Gerstenberger proposes that different religious dimensions of our present day social organization (any present day contemporary socio-religious situation) also serve, as the object of study in OT theology for the ultimate theological task thereof is to bring these theologies, those of ancient Israel in their various social settings, and ours in our social circumstances, into dialogue with each other.[62] This dialogue will enable the present and contemporary readers to appropriately read and integrate into the ancient texts like the Bible.

d) Walter Brueggemann: From a postmodern point of view the most challenging and stimulating work was done by Brueggemann in the area of the plurality of OT theologies or the presence of pluralism in the interpretive process of the Old Testament. To begin with Brueggemann affirms that it is high time that we realize and reject the hegemonic forces in the interpretation of the Old Testament. Before venturing into the idea of plurality in OT theology, Brueggemann talks about the polyphonic character of the biblical text that has to

61 Erhard Gerstenberger, *Theologies in the Old Testament* (Minneapolis: Fortress Press, 2002), pp. 16-17.

62 Ibid., pp. 15-17.

be borne in mind in today's interpretive and theologizing context. Taking a cue from Mark Coleridge whose quotation is cited by Brueggemann as follows:

> The Bible insists upon a common narrative, but one which includes a diversity of voices; many stories comprise *the* story. God's story is both single and several. It also insists upon a narrative which at times most disjointed and the connectedness of which is perceived only by way of struggle. The Bible is no easy read.[63]

On the basis of the above statement Brueggemann affirms that we need to be faithful to this polyphonic character of the Bible with the first listeners[64] or listening community, to understand their dialect and grammar and then look towards its openness for the second listening community without any way being subjected to any authoritarian closure or reductionism. "This quality of *many voices as the voice* of the text has let this text persist with such authority, and has enabled its first listening community to persist through time, through many 'toils and dangers.'"[65]

Brueggemann affirms that the basic interpretation of the Old Testament should and ought to happen in a pluralistic context. Thus, he calls for disestablishment from hegemonic interpretation to pluralism for which he further calls for disestablishment of institutional vehicles and mechanisms. At the outset Brueggemann calls for a critical examination of two kinds of establishment (hegemonic) assumptions that dominated Old Testament theological interpretation. On the one hand, OT theology as a Christian enterprise, could assume that it was dealing with normative socio-religious and moral convictions of the West. Due to this reason this Christian enterprise could allow the OT to flow continuously into the New Testament because the majority of Christians are from the West. Thus, the study of the text and its method was considered as normative as it comes from the West. On the other hand, OT theology in its centrist form, has been largely an academic matter shaped by the German Universities[66] slightly altered and taught

63 Mark Coleridge, "Life in the Crypt or Why Bother with Biblical Studies," *Biblical Interpretation* 2 (July 1994), p. 148, cited by Walter Brueggemann, *Theology of the Old Testament*, p. 89.

64 By this Brueggemann means that every biblical text has two listenings. One is the faithful community that received the text, whom he calls the first audience. Then the text is continued to be listened by the ongoing community that relates the text to its own grammar and dialect.

65 Brueggemann, *Theology of the Old Testament*, p. 89.

66 For this a classical example could be cited. In the eighteenth century, biblical scholars at the university sought to recover a universal or catholic Bible, one capable of fostering cultural and social unity. At the university the declining confessional Bible was reconstituted in academic

by the American universities. This academic shaping assumed that the Enlightenment theology should prevail over any novel way of reading and interpreting the Bible. In the light of this Brueggemann notes three epistemological assumptions that the interpretation of the biblical text was carried out: first, a historicism that could determine "what happened" and no meaning could be found beyond this "what happened;" second, evolutionism, under its influence it was viewed that religious development occurred in a straight line of unilateral progress from the primitive stage to the modern or sophisticated level; third, the influence of rationalism that went even beyond claiming something above naturalistic and scientific world.[67]

Therefore, Brueggemann wanted to move away from what he calls: a confessional shift and a hegemonic interpretation towards a pluralistic interpretive context, which is reflected in the texts themselves, in biblical interpreters, and in the culture at large. We shall make few observations in this regard in the paragraphs that follow:

Plurality of the testimonies in the text: Brueggemann talks about the plurality of testimonies concerning God and Israel's life with God. This is particularly reflected in a deeper way in the theological articulation concerning exile. The Priestly and Deuteronomic traditions compete with one another in articulating the exile from a different perspective. Several stances on the theodicy in the book of Job is yet another example of the existence of plurality of testimonies. Therefore, Brueggemann

---

form. The political goals of the German Enlightenment had a strong academic impulse: many universities were created or remade at this time to serve the interests of the state. German universities still retained their confessional identities and ecclesial origins. The main goal of these universities was to produce rational, tolerant and accommodative people who were capable of serving in the churches and government of progressive rulers in Germany's territories, kingdoms and electorates. Scholars like Johann David Michaelis (1717-1791) of Göttingen succeeded in creating frames of reference that allowed professors and students to engage the Bible and employ interesting frameworks not dependent of religious identity. In the broadest terms, Michaelis's project was to remake biblical Israel into a classical civilization. In order to do this Michaelis did three things in particular: first, he made it a mandatory Hebrew language study with the comparative use of Arabic, Syriac, and Ethiopic and imported scientific standards from the study of Greek and Latin; second, relying on the work of Robert Lowth, Michaelis used the invented concept of biblical poetry to recover the Bible as an anthology of sublime classical literature. This involved the work of aesthetic judgment by those who studied the biblical poetry; third, in the area of biblical law, Michaelis denied the theological normativity of the Bible, claiming that God never meant (the Mosaic law) to bind any other nation but the Israelites. On the whole the main goal of Michaelis was to recommend he use of critical scholarship to inoculate the German territories against fanaticism and religious violence. For more details on this subject read, Michael C. Legaspi, *The Death of Scripture and the Rise of Biblical Studies* (Oxford: Oxford University Press, 2010).

67 Brueggemann, *Theology of the Old Testament*, p. 708.

argues that in the so called final form of the text in the canonization process had not gained a complete hegemonic victory over any interpretive trajectory. This is because the canonization process itself is one of accommodation and compromise. Thus, Brueggemann concludes: "The decision to hold the Priestly and Deuteronomic traditions in tension, accepting and acknowledging both as truth, is a striking evidence of pluralism. Old Testament theology must live with that pluralistic practice of dispute and compromise, so that the texts cannot be arranged in any single or unilateral pattern. It is the process of dispute and compromise itself that constitutes Israel's mode of theological testimony."[68]

Dispute and Accommodation in interpretation: Having identified plurality of different voices in talking about God and Israel's relationship, Brueggemann is of the view that in a contemporary Old Testament theological interpretation we could notice proliferation of methods with different interpretive voices. These interpretations from OT theological perspective are coming from wide range of socio-political-economic contexts, therefore OT theology has to accommodate such wide variety of interpretive voices in ways that are unexpected yet very novel way than before. On this Brueggemann affirms: "Because different interpretations in different contexts—driven by different hopes, fears and hurts—ask different questions from the ground up, it is clear that there will be no widely accepted "canon within the canon," which is itself a function of hegemonic interpretation. As a consequence, we are now able to see that every interpretation is context-driven and interest-driven to some large extent.[69] However, Brueggemann believes that any context-driven interpretation is only a reality in a given and particular setting and it is also a temporary one. Such an interpretation must be willing to be open for accommodation as well as dispute, so it accentuates the point that Israel always arrives afresh at Yahweh for a new beginning and learning.[70]

The metaphor of testimony: having described that Israel's relationship with her God is exhibited in plurality of voices Brueggemann now talks about the very metaphor of testimony itself with some details. Brueggemann is of the view that in any serious courtroom trial, the testimony is challenged by other counter and competing testimony. This is an indication to say that no unilateral testimony of Yahweh by one voice in Israel need to be accepted. While commenting on the failure

68 Brueggemann, *Theology of the Old Testament*, p. 710.

69 Ibid., p. 711.

70 Ibid., pp. 711-712.

of the hegemonic interpretations of the Old Testament in the light of Western church sorry record of economics (be more self-indulgent and extravagant) and sexuality (still reeling under male-centred dominant structures) Brueggemann proposes an alternative understanding of Yahwism. He writes: "Thus, I have insisted that Yahwism in ancient Israel is a matter of communal praxis. We may expect, with emerging pluralism and collapsed hegemony, that the serious, intentional, disciplined practice of Yahweh may take many forms, some local and some larger, some ecclesial and some extraecclesial. Old Testament theology will perhaps on occasion be concrete and bodily enough to authorize such practices in the face of dominant metanarratives that resist such radical embodiment."[71]

The metanarrative of military consumerism: Brueggemann clarifies that pluralism in the public arena does not mean "anything goes." Such a notion of unmitigated freedom is itself a function of military consumerism. Brueggemann clarifies that it means concern for the individual's well-being, security, happiness are the result of getting, having, using, and consuming, all the activities that may be done without restraint or limit, even at the expense of others. In terms of the military metaphor Brueggemann is of the view that the one who is with consumerist attitude will eventually wants to achieve whatever it takes to enjoy well-being, security, and happiness. For this purpose the use of force, coercion, or violence, either to secure or to maintain a disproportion, is completely in agreement with the notion of happiness. Thus, the "military consumerism" has become a dominant metanarrative and also it becomes a hegemonic interpretation using the Old Testament for such a dominant self-serving and self-interest interpretive enterprise. Brueggemann converts this metanarrative and applies to the Israel's testimony of Yahweh. He writes: "Israel's testimony invites "the court" into a world of *undomesticated holiness*, marked by staggering sovereignty and inexplicable fidelity, but given in ways that are disjunctive and disruptive. Such an offer testifies against the hegemonic vision of military consumerism, which imagines that the world can be secured, explained, mastered, and controlled, and which makes convenient common cause with the domesticated divinity of bourgeois Christianity ... Israel's testimony invites "the court" into a world of *originary generosity* in which gifts are inexplicably given for "more than all we can ask or imagine" (Eph 3:20). Such an offer testifies against the grudging inclination of military consumerism, which concludes that no gifts are given, that there is no generosity,

71 Brueggemann, *Theology of the Old Testament*, p. 716.

> that everything is quid pro quo, and that one must have self-sufficient resources in order to get more ... Israel's testimony invites "the court" into a world of *indefatigable possibility*, in which promises are endlessly enacted beyond all visible circumstance, and in which new waves of promise are being uttered that permit passionate hope beyond every explanatory option. Such an offer tells against the closed-down world of military consumerism that imagines there are no more promises to be kept and no more words to be uttered, and so concludes in a self-destructive, world-destructive despair ... Israel's testimony invites "the court" into a world of *open-ended interaction*, a covenantal exchange that continually redeploys power between the strong and the weak and that even invites demanding, insistent interventions against Yahweh. Such an offer of lively covenantal existence testifies against the fixed, fated world of military consumerism, in which the poor only become poorer, the rich become richer, and together the rich and the poor end in a paralysis of pride, despair, and a futile death ... Israel's testimony invites "the court" into a world of *genuine neighborliness*, in which members in a community share without fear and practice justice that assures well-being for every member of the community. Such an invitation to community testifies against the harsh, definitional selfishness of military consumerism, in which every neighbor is reduced to a usable commodity, where the process of commoditization eventually empties even the subject of the individual of all human possibility."[72]
>
> In the light of the above lengthy argument Brueggemann concludes that in a world of self-serving, hegemonic, and dominant metanarratives, Israel's testimony opens up a possibility of sharing and caring, nurturing and upholding metanarratives about her relationship with Yahweh and with their neighbors defines an alternative model that we need to capture in our theological interpretation of the Old Testament.

On the basis of our foregoing discussion on the scholars' proposal concerning the theme of plurality of Old Testament theologies we now make the following concluding evaluatory comments and observations: first, the plurality of OT theologies was considered as a problem by some OT theologians since it may lead to loss of the sight of unity of the Old Testament unless the idea of pluralism is carefully delineated; second, the tradition history may be helpful to unpack the presence and growth of plurality of traditions even though such a task is not easy to be carried out; third, canon is a practical manifestation of accommodation of plural theologies as it either by force or with ease imposes canonical unity by bringing various traditions and books together; fourth, pluralism is not only seen in the canon but in the very faith of Israel in their daily living experiences and the

72 Brueggemann, *Theology of the Old Testament*, pp. 719-720.

way in which they appropriated their ancient West Asian traditions and cultures; fifth, pluralism has to be taken seriously in the very interpretive process of the Old Testament. For this theological interpretation of the OT we need to take into account: i) the polyphonic character of the text in which pluralistic voices have to be heard to make any unilateral presentation of God in ancient Israel; ii) disestablishment of the text from the hegemonic and dominant interpretation must happen for a liberative reading of the Bible; iii) the Bible is a record of plurality of testimonies and one need to capture this insight to avoid any one sided and dominant interpretation; iv) the biblical interpretation has to be seen in the light of dispute and accommodation so that multiple and plural voices can be heard of without any discrimination; v) the very metaphor of testimony invokes a discussion that counter testimonies are accommodated and heard to avoid any unilateral understanding of God's dealing with the people; vi) Bible can be misunderstood in the metanarrative of military consumerism and we need to liberate Old Testament interpretation from such a self-serving and individualistic interpretations. Thus, the issue of plurality of OT theology contains some unresolved issues open for further debate and discussion.

2.3 History, History of Tradition, Salvation History and Story in the Old Testament

Since the seventh century, when historians were forced to admit that biblical versions of history beginning with Adam and Eve, could do, no longer accommodate the accumulating evidence of a divergent picture of world history, the biblical history of world and Israel presented in the OT has been a matter of contention. Throughout the intervening centuries biblical scholars have sought to defend, modify, and explain biblical history, recognizing that the first editors of the biblical material were concerned, at least in a minimum fashion, with producing what, we would call "history" in several major blocks of Old Testament material, Genesis to 2 Kings being the most obvious example. That is, the material was structured in a more or less continuous narrative, causes s were stipulated and the story line follows a chronological outline.

Religionsgeschichte school was interested in the actual (factual) history before von Rad. For instance, Gabler was of the opinion that the final redactional form of the text is to be kept in mind. At the beginning of the nineteenth century, for example, De Wette was willing to give up on writing a history of Israel and its religion because he denied that we possess sufficient reliable biblical evidence. His contemporary like Wilhelm Vatke wrote in 1835. He was of the view that the Hebrews did not at all rise themselves to the standpoint of properly historical contemplation, and there is no book of the Old Testament, however much it may contain material that is otherwise objectively historical, that deserves the name of true historiography.

Theologians like Gottfried Menken (1768-1831) Johann Tobias Beck (1804-1878) and especially Johann Konrad von Hofmann (1810-1877) made significant contribution towards the debate on the salvation history. The theme of von Hofmann's work was the unity of the Bible, the integrating principle being defined in terms of a divinely guided history of redemption, a *heilsgeschichte* which had as its ultimate goal the establishment of the kingdom of God. The Old Testament contained the prediction or foreshadowing, in ever increasing intensity, of the fulfillment of God's purpose in the salvation eventually brought about in Christ. Its religion, in turn, he characterized as a progressively revealed saving truth which, it is important to note, was to be found not in the actual teachings of the Old Testament but, rather, in the events heralding the realization of the kingdom of God. Hofmann states: "we divide the study of the Old Testament into two different subjects, Old Testament history and Old Testament theology. The former reproduces the series of events recorded in the Old Testament as a continuous history. The latter describes the history of the proclamation of salvation implied in that history. The former one teaches the intrinsic connection of the revelatory facts, the latter one that of the divine revelation by word. While in both disciplines the understanding of the Bible as the document of salvation must precede its historical interpretation, yet the latter cannot be dispensed with either. The records of those events demand to be read as the record of the realization of actual salvation, yet of one which tends towards its full realization … The history recorded in the Old Testament is the history of salvation (*heilsgeschichte*) as proceeding towards its full realization. Hence the things recorded therein are to be interpreted theologically, i. e., as aiming at their final goal; and thus as being of the same nature as the goal yet modified by their respective place in history."[73]

On the basis of Gerhard von Rad's proposals for the Old Testament theology few important questions can be raised on the issue of the understanding of history. Von Rad was highly influential by his teacher von Hofmann in making the proposals of the Old Testament history. This can be noted in von Rad's sharp division of two versions of Israel's history: modern critical history and the confessional history on which Israel's faith has built up. Von Rad is of the view that the Old Testament is primarily a book of history concerned with the divine activity in history. The Old Testament writings confine themselves to representing Yahweh's relationship to Israel and the world in one aspect only, namely as a continuing divine activity in history. This implies that in principle Israel's faith is grounded in a theology of history.[74]

For von Rad history is a central and indispensible theme because he thinks that the OT is a history book. Moreover, for von Rad history is the place in which God reveals the secret of his person. Thus, OT theology ought to be charted out on

---

73 J. C. K. von Hofmann, *Weissagung und Erfüllung in Alten und in Neuen Testaments* (Nördlingen, 1841); *Interpreting the Bible* (Minneapolis, 1959).

74 Gerhard von Rad, *Old Testament Theology*, Vol. 1.

a historical grid because it is a definitive trait of OT texts that they are concerned with history. Von Rad operates his work in the framework of *heilsgeschichte* that is, faith as the history of actualization of traditions. For him history of traditions is history of Israel's effort of understanding herself; they have (Israel) done this by retelling the traditions in the light of their context, of what God has done in their life (it is a continuous process of reshaping and retelling of the traditions). In this process, Hexateuch was presented with addition of two blocks of materials namely, Deuteronomy and Chronicler history. Yahweh continued to act in the history by raising charismatic leaders, Judges, divine election of Zion, by choosing David as king, by raising prophets and even by sending people to exile because von Rad thinks that exile is a time for reflection, and the Deuteronomistic history is the product of this time, and during post-exilic reflection the material basically produced was Ezra-Nehemiah and Chronicles. In all these events Israel saw God's hand. All this von Rad calls as unfolding of traditions, that is, Israel's testimony to what God has done. But all these traditions are unfolded in their own way, not in a very systematic order of events, rather the growth and formation of traditions itself is a theological achievement. Thus, in von Rad, the history of growth of traditions takes precedence over systematization. Thus, for von Rad, OT theology is the unfolding of the testimony of Israel captured in retelling of traditions, and therefore OT theology should follow the sequence of events, not any systematic order.

The most vociferous criticism is against von Rad's dissociation of confessional history from factual history. Eichrodt accuses von Rad of violently wrenching apart the picture of history reconstructed by higher criticism and salvation portrayed in the utterances of OT faith. This leads to confession of 'spurious factuality' with 'historical truth.' Thereby the link between the testimony of faith and facts of history are seriously threatened. Eichrodt compares von Rad with Bultmann and asks if a valid revelation can be based on recitals which possess no links with historical reality. Eichrodt also raises the question whether the historical evidence is as fragmentary as von Rad assumes for the early period, and whether traditions history necessarily leads to the conclusion that Israel's history began with the amphictyony.

Frans Hesse criticizes von Rad for making confessional history which is erroneous, the object of real faith. Hesse feels that faith needs to be founded on what really happened and not what purportedly happened. So Hesse concludes that von Rad's theology is a history of religious study rather than theology, because theology would be occupied with facts and not testimonies.

***Further Debate*:** It was Wolfhart Pannenberg[75] who abandoned the idea of two histories and sought to argue that "revelation is history" and to extend the

75 Among many writings of Wolfhart Pannenberg some are worth mentioning here in relation to the debate on history. See his contributions: "Kerygma und Geschichte," in *Studien zur Theologie des altestamentlichen Überlieferungen*, ed. R. Rendtorff and K. Koch, Neukirchen,

concept of history to include "reality in its totality." However, Pannenberg is of the opinion that scientific history has its limitations in its scope, but strongly felt that there should be no dichotomy between that of actual history and the confessional history. Furthermore, Pannenberg opines that the connection between the OT and the NT is constituted by one history, namely, the universal history which is grounded in the unity of God who works in both the Testaments and remains true to his promises. In this universal history the destiny of human beings from the time of creation is unfolding according to a plan of God. Thus, Pannenberg presents a broader picture of Heilsgeschichte and makes it identical with universal history.[76] But, unfortunately no work has been done further along these lines.

In the light of the stalemate in the discussion over confessional and critical history two developments in the debate are worth mentioning:

First, much attention has been shifted to focus on tradition and the way in which traditions and streams of tradition have been shaped in the Old Testament. Hartmut Gese has argued that "theology must be understood essentially as an historical process of development." His program has been called "theology as tradition building." Gese describes his program, which in some ways simply follows von Rad's approach to its logical conclusion, as follows: "We are advocating that biblical theology has the task of determining the theology of the whole tradition and that it can accomplish this neither by isolating a dogmatic doctrine as the underlying factor of the whole, nor by descriptively rendering historical diversity as the assemblage of the whole but only attempting to grasp the totality as a cohesion. Consequently, this task confronts (a) the individual text with its preliterary antecedents (b) the development of the text as literature with its own literary classification, and (c) the growth of the text tradition into a corpus embracing the whole."[77] Gese wishes to trace the process of tradition building into the New Testament and thus produce a total biblical theology.

But unfortunately, this process of tradition building has some problems in itself: a) no continuation of traditions are seen in the Old Testament. Some materials/traditions came to an end at certain point, as for instance covenant, election etc. b) many of the OT material does not have any antecedent, that is, certainly many portions of the Old Testament are not the product of a prior tradition not have they a tradition history except as they became part of the canon of Old Testament scripture. For instance, some materials in wisdom and poetic literature in the OT. No one has yet produced a major OT theology along the lines of proposals made by Hartmut Gese.

1961, pp. 124-140; *Jesus—God and Man*, Philadelphia, 1966; *Revelation as History* (New York, 1968); *Basic Questions in Theology*, 2 Vols. Philadelphia, 1970-71.

76 Wolfhart Pannenberg, *Revelation as History*, pp. 132-133.

77 Hartmut Gese, "Tradition and Biblical Theology," in Douglas A. Knight (ed), *Tradition and Theology in the Old Testament* (Philadelphia: Fortress Press, 1977), pp. 301-326.

Second, a second development in the treatment of narrative material as a story rather than as history although it may be history-like in many places. Such an approach would not take in all the parts of the OT but only those narrative portions which have some similarity to history per se a unitary form, chronological framework, and so forth. In this regard James Barr has argued: "the long narrative corpus of the Old Testament seems to me, as a body of literature, to merit the title of story rather than that of history to put it another way, it seems to merit entirely the title of story but only in part the title history. This narrative spirals back and forward across what we would call history, sometimes coming closer to it and sometimes going far away from it."[78] Even before the proposal made by Barr, John Wharton had already argued that the word story can be replaced with history in understanding the material in the Old Testament. Wharton is of the view that story is what Israel "remembered in astonishing variety of modes reaching out to embrace most aspects of human life."[79]

To call the Bible or at least its narrative portions "a story book" certainly avoids many of the difficulties than calling it "a history book". The former takes the narrative as creative literature rather than as historical record. Moreover, story helps us to focus on the dynamics of revelation (story associated with people and their experience with the divine) that is, Old Testament is basically understood as collection of experiences of the people of God. In this way, the material in the OT can be understood as Israel's attempt to give honour and cohesion in its life by highlighting certain context for its present as well as its future. Therefore, to look Old Testament as a story means, to look what Israel wants to say about herself and not as actual history describes (not as other historians will say about Israel). Furthermore, story helps us to read the OT as a paradigmatic one for contemporary life and seeing its meaning just as we derive meaning from any other story.

The consequence of reading the narrative as story or as a literary form are several: a) it allows one to dispense with or hold in abeyance the issue of whether events happened as they were told; b) the locus or dynamics of revelation, if one chooses to use this word, can be seen as associated primarily with the people and the process which produced the story and secondarily with the story rather than with the events it tells about; c) the story can be seen as one of the ways in which Israel chose to give order and cohesion to its life by producing a symbolic context for its present and a basis for its future; d) the story, not the actual history of Israel can be viewed as what Israel wished to express about its own self-understanding.

78 James Barr, "Story and History in Biblical Theology," *Journal of Religion,* 56 (1976), pp. 11-17; reprinted in James Barr, *Scope and Authority of the Bible* (London, 1980), pp. 1-17.

79 John Wharton, "The Occasion of the Word of God: An Unguarded Essay on the Character of the OT as the Memory of God's Story with Israel," *Austin Seminary Bulletin,* 84 (Sept. 1968), pp. 5-54, esp. p. 22.

e) the OT story may be read by the contemporary person as paradigmatic and as informing just as any other meaningful story in world literature.

Exactly how such an approach to the Old Testament as story will work itself out has yet to be demonstrated in Old Testament theology. Does it mean that theology will consist of merely retelling the story or merely reading the story? If OT theology deals in some fashion with truth claims, how does this fact impact upon reading the narrative as if it were fiction or no more than history-like? Can the modern person, or could the ancient person, listen to and learn from a history-like story without becoming engaged in the question of factual information of its episodes? Is the resort to story as a description merely a means to avoid the issues over which the debates about history, salvation history, God's acts in history, and other matters have so long been raged? These problems remain and the debate will continue for some time.

2.4 History of Israelite Religion and Old Testament Theology

By the beginning of 20th century the history of Israelite religion and Old Testament Theology as two major disciplines/subjects in the study of Old Testament emerged. As was noted earlier in the history of the discipline of OT theology, the history of Israelite religions seems to have dominated all along that caused the decline of the OT theology until it was revived in the earlier part of 20th century. A brief review of the historical background of the OT theology in relation to the history of Israelite religion is inevitable in order to continue our discussion on the subject.

Historical Review: Johann Philipp Gabler (1753-1826) gave a major impetus for the understanding of Biblical theology as historical discipline. In his inaugural lecture at the University of Altdorf on March 30, 1787 Gabler defines Biblical theology as possessing historical character, transmitting what the sacred writers thought about divine matters. Understanding the Bible as historical document in fact had its roots from the age of Enlightenment. Since the Bible was considered as a purely historical literature, the development and influence of Historical Critical method was inevitable. As a result of this process Biblical theology has become a historical discipline replacing Dogmatic theology.

In 1796, George Lorenz Bauer (1755-1806) initiated the application of Historical Critical method and produced an Old Testament Theology with the title: *Theologie des Alten Testaments*. In his work Bauer made a clear demarcation between OT theology and NT theology. In 1801 Bauer again produced a work entitled: *Reliagen zur Theologie des Alten Testaments* in which he treated the history of Israelite religion rather inadequately. He divided the OT into fourteen parts and interpreted the history of Israelite religion "in terms of quasi-philosophical concepts rather than to appreciate the unique quality of Hebrew mind."[80] Nevertheless, Bauer's attempt was the first to sketch a historical account of the history of Israelite religion. And he was also the first to make a distinction

80 R. Dentan, *Preface to OT Theology*, p. 27.

between Old Testament Theology and history of Israelite religion. In the Old Testament theology, he treated the material systematically and in the history of Israelite religion he treated the material genetically and chronologically. In Bauer's treatment, history of Israelite religion was supplement to Old Testament theology. Bauer's presentation of the material in OT theology was however, follows the scheme of dogmatic theology.

The next great influence on the Old Testament was the impact of the idea of development mainly due to the influence of Hegel's dialectic philosophy and Darwin's theory of evolution. Wilhelm Vatke (1806-1882) was the first to adopt the philosophy of Hegel. He advocated that the biblical material should be arranged by adopting a system outside of the Bible. Consequently, he arranged the Old Testament material following the Hegelian principles of stages of development and dated the P material in the post prophetic period. Vatke's work greatly influenced the work of Julius Wellhausen.[81]

The History of Religion School: According the definition proposed by Richard N. Soulen, *Religionsgeschichte* can be defined as "history of religions" as a broad term which refers to "the application of the historical method of analysis, as developed in the late 19th century to the study of religion."[82] Soulen refers to *Religionsgeschichte Schule*, "history of religions school or religio-historical school" as "the name given to a group of Protestant scholars in Germany who, at the turn of the century sought to understand the religion of Old Testament and New Testament within the context of their historical development, including the other religions of that time and region."[83]

The publication of the *Prolegomena to the History of Israel* by Julius Wellhausen (1844-1918) marked the beginning of the triumph of the history of religions (*Religionsgeschichte*) approach to the Old Testament. R. C. Dentan points out two of the distinguishing features of the new discipline as follows: a) its exclusive use of the genetic method and; b) its tendency to treat the religious developments in the Old Testament period as merely particular examples of general *Religionsgeschichte* laws.

With the help of literary and historical criticism Wellhausen produced a critical and scientific history of Israelite religion. Subsequently, many works came up focusing in the light of history of Israelite religion. All these works dealt with the Old Testament religion in a developmental method. As a result of this trend, in general Old Testament theology became synonymous with history of Israelite religion.

H. G. Reventlow points out that by the turn of 19th century, the so called history of religions school, connected particularly with the name of Hermann Gunkel, become prominent. The decisive factor, says Reventlow, for this school,

81 R. Dentan, *Preface to OT Theology*, pp. 36-37.

82 Richard N. Soulen, *Handbook of Biblical Criticism*, p. 145.

83 Ibid.

was, apart from "the results of literary criticism and the idea of development was the influence of Herder."[84] Reventlow further notes that the history of religions school "understood itself as a thoroughly theological movement. It was opposed both to a purely philosophical and historical biblical exegesis and to the sort of traditional dogmatic biblical theology … instead of this it sought to understand and present the biblical religion of the two Testaments in the historical context it shared with other religions."[85]

G. W. Anderson is of the view that a change was introduced to the idea of development by Gunkel and Gressman. With the results of literary criticism Gunkel and Gressman "sought to show more clearly the relation of Hebrew religion to the mythology and eschatology of ancient east."[86] Anderson further notes the new approaches to eschatology. According to Wellhausen school, the "eschatological sayings in the pre-exilic prophets were post-exilic interpolations, and it was held that a developed eschatology was characteristic of a relatively late stage of religious development."[87] Whereas Gunkel in *Schopfung und Chaos in Urzeit und Endzeit*, 1895, argues that "the eschatological framework was derived from the Babylonian creation myth."[88] And Sigmund Mowinckel presented eschatology as "a projection into the future of what had been dramatically presented in the cult."[89] So Anderson points out that "no deep understanding of Israel's religion is possible without a study of its psychological and social background."[90]

On the basis of the foregoing discussion we may observe and conclude that in the history of religions school itself there has been tremendous change to look beyond the Hegelian idea of development.

Old Testament Theology and History of Israelite Religion: Apart from the points already mentioned by R. C. Dentan in the history of Israelite religion study, he further suggests three major factors that contributed to the renaissance of Old Testament theology: a) the general loss of faith in evolutionary naturalism, which resulted in a steadily increasing dissatisfaction with the *religionsgeschichtelich* attempt to explain Israel's religion as but one example of a universal law by which human beings inevitably progress from animatism to ethical monotheism; b) there was a reaction against the mid-nineteenth century conviction that historical truth

84 Henning Graf Reventlow, *Problems of Old Testament Theology in the Twentieth Century* (Philadelphia: Fortress Press, 1985), p. 7.

85 Ibid., p. 9.

86 G. W. Anderson, "Hebrew Religion," in *The Old Testament and Modern Study: A Generation of Discovery and Research,* ed. H. H. Rowley (London: Oxford University Press, 1951), pp. 283-310 and see especially, p. 284.

87 Ibid., p. 303.

88 Ibid.

89 Ibid., p. 304.

90 Ibid., p. 307.

can be attained by pure scientific "objectivity" or indeed that such objectivity is itself attainable; c) a trend which both rehabilitated the somewhat suspect term "theology" and gave a new impetus to biblical studies as being profoundly relevant to modern theological problems.[91]

As was noted earlier the beginning of the revival of OT theology was marked by an article written by Steuernagel in 1925 entitled: *Old Testament Theology and Religions of History of Old Testament.* In this he emphasized the independence of OT theology alongside the history of Israelite religion. According to Steuernagel, the study of general religion tries to grasp the nature of religion by means of comparison with other religions. Hence for him the history of Israelite religion should investigate and the factors that are effective in it. This task he assigned to History of Israelite Religion. But this is not sufficient. In the study of religion in general, he thinks that a systematic presentation of special and single development is needed. This task he assigns to Old Testament Theology.

Steuernagel points out that "both the disciplines have the same subject matter—Israelite religion, including the religion of the earlier Judaism—the same sources and the same method."[92] But the objective is different. History of Israelite Religion should present the totality of Israel's religion and the factors that are effective in it and the Old Testament Theology should follow up the "individual lines of development in particular complexes of themes."[93] Thus, Steuernagel puts both the disciplines side by side.

Otto Eissfeldt on the other hand, in his article entitled: *History of the Israelite and Jewish Religion and Old Testament Theology,* contrasts the two disciplines. According to him there exists "the tension between absolute and relative, transcendence and immanence."[94] Eissfeldt points out that this general tension in biblical science "has narrowed down to that of the tension between history and revelation of the Old Testament should be treated historically in the form of Religionsgeschichte or treated as the true religion, as God's revelation, as Old Testament Theology."[95] According to Eissfeldt faith is the means through which one understand, that which is absolute and transcendent. So when faith is applied to history, which is immanent and relative, it introduces confusion. N. W. Porteous attributes Eissfeldt's concept of faith and knowledge to Lutheran point of view, according to which, the faculty of knowledge is understood as activity and faith as passivity. Knowledge deals with that belongs to the world of space and time

91 R. C. Dentan, *Preface to OT Theology*, p. 61.

92 Reventlow, *Problems of Old Testament Theology*, p. 12.

93 Ibid.

94 Norman W. Porteous, "Old Testament Study," in H. H. Rowley (ed), *The OT and Modern Study*, p. 317.

95 Ibid., pp. 317-318.

whereas faith with human response to eternal world. Knowledge asks for proof whereas faith is personal and involves a leap in the dark.[96]

As a result of the above proposition of Eissfeldt, the historical approach avoids the question concerning truth and any valuation of the phenomena. On the other hand, theological approach is based on the understanding that only faith is able to grasp the nature of the revelation of the Old Testament and not through history. For Eissfeldt both these approaches are legitimate and necessary, but these should not be mixed up. For him the discipline of History of Israelite Religion is completely neutral, which means that anybody from any religious background can engage in the research. Whereas the discipline of Old Testament Theology is purely a confessional matter. It is each ones faith perspective.[97]

Eichrodt comes critically against the proposition made by Eissfeldt since it reduces the discipline of Old Testament Theology to a mere faith perspective. For Eichrodt OT theology is a descriptive science and he speaks against Eissfeldt's proposal of complete objectivity of historical approach. According to Eichrodt every science including historical critical discipline is subject to some subjectivity.

Georg Fohrer differentiates the task and purpose of history of Israelite religion and the Old Testament theology. According to him the purpose of history of Israelite religion is to depict the course of the history of Israelite religious development, without undertaking theological value judgments.[98] Fohrer is keen on depicting the course of Israel's religious development because he thinks that Israel's religion "underwent a process of historical evolution exhibiting a significant changes and developments occasioned by both internal and external influences."[99] Therefore according to Fohrer any presentation of history of Israelite religion, must first of all bring out the historical evolution and variety to light. And secondly it must also bring out that which was common in various periods and movements, which makes the Israelite religion as a single entity.[100]

The Old Testament theology according to Fohrer "must present the essential theological structures of a message, structures that, despite the variety of their historical manifestations, permeates the entire Old Testament and remain important even beyond the Old Testament period."[101] Fohrer exemplifies this by suggesting "the personal structure of faith ... belief in the dominion of God and communion between man and God."[102]

96 Norman W. Porteous, "Old Testament Study," in H. H. Rowley (ed), *The OT and Modern Study*, p. 320.

97 Ibid., p. 321.

98 Georg Fohrer, *History of Israelite Religion* (SPCK: London, 1972), p. 29.

99 Ibid., p. 23.

100 Ibid.

101 Ibid., pp. 23-24.

102 Ibid., p. 24.

Critical evaluation on the theme: From the time of Eichrodt, there has been a constant emphasis on the Old Testament Theology as an important part of Old Testament studies. But there has been various views which still emphasizes the priority of philology, literary and historical tasks in the study of Old Testament. According to those scholars who maintain that "the religious content of the Old Testament is material not for a theology of the Old Testament so much as for a critical account of Israelite religious history."[103] According to such scholars the task of Old Testament studies is "to provide factual data; on these data a theology might be constructed … but the task of construction itself would lie beyond the realm of Old Testament studies proper."[104]

At this juncture it would be appropriate to ask some basic questions: what is Old Testament Theology and the History of Israelite Religion? What are their roles? And whom these questions apply? By way of offering a critique on the foregoing debate we need to make the following proposal by way of the following argumentative evaluation.

In the 19th century there was a controversy between science and dogma. What was not empirically demonstrable was considered subjective. And the History of Israelite Religion was considered to be an objective study. As already pointed out by Eichrodt, can any discipline, even the historical descriptive approach be purely objective?

James Barr points out that even evolutionistic approach thought itself to be formulating elements of meaning for example, the concept of ethical monotheism derived by the evolutionary approach was considered to be of high meaning. But evolutionistic approach was discarded because its meaning was not considered as really meaningful and moreover the approach did not base itself on historical facts. Eventually, the evolutionist historicism was given up "to a kind of phenomenology in which it is recognized that a religion is at any given time a totality which is more than the sum of historical and environmental influences acting upon it."[105] And according to Barr this totality is ever changing and it is the task of History of Religions to investigate these changes, but it should treat the existence of this totality as a living consciousness, instead of just fragmenting it into more facts. Barr thinks that in this respect the study of the History of Religion is closer to the synthetic interest of Old Testament Theology, that is, their interest in the meaning of the religion for today.

Further, Barr thinks that the problem today between the Old Testament Theology and the History of Israelite Religion is quite different from the 19th century, where Old Testament Theology was needed to be separated from the evolutionist approach to the History of Religion. Today, the problem is the

103 James Barr, "The Problem of Old Testament Theology and the History of Religion," *Calvin Journal of Theology*, Vol. III (3) (1967), p. 141.

104 Ibid.

105 James Barr, "The Problem of Old Testament Theology," pp. 143-145.

distinctiveness of the Old Testament Theology from the study of History of Israelite Religion, because both concerns itself with religious meaning of the facts.[106]

C. R. North in his article "Old Testament Theology and the History of Hebrew Religion," looks at the problem from the question of the context or the need of the church today. He begins with the question: what is the demand of the church from the Old Testament? He answers that it is theology, which is what the Old Testament mean today to the church. North thinks that theology should be based on the history of Israelite religion. So the issue between Old Testament Theology and the History of Israelite Religion today is, according to North, "not one of principle. It is one of convenience, a question of form and method."[107]

Referring to Eichrodt's emphasis on the separation of the essential and non-essentials in order to make visible the total structure of the Old Testament's world of thought, H. H. Rowley writes that "here, then is a clear distinction between a History of Israelite Religion and the Old Testament Theology. For the former, every religious idea and practice which marked any period of the story demands full consideration. For the latter all that is not the essence of the faith of Israel is irrelevant."[108] Barr also thinks that it is the principle of selectivity which would differentiate Old Testament Theology from History of Israelite Religion.

On the basis of the foregoing discussion concerning the relationship between the History of Israelite Religion (HIR) and the Old Testament Theology (OTT) we make the following concluding observations: first, one needs to see the difference in intentions and goals of both HIR and OTT. The former's goal is to trace the development of religious phenomena including the development of religious ideas. The latter deals with theological concerns and a process of theological thought of a particular body of literature and tries to explicate theological ideas; second, both the disciplines differ in organizing principle of the material of the Old Testament. HIR deals with the materials of the OT as a progressive and linear development, whereas OTT deals with the materials on the basis of certain principles, concepts, with some theological perspective and focus; third, if we talk about the scope of HIR and OTT there is difference again in both the disciplines. The former discipline includes materials not only from the Old Testament but takes into account extra-biblical materials from the ancient West Asian context. The latter limits itself mostly to the canonical scriptures; fourth, in the light of above discussion Old Testament Theology was done in the subsequent years beginning from Walther Eichrodt and Gerhard von Rad with a clear focus

106 James Barr, "The Problem of Old Testament Theology," pp. 143-145.

107 C. R. North, "Old Testament Theology and the History of the Hebrew Religion," *Scottish Journal of Theology*, Vol. 2 (1949), p. 116.

108 H. H. Rowley, *The Faith of Israel*, p. 17 cited in James Barr, "The Problem of Old Testament Theology," p. 147.

and objective there by the History of Israelite Religion was clearly distinguished from the Old Testament Theology.

2.5 The Problem of a Center of the Old Testament

The effort to isolate a center, kernel, core or middle (German: *mitte*) of the Old Testament or other terms employed in this regard like a comprehensive or unifying principle according to which a presentation of the material might be organized has long been occupied the Old Testament theologians. Hasel points out that "the last two centuries of work in OT theology have indisputably demonstrated that the matter of the center and the unity of the OT has an extraordinary influence in the conception and doing of Biblical theology and OT theology in particular."[109] There are several opinions and proposals to center or unifying principle of OT. There would be little value in arguing in favour of one or another opinion since this has been done by scholars in their work. Thus, it would be helpful and appropriate to identify various proposals and make an evaluation on them.

D. L. Baker[110] classifies the term center into two categories: a) centre, mitte etc.; b) unity, unifying principle etc. Th. C. Vriezen uses both categories to mean the same as, 'unifying idea' 'essential root idea' 'key-stone' and 'fundamental idea'. D. L. Baker shares the difference in the use of the term such as some of the writers are interested in: a) center of the OT; b) center of OT theology; c) center of the whole Bible. Walter C. Kaiser rightly observes that "in spite of the terminological variation a similar note is sounded in all these terms" and that "perhaps the word 'center' is most useful."[111]

In the formative years of the OT theology, God-Man-Salvation was the general pattern under which the entire materials of the OT was organized. Scholars who come under this pattern include L. Köhler. J. Hänel and others. But a new era of awareness reached through at the beginning of Walther Eichrodt's theology in which he deliberately rejected all patterns derived from Christian dogmatics and sought to plot out the course of doing OT theology along the lines of the OT's own dialectic. We shall now venture into various proposals made by scholars and see their strengths and limitations in the paragraphs that follow.

Single center pattern: Walther Eichrodt began the revolutionary approach in which he broke with the dogmatic structure in as much as it superimposed external categories of the OT. He replaced it with the biblical concept of 'covenant' as center which determines everything, and which is capable of demonstrating the structural unity and the unchanging basic tendency of the message of the Old Testament.

---

109 G. F. Hasel, *Old Testament Theology*, p.

110 D. L. Baker, *Two Testaments. One Bible: The Theological Relationship between the Old and New Testaments* (Downers Grove, IL: InterVarsity Press, 1977).

111 Walter C. Kaiser, *Towards an Old Testament Theology* (Grand Rapids: Zondervan, 1978), p. 20f.

Those who nevertheless believed that there was easy evidence for the concept of covenant include McCarthy and others. Beauchamp begins from the covenant formula and Fensham sees the 'covenant' as the binding link between testaments.

The central concept of OT theology in a similar, though in a broader way is put forth by Th. C. Vriezen. For him 'communion' between 'God and Man' is the fundamental principle of the Israelite religion, and thus the best starting point for a biblical theology of the Old Testament. Jesper Høgenhaven feels that Vriezen's definition of the center is more open and inclusive than Eichrodt's. Samuel Terrien poses a major challenge to the 'Covenant' concept. He makes a shift of emphasis from covenant to the presence of God and says that this stands at the center of biblical faith. He stresses that the Hebraic theology of presence rather than the ideology of the covenant which provides a key to understanding the Bible. He explains that the motif of divine presence is same as a dynamic 'principle of coherence' or of continuity and unity within the Old Testament and between the two testaments.[112]

The covenant concept of Eichrodt and those who followed after him does not exhaust the suggestions of single center for the OT. Among other single-centered suggestions some prominent ones include the following: H. Seebas who makes 'rulership of God' starting from the OT but aiming beyond it at a biblical theology of both testaments. G. Klein begins from the New Testament, also considering the OT argues for the 'Kingdom of God' as the central concept. Walter C. Kaiser also employs the cross-section method of Eichrodt but calls it an inductive approach which he claims, can be textually demonstrated and which is an ubiquitous concern, a central hope, and a constant measure of what was theologically significant or normative, which New Testament eventually calls as the 'promise' which he says was known in the OT under a constellation of terms. Kaiser thus replaces covenant with promise.

Literary unit as a single center: In this approach, rather than a concept of a formula as the center of the OT literary unit is introduced. W. H. Schmidt postulates the first commandment of the Decalogue (Exod 20:2) as a guideline which runs through the whole history of the Old Testament understanding of God serving as a structure of an OT theology. This he picks up because it is exclusive and without analogy in the ancient West Asia and thus being genuinely Israel. Similarly Zimmerli believes that, with the sentence 'I am Yahweh your God' (Exod 20:2) and the response of Israel 'the LORD your God' (Deut 26:1) has come to view the center which is uniquely held onto the entire OT history of tradition and interpretation.

Single center observations: From the knowledge of the above mentioned proposals for the center in the OT theology, the inner unity or central concept

112 For more details on this see Samuel Terrien, *The Elusive Presence: Toward a New Biblical Theology* (San Francisco: Harper & Row, 1978).

appears to have remained hidden beneath the diversity of form and content in the OT. It is evident that even the most carefully worked out single center or formula will prove itself finally, as one-sided, inadequate, and insufficient. For example, in the work of Eichrodt, the wisdom literature remains an acute problem. R. C. Dentan observes that "the idea of the covenant is far from omnipresent in OT literature and only by a *tour de force* can it be made to appear so."[113] Regarding the literary unit being the center, Hasel observes that if Schmidt argues in favour of his proposed center on the basis of its lack of West Asian analogy, then this has insurmountable deficiencies. Hasel remarks that ever book and every author's purpose was not necessarily to prove Yahweh's exclusiveness.

At this juncture, a crucial question arises whether or not a single center concept, even though taken from the biblical material, is sufficient and adequate in bringing about an organization of the OT material in terms of a systematized structural unity? The problems in this are seen as follows:

a) The subjective nature of the understanding must be first acknowledged, because a particular individual chooses a theme.
b) Operating with such single category provides only single static unity and does not do real justice to the dynamic unity, growth and development of OT faith.
c) It becomes an artificial imposition of unity which the materials themselves may not see the growth and development in such a way.
d) The governing category when imposed upon the materials rather than read out of it. Then some materials are left out like Wisdom and Psalms.

Plurality of Centers: The exercise of finding a center deemed a failure. Many scholars have showed their skepticism and saw the possibility of several centers. James Barr has suggested that the theologies of the Bible are extremely complex entities and thus explorations should be centered in more than one particular aspect. In this regard we shall make few summaries of the proposals made by certain scholars.

Gerhard von Rad: He out rightly rejects the possibility of determining a center of the OT by means of which the contents of OT books might be theologically systematized. According to von Rad, the most typical feature of the OT is that it unites its different theologies in the process of tradition leading to the fulfillment of God's promise. Von Rad then explicitly states that the Deuteronomistic theology has given the clearest expression to the idea of salvation history. Although von Rad sys that he is not operating with a center to organize the material of the Old Testament, some scholars doubt whether von Rad is so doing.

113 R. C. Dentan, *Preface to the OT Theology*, p. 61f.

Hasel points out to the secret center of von Rad when he says "von Rad proceeds from a kind of secret center, which reveals itself in his basic thesis, namely that the establishment of God's self-revelation takes place in his acts in history."[114] Thus, there are limitations in von ad's work, yet the idea of no single center itself has been supported by others such as R. E. Clements who refuses to follow a center oriented approach to the OT theology. Claus Westermann justifies von Rad's 'no' to the center, and AHJ Gunneweg does the same.

Broader Center: Siegfried Hermann emerges with the broader conception of a center for the OT. He suggests that Deuteronomy be declared the center of biblical theology. Jesper Høgenhaven explains Hermann's argument that in Deuteronomy there is summary of the most central themes in the OT, which points backwards to the essence of Israelite traditions and forward to post-exilic developments. H. G. Reventlow observes that this broader center approach does not consider other significant areas of traditions within the OT which are far removed from those of Deuteronomy and the Deuteronomistic history, such as the priestly tradition, or in the prophetic sphere, the school of Isaiah.

Dual concept center: some scholars instead of single center argues for dual center for the OT. Two such scholars could be named under this category.

a) Georg Fohrer: sees the unity of the OT in the dual perspective of the 'divine rule' and the 'divine communion'. This forms the unifying element in the plurality of theological view points and tendencies found in the OT. Hasel observes that this dual concept falls short, that is, Fohrer was forced to structure his theology, and that there is no integrated place for wisdom theology.

b) Rudolf Smend: he takes the so called covenant formula that is, *Yahweh the God of Israel; Israel the people of Yahweh* (this idea goes back to J. Wellhausen). Hasel reports that the large sections of OT material such as Psalms, Wisdom Literature and Deutero-Isaiah are very distant from this *mitte*. Hasel is of the view that the particularism of this formula with its virtually exclusive stress on the unique relationship of Yahweh-Israel-Yahweh does not have sufficient room for the universalism present so widely in the Old Testament (Gen 12:1-3; Isa 2:2-4; Amos 9:11f etc.). Therefore Smend's proposal fall short of being a genuine center of the Old Testament.[115]

c) Other scholars: N. W. Porteous advocates the relational concept of God and people as the axis of a theology of the OT; Roland de Vaux sees the relationship of God and Israel in the dual idea of 'election and covenant;' F. C. Prussner juxtaposes the covenant of Sinai and the covenant with David as the center.

114 G. F. Hasel, *Old Testament Theology*, p. 74f.

115 Ibid.

Tripolar center: Hasel reports that R. M. Achand has proposed a threefold 'axis' hat is, three lines of thought, the doxological, the polemical, and the soteriological, around which the OT material may be grouped. However, Reventlow rules out this proposal as having any prospect of a 'center'.

Fourfold approach as center: Hasel notes that the fourfold approach employed by Elmer A. Martens with God's design that incorporates four components: deliverance, community, knowledge of God, and the abundant life. This study is unique in the sense that it takes a single passage that is, Exodus 5:22-6:8 as the starting point. He believes that these components are implemented and tested during monarchy, reaffirmed during post-monarchic period and continued it to the New Testament.

Multi-dimensional approach for a center of the Old Testament: D. L. Baker's basic presupposition is that the Old Testament is all part of the national literature of Israel. In this regard Baker proposes diagrammatically by an elliptical cylinder which is an image of the multiform unity of the OT, with the center as Christ, God and people as the two foci pointing to various concepts like: election, promise, covenant, kingdom, communion, exclusiveness and redemption as the concentric layers of the cylinder. Baker further observes that in spite the idea of center, Barr, von Rad, and Vriezen do not completely do away with it. Baker pints out that Barr accepts 'creation story' as the starting point for understanding the OT, von Rad Deuteronomy and Vriezen God. Baker also observes that in the unifying themes found as the OT's presentation between God and Israel, sometimes the emphasis falls on God and other times on Israel.

On the whole two motives govern scholars' proposals in suggesting a center: a) the need to recognize a systematic presentation of the main contents of the OT materials; b) the desire to establish the theological relevance of the OT by asserting its center. But no consensus as to what constitutes the organizing center of the OT has emerged. Hasel questions: on what basis is a single or dual centers are selected that function as an adequate norm for the richness of the OT? Hasel is of the view that "unconscious philosophical-speculative premise that the diverse and manifold OT testimonies can be organized into a systematic structure by means of a single or dual center or formula must be radically questioned. Any center he calls is but a *tour de force*."[116] Walter Kaiser in such a context questions: "does a key exist for an orderly and progressive arrangement of the subjects, themes, and teachings of the OT?" and "were the writings of the OT consciously aware of such a key as they continued to add to the historical stream of revelation." If not Kaiser says, "the idea of an OT theology as such must be permanently abandoned. Not only would it be necessary to acknowledge that there is no unity to be found in

116 G. F. Hasel, *Old Testament Theology*, p. 139f

the OT, but the search for the legitimate and authoritative lines of continuity with the NT would need to be abandoned as well."[117]

New proposals: In the light of the above discussion the problem of discovering and identifying a center has become more and more a complex question. However, scholars continue to make new proposals and we shall see few of them in the following paragraphs.

a) G. F. Hasel: While Kaiser in the above discussion sounds too harsh, Hasel proposes that "our approach to OT theology follows the model of multitrack presentation of the various OT books or blocks of writings and a resultant summarizing presentation of various longitudinal themes, motifs, or concepts so as to elucidate their development and transformations throughout the entire period of biblical history. Each of the OT aspects of thought, life and faith must be seen as expressions of OT realities in their dynamic interrelationships."[118]
b) B. S. Childs's canonical approach: The new proposal of Childs is that biblical theology would have its basis in the canon of scripture, the canon being taken as, instead of seeking a structural principle or a center around which a statement of theology of the Bible is to be built, must work with the formal fact of the canon and follow the pattern imposed by the actual outlines of the canon. Childs approach has nay limitations which only rests on the redaction criticism therefore obscuring the theology which could be derived from the *ipissma verba* of the authors. James Barr makes a critique of Childs to the extent of calling it as being no OT theology.
c) John Goldingay: He is surprised that some central themes of OT faith have been neglected by many OT theologians. Themes such as the land, blessing and death are the neglected themes. He notes that the diversity in the literature written over hundreds of years against a variety of cultural, historical, geographical and religious backgrounds and raises the question of how the viewpoints within the Jewish scripture be acknowledged, interrelated, and allowed to function theologically? Goldingay proposes two approaches in this regard.[119]

    1. Historical or Contextual approach: Goldingay stresses that "one approach to theological diversity in the OT is simply to acknowledge the variety of viewpoints and to accept all of them as

117 Walter C. Kaiser, *Towards an Old Testament Theology* (Grand Rapids: Zondervan, 1978), p. 20f.

118 G. F. Hasel, *Old Testament Theology*, p. 205.

119 John Goldingay, *Old Testament Theology: Israel's Gospel/ Faith*, 3 Vols. (Downers Grove, IL: InterVarsity Press, 2003-2009).

potentially instructive when understood against their appropriate context." For example, he explains: "The motif of creation, is applied within the OT to question such as the relationship of Israelite to Babylonian religion (Gen 1), the apparent insecurity of this world (Psalm xciii), the need to maintain trust when God's faithfulness seems to fail (Job), the possibility of judgment (the creation hymn in Amos), or of restoration (Isa xi), and to various other issues that concerned Israel in different contexts." This approach is almost similar to Childs which does OT theology in a framework of issues selected subjectively.

2. This approach requires consideration of the relationship between the related polarities, such as universalism and election, politics and religion, cultic piety and prophetic piety, suffering and confidence in God, creation redemption, exodus and exile. This approach, says Goldingay, involves seeking to clarify their interrelation rather than abandoning one member of each pair.

   First of all, Goldingay has not developed an OT theology based on his proposal to really study the merits and limitations of this method. Yet it could be said of what would be of the material/ themes which are not in polarity with any other? Secondly, for instance why election should be seen in relation to universalism, why not in relation to the motif of rejection? Hasel's question reappears that on what basis is a dialectic/polarity is comprehensive enough to encompass the entirety of OT scriptures?

d) Jesper Høgenhaven: He divides the work of scholars of OT theology into two groups according to their predominantly 'historical' or 'theological' interests. He points out that on the historical level the attempt at establishing a sort of common denominator for all the documents in the OT "anthology" can hardly be regarded as a very meaningful enterprise in itself. But he believes that theologically, the idea of a 'center' of OT may indeed have a certain justification. And thus he proposes that "OT theology should not be structured in accordance with theological categories or concepts more or less like those found in a traditional course book on dogmatics, but should follow a historically oriented scheme.[120] The scheme he proposes is as follows: i) Wisdom; ii) Psalmic literature; iii) Narrative literature; iv) Law; v) Prophecy. According to Høgenhaven "this scheme is not chronological order rather, the arrangement suggested here reflects certain basic viewpoints

120 Jesper Høgenhaven, *Problems and Prospects of Old Testament Theology* (Sheffield: Sheffield Academic Press, 1992).

as to what is primary and secondary in Israelite religion as it is exhibited in the Old Testament."[121]

In the above light of Høgenhaven a brief explanation of his proposal would in order at this point: i) Wisdom: Wisdom literature is sad to form an important part of the background for most of the literature in the OT; ii) Psalmic literature: this corpus is said to preserving all the historical experiences and also the Canaanite polytheistic traits; iii) Narrative literature: most of it is dated relatively late around Babylonian exile; iv) Law is taken next; v) Prophets from the time of Northern Israelite prophets to the time of Daniel, hat is second century BCE is taken up.

The way the above proposal for OT theology is structured is purely dependent on the current state of historical and exegetical research and very much prone to subsequent modifications and alterations which poses a greater threat of providing freedom for every generation to be theologizing.

On the basis of our foregoing discussion on the issue of center of the Old Testament and its theological discussion two things become clear. First, the scholars' assumption that there is unity in the diversity of materials of the OT, and second, that this unity can be brought about by a 'central concept' or a unifying principle. However, the question of the problem of a center of the Old Testament remains open-ended.

2.6 The Relationship Between the Old Testament and the New Testament

The debate on the relationship between the Old and the New Testaments has been an age old one, from the second century classical heretic Marcion to modern times. The need for establishing a relationship emerged from the extreme acts of violence to the text when the Old Testament was ruthlessly rejected and cut off from the holy scripture. The fact that canon does not provide a sufficiently binding factor for many scholars to accept the OT without proper theological reasons of doing it. It would have been an easier task if the OT would have been accepted as a timeless revelation by concentrating on its existential character. But it would be depreciating the historical character of the OT which has a great deal to offer theologically. A satisfactory solution to the problem of relationship remains an ongoing struggle with certain questions like: is there a single formula or solution to answer this relationship satisfactorily? What is the authority of the OT for doctrines and ethics? What is the nature and purpose of revelation? Is doing a biblical theology possible? What is the real nature and importance of the

121 Jesper Høgenhaven, *Problems and Prospects of Old Testament Theology* (Sheffield: Sheffield Academic Press, 1992).

history as it is recorded in the OT? Several such questions need to be tackled and answered in this topic in a general way.

Historical Background: Second century heretic Marcion was the first one who attacked the Old Testament and rejected it as a part of the holy scripture. During eighteenth century with the background and under the influence of Pietism, Rationalism and Romanticism, a Christian rejection of the OT came from Fredrick Schleiermacher (1768-1834). He claimed that there is no possibility of any relationship between the New and Old Testament because the OT is equal to heathenism (Greek and Roman thought). After a century of Schleiermacher the scholars of higher criticism took up his views and refined them to declare that there is no theological relationship between the two testaments but there is a historical relationship, that is, that OT contains the history of theocracy which is finalized in the NT by the coming of Jesus Christ. This led to a developmental approach towards the relationship of the two testaments. It claimed that there is a progressive revelation from the OT to the NT. Therefore, the OT is incomplete, imperfect and developing, it must be judged from the final stage. On the political front, after the first world war, anti-Semitic thought was dominant in Germany which aimed to remove the traces of Judaism from Christianity. They totally rejected the OT and replaced it by Nordic and Aryan literature, on an assumption that Luther would have done the same, had he lived in 20th century. Fredrich Delitzsch and Harnack are the two scholars who are of the opinion that the OT was produced by lazy cattle breeders who made Yahweh as a god in their own image.

A defense arose for the OT in the early 20th century by scholars like Wilhelm Vischer, Karl Barth, and Otto Procksch. They tried to divert people's attention from the relevance of OT for the Jews by claiming and interpreting OT as a witness to Christ, and thus they tried to claim back the OT for the church. In the same wake, Emil Brunner (1930) tried make an understanding of the OT as mandatory and preparatory for the understanding of the NT, because many OT ideas are presupposed and not explained in the NT like creator, Lord, the one who chooses and reveals God-self personally, eschatological elements, importance of community, people of God etc. Otto Eissfeldt and many other scholars continued to pursue OT studies with a clear emphasis on its importance for faith.

Again OT was attacked in an implicit way. The anti-OT tendencies were still operating in a subtle guise, when a generosity towards OT was shared and it was given back to the Jews. It was implied that the OT has no use for the Christians. Isaac G. Mathews in 1947 wrote a history of Israel up to AD 135 without any reference to Jesus or Christians, assuming that the natural continuation of OT religion was Judaism. In a way he tried to give the OT back to the Jews. The other subtle and implied (under the influence of Marcionism) ways of rejecting the OT are still evident in various manifestations. Many missionaries substituted the OT by natural religions and literatures as the basis for their preaching. In the West, modern thought and culture are used as a preparation for Christian message at the expense of biblical studies, especially the OT studies, instead social sciences were introduced in various theological colleges. The church, except for few messianic passages of Isaiah and few psalms, grossly ignored the OT.

In the light of the above historical background, our task lies ahead to define a theological relationship between the two testaments, which will provide a paradigm for the biblical theology, and will bridge the gap that is, historical and theological relationship between the two testaments. We shall make an attempt in these lines with the help of scholarly opinions and proposals in order that we may be able to see a reasonable and logical conclusion on the relationship between the Old and New Testaments.

Theological Relationship – the OT over the NT:[122] In the light of the above discussion on the overview of the historical background over the relationship debate, it was obvious and natural for the scholars to suggest the priority of the OT over the NT, because in the past the OT was subjected to a total negligence and rejection as a scripture. Scholars like Arnold A. van Ruler, K. H. Miskotte, James Barr, H. Wheeler Robinson and Claus Westermann asserted the supremacy of the OT over the NT due to the following reasons:

a) The legitimation of Jesus as Christ depends on the OT.
b) Interpretation of the gospel concepts in historical, concrete, and worldly expressions depends on the OT ex-kingdom of God.
c) The concept of history is a continuing one link, and Jesus Christ is to be seen as part of history with Israel which is a historical fact.
d) The eschatological hope started from the OT and it goes beyond the NT. In OT, God created the world and the consummation of the world goes beyond the NT, and is yet to come.

For reaching the above conclusions scholars have used the methods of allegory, typology, and a new interpretation of the concept of history. We shall briefly summarize the opinion of each scholar below:

1. Arnold A. van Ruler: He asserted the reality of revelation as a tradition which has been passed on from the OT to the NT. Yahweh of Israel is also the father of Lord Jesus Christ, and the salvation is passed on from Israel to Christians as a tradition. It is not a progressive revelation but equal. Van Ruler defined the task of scholarship to determine what OT says about and it is the faith that decides what revelation in it is. He

122 For a general discussion on the various proposals on this topic see G. F. Hasel, *Old Testament Theology*, p. 172f.

uses allegory and typology, and assumed that the OT is the word of God.[123]

2. K. H. Miskotte: According to him, the relationship between the two testaments is a relationship of priority because the meaning and intensity of Christ, the OT looking forward to it and the NT looking back at it. But the NT depends on OT references and quotations to authenticate Jesus as Christ, whereas the OT independently speaks for itself. Miskotte is of the view that the church is a repetition of Israel as gentiles are grafted to the old vine of the covenant people.[124]
3. James Barr: He claims that the problem of the NT is to understand Christ in the light of the OT and by the help of the OT. Though both the testaments are equally important because they speak of the same God, nonetheless the OT has priority over the NT.[125]
4. Claus Westermann: He establishes a relationship between the two testaments by defining history as event in dialogue between God and human beings. For Westermann there is no distinction between the reality and the faith. Thus, he could see a continuation of the OT into the NT, both as 'historical' as well as theological.[126]

Theological Relationship – the NT over the OT: At the face of strong anti-Semitic movements, scholars like R. Bultmann tried to divert people's attention from the OT as a Jewish book by interpreting it as a witness to Christ. There are other scholars who followed the line of Bultmann due to the following reasons:

a) They questioned the significance of the OT for Christian faith.
b) They proposed 'developmental model' to explain the relevance of the OT in the light of the NT with the following: progressive revelation, promise and fulfillment and law ad gospel.
c) They came up with contrasts as a relationship between the two; and obviously it highlighted the NT over against the OT, cultic and nationalistic, refined (national) and universal etc.

We shall briefly summarize the opinion of each scholar in this regard below:

---

123 For more details on the proposals of A. A. van Ruler see his work entitled: *Christian Church and the Old Testament* (Grand Rapids, MI: William B. Eerdmans Publishing Company, 1971).

124 K. H. Miskotte, "Das Problem der theologischen Exegese," in *Theologiesche Aufsätze. Festschrift für K. Barth.* Munich, 1936, pp. 51-77 and Idem, *Wenn die Götter schweigen.* Munich, 1963, trans. *When the Gods are Silent.* London, 1967. Miskotte's works are cited by G. F. Hasel, *Old Testament Theology.*

125 James Barr, *Old and New in Biblical Interpretation* (London: SCM Press, 1966).

126 Claus Westermann, *Elements of Old Testament Theology* (Atlanta; John Knox Press, 1982).

1. Rudolph Bultmann: He posed a question that whether and to what extent the OT can be a revelation for Christian faith. It is only possible in an indirect way because basically the OT is not a Christian book and it is only a presupposition of the NT and Christianity. The OT is a revelation in a historical sense to the Jews, and in a direct eschatological sense to the NT. For Christians the OT is indirect revelation in this way: Jesus Christ is God's word to human and any other word which elucidate this word are indirectly God's word.

   In his developmental approach, Bultmann claims that the relationship between the two is of improvement and progression. He also suggests an existential approach because both the testaments deal with human existence and the law culminates in the gospel and the OT is an important part of the world history.

   Bultmann further explains the relationship between the two testaments in terms of prophecy and fulfillment. For him, the prophecy is a declaration about the eschatological and of salvation history. The prophecy as promise arose from the miscarriage of the OT history, which are understood eschatologically in the NT that is in the themes of covenant, kingdom, the people of God etc.

   In explaining the relationship between the two testaments, Bultmann proposed an antithesis to Luther's law versus gospel theory. He proposed that the existence under the law is the presupposition of existence under grace. Therefore grace can only be appreciated and enjoyed by the one who is under law. So, both law and gospel (grace) are complimentary to each other. Because what was impossible (miscarriage) under the law was made possible under the grace. Thus, OT can be reflected as several such miscarriages and the complete picture can only be seen in the NT.[127]

2. Friedrich Baumgartel: He is of the view that the prior understanding of the NT is mandatory to recognize the OT as a witness of God's promises in Jesus Christ.[128]

---

127 Rudolph Bultmann, "The Significance of the Old Testament for the Christian Faith." In *The Old Testament and Christian Faith: A Theological Discussion,* ed. Bernard W. Anderson (London: SCM Press, 1964), pp. 8-35 and "Prophecy and Fulfillment." in *Essays Philosophical and Theological* (London, 1955), pp. 182-208. Both these sources of Bultmann are cited by G. F. Hasel, *Old Testament Theology.*

128 Friedrich Baumgartel, *Die Bedeutung des Alten Testaments für den Christen* (Schwerin, 1925) cited by G. F. Hasel, *Old Testament Theology.*

3. Emmanuel Hirsch: For him, the OT is anti-thesis of NT. It serves to illuminate the distinctive nature of Christianity as gospel by presenting its opposite, the legalistic Judaism.[129]

Theological Relationship – A Biblical Solution: Beside the two above discussed lopsided ways of explaining the relationship between the two testaments, there is a third approach to this debate in the form of a biblical solution. This method tries to incorporate the two testaments as equally valid and important which are historically and theologically linked in a complimentary way. This approach is suggested by scholars on the basis of the following reasons:

a) Typology and analogy are used to explain the relationship the relationship as Christological solution. Though the Christological solution implies a New Testament emphasis but still the unity of both in terms of language, structure, and message are maintained.
b) Salvation history is taken to define the theological relationship between OT and NT.
c) The relationship between the two testaments is a relationship of tension, it has a continuity as well as discontinuity.

We shall briefly summarize the opinion of each scholar in this regard below:

1. Wilhelm Vischer: He applied historical and linguistic approach to come up with a typology in categories like: synagogue-Church; Promise-Fulfillment; OT looks forward to Christ-NT looks back to Christ. He explained his Christological solution by saying that "Jesus is Lord" as the formula that links both the testaments. The first creed of the church explains the unity of the two testaments in this formula: the OT defines the word Lord and the NT supplies the name Jesus. The testimony of the NT (in the Gospel of Luke) is that this happened according to the scripture. The unity of the two testaments lies in the death of Jesus that makes Jesus really Christ.[130]
2. Karl Barth: He explains the relationship between the two testaments that there is an essential identity—the same God Jesus of Nazareth is the Messiah of Israel. The same method is followed by E. Jacob, J. L. McKenzie and H. W. Wolff who used typology and analogy to establish the Christology on the relationship between the two testaments.[131]

---

129 E. Hirsch, *Das AT und die Predigt des Evangeliums* (Tübingen, 1936), cited by G. F. Hasel, *Old Testament Theology.*

130 Wilhelm Vischer, *The Witness of the Old Testament to Christ* (London, 1949), cited by G. F. Hasel, *Old Testament Theology.*

131 G. F. Hasel, *Old Testament Theology.*

3. Salvation History groups: under this broader framework several scholars and biblical groups can be considered as follows:

   a) Gerhard von Rad: He explains the relationship between the two testaments as "the way in which the OT is absorbed in the NT is the logical end of a process initiated by the OT itself, and that its laws are to some extent repeated in this final reinterpretations." Von Rad's basic approach was traditio-historical and he explained that it is a tradition history or re-telling of God's saving acts or events that are actualized which is also viewed as a kind of representation of the God's saving deeds. In the OT itself the saving events were actualized in the cultic celebrations (as for example in the Passover).
   b) Biblisher Kommentar Group (1955): This group also dealt with the question of relationship between the two testaments in the salvation history solution with the help of traditio-historical method. Martin Noth claimed that in the OT the historical events were represented for proclamation, like Exodus event was represented as the peripheral feast of Passover. So the OT's saving acts and demands of God in a way, are represented in the NT (von Rad's actualization method). Another member of this group Walther Zimmerli explained that in the Bible there is great history of movement from promise to fulfillment.
   c) Pannenberg Group: This group used the categories of salvation history and promise-fulfillment scheme to express relationship between the two testaments. They believe that it is one, actual history from creation to consummation, and God's self-revelation through historical acts that are recorded in the Bible. The Christ event in the anticipated and that makes the revelation in the history understandable, which is recorded in the Old Testament. Scholars who come under this group include: Samuel Amsler, Oscar Cullmann, G. E. Wright, W. Eichrodt (though Eichrodt starts with a different methodology, from a different point of view, yet he reaches the same conclusion like von Rad that the OT is continued in the NT).

Theological Relationship – A Tension – Continuous and Discontinuous: This approach seeks to highlight the validity of revelation in both the testaments in their own light. The two belong to one another and neither is complete without the other. There is a continuity of traditions but there is also discontinuity where the Old Testament is reinterpreted and modified and surpassed by the New Testament. The primitive elements like sacrifice, old cultic and social laws are dropped and new interpretations are added. This approach tries to balance the extreme and opposite stands on the one sided way of defining the relationship between the two testaments. Scholars that fall under this category include: Th. C. Vriezen, H. H. Rowley, C. H. Dodd, B. S. Childs and others.

Evaluation and Conclusion: It is obvious that from the above discussion that the OT is unfulfilled and incomplete historically as well as theologically. And the NT affirms the fulfillment of hope and expectancy in the background of OT. Any attempt which seeks to establish a theological and historical relationship between the two cannot afford to neglect the importance of either. There have been a strong socio-political reasons for scholars to assert the importance of one over against the other, and those attempts were valid in their own context. But, still the debate is open and ongoing for each generation to decide for itself.

Among many, three important issues need to be considered in any attempt to establish a theological relationship between the two testaments:

a) Contradictions: There are obvious contradictions between the two testaments with regard to certain key theological elements and their interpretations. There is also a paradigm shift with regard to the point of emphasis. Some of the contradictions can be listed as follows: creation-salvation, theocracy-soteriology, earthly-spiritual, law-gospel, community-individual, wrath-love, glory-suffering, human messiah-divine messiah. These incongruities and paradoxes should be taken into account when defining the relationship between the two testaments.
b) History: The problem of relationship between the two testaments needs the consideration to the issue of "history" in the Bible, its interpretation and understanding. We need to have a theological understanding of history which runs across the two testaments.
c) Promise and fulfillment: Though this had been the most common way of establishing a relationship between the two testaments, but it is far from sufficient because the OT has more to say and offer than mere promises, and the NT goes beyond the expected fulfillment of the OT.

In the light of the above, we may conclude that the issue of relationship between the two testaments is continues one for further debate and thus stands an open-ended problem.

Chapter 3

Some Major Theological Topics in the Old Testament in an Integrated Perspective in the Light of Indian Context

Introduction

In the previous two sections we dwelt on various issues and concerning the history and normative issues of Old Testament Theology. In those two sections we were left with little or no option of integrating the OT theology and the issues connected with Old Testament. In the discipline of OT theology we have little option since they also cover some historical antecedents. But in this thematic section we will be concentrating on the theological themes of the OT and we will make an earnest attempt to examine and analyze each theme in the light on an integrated approach. Before we venture into that task we must clarify and add a note on the distinct features of our approach.

The integrated approach to the study in social sciences is not new venture. Even in the time of Enlightenment (see for details note 66 above) such attempts were made both in the academia and in the church and these attempts in their own way yielded some fruits in a broader scale. It is not the purpose of this topic to dwell on the details what integration means in historical sense, but we shall clarify this idea in so far as our discussion on the themes of Old Testament theology. Following general features encompass what we mean by integration and how these integrative principles are operative and functional in our theological discussion on the themes of the Old Testament. Following features can be noted:

First, integration is not exclusively a combination of various disciplines or disciplinary insights into one whole or a bundle of ideas. Although we may derive insights from various fields (mostly from allied disciplines) in our effort to delineate various topics for a holistic understanding, it will not be done like a mixed 'fruit-salad.' A careful consideration will be given to draw various insights from several fields to see how they are interconnected and are complimentary to one another.

Second, our approach to the themes of the Old Testament in this book has to happen in a way that enhances the life in all its fullness. In other words, our life experiences should be reflected in our integration process as we deal with the issues of the biblical text. In our contemporary times, the biblical studies has very much shifted its focus on this life-experiences of the reader rather than simply dealing with the text of antiquity in ways that was already done by the historical criticism in reading a biblical text. This will be reflected all through our thematic approach of our theological discussion of the Old Testament. This means then the life-experiences of the ancient Israelite community should be seen in the light of the contemporary living communities and vice versa.

Third, the integrated approach that we will be employing in this thematic section has to do with the building up of the individuals and the communities with values and value system that will take its roots for building up a just and equal society. Whether that becomes a simple ideal or how much we can envisage such a model value system depends on the readers of this material to appropriate what is read.

Fourth, somewhat related to the above point, what we need today in the integrated learning and approach to the biblical text is to build up communities of love, caring and sharing. At the heart of the Old Testament these ideals are deeply seated and our task is to explore such ideas of equality, justice and egalitarian ideals so that we can inculcate the values of the Kingdom of God here on the earth.

Fifth, our approach to the theological themes of the Old Testament is based on the canonical, chronological, theological and thematic perspectives in order to get a comprehensive and integrated treatment on the subject. Each of these perspectives cannot be studies in isolation, but we will demonstrate how they are complimentary to each other. Thus, these approaches can be seen as one integrated whole. It will be demonstrated in our study of themes in this section.

In the light of the above discussion we shall now venture into some topics and themes in the Old Testament from a historical (in a broader sense) and theological perspective.

3.1 Socio-Cultural Background of the Old Testament Themes: Ancient West Asian/Indian Parallels: A General Discussion

Although we will use the parallel stories and case studies for our OT theological themes at relevant and appropriate places when we deal with individual themes a general discussion with some examples will be of immense help to clarify our view point.

Ancient West Asian Parallels

The Bible is not an isolated book without any socio-cultural background. In fact, it was strongly influenced by its surrounding cultures and religious milieu. The ancient West Asian and Indian culture has several or some similarities with the culture and religion of the Bible. We shall dwell on the examples from the Prophetic literature of the Old Testament and their parallels from the ancient West Asian and Indian examples.

The literary documents are discovered along with some epigraphic and archaeological findings that will enhance our knowledge on the ancient West Asian parallels. The texts from this context involve predictions or apparent predictions, eschatological and apocalyptic sayings, social and religious criticism and commissioned messages from deities. Few examples from these will suffice to prove our point how the parallel world to ancient Israel existed. Sometimes these parallels are not exact but somewhat similar to ancient Israel.

In **Phoenicia** in the name of gods Baal or Asherah the prophets existed and performed their prophetic function. The Baal prophets share ecstatic behaviour with the Israelite prophets, but they are not identified as giving oracles. However, the **Egyptian** report of *Wen-Amun* (ANET, pp. 22-29)[132] states that while Wen-Amun was in Babylon (in 1090 BCE) one of Phoenician's prince's young attendants became ecstatic and delivered an oracle authenticating Wen-Amun's mission from God Amun, primarily because of these references it was at one time argued that biblical prophecy was derived from Canaanite (Phoenician) prophecy.

In **Mesopotamia** a rich variety of texts are discovered that have several parallels to Israelite prophetic phenomena.

Several thousand texts are published from *Mari* (middle of Euphrates) which are dated in the first half of the 18th century BCE. In these texts there are many references to prophetic activity and variety of titles are used for more than a dozen deities were involved in the prophetic activity. Both male and female prophets of about eighteen of them seem to have involved in the prophetic activity. Some of the titles include the following: *Āpilu/ăpliltu* (answerer) is an ordinary Akkadian form. This title is applicable to both male and female prophets. The meaning of the title implies that the person provides an answer to an explicit or implicit inquiry, although texts do not exemplify the process. For instance, one of the most important letters sent from Aleppo, concerns the answer of Addu, Lord of Kallassu who "reclaims the territory of Alahtum as property", The answerer is the one who "came and spoke" or "got up (in the temple) and spoke" addressing a court official with message for the king (ANET, 623-632).

132 James B. Pritchard, *Ancient Near Eastern Texts* (Princeton: Princeton University Press, 1955), henceforth cited as ANET.

Assinu (cult functionary): The two Assinu attested are affiliated with annunitum, a form of Ishtar. One of these speaks in a state of ecstasy. Another Assinu apparently resides in an abandoned and partly ruined sanctuary. *Nabu* (diviner?) this appears for the first time as a "prophetic" title in the Mari texts. A Mari functionary advises the king and he went to meet with a Hanaean leader. He then assembled the Nabu (plural) of the Haneans and had an omen taken on king's behalf, putting a binary question to them and obtaining apparently, a favourable answer.

The context of the above prophetic titles and their message is provided within the oracles. The typical locus of the revelation is a temple, either in reality or by dream visit by one correspondent advises the king (when) I offered a sacrifice to Dagan for the life of my lord the 'answer' (masc) of Dagan Tuttal got up and spoke as follows: 'O Babylon…' then follows an oracle against Babylon. The message is usually communicated to a royal official, but on two occasions a temple administrator (Sangu), who is not a cultic priest serves as intermediary with the royal official. The Sangu presumably had some jurisdiction over such temple activity. A number of oracles are uttered in public in the presence of assembly elders.

The content of the oracles mainly consists of or exclusively deal with the kings' affairs. Normally, the message is communicated by the prophets, who were sent by a deity and usually begins with a formula "thus says the deity." The content is generally an assurance to the king or a warning to the king of dangers, an assurance of divine assistance, but number of messages deviate from this pattern.

On the basis of the above discussion it is clear that there are some resemblances of ancient West Asian prophetic phenomena with that of ancient Israel and certainly there must have been an interface between them at some point.

Indian Parallels: If we compare the Hebrew prophets with the so-called 'rishis' or saints of India, we see some similarities as well as contrasting features between them. In ancient India several rishis were popular, and some of the prominent ones include: Kashyapa, Athri, Bharadwaja, Gowthama, Viswamitra, Jamadagni, and Vasista. Hindus respected them and even worshipped them. It was believed that these are the authors of Vedas and perhaps lived even before the Vedas came into existence. It was also believed that there rishis are always in praise of gods and angles. Some among them were very intelligent poets. The character of these rishis is very generous in nature, whoever approaches them for help they provide in abundance. They possessed some extra powers and always used to transcend human and natural realm due to the possession of such powers. Like gods they possessed eternal life, fertility, victory, property, all kinds of physical and material blessings. By virtue of their drinking of *soma pāna*, they uttered wonderful and life-giving words possessed with extraordinary powers. The rishis always maintained a good relationship with the kings and their court. Usually they live in ashrams with a bunch of disciples around them. Whenever there is a problem or a matter to be resolved in the king's court, rishis visited them and gave advise. For certain wars with other nations or as peacemakers between two enemy nations in case war breaks between them rishis played a decisive mediatory role. When they met public they used devotional methods to inspire them with devotional messages. When they found undesirable way of walking in the people, they exhorted them with divine injunctions. They claimed certain privileges of food, shelter and other provisions required for their daily bread.

Despite these seemingly similarities existing between the rishis and Hebrew prophets, there are some contrasting features between them. In the case of Hebrew prophets they receive a definite call from God and in obedience to such a call they dedicate their entire life to the service of God. But we do not find such a definite call in the case of rishis. Moreover, Hebrew prophets were ordinary persons in virtue of their calling from God, God endowed with best gifts in them and filled them with God's spirit. Also, the prophets are effective in communicating the message God to the people. Whereas the rishis, most often due to their own and self-effort, especially through rigorous meditation and concentration (tapas) are endowed with special gifts (varas) by the deities which they worship or performed their tapas. The Hebrew prophets proclaimed the message of doom and judgment without fear. They even faced the rulers boldly and courageously. They too preached about God's salivific acts that followed after the punishment. However, the rishis are always anxious and eager to declare their glory and power which resulted in terror and destruction even among the deva-loka. The Hebrew prophets predicted the future messianic hope and the new age that will bring comfort among the people. Whereas, the rishis hardly mention anything about the future apocalyptic message.

On the basis of the above discussion, we make the following observations on how the ancient world lived in parallel thinking with one another.

First, in a world of similarities and differences, it is natural for the Hebrew world to face such similarities and contrasting features in all their endeavours in the midst of other nations or surrounding nations. Either the prophetic phenomena, or wisdom thinking or any other aspect among the Hebrews is applicable and is governed by the parallel as well as contrasting framework.

Second, the socio-cultural context most often was similar in the case of the Hebrews and other nations surrounding her. In several instances the socio-cultural phenomena was almost similar and it would be a daunting task to find out who is influenced by whom, but certainly we will have to go by the date of the archaeological and literary sources.

Third, in view of the above two concerns it is then clear that the contact and the contrast between the Hebrew and other West Asian or Indian socio-cultural phenomena is an indication that we need to take these situations into serious consideration so that we present the socio-religious ideas among Israelite and their other corresponding or counterparts as a whole impacting one another.

3.2 Laws and Legal Codes in the Pentateuch: A Theological Perspective and their Implications and Parallels in the Indian Legal Systems

Ancient Israelite society was a theocratic society and their community life was intact with stringent regulations and rules that governed all their walks of life. God, through various means and ways and also through various leaders like Moses, Aaron, Joshua and through Judges and at later times through prophets, kings, wise people and so on, guided them so that they are always expected to live a life that is both distinct and holy in comparison with their surrounding neighbors. One should not look at these legal systems in the Israelite society as something that was used by coercion rather it as to be seen in the light of their overall community life that affirms the covenant relations and principles and at the same time equality and justice. These legal injunctions and procedures are aimed at Israelite society as an egalitarian one where every member of the society are treated equally without any discrimination. Additionally, these laws are aimed towards assisting the poor and vulnerable in their society in particular. Because of the bondage experience of Israelites in Egypt, they in turn should not oppress the aliens or foreigners among them rather to be kind and just towards them and thus these laws are geared towards that purpose. Moreover the legal injunctions are aimed towards not just charity purpose rather they are for the purpose of establishing the systems and structures towards building a just and egalitarian society in ancient Israel. Additionally, these law codes have to be seen in the wider context of Israel's response and obligation towards what God has done in their liberation experience from the Egyptian bondage.[133] The law codes are also God's manifestation and demonstration of love towards his people to guide and lead them in their community life. In the following pages we shall explain briefly each of the laws and their theological and sociological significance and then we shall talk about Indian laws in general to see some significant similarities with the Israelite law codes.

Covenant Code and its theological focus

The Covenant Code (abbreviated as C) is found in Exodus 21-23 chapters, deriving its conventional title from Exodus 24:7 where it is stated: *Then he (Moses) took the book of the covenant, and read it in the hearing of the people;* It is believed that this code is the oldest among all the codes mentioned in the Pentateuch. This code can be divided into two halves, the first of which (Exod 21:1-22:17) is formulated mainly in conditional sentences (known as "casuistic form") wherein protasis ("if"

133 There are some historical and chronological problems in the different law codes found in as part of Pentateuchal laws in ancient Israel. It is beyond the scope of this writing to deal with such complex issues.

clause) states circumstances and the apodosis ("then" clause) the legal consequences are mentioned. The second half of the code (Exod 22:18-23:19) expressed largely in the "apodictic" form (direct, second person commands, unaccompanied by any statement of sanction). The use of "if" clause and "then" clause in the protasis and apodosis respectively is predominant in the legal materials of the ancient West Asian codes. There is so much similarity in the content and form between the Covenant Code (Exod 21:35) and Laws of Eshnunna 53. The C contains (in the first half Exod 21:1-22:17) rules on slavery, homicide, various types of assault, death caused by animals, cattle theft, agricultural damage, deposit of property, shepherding, loan of animals, and seduction of virgin. The rule "eye for an eye..." is found earlier in the laws of Hammurabi. In the second half of the code (Exod 22:18-23:19) we find the material on social offenses, humanitarian injunctions, standards for the administration of justice, the laws of seventh year, the Sabbath, and the three pilgrimage festivals (see Exod 23:14-17) and regulations regarding sacrifice; it may be significant that the ban on seething (boiling) a lad in its mother's milk is found in this latter context. It is likely that the code as a whole was compiled from discrete sources, and it is widely believed perhaps it is an elaborated version of the original Sinaitic narrative, to which it now belongs.

Within the framework of the covenantal ceremony in Exod 19:1-24:11, the law code as mentioned earlier (20:22-23:19), conventionally termed as the "Book of the covenant", on the assumption that this is the document referred to in Exod 24:7. The content of this legal code presupposes, a settled community living in houses (22:2,7), frequenting fixed sanctuaries (23:17,19), possessing cattle as well as sheep (21:28), fields with their crops, vineyards and olive orchards and the necessary installations for pressing grapes and olives (22:19). There are four main types of formulations within C. This process has been noticed as a process of gradual development of the material before it took a definite form and systematization. We shall briefly present these stages as follows:[134]

First, 'when ... if, then ...' type: (Exod 21:18f), this is discursive variety of law which begins with a general situation (when men quarrel), introduces a particular circumstance (if the man rises again) and concludes with an appropriate legal sentence (then he shall be clear). The whole context is expressed in the third person (the men, the man, he) and thus adheres to the standard form of legal formulation in the ancient West Asia. Another example that might belong to this type is Exod 21:1-11. The technical term for this term of legislation is given in the heading of 21:1: *mishpat*, 'ordinance.' Albrecht Alt identifies this kind of law as 'casuistic' (case) law.

Second, the 'whoever' type: (Exod 21:15), this is terse n formulation. It begins with a participle (in the example 'whoever' strikes) and is expressed in the third person. Exod 21:12-17 and 22:18-20 belong to this type (21:13f seems to

134 For a detailed discussion on the four stages of development of the material in C see, W. Johnstone, *Exodus (OT Guides)* (Sheffield: JSOT Press, 1990). Reprint 1995.

be a secondary qualification separating manslaughter from murder, the second person 'you' in 22:18 is again a secondary contamination from the surrounding context, cg 22:21). It may be supposed that the technical term for this type of legislation is *h(ch)oq* (statute). Since, it is a statute it is frequently paired with 'ordinance' type discussed above. Both these words, statute and ordinance are synonymously used in the Hebrew for law code (Exod 25:15b and Josh 24:25).

Third, 'you (masculine plural) shall not ...' type: (Exod 20:23a), a prohibition addressed to the second person plural. A possible technical term used for this type would be *mitzwah* (commandment).

Fourth, 'you (masculine singular) shall not...' type: (Exod 20:24), a prohibition addressed to the second person singular. This is the same form as Decalogue, or 'ten words' (e.g. Exod 34:1; Deut 4:13) hence the technical term for this variety might be *dabar* (word).

The *mishpatim* (ordinances in Exod 21:1-11, 21:18-22:17) are wholly at home in the age-long legal practice of the ancient West Asia. *Mishpat* means both custom and precedent as the judgment based thereon. The *mishpatim* thus cover a wide range of civil and criminal cases 9 slavery, personal injuries, goring oxen, theft, damages, to crops, deposits, loans, seduction etc.) on which there is established practice. It is striking that in this range of inter-human, mundane, communal issues there is prevailingly a secular tone, in these there is not a single reference to God as the source of revelation. Jurisdiction in these cases is vested with the elders in the gate that is, the council of the heads of household within the community attended in Exodus 21:22 and more fully described in Deut 16:18-20; 17:2-7. It is only when the requisite two or three witnesses are lacking that the case must be referred to the sanctuary for decision by the drawing of the sacred lots or affirmation by oath before God (Exod 22:7-13).

The *huqqim* 'statutes' (Exod 21:12-17, 18-20) concern actions which threaten the established order of society—the sanctity of life and freedom of the individual and duty to parents and God. Infringements of these are absolutely prohibited and necessarily incur the death penalty. Jurisdiction in these matters again belongs to the elders in the gate, as the parallel legislation in Deuteronomy on the case of the unruly son makes clear (Deut 21:18-21; cf. Exod 21:15,17). These seven *huqqim* have their counterparts in anathemas pronounced in the curse liturgies in Deut 27:15-26, but it is clear that this passage in Deuteronomy is concerned with the prevention of such practices even in secret, that is, when there are no witnesses to bring a case to the court.

The outer framework of *dabar* and *mitzwah* (Exod 20:22-26; 22:21-23:19), however, introduce a completely a new factor: they are not expressed in the objective third person formulation of the law-code but as direct address by God to Israel, both individually and corporately. They are thus cast in the form of the code of the covenant between God and Israel. The stipulations are matters concerning divine-human relationship. The opening part of the framework (Exod 20:22-26) states the exclusiveness prescribes the appropriate mode of constructing the altar, the means by which that relationship is expressed and maintained. The materials in the concluding part (Exod 22:21; 23:19) are more miscellaneous in character and are disposed in four sections. Section one and three (Exod 22:21-27; 23:1-9) concern a variety of interpersonal relationships, the care for the weak in the society, the stranger, the widow, the orphan, the poor and even , the domestic animal; the safeguarding of the judicial process. Sections one and three are linked together by the prohibition 'you shall not oppress a stranger', with which section one begins and section three ends (Exod 2221; 23:9), and by interweaving the humanitarian concern for the domestic animal (Exod 23:4f) with the demand for the upholding of justice. These humanitarian concerns are held within the context of the specific duties of Israel towards God enjoined in sections two and four (Exod 22:18-31; 23:10-19); the prohibition of cursing God; the acknowledgement of God's love by offering of firstlings and first fruits; the eating of flesh only if offered according to the approved sacrificial rites; the observance of sabbatical year, the Sabbath, and the three annual pilgrimage festivals.

Priestly Code and Holiness Code and their theological foci

Apart from the Covenant Code discussed above, much of the rest of the book of Exodus, Leviticus and Numbers is often broadly called "Priestly Code" associated with the literary source "P" of the biblical source criticism. Very generally, the priestly source emphasizes religious and ritual concerns, while the Covenant Code as noted above deals with civil law and Deuteronomic Code shows special interest in matters of public law. But these characteristics are by no means exclusive: both the Priestly Code and Deuteronomic Code also deal with slavery and homicide; Deuteronomy alone deals with remarriage. Within the priestly corpus, there is a distinguishable text in Leviticus 17-26 known as the "Holiness Code" (abbreviated as H) in view of the reiterated motive for obedience to its laws: "Be Holy." We shall now consider some important characteristic features of H in the paragraphs that follow.

Leviticus 17-26 is usually distinguished from the rest of the book and designated as the Holiness Code; Lev 27 is viewed as a later appendix to this. Lev 17-26 give a different perspective from Lev 1-16. A number of sections are devoted to clear themes: the shedding and treatment of blood (17), prohibited sexual relations (18), regulations for the priests (21-22), festivals (23), sabbatical and jubilee years (25), and blessings and cursing (26). Other chapters, especially 19 and 20, have a miscellaneous character in terms of modern ideas about organization. We shall now make a brief survey of some individual sections and examine their content in the light of the overall focus of the H.

Leviticus 17:1-16: The shedding of blood and its treatment is discussed in this section. It was envisaged that all slaughter was to be done at the altar so that the blood could be dashed against the altar and the fat burned on it (17:3-7).

Thus, all slaughter of animals for food would take place in a sacrificial context and no butchering or consumption of meat could be done away from the shrine. How could this stipulation be carried out in practical terms? This difficulty is highlighted by Deut 12:20-25, which seemed to change just such a regulation when it stated that profane slaughter was allowed, as long as the blood was drained out of the animal. This means that Leviticus 17 must either be an idealized system divorced from reality or have envisaged a society small enough in numbers and territory to allow a trip to the altar and back within a day or so. Although no specific site is mentioned in Leviticus, it is clear that only one altar was envisaged, the context being tabernacle in the wilderness. Sacrifices were not to be carried out elsewhere (Lev 17:7-9). The exception to this rule about laughter at the altar was the case of clean wild animals or birds which could be hunted, killed and eaten apart from the shrine as long as the blood was drained out into the earth (Lev 17:13-14).

Blood itself is a central element in Lev 17. The life of both human beings and animals is in their blood. For that reason, blood should not be eaten, but dashed at the altar or poured on the ground and covered with dust. Blood functions as a potent symbol within the sacrificial cult. For the same reason that blood was not to be eaten, that which dies of itself or is killed by animals was not to be eaten since it polluted the eater (Lev 17:15-16).

Leviticus 18:1-30: This passage talks about the forbidden sexual relations. Much of the chapter covers what is usually referred to as incest, that is, sexual relations forbidden because of the closeness of kinship of the persons involved. The following are forbidden to the Israelite male: first, sexual acts with his own flesh (near of kin): mother or step-mother (Lev 18:6-8); sister, half-sister, step-sister, or sister-in-law (Lev18:9,11,16), daughter-in-law or granddaughter (Lev 18:17). Second, other regulations seems more concerned with what was deemed appropriate: not to take a wife's sister as rival wife (Lev 18:18), not to indulge in sexual intercourse during the menstrual period (Lev 18:19) or with the neighbor's wife (Lev 18:20), with another male (Lev 18:22), or with animals (Lev 18:23). It was forbidden to offer one's children to Molech (Lev 18:21).

Sexual relations are at the heart of social practice within any community. Each society has strict views about which kinds are allowed and which are not. Israel's rules here are lenient despite the claim that the Canaanites allowed sexual relations with close of kin, allowing even first cousins to marry. Israel was thus an endogamous society. This fits with their emphasis on rigid barriers to non-Israelites.

Leviticus 19:1- 20:27: This section deals with miscellaneous laws. It has a number of parallels with the Covenant Code and with Deut 12:26, as well as with the laws known elsewhere in the ancient West Asia. It has been suggested by some scholars that the regulations in Lev 19:1-20:9 have parallels with the Decalogue. It is true that the contents of some of the ten commandments are echoed here

(Lev 19:11-12; Exod 20:7,13 for example), but this seems to be fortuitous. There is no obvious relationship between the structure and wording of Leviticus 19-20 and the Decalogue.

Leviticus 21:1-24: This chapter deals with laws on priesthood. The presumption was that all Israel was to be holy, but the priests had to be even more rigorous. They were not allowed to defile themselves by contact with a corpse though participating in funerals other than close relations like mother, father, son, daughter, brother, or an unmarried sister (Lev 21:1-4). They were not to carry out mourning rites by disfiguring their hair, beards, or flesh (Lev 21:5-6). They were not allowed to marry a harlot or a divorcee and the priest's daughter who became a harlot was to be burned (Lev 21:7-9). Leviticus does envisage certain regulations for a high priest (Lev 21:10-15). This person had been anointed by the sacred oil. He was not to participate in a funeral, even for a close relative, or engage in mourning rites of any kind. He was to marry only a virgin of his own people. In the light of the above discussion it is clear that those who preside the alter functions (apart from the priests and high priests) were also rigorous (Lev 21:16-23). Just as animals to be sacrificed were to be without physical defect, so the officiating priests were to be without physical blemish.

Leviticus 22:1-33: This text talks about the regulations concerning the sacred gifts. Certain portions of sacrificial animals and other offerings were to go to the priests. These were sacred and to be eaten only by those qualified and only under certain conditions. The priests and their families who were in the state of purity , and they alone, were to take part of them (Lev 22:3-16). Lay persons were not to eat of these holy things. Hired servants also were forbidden to do so, but slaves owned by the priests were considered a part of the family and could eat them. The priestly portions were prohibited to the daughter of a priest who married a layman, unless she became divorced or a widow and returned to her father's house. If a layman unwittingly ate of the sacred gifts he was to restore them, together with an additional twenty percent of their value (Lev 22:14).

All offerings were to be of whole, normal animals without major physical defects (Lev 22:17-25). Anything which was blind, injured, maimed, or had certain sorts of disease was rejected. Neither was a castrated animal to be accepted (the implication being that Israelites did not castrate their animals, contrary to the normal practice of around them). An animal with a limb extraordinary short or long could be accepted for a free-will offering but not for a vow. This was only explicit concession made about blemishes, though how these regulations might have been interpreted in practice is unknown. A new born animal was not to be sacrificed until it had been with its mother seven days (Lev 22:26), nor was its mother to be sacrificed on the same day (Lev 22:27). Any thanksgiving offering had to be eaten on the day it was offered, anything left over was to be burnt (Lev 22:29-30, in agreement with Lev 7:15).

<u>*Leviticus 24:1-9:*</u> It talks about lampstand and bread of presence. The first part of Lev chapter 24 relates to the area inside the holy place but in front of the certain separating the Holy of Holies. A very pure olive oil was to be provided to keep the lampstand burning continually (Lev 24:2-4), there was also to be a table on which twelve loaves (together with frankincense) were to be placed each Sabbath. The frankincense was evidently burned at the end of the week, and the priests were allowed to eat the loaves. This was known as the bread of presence or show bread.

<u>*Leviticus 24:10-23:*</u> Blasphemy: At times within Leviticus there occurs a narrative rather than a specific law. In such cases, the episode in question seems to have been intended to explain what should be done by example rather than by direct instruction. In Lev 24:10-23, an Israelite whose father was Egyptian used God's name in a blasphemous way. He was put in custody until God could be consulted. God's reply was that that man should be stoned by the entire community. In future, anyone blaspheming with God's name was likewise to be executed by stoning. Within this section, there is an insert paragraph about life and reciprocation of punishment, otherwise known as the *lex talionis*. Lev 24:17-27 stresses the importance of life, especially human life. One who kills another person is to be compensated a reciprocal injury to the perpetrator, the famous 'eye for an eye and tooth for a tooth.' This law has often been misunderstood as a primitive barbaric practice, which embarrassed legislators later did their best to soften.

In fact, the earlier principle was that a person injuring another was to pay compensation. In the case of an extended family or community, that was the simplest way of handling the matter. The injured party, or the family, received some benefit. The *lex talionis* was an important advance in jurisprudence for two reasons. Firstly, it made everyone equal before the law; the rich could not get away with the crime of injuring another simply by making monetary payment. The 'eye for an eye' principle was a great leveler. Secondly, the law marked the stage at which the tribe or state took over the function of justice from the local community.

<u>*Leviticus 26:1-46:*</u> This is the concluding section of the H with blessings and curses. An appropriate literary closure of a book such as Leviticus is a section demonstrating the consequences of heeding or ignoring the commands contained in it. In Lev 26 the blessings for obedience come first (26:3-13), with promises of peace, plenty of fertility, the section given over to the curses for disobedience is longer and more clearly structured (26:14-38). Five sections are marked off with the phrase: 'If you (still) disobey, I will punish you sevenfold' or similar words (26:14-16, 18-20, 21-22, 23-26, 27-38). The aim seems to have been to create a crescendo effect, so that the longer the Israelites refused to obey, the stronger became the punishments, multiplying sevenfold each time. Finally, hope is expressed for repentance and a return from captivity (Lev. 26:39-45).

Such blessings and curses are well known from other ancient West Asian literature. International treaties usually ended with a list of blessings and, especially, curses for disobedience. The so-called law codes often included a similar section. For example, the epilogue to the Code of Hammurabi spelled out how the gods would punish the king in various ways for not heeding the marvelous laws which had just been listed. As with the list in Leviticus 26, the curses tended to dominate with the blessings listed only briefly. Lev 26:31-45 ends with reference to an exile and return, which led many scholars to claim that this showed knowledge of the exile of the Jews in 587/586 BCE and their return in 538 BCE.

Leviticus 23:1-44: This chapter talks about the important festivals of Israelite religious calendar. Before presenting some details of the religious festivals and their theological significance we shall briefly make some observations on the importance of the sacred time in the ancient Israel and its related concerns.

The concept of sacred time is found in most religions and is taken for granted in most forms of liturgical worship. It was not simply how God was worshipped but also when God had marked off certain periods of time as different as holy with rules as to how they should and should not be used. Several sections of Leviticus are concerned with the proper times for various observances: the weekly Sabbath and annual festivals, as well as the sabbatical year and jubilee year.

The determination of times—the calendar—is important in regulations about festivals and holy times but, surprisingly, the calendar is nowhere discussed in the Old Testament. It seems to have been taken for granted, and was mentioned only in passing reference. In some texts, the months are listed only by number like seventh month, first month and so on. Occasionally, the old Hebrew names are mentioned, although only some of these are known. Mainly, when the actual name of a month is used in the Old Testament the later Jewish name which had been borrowed from the Babylonians is used. For instance the list of names mentioned here are from Babylonian names and only for some Old Hebrew name mentioned in the brackets is mentioned: Nisan (Abib), Iyyar (not mentioned in the OT - Ziv), Sivan, Tammuz (not mentioned in the OT), AV (not mentioned in the OT), Elul, Tishri (not mentioned in the OT - Ethanim), Marchesvan (not mentioned in the OT - Bul), Kislev, Tebeth, Shebat, Adar.

Most of Leviticus 23 is taken up with the annual festivals (appointed times). These follow the agricultural year, most being related to specific events in the annual round of planting and harvesting. They all fall within the main growing period and avoid winter months. Holy days were treated like the Sabbath, could also be referred to annual Sabbath with no work being done. One apparent difference from the weekly Sabbath was that the preparation of food was allowed (see Exod 12:16).

We shall now examine briefly the significance of some important festivals in the ancient Israelite religious calendar. These festivals in general are to be seen in the light of Israelite experience of remembering and celebrating the liberation experience received. These festivals are therefore needs to be seen as a demonstration of celebration of God's liberative activity.

Festival of Passover and the Unleavened Bread: Lev 23:5 briefly mentions the Passover, but no details about this festival are furnished. In Leviticus the Passover is tied up with the festival of Unleavened Bread (23:6-8), the seven-day period when only unleavened bread (massôt) was eaten and no leavening or leavened products were allowed in the land. The festival was inaugurated by the Passover meal, at which unleavened bread was eaten, on the evening between the fourteenth and fifteenth of Nisan. The first full day (fifteenth) and the last day (twenty-second) were holy days.

An important day within the festival of unleavened bread was the wave sheaf ('ōmer) day (Lev. 23:9-14). On this day a symbolic sheaf of grain was cut as the first fruits of the harvest and presented before God. In addition certain specific offerings were enjoined: a male lamb as a burnt offering, a cereal offering of two *ephahs* of flour mixed with oil, and a quarter *hin* of wine as a divine offering. This ceremony marked the start of the grain harvest. No bread or grain from the new crop was to be eaten until the first sheaf had been brought. The ceremony took place on the Sunday (a day after the Sabbath) during the days of unleavened bread. In later centuries, various sects disagreed over whether the day after Sabbath meant the day after the first annual Sabbath (the holy day on 15 Nisan) or after weekly Sabbath, the most natural reading of the Hebrew text being that which interpreted it as the weekly Sabbath. This day also affected the date of Pentecost.

This festival is celebrated basically to remember the liberation experience of the way in which Yahweh delivered Israelites from the Egyptian bondage, to retell the people how bitter and insecure was their life under Egypt and now by the grace they remain free to celebrate Yahweh's goodness in the land. Moreover, the sheaf day reflects the idea of thanking and expressing the gratitude to Yahweh on the part of Israel.

Feast of Weeks or Pentecost: The spring grain harvest began on the wave sheaf day and continued for seven weeks until the feast of weeks (Lev 23:15-21). For some reason no specific term occurs for this festival in Leviticus. The Feast of Weeks did not fall on a specific day of the month but was counted from the wave sheaf day, reckoning seven Sabbaths. The Feast of Weeks (Exod 34:22) was on the day after the seventh Sabbath, called the fiftieth day when counting inclusively (that is, including both the starting and finishing day in the total). Hence, in later times the day was given the Greek name πέντήκοστή (fiftieth) day, from which the English Pentecost comes.

From later Jewish sources, it is known that there was disagreement among the sects about the day of this festival. The dispute concerned whether seven weeks from a floating annual Sabbath on 15 Nisan or seven Sabbaths from the first day of the weeks should be counted, to arrive at another first day of the week. Some translations and lexicons render the Hebrew phrase *Sabbātôt* as 'seven weeks', but this would be the only place where *sābbāt* means 'week' on the Old Testament; it is more likely that the word means 'Sabbath' here, as elsewhere. Only in Second Temple times did this meaning 'week' develop, allowing some sects to count from a fixed day of the month. Hebrew wage system and later priestly practice indicate that Shavuot was always celebrated on a Sunday as long as the temple stood and only later became fixed on the sixth of Sivan as it is among most Jews today.

Shavuot also had its own specific offerings. Two loaves of bread were baked from flour made from the new grain and presented before God. Usually, they were to be baked with leaven, this seems to be the only exception to the requirement that cereal offerings were to be unleavened, though nothing is said about their being burnt on the altar. Accompanying this were a burnt offering of seven lambs, a bull, and two rams; a sin offering of a male goat; and a well-being offering of two male lambs. In Exod 23:16 this festival is called as 'the feast of the harvest, the first fruits of your labor of what you sow in the field'. In Exod 34:22, the feast of weeks is further defined as 'the first fruits of wheat harvest'. These phrases indicate that the Feast of Weeks was originally agricultural festival, an occasion on which the community was expected to show gratitude to God for the first fruits, that is, the early harvest.

The Feast of Booths or Tabernacles (Sukkôt): The Feast of Booths or Tabernacles was the final festival of the year, celebrated after the autumn harvest (Lev 23:33-36, 39-43) on 15-22 Tishri (from the 15th of Tishri: late September or early October). It was Israel's joyous, thanksgiving , autumn harvest festival for the ingathering from the threshing floor and the wine press (Exod 23:16; 34:22; Deut 16:13-15). Its main distinctive ritual is the requirement to "dwell in the booths" in commemoration of God's protection of Israel during the wilderness wanderings (Lev 23:39-43; Neh 8:13-18). It probably arose from the practice of farmers who would build a temporary shelter (booth) in the field to sleep in, enabling them to protect the harvest and make best use of the daylight until the harvest was gathered. The people were to take fruit, palm leaves, tree branches, and willows and make booths as a part of celebration. The first and eighth days were holy days on which no work was to e done.

As with the Day of Trumpets, no sacrifices are listed for Sukkôt in Leviticus. In Numb 29:12-39, however, an elaborate series of sacrifices was mentioned that needs to be followed, each of the eight days having its own particular ceremony. This followed a diminishing series, beginning with 13 bulls on the first day, 12 bulls on the second, and so on down to seven bulls on the seventh day. Accompanying these were daily sacrifices of two rams and 14 yearling lambs, plus cereal and drink offerings. The eighth day had its own separate ceremony.

Sabbath and its significance: The word Sabbath is derived from the Hebrew root *šbt* which means "rest, cessation." The basic characteristic of the Sabbath was that no work of any kind was to be done. What made up that prohibited work is not precisely stated anywhere. Outside Leviticus, one passage notes that which is also prohibited on the holy days except 'that which each person must eat' (Exod 12:16), suggesting that the preparation of food was allowed on these annual Sabbaths but not on the weekly Sabbath.

Much later, contain other types of activity were allowed by some groups of Jews but forbidden by others. For example, one could aid the 'ox in the ditch' on the Sabbath according to general custom (Matt 12:11), though other Jews actually forbade it (Damascus Document = CD11:13-14). The saving of human life seems to have been almost universally allowed (cf. CD 11:16-17), but even here there was a qualification: in one instance, a group of Jews refused to fight in self-defense on the Sabbath (1 Macc 2:32-38), a fact which caused others to make the explicit decision that defensive warfare was permissible on the Sabbath, but not offensive (1 Macc 2:39-41). This custom was taken as an advantage by some Gentile generals, who used the Sabbath to extend and strengthen their siege works, knowing that they could proceed unmolested as long as they did not attack the Jewish defenders directly (for more details see Josephus, *War* 1:7-3:146).

The Sabbath seems to have had a long history in Israel and was not invented by the Priestly writers, but it is difficult to sustain that argument since we do not have sufficient evidence to prove it. It was once common to regard the Sabbath as primarily a post-exilic innovation. Sabbath observance is emphasized mainly in exilic and post-exilic texts (Isa 56; Neh 13:15-22 for example). The question of the origin of the Sabbath, is a difficult one. The number seven had a symbolic significance in many ancient West Asian cultures, including Ugarit and Mesopotamia, as well as in the Old Testament. Some festivals lasted seven days (Tabernacles, Unleavened Bread) and the date of the Pentecost is computed on the basis of seven times seven days. A seventh day celebration is, therefore, not surprising. More puzzling is the fact that there seems to be no relationship between the week and the rest of the calendar.

One suggestion is that the Sabbath arose originally as a periodic day of observance unrelated to the lunar or solar cycle. For example, a market-day cycle of a fixed number of days is known, in a variety of cultures, often from five to eight days in length and having nothing to do with the month or with other calandrical events. Nonetheless it has been suggested that there may once have been a relationship between the week and the month. The seven-day week is intriguingly close to a quarter of a lunar month, suggesting that the Hebrew Sabbath, originated from a four-times-a month-celebration.

The Hebrew word 'Sabbath' (Šābbāt) is similar to the Akkadian *Sapattu* or *Sabattu* meaning 'full moon' or fifteenth day of the month. There also Babylonian menologies, a cycle of ominous days which occurred four or five times a month, at approximately seven-day intervals. It is not clear that *Sapattu* is related to this cycle; however, no OT texts connect the Sabbath with the lunar cycle any way.

The Sabbath is to be both a sign of and a time for remembering the distinct relationship between Yahweh and the people of Israel (Exod 31:13; Ezek 20:20).

Because of the command that slaves should not be put to work on that day, it is a reminder of Israel's enslavement in Egypt and subsequent deliverance by God (Deut 5:15). In particular, God's creation of the world in six days and his resting on the seventh is to be called to mind (Gen 2:2-3; Exod 20:11, 31:17). The Sabbath is to be a time when the worshippers of God are gathered (Lev 23:3). The Tabernacle's Bread of the Presence was to be set on its table on the Sabbath (Lev 24:8; 1Chr 9:32) and special sacrifices were made in the temple (Numb 28:9-10; Ezek 46:4-5). In the synagogues the Sabbath became a time for teaching directed to the whole community (cf Mark 6:2; Luke 6:6, 10:10; Acts 13:14,27, 42,44).

Sabbatical Year and Jubilee Year: Leviticus 25 is a mixture of Holiness Code (H) and Priestly source (P). Verses 1-7 belongs to H; verses 8-16 mostly belongs to P; verses 17-34 and 35-40a are mostly H, and the rest are mostly H.[135] It may be noted that the H was thought of an independent law book that may have been composed between the end of pre-exilic cultus and at the beginning of post-exilic cultus. But H does not show any unity in terms of the content, but appears to be composition of smaller units, originally independent collection of laws. It may be that the priestly school had attempted on this earlier collection of H more editing, by way of expansion and modification.[136] Because Šemitta institution referred in Exod 21 and Deut 15 was never practiced in the pre-exilic times, the priestly school would have once again emphasized the need for sabbatical institution (Lev 25:1-7) and later Jubilee year institution (Lev 25:8-55). Based on the foregoing discussion it may be concluded that Lev 25 can be placed in a historical setting that is in the post-exilic composition.

In Nehemiah 5, there is a mention of Sabbatical year, which is an indication that Jubilee was not yet known by then. Since Jubilee year requirements were already taken care in haptad-institutions (land release: Exod 23:10, Deut 31:10; slave release: Exod 21:1-11, Deut 15:1ff; debt release: Deut 15:1-15) the possibility may be that Jubilee year was practiced when, there was a time that other seventh year institutions were not practiced and this must have happened in the post-exilic historical setting.[137] This fact is further illustrated if one counts the captivity from 587 BCE up to the time of Edict of Cyrus in 538 BCE. The period of exile is thus counted exactly as 49 years, which is the same as jubilee period. The year of returnees from exile would then be the fiftieth year. During this time a total freedom of the community should be restored and a redistribution of the land and wealth had to be implemented.[138] It is precisely at this point, there was a need that prompted the priestly writer to go for jubilee legislation.

135 Norman H. Snaith, *Leviticus and Numbers* (London: Thomas and Nelson Sons, 1967), p. 161.

136 J. R. Porter, *Leviticus* (Cambridge: Cambridge University Press, 1976), p. 135.

137 Gnana Robinson, "A New Economic Order: The Challenges of Biblical Jubilee," in Samuel Amirtham (ed), *A Vision for Man: Festschrift for J. R. Chandran* (Madras: CLS, 1978), p. 375.

138 Ibid., p. 368.

Now the question arises in the light of the foregoing discussion: how the institutions of sabbatical year were promulgated by the kings in the pre-exilic period? There is no proper evidence available to address this question. Probably if we study some ancient West Asian parallel customs we can get some clues on the question raised above. For instance *misārum* was an institution in Babylon, coming from the edict of *Ammisaduqa* the 10th ruler of Hammurabi's dynasty in Babylon (1664-126 BCE). The word *misārum* means equality and justice. This was used by the kings for maintaining a just economic order in their kingdom. Perhaps all the Babylonian kings promulgated *misārum* at the beginning of their reign, and afterwards when the occasions demanded it (as in the case of Zedekiah in Judah, see Jer 31:31). Moreover slave and debt release in the seventh year institution of Israel is in many respects analogous to the Babylonian *misārum*. During the reign of *Ammisaduqa* there are prescribed rules for the release of debts and release of slaves (as in Deut 15:1-11 and 12-18). In the case of Israel it is Yahweh who is portrayed as the king, the promulgator of equality and justice (Exod 22:21-27; 23:6-9). During the post-exilic period, the idea of kingship of Yahweh is renewed, thus, the liberation of slaves and restoration of their fortunes like their property and so on were seen as marks of inauguration of Yahweh's kingship.[139]

Implications and relevance of Sabbatical and Jubilee in our historical setting: Three basic elements of sabbatical year and jubilee year that is, rest for the land, release of debts (property mortgaging), and release of slaves are meant to be the elements of equality and justice, especially for the returnees of the exile, who were deprived of their rights by their fellow country people. We shall now focus on these aspects to show their implications and relevance in the preset day Indian context.

Rest for the land: It may be stated at the very outset that the sabbatical and jubilee years are God's *conservation strategy* for God's creation on this planet. Today, the principle of fallowing has almost disappeared from the agricultural practices causing unproductive and less yielding agricultural lands.[140] H. F. Beck states that fallow ground is usually broken up with plough and harrow, but it is left unseeded for the purpose of destroying weeds and insects, thus allowing the fertility of the soil to be restored.[141] V. R. Reddy comments that in the name of development and sustainable agricultural practice, intensive methods in agriculture is practiced by means of using chemical fertilizers and pesticides resulting in degradation in

139 Gnana Robinson, "A New Economic Order: The Challenges of Biblical Jubilee," in Samuel Amirtham (ed), *A Vision for Man: Festschrift for J. R. Chandran* (Madras: CLS, 1978), pp. 375-76.

140 Jürgen Moltmann, "The Ecological Crisis: Peace with Nature," *Scottish Journal of Religious Studies* 9 (1988), p. 13.

141 H. F. Beck, "Fallow Ground," *Interpreter's Dictionary of the Bible,* Vol. 2 (New York: Abingdon Press, 1962), p. 237.

the quality of soil.[142] A. Nadkarni suggests an alternative solution to use herbal pesticides in the place hazardous chemical fertilizers, especially herbal pesticides from neem. This, Nadkarni says will guarantee the food security and is very helpful for the majority of Indian rural farmers and population.[143]

In ancient Israel, rest for the land during the seventh year is a sign of God's *restitution in integrum* that is, restoration to an original state.[144] In other words, there is an echo of creation principle reflected in the institutions of sabbatical and jubilee years that is human beings as God's stewards of God's creation.

Release of debts/property and release of slaves: Both the sabbatical and jubilee year institutions are intended in Israel for an economic system which was geared to the needs of the poor and underprivileged in their society, thus giving a maximum assistance to such people, ultimately leading to an ideal state where there will be no poor (Deut 15). Furthermore, redemption of property is an indication that land should not be sold permanently, because ultimately the land belongs to Yahweh (Lev 25:23). Prohibition on taking interest on loans, especially from the poor to enable the poor farmer to buy enough seed for the next season (cf. Exod 22:24).[145] Redemption of slaves is in effect worked to advocate social justice (Deut 21:2-6; 15:12-18). In the light what is discussed thus far few important observations can be made with reference to the Indian context.

First, sabbatical and jubilee year institutions in the Bible serve as a critique against the massive private accumulation of the land and the wealth in Indian today. C. T. Kurian rightly observes that, "the socio-economic phenomena whereby the resources available to a society are used to satisfy the wants of the few, while many do not have their basic needs met."[146] According to a survey of Reserve Bank of India in 1971-72, the lowest 10% of the rural population have only 0.21% of the total assets of the country, whereas the top 10% of the rural population have 62% of the total assets. Similar way, top 75 industrialists have 50% of the industrial assets in the country.[147] In the name of development many people are uprooted from their land, several forests are wiped out. For example, "requirement of land for coal mining projects envisaged during VIII five year

142 V. Ratna Reddy, "Environmental and Sustainable Agricultural Development: Conflicts and Contradictions," *Economic and Political Weekly* 30, March 25 (1995), pp. A21-A27.

143 Avadhoot Nadkarni, "The Green Revolution: Twenty Five Years Later," *Social Action* 43 (1993), pp. 290, 293.

144 Martin Noth, *Leviticus* (London: SCM Press, 1965), p. 183.

145 R. P. Maloney, "Usury and Restrictions on Interest-taking in the Ancient Near East," *Catholic Biblical Quarterly* 36 (1974), pp. 1-20.

146 C. T. Kurian, *Poverty, Planning and Social Transformation* (New Delhi: Allied Publishers, 1978), p. 8.

147 Results of RBI. All India Debt and Investment Surveys, reported in *Economic and Political Weekly* 12, March (1977), cited with analysis by P. N. Varughese, "The Poverty Removers," *State and Society* 2, Jan-Mar (1981), pp. 42-54.

plan is about 116470 hectares, out of which the forest land is 36,170 hectares."[148] This result in disturbance in the ecosystem causing severe atmospheric changes, particularly the poor are affected in the sense that there may be any substantial benefit for them from coal mine industry.

If we analyze further the deep rooted causes of poverty in India in particular we may cite an example of hunger since hunger may lead to low output and hence poor wages. Hunger in India has gender and age dimensions too. Women, children and old people are less likely to receive the full nutritious meals needed for their survival. This can be noted very clearly in the following statement that the poverty and:

> [...] destitution, leading in extreme cases to starvation deaths but in any case to a life in misery, is more endemic amongst certain groups. These include persons with disabilities, persons with stigmatizing illnesses such as leprosy or HIV/AIDS, the elderly and the young who lack family support and single women. Social and employment factors causing destitution include scheduled caste population, tribal populations, manual scavengers, beggars, sex workers, landless labourers and artisans. Persons displaced by natural disasters or development projects are also often in this group. Due to prolonged deprivation of sufficient food and recurring uncertainty about its availability these people are forced to lose their dignity through foraging and begging, debt bondage and low end highly underpaid work; self denial; and sacrifice of other survival needs like medicine or children's education, and thus they transfer their misery to the next generation.[149]

Moreover, poverty has particular dimension of caste. While all the poor are affected by the drastic conditions of poverty, poor among the Dalits and tribals are still the worst victims.

> In social group terms, over 80% of the poor in the country now belong to socially disadvantaged groups like SCs, STs, the most backward castes among OBCs and weaker sections among the Muslims. More than 92% of SC farmers, a similar percentage of ST farmers and 84% of OBC farmers possess less than 2 hectares of land. The same is true for 78% of farmers from the 'others' category, which includes rural households from the upper castes and minorities. Access to land is

148 B. C. Misra, "Economy, Energy and Environmental Interface with Particular Reference to Socio-Economic Dimensions and Impacts," in *Socio Economic Impacts of Environment* (New Delhi: Ashish Publishing House, 1994), pp. 111-115.

149 Harsh Mander, "Living with Hunger: Deprivation among the Aged, Single Women and People with Disability," *Economic and Political Weekly* 43:17 (2008), pp. 87, 89-98.

> an important determinant of access to economic resources such as credit, as well as other resources that determine outcomes in terms of income. Further, the social identity of farmers is also seen to mediate access to economic resources and delivery of public services. Together, these factors account for lower levels of living of farmers in these groups, pointing to the need for concerted and multifaceted state policies and actions to ameliorate their disadvantages. Investing in infrastructure, knowledge generation and extension to support and empower marginal farmers, many of whom are women, so as to increase productivity on these marginal holdings, can be an important source of food security[150]

Poverty is the largest and most serious development challenge facing India. Although there has been sustained overall economic growth performance since the early 1980s in the country, the reduction in the rate of incidence of poverty has been extremely slow. Performance has been unsatisfactory, not only with regard to income poverty but also with regard to measures such as life expectancy and literacy. There is some misunderstanding on the whole concern of poverty and the poverty line in the recent data given by the Indian planning commission. S. P. Talukdar makes following incisive comments in this regard:

> India's Planning Commission and the system of statistics denote the utmost cruelty to the poor. As if by a magic wand, the number of the poor is raised or decreased by the adjustment of the Poverty Line. The latest poverty line of Rs. 22.43 per person per day for rural areas and Rs. 28.65 for urban areas has brought down poverty by 7.3 percentage points to 29.8% in 2009-10 from 37.2% in 2004-05. In terms of this absurd and ridiculous poverty line, or call it 'survival line' if you will, 50 million Indians have risen above poverty line in the last five years. In absolute numbers, after this "great" achievement, we still have 355 million below the Line against 470 million five years earlier. Even after hiding real poverty behind crazy statistics, India is still harbouring the maximum number of the poor in the world. As many as 355 million poor in a global population of 7000 million is a shockingly high number.[151]

---

150 Aasha Kapur Mehta, Andrew Shepherd, Shashanka Bhide, Amita Shah and Anand Kumar, *India Chronic Poverty Report: Towards Solutions and New Compacts in a Dynamic Context* (New Delhi: Indian Institute of Public Administration/Chronic Poverty Research Centre, 2011), pp. 34-35.

151 S. P. Talukdar, "Toying with the Poor," *Indian Currents* 24:14 (26 March - 1 April, 2012), p. 27.

It was right that the poor are mocked in the way in which r\the data on poverty is often presented. Thus, "the poverty management is characterized by duplicity, insensitivity, and cruelty."[152] In a world of subsidies, the poor are often neglected and favoritism and nepotism is the rule of the day in all the implementation of the subsidy programs. The net result of all these can be noted in several mega scams liker Commonwealth games, 2G scam and Adarsh project in Maharashtra. Thus, what is needs is a thorough shaking of the entire administrative system so that real benefit goes to those who are really suffering poverty in India.

Second, according to the new agricultural policy drafted by the government of India on March 6, 1993 and was presented at the Chief Ministers' conference envisages the agricultural growth resulting in higher income of the rural areas, which will ultimately improve the quality of life in villages. In view of this policy, contract farming was given to big firms like ITC, Pepsi etc. Due to this the traditional crops of the poor farmers are replaced with higher technology production of pulses was stopped, instead high yielding varieties of cotton and tobacco are grown, forcing poor farmers to by their rice from market, which is very expensive. The new agricultural policy caused damage to the land, depriving the rights of the poor farmers at the same time.[153] Contrary to all the plans giving priority to agricultural sector by the Indian government, the suicide rates of the farmers boomerangs the actual expectation. Recent data indicate a rise in farmer suicides owing to financial distress, for instance in the hill district of Wayanad in Kerala in South India. The amount of expenses invested in the farming is steeply rising than the profit and thus the farmers resort to end their lives due to huge debt incurred by them.[154]

Third, the issue of bonded labour system in India is an important concern to be discussed briefly at this point. Slavery abolition act of 1843 failed to curb the system of slavery and bonded labour practice in India. In 1976, Indian government promulgated bonded labour legislation act, which is an indication that it is practiced harshly by the oppressive class on the poor and marginalized. The landlordism and zamindari system continues to exist in several parts of India even today. To cite one specific example, in a village called Chinnappa Naicken Palayam of South Arcot district in Tamilnadu, a thirty old man was compelled to serve a landlord due the loan taken by his father from the age of thirteen. At the age of twenty five the landlord spent some money for the marriage of this young man, thus making him life-long bonded labourer. This young man is made to work 12 to 13 hours per day and he is paid only Rs. 30/- per month. Moreover

152 S. P. Talukdar, "Toying with the Poor," *Indian Currents* 24:14 (26 March - 1 April, 2012), p. 27.

153 T. Palakudy and S. Singh, "The New Agricultural Policy and the Rural Poor," *Social Action* 43 (Sept 1993), pp. 330-335.

154 For some details on the recent incidents on the farmers' suicide see *The Hindu* February 03, 2012, New Delhi Edition.

the landlord took away the inherited fertile land of this young man. This landlord owns 26 acres of land and six bonded laborers.[155] S. P. Gupta reports that, due to uneven distribution of the land in India, majority of the population do not hold land. The landless poor is estimated to be 66.3% in India, and 17.7% of the poor have only one bigha of land per head. This is an indication that only very few people own almost all cultivated land in India.[156]

In the year 2007 Thorat Committee reported the then status of Dalits in India in relation to their land ownership and the related issues. 75% of Dalits either own no land or less than one acre of land. Only 16.8% of Dalits are self-employed as cultivators of lands against 41% of non-Dalits. 62% of Dalit households are daily wage earners because of lack of any fixed capital. 35.4% of rural Dalits are below poverty line as against 21% of non-Dalits. In urban areas 39% of Dalits are below poverty line as against 15% of non-Dalits. 69.5% of Dalits in urban areas are casual laborers. Lack of food and sanitation leads to 83% infant mortality among Dalits compared to 61% non-Dalits. 75% of Dalit children are anemic. The literacy rate among Dalits is 54.7% while it is 68.8% among others.[157]

The plight of Dalits is so horrible that once they are the land owners are now made to migrate to other places due to the loss of land. The cumulative effect of their landlessness is graphically described by Dayanandan as follows:

> In a country with an agrarian economy the Dalits have no financial means to cultivate the land they possess profitably. The rich and powerful in India and abroad are ready to pay any amount to buy their lands for a variety of profit making ventures. The deprived Dalits have no alternative but to move to cities and become slum dwellers, servants, beggars, hawkers, or worse.[158]

Thus, it is clear that while all the poor people are affected by the worst and ill effects of nature and poverty in India it is the Dalits and tribals who are the most and drastic victims in the process. It is also to be noted that Dalits have no 'God fathers' to support and defend and most often they had to fight their own cause and emerge successfully out of their own problems. First of all Dalits own very little land given to them by their forefathers and even that is land is either

155 R. Vidyasagar, "Debt Bondage in South Arcot District: A Case Study of Agricultural Labour and Handloom Weavers," in *Chains of Servitude: Bondage and Slavery in India* (New Delhi: Sangam Books, 1985), pp. 150, 153-154.

156 S. P. Gupta, *Structural Dimensions of Poverty in India* (Delhi: Mittal Publications, 1987), p. 165.

157 Sukhdeo Thorat, "Economic and Educational Empowerment of the Scheduled Castes," *Planning Commission*, Government of India, 2007.

158 P. Dyanandan, *Dalits, Land and Environment* in Dalit Daniel Gnanasekaran (ed), *Let Me Own My Land: Dalit Voices in India* (Tiruvannamalai: Department of Dalit Concerns/Arcot Lutheran Church, 2009), p. 71.

confiscated or grabbed from them by illegal means and often they are killed in the process or made to be silent if they revolt against any atrocity. Dalits once lived as land owners are made as landless labourers or tenant farmers by the dominant caste people. Due to their vulnerable condition and lack of any support in the system Dalits remain silent and work within the system as tenant farmers and bonded labourers in the land of dominant caste people. The 'panchami' lands allocated to them by the government are kept only records while the actual beneficiaries of those lands are someone else than those to whom the land is allocated. The political system is so corrupt that nothing can be done to address this anomaly and Dalits continue to remain landless.

In the light of the above discussion, we now make the following observations and comments on the significance of Sabbatical and Jubilee years mentioned in the Holiness Code of Leviticus 25 and its historical antecedents:

First, it has been observed that God is the owner of the land given to the human beings as a gift and thus human greed and unnecessary want cannot be justified. This principle has been neatly reflected in and through the institutions of sabbatical and jubilee years. While the Deuteronomic reformers affirmed that the land is a gift given to the people by Yahweh the priestly writer from which the sabbatical and jubilee years have been introduced affirm that God alone owns the land and Israel was merely a tenant. Thus, the question of land ownership by the rich landlords does not arise. The land cannot be sold from one to another as that would deny the fundamental right of a person. Even if the land has been sold due to some economic crisis it has to be returned to the original land owner in the sabbatical year or at least during the jubilee year (Lev 25:25-28). While the final ownership of the land is rested with God, human beings are trustees and stewards called to preserve God's creation. Everyone has the right to have their own vine and fig tree, and eat their own harvest. No one is enslaved to another. No one is supposed to exploit other person by grabbing others' property. Debts are to be cancelled and covered up, particularly the debts of poor and marginalized. Land and animals are allowed to rest. Thus, humanity, natural resources, and living beings upon the earth are expected to live in justice and peace with one another.[159]

Second, the mandate for eco-justice is not only present in the Bible but in the every major religious tradition in India and elsewhere. Eric Lott states that in Hinduism, earth is respected as mother earth (*bhumaata*). In Vaisnavism this *bhumaata* is found in close association with Lakshmi, who is portrayed as gracious mother, by whose intercession God's grace is secured on all people of the earth. The Jain and Buddhist understanding of non-violence and compassion for life are

159 David C. Scott, "Some Reflections on 'a Theological Response to Ecological Crisis," *Masihi Sevak* 18 (June – Sept 1994), pp. 11-16.

the valuable resources for our eco-justice action.[160] The Buddhist understanding in particular affirms that the land cannot be owned by human beings and thus to exploit the rich resources of the land for human greed amounts to the violation of land, the violation of life sources and the divine.[161]

Third, we need to develop a holistic vision of our interconnectedness with the entire eco-system that will promote a 'shared existence' on this planet. This has been explained beautifully by Saji Mathew Kanayankal as follows:

> Therefore, our idea of wholeness appeals to see realities above their material realm and frame the concept of happiness and welfare in the context of one's right relationship with God, neighbour, him/herself and the earth. A true and genuine welfare consists neither in the progress of material goods and its consumption or maximisation, nor in the construction of great monuments and architects; instead, it does focus on the building up of richer relationships between persons not excluding the creator and different creatures on the earth. In this view, the ecological task of Christian theology is to enhance and enrich the different spheres of relationships that promote the human and ecological flourishing.[162]

This way of understanding leads us to promote dignity of life at all levels and "affirms the intrinsic relationship between the well-being of the individual self and the productivity, diversity, and dynamic stability of the natural world.[163]

Fourth, the urgent task of the church today is to respond to the ecological crisis as the survival problem of humanity, by responding positively to the eco-justice crisis, not simply as peace with nature, also peace within the human relationships, expressed in justice concerns. It has been pointed out that the churches must come together for united action on eco-justice. This must happen in the overall framework of need against greed, enabling power against dominating power, conservation against consumerism.[164] If these principles are followed today in our church and society, there will be a radical change in the restoration of God's creation and its resources.

To conclude our discussion on the topics of the sabbatical and jubilee years, coming from a concrete life experience of ancient Israel affirm that they serve as

---

160 Eric J. Lott, "An Eco-theology for the Future: Resources from India's Past," in Arvind P. Nirmal (ed), *Adventurous Faith and Transforming Vision* (Madras: Gurukul, 1989), pp. 29-52.

161 Wesley Ariarajah, "World Religions and the Wholeness of Creation," in *The Ecumenical Movement Tomorrow* (Geneva: WCC, 1993), pp. 159-171.

162 Saji Mathew Kanayankal, "Being in Harmony: Biblical Vision of Interconnected Existence," *Journal of Dharma* 36:3 (2011), pp. 286-287.

163 Ibid, p. 287.

164 K. C. Abraham, "Ecology and Mission," in J. R. Chandran (ed), *Third World Theologies in Dialogue* (EATWOT, 1991), pp. 114-119.

life-giving institutions and also God's creative act for the entire cosmos. Israel was aware that God's continued creative action can be experienced in and through these institutions. These two institutions also remind ancient Israel and everyone of us to realize our primary social and ethical responsibilities, thereby create a new people who are not only conscious about their God and the creation but about their neighbor.

Deuteronomic Code and its theological focus

The heart of the book of Deuteronomy is to be found in the central law code in 12:1-26:15. This consists of a revised and updated form of earlier laws, chiefly drawn from the Covenant Code of Exod 20:22-23:19, and partly of a range of civil laws which appear in Deuteronomy for the first time. What is most original in Deuteronomy, however, and constitutes the most striking feature of the book, is the large number of rules governing worship and prohibited practices of alien worship, which are closely integrated into the overall structure of the law codes. We now present this outline and contents of the code.

1. Laws governing worship: a) 12:1-32: the law of the central sanctuary; b)13:1-14:2,16:21-27, 18:9-14: the avoidance of false worship; c) 14:3-20: clean and unclean animals; d) 14:22-29,15:19-23: tithes and firstlings; e) 15:1-18: the year of release and the freeing of slaves; f) 16:1-17: the festival calendar.
2. Offices and Institutions: a) 16:18-20; 17:8-13; 19:14-21: the administration of justice; b) 17:14-20: the appointment of the king; c) 18:1-18: provision for Levitical priests; d) 18:9-22: the role of prophets; e) 19:1-13: the cities of refuge; f) 20:1-20: the conduct of war.
3. Miscellaneous Laws: a) 21:1-9: unaccounted death; b) 21:10-22:30: marriage and family life; c) 23:1-25: persons excluded from the community and other laws; d)24:1-22: the protection of persons; e) 25:1-19: the maintenance of order and justice; f) 26:1-15: the offering of first fruits.

We can notice three significant features in the central law code of Deuteronomy. We shall summarize the major concerns of each in the paragraphs that follow.

Deuteronomic revision of earlier laws: As noted earlier that the law code of Deuteronomy is built upon a revision of many of the earlier laws to be found in the Book of the Covenant (Covenant Code in Exod 20:22-23:19). The following list[165] indicates the correspondences between D and C as follows:

165 The list is presented by Gerhard von Rad, *Deuteronomy: A Commentary* (London: SCM Press, 1966), p. 13.

Exod 21;1-11	Deut 15:12-18
Exodus 21:12-14	Deut 19:1-13
Exod 21;16	Deut 24:7
Exod 22:16f	Deut 22:28-29
Exod 22: 21-24	Deut 24:17-22
Exod 22:25	Deut 23:19-20
Exod 22:26f	Deut 24:10-13
Exod 22:29f	Deut 15:19-23
Exod 22:31	Deut 14:3-21
Exod 23:1	Deut 19:16-21
Exod 23:2f; 6-8	Deut 16:18-20
Exod 23:4f	Deut 22:1-4
Exod 23:9	Deut 24:17f
Exod 23:10f	Deut 15:1-11
Exod 23:12	Deut 5:13-15
Exod 23:13	Deut 6:13
Exod 23:14-17	Deut 16:1-7
Exod 23:19a	Deut 26:2-10
Exod 23:19b	Deut 14:21b

This series of correspondences can either be increased or decreased or decreated depending on the degree of closeness we expect to find in different law codes. We should also naturally expect to find a certain measure of overlap.

When we examine in detail the nature of this Deuteronomic revision of earlier laws taken from the Book of Covenant we are brought face to face with a number of interesting features of the development of Israel's legal system. It becomes clear in the first place that the Deuteronomic law is the latter version and has been designed to take account of wider range of features than those reflected in the earlier laws. This becomes clear for example, when we examine the law concerning homicide and the importance it demonstrates of the necessity of distinguishing between accidental and intentional killing. This law in the Book of the Covenant reads as follows:

> *Whoever strikes a man so that he dies shall be put to death. But if he did not lie in wait for him, but God let him fall into his hand, then I will appoint for you a place to which he may flee. But if a man willfully attacks*

> *another to kill him treacherously, you shall take him from my altar, that he may die* (Exod 21:12-14)

When we compare this with the revised form of the law as set out in Deut 19:1-13, we find that it has been incorporated into a larger set of provisions concerning the allocation of six cities to serve as the specified places of refuge (they are called 'cities of refuge' in Numb 35:6,11). These are to serve as substitutes for the sanctuaries of the older law (cf. the reference to the 'altar' in Exod 21:14). We notice that the whole question of investigation of the crime and of establishing the guilt by showing a motive for murder has been dealt with more extensively. A matter of prime concern in dealing with cases of murder was the need to assess the culpability. This could only be achieved by establishing some idea of motive; and this required a knowledge of both the circumstances of death and the culprit's intentions towards the victim. From the more advanced legal system presupposed by Deuteronomy we can see that much less responsibility has been placed upon the 'avenger of blood' and upon the priests of the cultus. M. Fishbane[166] is of the view that in Deuteronomy we can notice an increasing rationalization of the juridical process. This led to the establishment of a system of officers and judges (Deut 16:18) who were to handle all normal legal cases. They were clearly expected to make whatever assessments they could in the light of what they could discover about the relationships between the culprit and the victim, much as a modern murder investigation would be expected to do. Only when these officers were unable to reach a satisfactory verdict was resource to be made to the Levitical priests who were to be found at the central sanctuary (Deut 17:8-13).

The ruling of the law of evidence in Exod 23:1-3 runs quite tersely:

> You shall not utter a false report. You shall not join hands with a wicked man, to be a malicious witness. You shall not follow a multitude to do evil, nor shall you bear witness in a suit, turning aside after a multitude, so as to pervert justice; nor shall you be partial to a poor man in his suit.

When we compare this with what we find in Deut 19:15-21, we can see that it has been elaborated to a quite considerable degree. The 'revised law' demands that a charge be supported by at least two, and if possible three, witnesses for it to be sustained. The Deuteronomic provision also envisages the further examination of witnesses to check on their veracity (Deut 19:18). The new law then further lays down penalties where perjury has been committed (Deut 19:19) and this is amplified by the mention that such penalties are to serve as deterrent. Quite clearly the need to check on witnesses, combined with the difficulty of weeding

166 Michael Fishbane, *Biblical Interpretation in Ancient Israel* (Oxford: The Clarendon Press, 1985), p. 244.

out malicious cases of collusion between unprincipled witnesses had to be taken fully into account. In this respect we can see how the Deuteronomic legislation has become conscious of the need to resort a principle of deterrence in its efforts to establish a rational and fair judicial system.

We can see further aspects of the way in which Deuteronomy has built upon the greater simplicity of the older Book of the Covenant when we note the way in which the latter law presupposes a more advanced economic order. Ownership of property and systems of sale and exchange in the Book of the Covenant are relatively unsophisticated. They have become much more sophisticated in the Deuteronomic code. This is reflected in the development of the law concerning the release of slaves after they have fulfilled their allotted time of servitude.

The law in Exod 21:2f envisages the case of a slave bought from a previous owner, who is then obligated to fulfill six years of slave service. The development of this in Deut 15:12f, recognizes rather different situation of debt-slavery. In this the person concerned is considered to have sold himself into slavery in order to clear debts that have been incurred. The Deuteronomic legislation also considers the possibility of woman being entitled to inherit and own property in a manner which is not envisaged in the earlier code. Several examples of this sort can be cited both from the Covenant Code and Deuteronomic law Code.

Regulations Governing Worship: In the book of the Covenant a short calendar of the major religious festivals which Israelites were bond to observe is given (Exod 23:14-17). An impressive and striking feature of the Deuteronomic law Code is that a more elaborate version of this festival calendar (Deut 16:1-17) has been incorporated into the very heart of the collection. Moreover, other features regarding the worship , for example, the law of altar of Exod 20:24-26, have been expanded extensively and woven fully into the Deuteronomic legislation (Deut 12:2-14). Laws relating to religious observance have been set alongside more strictly legal matters and incorporated into a code in which both are given similar importance. The law of the central sanctuary in Deut 12:2-14 must certainly be regarded as one of the most distinctive features of the Deuteronomic legislation. It represents a milestone of great significance in the development of worship in ancient Israel. The toleration of a wide variety of altars and sanctuaries can be described as 'pre-Deuteronomic', whereas insistence on a single sanctuary can be recognized as belonging to a period after this Deuteronomic demand had become an established fact.

It is also significant that the manner in which most of Israel's and Judah's kings are criticized in the history of 1 and 2 Kings up to the time of Josiah's great reform (2 Kings 22-23), demonstrates the influential outworking of this Deuteronomy has sought to introduce such a restrictive rule concerning sacrificial worship which in other respects must have proved highly inconvenient (cf. Deut 14:24-26). It is part of its endeavor to implement a wide spread purification of worship of God in Israel by removing the opportunity and occasion for retaining any vestiges of the older Canaanite worship of Baal and other gods and goddesses (Deut 12:2-3; see also 13;1-5, 6-11 and 12-18). By restricting sacrificial worship to one single sanctuary far greater control could be exercised over its activities.

It is wholly in keeping with the Deuteronomic concern to bring together a wide range of religious and social concerns that it should include a comprehensive calendar of religious festivals (Deut 16:1-17). This clearly represents an expansion and development from the laid down in the older shorter festival calendars preserved in Exod 23:14-17 and 34:8-24. At the same time it is lees developed than the much fuller calendar in Lev 23:1-44, showing how Deuteronomic legislation represents a middle position in the records of Israel's developing system of worship.

What is especially noteworthy about these Deuteronomic rules for worship is the manner in which they combine into one single spring festival, the celebration of the Feast of Passover (Heb. *Pesah* Deut 16:1-2,5-7) with that of the Feast of Unleavened Bread (Heb. *Massot* Deut 16:3-4,8). There can be no doubt that this marks a carefully considered concern to bind together tow festival celebrations which were originally separate in their origin. One of these was a shepherd's sacrificial rite, most probably occurring at the time when the flocks were moved into new pasture lands. The rites relating to the eating of unleavened bread on the other hand, were celebrated by those living off the sown land and marked the consumption of the last of the previous year's grain stocks. It would appear that an economic situation had developed in which both patterns of agriculture had come to exist side by side, the accompanying religious rites were linked together.

Two other features relating to this spring festival deserve special mention. The *first* of these is that the purpose of such a celebration is very firmly laid down as an act of remembering the event of the Exodus from Egypt (Deut 16:1-8). In this way the more surface aspects of the agricultural significance are left in the background. The *second* is the firm insistence that the Passover should be celebrated at the sanctuary which God would choose (Deut 16:6-7), and not the domestic settlements of the worshippers. It is probable that, by combining these spring celebrations, Deuteronomy was simply acknowledging a practice that had already become an established convention for some groups in Israel.

Distinctive Laws in Deuteronomic Code: Besides developments and modifications of earlier laws and elaboration of regulations governing worship there are in Deuteronomy many legal prescriptions which do not appear in earlier texts. Of special interest among these is a series of laws relating to the conduct of war and the obligations for military service. These cover such issues as circumstances entitling a man to exemption from military service (Deut 20:1-9), the conduct of an army when besieging a city (Deut 20:10-20) and the necessity for maintaining firm hygienic discipline in a military camp (Deut 23:9-14).

The inclusion of these regulations governing warfare would certainly suggest that Deuteronomy arose at a time when Israel was facing something of a military crisis. It is also significant that such regulations presuppose that Israel's defence was primarily a matter for the civilian conscripted militia, rather than for a central corps of professional soldiers, such as must have grown up as a part of Israel's royal establishment from the time of David and Solomon.

Besides a number of miscellaneous laws which appear in Deuteronomy for the first time aimed at protecting the environment (cf. Deut 22:6-7) and requiring a responsible attitude towards the building and maintenance of property (cf. Deut 22:8), the most striking new introduction in a law defining the position of the king (Deut 17:14-20). This is the only biblical statement concerning the constitutional position of the monarch, and it contains a number of striking features. In the first place the requirement that he should be 'one among your brethren' (Deut 17:15), excludes a foreigner from such office. At the same time there is no hint that he is anything other than an ordinary mortal human being, so that all traces of an older divine mythology concerning the king's status are set aside. The highest that is affirmed regarding him is that he must be one whom God himself has chosen. This indicates divine election.

Decalogue and its Theological Focus

A series of commandments from God to the chosen people is mediated by Moses. The text of the Decalogue (Gk. 'ten words') or Ten Commandments is given in its entirety twice in the OT with only slight variations. In Exod 20:1-17 the setting is Mount Sinai; Moses brings down to the people the two tablets of law written down by the very hand of God (Exod 24:12). In Deut 5:6-21 the text is part of Moses' recitation of the history of salvation with which he prefaces his last will and testament.

Origin and setting: Everything about the Ten Commandments suggests that it was a text intended to be memorized and publicly recited by the covenant community. Not only are the commandments in number equal to the fingers of both hands, but a similarity of form also pervades most of the list: "you shall not" is followed by a verb. Placed at the very beginning of the lengthy block of legal materials known as the Sinai Passage (Exod 19:11-numb 10:10), the Decalogue functions as a summary of the covenant tradition suitable for recitation on public occasions of national reaffirmation of loyalty to the sovereign God. Although OT makes no specific mention of a regular 'feast of covenant renewal', the events recalled in Deuteronomy 27 and in Joshua 24 appear to be such occasions: the people gather at Shechem, swear their allegiance to the law, and watch as inscribed stones are set up to preserve the terms of the covenant. We may even suppose that certain religious officials were responsible to lead the recitation of the law on these occasions, and that these 'covenant mediators' may have interpreted the Ten Commandments for their own generation.

Function: Israelite law can be separated into two broad categories: case law and categorical law. The former, represented for example, in the Book of the

Covenant (Exod 20:22-23:33), preserves decisions about actual cases reached through judicial processes of a settled agricultural community. Biblical case law is roughly equivalent to our common law. Categorical law, on the other hand does not seem to emerge from actual cases but sets forth the broad principles of community life. The Ten Commandments and similar lists of legal sentences (see Deut 27:15-26; Lev 19:13-18) amount to something like the constitutional law of ancient Israel. In function the Ten Commandments can be compared to ten posts supporting the fence separating the viable community of Israel from the breach of disorder in the society's confusion and bloodshed. Of all the statutes needs to regulate the life of the community, these ten were deemed essential beyond all others. Should any one of these ten fence posts collapse, chaos could break in and results create havoc in the community. For Israel, survival itself was at stake with every one of these ten categorical imperatives.

Brief survey on the commandments: The commandment reckoned to be the first one by most Protestant and Eastern Orthodox Christians, "you shall have no other gods before me" (Exod 20:3; Deut 5:7) is considered the first half of the second commandment in Jewish tradition. In Lutheran and Roman Catholic traditions this commandment is combined with prohibition against graven images to form the first commandment: Exod 20:17 is then divided into two commandments to make up the ten. This commandment does not deny the existence of other gods, but it demands total allegiance on the part of Israel to her own God, the covenant giver. The prohibition against graven images (Exod 20:1-6; Deut 5:8-10) may be in the first instance having been aimed at images of Israel's own God, Yahweh. God will not be localized in an object such as a golden calf (see Exod 20:4-6; 1 Kings 12:28), because to permit this to happen would make God an object of manipulation. God has the images in the world (Gen 1:26), but they walk on two feet and they love God and keep the commandments (Exod 20:6). The prohibition against the misuse of the name of God (Exod 20:7; Deut 5:11) is directed at another form of manipulation of the deity for personal interest. Magical, imprecatory, and other trivial cultic uses of the sacred name are forestalled.

The commandment to rest on the Sabbath is motivated in Exod 20:11 by the creator's own Sabbath rest. In Deut 5:12-15 the Sabbath is a day of remembrance of liberation from Egyptian slavery. The commandment to set one day apart from all others ('to keep it holy') stands as a bulwark against endless self-destructive human greed, and spares Israel the honor of being a sabbathless culture. The command to honor father and mother (Exod 20:12; Deut 5:16), the only one accompanied with a promise, promotes a community climate in which the chances of survival are enhanced by a tradition of tender solicitude shown by the young towards the older generations. The uninterrupted flow of community tradition from one generation to the next is also ensured by the 'honour' shown to the father and—in a perfectly equal way—to the mother. Technically speaking, "you shall not kill" (Exod 20:13; Deut 5:17) prohibits only that kind of antisocial killing, done in vulgar self-interest, that poses a threat to the very existence of the community. Jesus' radicalization of this commandment in Matt 5:21-26 suggests that the definition of antisocial murderousness could evolve and that the commandment could come to mean more than it originally meant.

"You shall not commit adultery" (Exod 20:14; Deut 5:18) guards marriage and family against the intrusion of third parties and the socially disruptive questions of the legitimacy of children and the transfer of the family legacy. "You shall not steal" (Exod 20:15; Deut 5:19) may originally have included, as the object of the verb, the term "a man" (see Exod 21:16). As it stands however, this commandment protects private property from illegal attachment. The prohibition against bearing false witness (Exod 20:16; Deut 5:20) is aimed not so much at living in general as it is at perjury at court. The very survival of a community is threatened when the weak, disadvantaged and falsely accused can find no remedy before impartial judges informed by credible witnesses. Finally, the commandment against the covetousness (Exod 20:17; Deut 5:21) points for the first time beyond public and overt acts to private attitudes. Like all Hebrew verbs the mental activity, however, 'to covet' also includes an element of enactment. It is action rehearsal. Unenforceable as it may be, in its attach upon inordinate desire this final commandment seeks to forestall the conspiracies that led to illegal, ruthless seizure of persons and property.

On the basis of our foregoing discussion on the various law codes and the Decalogue in the Hebrew Bible it is clear that they are the basic foundation for the community of Israel in their daily walk of life. Though the laws and law codes in Israel came from an agrarian and pre-industrial society, they are certainly relevant and appropriate for our modern context today.[167]

Indian Parallels on Legal Systems and Practices with Some Examples

It is very hazardous two compare two legal and social systems that are totally from different periods of history. However, it is worth trying to see how the legal system in India has some parallels to that of ancient Israelite legal practice so that we can see some resonances between them. Being a democratic country like India there are ample number of laws and legal procedures that are available even before the time of its independence. Law in India refers to the system of law in modern India. Some of contemporary Indian laws show substantial European and American influence. Various legislations first introduced by the British are still in effect in modified forms today. During the drafting of the Indian Constitution, laws from Ireland, the United States, Britain, and France were synthesized into a refined set of Indian laws. Indian laws also adhere to the United Nations guidelines on human rights

167 On this point of relevance of Torah and its legal codes see Frank Crüsemann, *The Torah: Theology and Social History of Old Testament Law,* trans. Allan W. Mahnke (Minneapolis: Fortress Press, 1996), pp. 5-6.

laws and the environmental law. Certain international trade laws, such as those on intellectual property are also enforced in India. Indian family law is complex, with each religion adhering to its own specific laws. In most states, registering of marriages and divorces is not compulsory. Separate laws govern Hindus, Muslims, Christians, Sikhs, and followers of other religions. The exception to this rule is in the state of Goa, where a Uniform Civil code is in place, in which all religions have a common law regarding marriages, divorces, and adoption.

There are about 1221 laws as of May 2010. However, since there are Central laws as well as State laws, it's difficult to ascertain their exact numbers as on a given date.

Ancient India represented a distinct tradition of law, and had a historically independent school of legal theory and practice. The Arthashastra, dating from 400 BCE and the Manusmriti, from 100 CE, were influential treatises in India, texts that were considered authoritative legal guidance. Manu's central philosophy was tolerance and pluralism, and was cited across Southeast Asia. Early in this period, which culminated in the creation of the Gupta Empire, relations with ancient Greece and Rome were not infrequent. The appearance of similar fundamental institutions of international law in various parts of the world show that they are inherent in international society, irrespective of culture and tradition. Inter-State relations in the pre-Islamic period resulted in clear-cut rules of warfare of a high humanitarian standard, in rules of neutrality, of treaty law, of customary law embodied in religious charters, in exchange of embassies of a temporary or semi permanent character.

When India became part of the British Empire, there was a break in tradition, and Hindu and Islamic law were supplanted by the common law. As a result, the present judicial system of the country derives largely from the British system and has little correlation to the institutions of the pre-British era.

Constitutional and administrative law

The Constitution of India, which came into effect from January 26, 1950, is the lengthiest written constitution in the world. Although its administrative provisions are to a large extent based on the Government of India Act 1935, it also contains various other provisions that were drawn from other constitutions in the world at the time of its creation. It provides details of the administration of both the Union and the States, and codifies the relations between the Federal Government and the State Governments. Also incorporated into the text are a chapter on the fundamental rights of citizens, as well as a chapter on directive principles of state policy.

The constitution prescribes a federal structure of government, with a clearly defined separation of legislative and executive powers between the Federation and the States. Each State Government has the freedom to draft it own laws on subjects classified as state subjects 1. Laws passed by the Parliament of India and other pre-existing central laws on subjects classified as central subjects are binding on all citizens. However, the Constitution also has certain unitary features, such as vesting power of amendment solely in the Federal Government, the absence of dual citizenship, and the overriding authority assumed by the Federal Government in times of emergency.

Criminal Law

The Indian Penal Code formulated by the British during the British Raj in 1860, forms the backbone of criminal law in India. The Code of Criminal Procedure, 1973 governs the procedural aspects of the criminal law. Jury trials were abolished by the government in 1960 on the grounds they would be susceptible to media and public influence. This decision was based on an 8-1 acquittal of Kawas Nanavati in K. M. Nnavati vs. State of Maharashtra, which was overturned by higher courts. In February 2011, the Supreme Court of India ruled that criminal defendants have a constitutional right to counsel. Capital punishment in India is legal. The last execution was conducted in February 2013, when the mastermind of 2001 Indian Parliament Attack, Afzal Guru was hanged for the same in Tihar Jail, New Delhi.

Contract Law

The main contract law in India is codified in the Indian Contract Act, which came into effect on September 1, 1872 and extends to all India except the state of Jammu and Kashmir. It governs entrance into contract, and effects of breach of contract. Indian Contract law is popularly known as mercantile law of India. Originally Indian Sales of Goods Act and Partnership Act were part of Indian Contract act, but due to needed amendment these acts were separated from Contract Act. Contract act is the main and most used act of legal agreements in India.

Tort Law

Development of constitutional tort began in India in the early 1980s. It influenced the direction tort law in India took during the 1990s. In recognizing state liability, constitutional tort deviates from established norms in tort law. This covers custodial deaths, police atrocities, encounter killings, illegal detention and disappearances. Law commission of India's first report was relating to the Liability of the State in Tort. This report was submitted by the Law commission of India on 11.5.1956. State owes tortuous Liability under Article 300 of Indian Constitution.

Tax Law

Indian tax law is an extremely complex body of law, with several different taxes levied by different governments. Income Tax is levied by the Central Government under the Income Tax Act, 1961. Customs and excise duties are also levied by the Central government. Sales tax is levied under VAT legislation at the state level.

Trust Law

Trust law in India is mainly codified in the Indian Trusts Act of 1882, which came into force on March 1, 1882. It extends to the whole of India except for the state of Jammu and Kashmir and Andaman and Nicobar Islands. Indian law follows principles of English law in most areas of law, but the law of trusts is a notable exception. Indian law does not recognize "double ownership", and a beneficiary of trust property is not the equitable owner of the property in Indian lawn.

Family Law

Family laws in India are different when Warren Hastings in 1772 created provisions prescribing Hindu law for Hindus and Islamic law for Muslims, for litigation relating to personal matters. However, after independence, efforts have been made to modernize various aspects of personal law and bring about uniformity among various religions. Recent reform has affected custody and guardianship laws, adoption laws, succession law, and laws concerning domestic violence and child marriage.

Hindu Law

As far as Hindus are concerned Hindu Law is a specific branch of law. Though the attempt made by the first parliament after independence did not succeed in bringing forth a Hindu Code comprising the entire field of Hindu family law, laws could be enacted touching upon all major areas that affect family life among Hindus in India. Jains, Sikhs and Buddhists are also covered by Hindu law.

Muslim Law

Indian Muslims' personal laws are based on the Sharia, which is partially applied in India. The portion of the *figh* applicable to Indian Muslims as personal law is termed Mohammedan law. Despite being largely uncodified, Mohammedan law has the same legal status as other codified statutes. The development of the law is largely on the basis of judicial precedent, which in recent times has been subject to review by the courts. The contribution of Justice V. R. Krishna Iyer in the matter of interpretation of the statutory as well as personal law is significant. The very Source of the Muslim law are divided into two categories: (1) Primary Source (2) Secondary Source.

1. **"Primary Source"**

   As per Sunni Law:

   - Quran
   - Sunna or Ahdis (Tradition of the Prophet)
   - Ijma (Unanimous Decision of the Jurists)
   - Qiyas (Analogical deduction)

As per Shia Law:

- Quran
- Tradition (only those that have come from the family of the Prophet)
- Ijma (only those confirmed by Imams)
- Reasons

2. "Secondary Source"

- Custom
- Judicial Decisions
- Legislation

Salient Feature of Quran: It is based on the following aspects: Divine Origin; First Source; Structure; Mixture of Religion, Law and Morality; Different Forms of Legal Rules; Unchangeable.

Christian Law

For Christians, a distinct branch of law known as Christian Law, mostly based on specific statutes, applies. Christian law of succession and divorce in India have undergone changes in recent years. The Indian Divorce (Amendment) Act of 2001 has brought in considerable changes in the grounds available for divorce. By now Christian law in India has emerged as a separate branch of law. It covers the entire spectrum of family law so far as it concerns Christians in India. Christian law, to a great extent is based on English law but there are laws that originated on the strength of customary practices and precedents. Christian family law has now distinct sub branches like laws on marriage, divorce,restitution, judicial separation, succession, adoption, guardianship, maintenance, custody of minor children and relevance of canon law and all that regulates familial relationship.

Nationality Law

Nationality law or citizenship law is mainly codified in the constitution of India and the Citizenship Act of 1955. Although the Constitution of India bars multiple citizenship, the Parliament of India passed on January 7, 2004, a law creating a new form of very limited dual nationality called *Overseas Citizenship of India*. Overseas citizens of India have no form of political rights or participation in the government, however, and there are no plans to issue to overseas citizens any form of Indian passport.

Law enforcement

India has a multitude of law enforcement agencies. All agencies are part of the Internal Affairs Ministry (Home Ministry). At the very basic level is the local police force, which is under state jurisdiction. The following are the main law enforcement agencies: Central Bureau of Investigation (CBI); Indian Penal Code

(IPC); Law enforcement in India; Legal systems of the world; Supreme Court of India; Cyber Crime Bureau of Investigation.

Indian Penal Code (IPC): Is the main criminal code of India. It is a comprehensive code, intended to cover all substantive aspects of criminal law. It was drafted in 1860 and came into force in colonial India during the British Raj in 1862. It has since been amended several times and is now supplemented by other criminal provisions. In the state of Jammu and Kashmir, the IPC is known as Ranbir Penal Code (RPC). After independence, Indian Penal Code was inherited by Pakistan (now called Pakistan Penal Code and Bangladesh, formerly part of British India. It was also adopted wholesale by the British colonial authorities in Burma, Sri Lanka, Malaysia, Singapore and Brunei, and remains the basis of the criminal codes in those countries.

History of IPC

During the Moghul rule courts administered the "Sharia" to the exclusion of Hindu law, Islamic law gave way to English criminal law with the increase of British influence in the Indian subcontinent. Before 1860, The English criminal law, as modified by several acts was administered in the Presidency-Towns of Bombay, Calcutta and Madras.

The draft of the Indian Penal Code was prepared by the First Law Commission, chaired by Thomas Babington Macaulay. Its basis is the law of England freed from superfluities, technicalities and local peculiarities. Elements were also derived from the Napoleonic Code and from Edward Livingston's Louisiana Civil Code of 1825. The first final draft of the Indian Penal Code was submitted to the Governor-General of India in Council in 1837, but the draft was again revised. The drafting was completed in 1850 and it was presented to the Legislative Council in 1856 but it did not take its place on the Indian statute book until a generation later, following the Indian Rebellion of 1857. The draft then underwent a very careful revision at the hands of Barnes Peacock, who later became the first Chief Justice of Calcutta High Court, and the future puisane judges of the Calcutta High Court, who were members of the Legislative Council, and was passed into law on 6 October 1860. The Code came into operation on 1 January 1862. Unfortunately, Macaulay did not survive to see his masterpiece come into force, having died near the end of 1859.

Objective of IPC

The objective of this Act is to provide a general penal code for India. Though it is not an initial objective, the Act does not repeal the penal laws which were in force at the time of coming into force in India. This was so because the Code does not contain all the offences and it was possible that some offences might have still been left out of the Code, which were not intended to be exempted from penal consequences. Though this Code consolidates the whole of the law on the subject and is exhaustive on the matters in respect of which it declares the law, many more penal statutes governing various offences have been created in addition to the code.

Structure of IPC

Indian Penal Code, 1860, sub-divided into twenty three chapters, comprises five hundred and eleven sections. The code starts with an introduction, provides explanations and exceptions used in the code, and covers a wide range of offences. The Outline of IPC is as follows:

Indian Penal Code, 1860 *(Sections 1 to 511)*

Chapter	**Sections covered**	**Classification of offences**
Chapter I	Sections 1 to 5	Introduction
Chapter II	Sections 6 to 52	General Explanations
Chapter III	Sections 53 to 75	of Punishments
Chapter IV	Sections 76 to 106	General Exceptions *of the Right of Private Defence* (Sections 96 to 106)
Chapter V	Sections 107 to 120	Of Abetment
Chapter VA	Sections 120A to 120B	Criminal Conspiracy
Chapter VI	Sections 121 to 130	Of Offences against the State
Chapter VII	Sections 131 to 140	Of Offences relating to the Army, Navy and Air Force
Chapter VIII	Sections 141 to 160	Of Offences against the Public Tranquillity
Chapter IX	Sections 161 to 171	Of Offences by or relating to Public Servants
Chapter X	Sections 172 to 190	Of Contempts of Lawful Authority of Public Servants
Chapter XI	Sections 191 to 229	Of False Evidence and Offences against Public Justice
Chapter XII	Sections 230 to 263	Of Offences relating to coin and Government Stamps
Chapter XIII	Sections 264 to 267	Of Offences relating to Weight and Measures
Chapter XIV	Sections 268 to 294	Of Offences affecting the Public Health, Safety, Convenience, Decency and Morals.
Chapter XV	Sections 295 to 298	Of Offences relating to Religion
Chapter XVI	Sections 299 to 377	• Of Offences affecting the Human Body

Chapter	Sections	Content
		• Of Offences Affecting Life including murder, culpable homicide (Sections 299 to 311) • Of the Causing of Miscarriage, of Injuries to Unborn Children, of the Exposure of Infants, and of the Concealment of Births (Sections 312 to 318) • Of Hurt (Sections 319 to 338) • Of Wrongful Restraint and wrongful Confinement (Sections 339 to 348) • Of Criminal Force and Assault (Sections 349 to 358) • Of Kidnapping, Abduction, Slavery and Forced Labour (Sections 359 to 374) • Sexual Offences including rape (Sections 375 to 376) • Of Unnatural Offences (Section 377)
Chapter XVII	Sections 378 to 462	Of Offences Against Property • Of Theft (Sections 378 to 382) • Of Extortion (Sections 383 to 389) • Of Robbery and Dacoity (Sections 390 to 402) • Of Criminal Misappropriation of Property (Sections 403 to 404) • Of Criminal Breach of Trust (Sections 405 to 409) • Of the Receiving of Stolen Property (Sections 410 to 414) • Of Cheating (Section 415 to 420) • Of Fraudulent Deeds and Disposition of Property (Sections 421 to 424) • Of Mischief (Sections 425 to 440) • Of Criminal Trespass (Sections 441 to 462)
Chapter XVIII	Sections 463 to 489	Of Offences relating to Documents and Property Marks • Of Property and Other Marks (Sections 478 to 489) • Of Currency Notes and Bank Notes (Sections 489A to 489E)
Chapter XIX	Sections 490 to 492	Of the Criminal Breach of Contracts of Service

Chapter XX	Sections 493 to 498	Of Offences Relating to Marriage
Chapter XXA	Sections 498A	Of Cruelty by Husband or Relatives of Husband
Chapter XXI	Sections 499 to 502	Of Defamation
Chapter XXII	Sections 503 to 510	Of Criminal intimidation, Insult and Annoyance
Chapter XXIII	Section 511	Of Attempts to Commit Offences[168]

By now it is clear from the above presentation that the Indian legal codes, legal systems and mechanisms as well as the legal procedures are very comprehensive and complex in nature. These legal codes are geared towards the protection of rights and values of the Indian society as a whole. At the same time these laws are aimed towards the protection of religious and social minorities both as groups and as individuals. It is also clear that in both the ancient Israelite and the modern Indian society the vulnerable and marginalized sections of the communities and individuals were protected in particular than other people. The law codes and their mechanisms were operated in such a way that the culprits are caught of their offence and they are surely punished. However, like any other legal and social system the enforcement part is always a problem in the modern Indian legal system. It has been stated, 'justice delayed is justice denied' is true in many practical cases. Due to cumbersome and complex procedures involved in many legal trials the process gets dragged from several months to several years. By the time the sentence is passed on the offender it becomes too late and at times the offender even dies. Despite several enforcement agencies this has not changed in India. But in ancient Israel the process seems to be much quicker so that the punishment is delivered soon.

3.3 Judges and Kings in the Old Testament in their Historical Period: Some Parallels from a Leadership Perspective in the Indian Context

Israelite history has seen many faces of ups and downs with many ways in which God communicated God's will and intentions to Israel. Even before there are some mediating persons like: judges, kings, prophets and sages, there was a time when Yahweh is available directly in Israel without any mediating agents. Walter Brueggemann[169] talks about some such aspects briefly. We shall summarize his view as follows:

168 The section on Indian Penal Code and general, civil, religious and social laws are adapted with some modifications from the following web sites: http://en.wikipedia.org/wiki/Indian_Penal_Code and http://en.wikipedia.org/wiki/Law_of_India. Both these sites accessed on May 3, 2013. For some critical observation on the Indian law codes see, Surraj Nandan Prasad, *Ambedkar* and *Indian Code of Laws* (Jaipur: ABD Publishers, 2010); Girish Agrawal and Colin Gonsalves, *Dalits and the Law* (New Delhi: Human Rights Law Network, 2005).

169 Walter Brueggemann, *Theology of the Old Testament*, pp. 567-577.

First, Yahweh is available through theophanic manifestations. By many theophanic manifestations many times Yahweh intruded into the history of the people of Israel to lead and guide them at critical moments. Due to this intervention Yahweh discloses his awesomeness, ferocious power and his exclusive claims puts the people in an uncompromising obedience and loyalty to Yahweh. In places like Judg 5:4ff; Deut 33:2; Hab 3:3; Ps 68:8ff; Micah 1:3ff; Amos 1:2; Isa 19:1 and so on indicates that through theophanic manifestation Yahweh demonstrates his sovereignty in ways that are marvelous in the eyes of Israel and also made them speechless.

Second, Theophany at Sinai is a special and unique moment in the history of Israel. It began in Exod 19:9-25 and its peculiar culmination in Exod 24:9-18. In these places, Israel was gathered as a community under the leadership of Moses. In this theophanic encounter between God and Israel it evoked both fear and communion and the people's experience of God seems to be intimate and immediate. It was indeed an awesome and physical presence of Yahweh that even scared Israel but at the same time assured them of God's protection. Later this direct presence of Yahweh is very much limited or rather gradually faded away with the mediatory role of Moses and written Torah has increased.

Third, through personal encounters between Yahweh and some individual the mediatory role between God and people is expressed in definitive terms. With people like Abraham (Gen 12:1-3, 15:1-6, 22:1-2), Moses (Exod 3:1-6, 3:7-4:17, 32:11-14, 33:7-11), and Elijah (1 Kings 19:5-18) God's encounter was decisive and their mediatory role on behalf of the community of Israel was also significant.

Then at a later point Torah has become a decisive and fundamental way of mediation between the people of Israel and Yahweh. It is through Torah the purpose, presence, and power of Yahweh is manifested to Israel. The words of Brueggemann are clear on the dynamic practice of Torah in the lives of the Israelites: "It is evident that Torah as a concrete interpretive practice in Israel is enormously dynamic and supple, and it has the capacity to impinge on every aspect of Israel's imaginative life. Christians who seek to understand what is intended in Torah will have to move beyond conventional, polemical caricatures of legalism, in order to ponder an interpretive practice that is (a) intransigently normative and yet enormously open to adaptation; and (b) has an uncompromising sovereign at its center, but with a capacity to attend in delicate ways to the detail of its daily existence."[170]

In the light of the above discussion it is to be stated that the even before any formal mediators appointed, it is the awesome presence of God that made manifest in different theophanic occurrences. Then when the mediators were appointed from the time of Judges in the Israelite community they maintained an intimate and close communion with Yahweh in ways that brought in peace

170 Walter Brueggemann, *Theology of the Old Testament*, p. 595.

and prosperity to the community. At the same time, they gave stern warnings to the people when things went wrong. We shall look at some figures in the pool of judges and Kings and later in our next topic we shall examine the role of priests, prophets and sages.

The Role of Judges: the role of judges intended to account for the period between the death of Joshua and the appearance of Samuel. Because the narratives concerning the judges are of such unequal length, it has become customary to use two different terms for the judges. The heroes of the detailed narratives are called the "major" judges like: Othniel, Ehud, Deborah (and Barak) Gideon (and Abimelech), Jephthah and Samson. Those that are merely mentioned in brief notices are called the "minor" judges like: Shamgar, Tola, Jair, Ibzan, Elon and Abdon. Within the framework of their presentation, they appear to exercise their judgeship over the entire nation as regents of Israel and forerunners of the kings. More precisely, we can distinguish two types of figures included under judges. The Hebrew term for judge usually means "executor of justice", "helper", "ruler". On this basis the first group mentioned in the Hebrew Bible are war-like heroes, be they leaders of tribes, militants, tribal heroes, or individuals about whom we have sufficient information. They are Othniel, Ehud, Shamgar, Deborah, Gideon, Abimelech, Jephthah, and Samson. A second group consists of the data concerning the length of time the person lived and judged Israel, his family and his burial place, obviously represents a different type.

The core of the book of judges contains the exploits of the heroes of the time who are raised up by Yahweh to "save" Israel and who "judge" Israel for the reminder of their lifetime. These judges are endowed with the spirit of God and because of that spirit they are able to judge the people of Israel and perform other heroic acts (Judg 3:10; 6:14; 11:20; 14:6).

These judges in Israel also come from simple family background. Gideon was the youngest in his somewhat obscure family background, and his clan is the smallest in his tribe. Deborah was a woman to whom in the normal case the leadership position would not have been assigned. Jephthah was a dubious descent and a bandit by profession. Only in the case of Ehud (Judg 3:15) is something like 'genuine' genealogy was present. But none of these judges seems to have been associated with significant power base like Gilgal, Shechem, Bethel or Shiloh.

The purpose of the judges in Israel can be stated in four different points as follows:

First, Judges and the Book of Judges maintains a general antimonarchical stance of the Former Prophetic books. Kingship is ridiculed in the fable of Jotham (Judg 9:7-15). The rejection of Gideon to be the king of Israel, more particularly the dynastic kingship (Judg 8:23) is another example towards the negative attitude towards the kingship. The only real king Abimelech is also presented as the one who brutally seizes power after the death of his father and exercises an abortive reign in Shechem (Judg 9:1-6).

Second, the Judges in Israel appeared spontaneously always in situations of extreme need. They do not hold any office in the institutional sense and there is no continuity between the individual judges. They are therefore often describes as "charismatic military leaders." This also denotes that their function is essentially military, namely to summon and lead the army of Israel, to organize able men capable of bearing arms (Judg 1:27; 3:27; 4:10; 6:34; 11:29). Moreover, the use of the term 'charismatic' is particularly applicable to their delivering activity (Judg 3:10; 6:34 and 1129).

Third, Israel as a theocratic nation is reflected in and through the role of judges. William Dumbrell summarizes this aspect of judges more clearly: "Everything in these bizarre accounts commands God's direct leadership of God's people as the sole guarantee that Israel will have a future. The real Judge behind the scenes is Yahweh (11:27). It always had been and always will be the kingship of God that sustains the nation."[171]

Fourth, the lesson that one can learn from each of the judge is that those who are dedicated to Yahweh can be used by Yahweh, the individuals, despite their shortcomings on account of their dedication. Yahweh could use the judges even in the face of apostasy of Israelites, to deliver them from the hands of her enemies. Yahweh never wants to give up on Israel. Thus, in and through the activities of the judges, Yahweh wants to keep the tribal federation alive until Israel is ready for the next stage in Yahweh's great redemptive act.

The Role of Kings: Just as judges played a pivotal role in shaping the character and national spirit of Israel, kings continued this mission of God in a way that sustained Israel as a nation. The emergence of kingship in Israel is not sudden, rather it is the sum total of a long process of various political and religious developments. The opening chapters of 1 Samuel reveal that Israel was in crisis due to various reasons. As was noted above the crises began even during the time of judges.

There are some *internal pressures* that reached a crisis point when it was reported that the sons of Eli were highly corrupt (1 Sam 2:11-17). Eli seems to be powerless to change the situation (1 Sam 2:22-25). Periodical threats for the tribes involved judges fighting against the enemies of Israel, but only for a limited period as long as there was a crisis situation. Moreover, the sociological and anthropological studies on the premonarchic Israel reveal that "there were growing pressures on the tribal groups of early Israel toward centralization even before the events of 1 Samuel. These probably included increased population, incorporation of diverse cultural groups, and the agricultural limitations of the hill country."[172] Added to these problems, demands for the centralization came

171 William J. Dumbrell, *The Faith of Israel: A Theological Survey of the Old Testament* (Grand Rapids: Baker Academic, 2002), p. 80. Second Edition.

172 Bruce C. Birch, et al., *A Theological Introduction to the Old Testament* (Nashville: Abingdon Press, 1999), p. 216.

from a wealthy class, who wanted centralization of governance that will serve their own profit and market interests. The final chapters of the book of Judges (17-21) "reflect violent conflicts between tribal groups and suggest there is no authority to give unity, governance, and moral guidance in such times."[173] That is why the book of Judges reflect and evaluate such a situation when it states: "In those days there was no king in Israel; all the people did what was right in their own eyes." (Judg 17:6; 21:25).

There are some ex*ternal pressures* that were responsible for the transition from a tribal to kingship situation in Israel. This was mainly from the Philistines. Even though during the time of judges, a number of battles were fought by the leaders to contain the threats from the enemies, the Philistine threat was of a different kind. The Philistines established themselves on the Mediterranean coastal plain at the beginning of 12th century BCE as part of general migration out of the Aegean of the Sea Peoples attempting to settle coastal territories throughout eastern Mediterranean. The Philistines as part of these Sea Peoples seemed to have replaced the ruling class of Canaanite population and thus exert a tremendous influence in that region. Military wise Philistines were well organized, utilizing both professional standing armies and the hiring of mercenary troops. Philistines had a strong economic base on the coastal plain and possessed iron weapons. In the book of Judges there was a report that conflict arose between Israel and Philistine even to the extent of relocating the tribe of Dan as far as north of Israelite territory (Judg 17-18 chapters). The Philistine threat became more serious when they embarked on a military campaign aimed at establishing their sovereignty over all the Israelite central hill country. 1 Samuel chapters 4-6 records a major defeat of Israelites in the hands of Philistines in this direction.[174]

In the light of the above discussion it is clear that the Israelites have determined to go for a centralized leadership due their dire and pressing need. Thus, in 1 Sam 8:19 b-20 they state: "We are determined to have a king over us, so that we also may be like other nations, and that our king may govern us and go out before us and fight our battles."

It was a necessary option for the Israelites to choose a king and institutionalized structure over against their tribal system so that they would face the context and its challenges. We shall now talk briefly about the role of kings in such a situation, the way they mediated between Yahweh and the people to communicate Yahweh's

173 Bruce C. Birch, et al., *A Theological Introduction to the Old Testament* (Nashville: Abingdon Press, 1999), p. 217.

174 Ibid., pp. 217-218. Norman K. Gottwald, *The Hebrew Bible: A Socio-literary Introduction* (Philadelphia: Fortress Press, 1985), pp. 319-323 states that the Philistines had the advantage of oligarchic leadership, unlike the divisive Canaanite city-states, and their iron weaponing and mobile strike force made them effective fighters in the hill country to this highly organized military force there was a need for a strong counter force and military defense on the part of Israel.

purpose and will, to fight battles as people expected and at the same time the kings also became oppressive among the Israelites, and eventually the kings became a real burden for the people.

Till the people adopted kingship there was a model kingship, for all practical purposes, Yahweh is the real king and also guide in all departments of Israel's life. But the earthly king was altogether seen in different light in the lives of Israelites. Initially, Yahweh granted the request of the people's desire to have a king through Samuel (1 Sam 8:22). However, Samuel sternly warns the people that by choosing a king the people are opting for autocratic, oppressive and rigid structures that they can no longer enjoy the same freedom as before (1 Sam 12).

King Saul: Saul was a 'military' king of Israel, must have had some role in the cultic activities. Saul's major achievement was to drive back the Philistines for a time from the central hill country. Saul can also be given the credit for his victories over Ammonites, Edomites, Moabites, Amalekites, and Arameans of Zobah (1 Sam 14:47-48). Saul was operating as a military leader with the corps of Benjaminite warriors, to which other tribes were added as and when needed. Saul had not set up very elaborate administrative machinery. Sophistication was still lacking in terms of his administrative system and he was functioning more like *nāgīd*, prince or a commander rather than *melek*, as a king. Saul functioned like a chieftain in one of the ancient West Asian countries.[175]

At a later point the clash between Saul and Samuel is an indication that the experiment on kingship had failed with Saul's performance. Samuel "represents an ideological commitment in the older tribal system in Israel, and therefore stands in opposition to the new future God may bring."[176] There is an obvious clash between the older and emerging ideologies on the leadership in Israel. Saul was also at the cutting edge of the leadership that was so far managing all the affairs, be it religious or political. Saul's intrusion into the religious realm of Samuel obviously brought clash between them. The episodes of 1 Samuel 13-15 exposes Saul's weaknesses. Though Saul made several attempts as a warrior king and thus considered to be the people's king, he was not successful in his political and religious strategic moves. Thus, Samuel clearly communicates the divine decision on Saul that Saul cannot be the future hope Israel and God regrets in approving Saul's appointment as the king of Israel. For God it is David who is the "man after God's own heart" sought out to rule after Saul in 1 Sam 13:14, and it is David who is the "neighbor of yours, who is better than you" and will receive the kingdom torn from Saul's grasp.[177]

King David: David emerged as a choice king when the split between Samuel and Saul became wide open. For more than seven years there was a contest between

175 Bruce C. Birch, et al., *A Theological Introduction to the Old Testament* (Nashville: Abingdon Press, 1999), p. 217.

176 Ibid., p. 235.

177 Ibid.

Saul and David in the south and eventually David has emerged as successful when the tribal leaders of north entered in a treaty with David as king of all Israel.

David's achievement began when he decisively defeated Philistines by restricting them to coastal plain. He further was swift in strengthening the state apparatus by setting up its administrative center at Jerusalem. He prioritized Jerusalem as a significant center by bringing the ark of the covenant. He appointed Abiathar and Zadok as state priests who may have represented respectively the old Israelite and new Canaanite components of the territorial of Israel. It has been pointed out that by establishing Jerusalem as a capital city of his state David was shrewd in approach that he gained a politically neutral capital but at the same time it was an urban Canaanite (Jebusite) center with many of the scribes, tradesmen, architects, and managers necessary to establishing a full-scale monarchy with its bureaucracy.

David was also successful in his wars in Transjordan against Ammon, Moab, and Edom and against Aramean states north into Syria establishing his hegemony as far as the Euphrates river. Thus, David emerged as a significant force in the entire region of Syria-Palestine and filled in a political vacuum that was there for some time after Joshua's conquests in the region. Although David made use of some chariotry, his main strength was on the highly mobile infantry. Moreover David was able to put down all the opposition to his rule by northern tribes and rebellion of his own son Absalom. Unlike Saul David could be called as a king in the proper sense of the term. He ruled over the territorial state that embraced the Canaanites who were not part of the old intertribal confederacy. He was successful in extending his battles by spreading and expanding the borders of Israelite nation to Transjordanian and Syrian states. David was successful in organizing and setting up a proper state administration. For all this he needed to improve the state revenues, David drew his resources from the tributes of the foreign nations. Thus, David emerged as an all-round successful person who lifted the status of the Israelite state in the entire West Asian region.

However, all is not well with David and there are clear signs of his being an ordinary human being susceptible to tragedy and fall. David-Bathsheba's episode in 2 Sam 11 is an example of a personal tragedy in his life. Of course David receives an indictment from the prophet Nathan in 2 Sam 12:1-7 with the announcement that the violence in David's family will be the dire consequence for what he has done to the family of Uriah. 2 Samuel 13-20 chapters records the tales of family tragedies of David. The final moments of David were not that powerful and glorious compared to his younger days or the days when he assumed the throne of entire Israel. He was as vulnerable as any other human being. It is therefore stated by Walter Brueggemann that in the David's story we can find on God's willingness to risk human freedom and responsibility while yet pursuing the divine purposes through these "trusted creatures." Thus, David simply becomes an exemplary figure that we can take it to look at in the light of human freedom, responsibility, and at the same time sin as it was described in the opening chapters of the book of Genesis.[178] Thus, it is concluded that "A heroic David demonstrates such freedom and giftedness at its best, but the David of Succession Narrative/Court History shows all too well the temptation of every human to sinful grasping and its painful consequences. David's portrait is a full human portrait in these stories."[179]

King Solomon: Solomon became a successor to David after a bitter dynastic fight in which he had to forcefully support a powerful faction that backed his rival brother Adonijah. Solomon opened his rule with an "iron fist" in order to gain his control in Judah and also filled him with courage to launch an ambitious political program that was about to increase the wealth of his kingdom in a dramatic way. Solomon began his ruthless and violent reign by consolidating himself as the successor of David. He meticulously planned to kill his half-brother Adonijah along with his influential supporters, including David's general Joab. David's priest Abiathar is also banished for the same reason.

He depended on the agricultural resources of peasants and also by increasing trade deals with the other nations that he was in contact with. In order to secure more resources for his booming economic empire, he started to increase his military superiority by building massive fortifications and equipping a large chariot forces. With his new found resources he undertook huge construction projects in Jerusalem, including a temple constructed on the Phoenician lines of architecture and a palace for himself that exceeded the temple in size. For some time after his accession to the throne he relied on the old tribal administrative districts that his father David had followed, but soon he revamped the entire system by redistricting his kingdom and appointing officials in each of the new districts, thereby centralizing the command structure. "By this new system he provisioned his court with sumptuous food and the temple with lavish sacrifices supplied from districts of roughly equal economic clout (the tribes had been unequal in size and productivity) and also hoped to control or neutralize the dangerously powerful northern tribes. Furthermore, to accomplish his construction of fortifications and to expedite his beautification of Jerusalem architecturally he forced his subjects into corvée labor gangs."[180]

The enthusiasm with which the economic surge began at the beginning of Solomon's reign soon ran into difficulties and also resulted in diminishing profits. In order to create a privileged upper class of economic non-produced, Solomon had to depend heavily in the agricultural and commercial surpluses. For his building projects Solomon needed timber and metals from abroad and in return

178 Walter Brueggemann, "The Trusted Creature," *Catholic Biblical Quarterly* 31 (1969), pp. 481-501.

179 Bruce C. Birch, et al., *A Theological Introduction to the Old Testament* (Nashville: Abingdon Press, 1999), p. 246.

180 Norman K. Gottwald, *The Hebrew Bible*, pp. 319-323.

he could offer agricultural products. For this purpose Solomon demanded the labor class to produce more and more than what they could normally do. Most of the things were produced for the purpose of export. Moreover Solomon taxed the people heavily in order to meet the needs of his extravagant building projects. This along with corvée had created displeasure and anger among the common populace. Moreover Solomon had biased attitude towards the northern tribes and exempting Judah from the compulsory labor. This also angered the northern tribes in particular. Jeroboam has particularly organized a resistance against all these exploitative moves of Solomon and because of a threat from the ruling party he fled to Egypt, only to be returned later as a first king of the divided kingdom, the northern Israel. Moreover the rebellion also came from another quarter. With the revolt from Edom and Arameans (1 Kings 11:14-28) the vital monopoly on trade in the inter-territorial corridor was jeopardized. Moreover Solomon made an unwise decision to give twenty cities in Asher area to Phoenicia in return for precious metal.

On the whole, it is clear that Solomon was successful in securing a luxurious and extravagant life for a small minority upper class in government and trade, whereas the economic development of the majority of marginal class was almost nil. Solomon's reign in practical terms made the gap between the minority rich and majority poor more wider than ever before in the history of Israel.

Solomon's rule has totally displaced the emphasis on justice that was engraved in the covenant law codes given by Yahweh to the Israelites and the rulers are supposed to uphold the same. The weak and the poor during the reign of Solomon no longer have real access to the precincts of royal decision making. Significantly the people play no role in the elevation of Solomon to kingship as they did for Saul and David. Solomon comes to power completely as a product of politics inside the royal court. His policies clearly weigh on the common people because as was pointed above, rebellions break out toward the end of Solomon reign (1 Kings 11:14-40).

In the light of the above discussion one wonders what happened to Solomon's wisdom. Was he not endowed with God's wisdom to rule over the people of Israel? Is it a mere idea that Solomon was considered as a wise king among all other of that time in the Mediterranean and Syria-Palestine region? But the way in which Solomon used the gift of wisdom endowed by God is not proper. There lies the real problem with Solomon. He virtually did not use his wisdom for a good governance. However, it is reported that Solomon became renowned for his encyclopedic knowledge, his telling of proverbs, and his trading of observations with wise teachers (1 Kings 4:29-34); the queen of Sheba also comes to experience and test his reputation for such wisdom (1 Kings 10:1-10). Thus, we are left with Solomonic wisdom sayings and his international reputation in parallel and equally competent wisdom tradition like Mesopotamian and Egyptian wisdom traditions. But he thoroughly failed in his strategic moves to give a just governance and enduring values of the covenant principles. After all the legacy of Solomon was not remembered at all except for his wisdom contribution both at the national and international levels. Inevitably such a ruthless way of administering led to a thorough frustration and the kingdom was ready for split and we see that instantly happened soon after his death with the beginning of his son Rehoboam's reign. Therefore the overall impact of such a drastic rule of Solomon may be summarized as follows:

"In Saul the kingship experienced an abortive birth. Under David we glimpsed the promise of kingship. With Solomon the promise of kingship was broken. All of the themes of royal ideal and royal reality, covenant faithfulness and covenant disobedience in a time of Israelite kingdom, are introduced in the stories of these three kings. In a time of shattered Israelite unity we must now watch these themes played in many variations as kings, prophets, and people move down a road that tragically will lead to oblivion for the northern kingdom and exile for the southern kingdom."[181]

Such is the drastic impact of Solomonic reign continued throughout the history of divided kingdoms of Israel and Judah. On the one hand Solomon seems to have increased and improved the international relations between the Israelite kingdom and other nations surrounding it and on the other hand did badly on the internal matters of administration and policy making.

Space will not allow us to present the details of all other kings of the divided monarchy followed by Solomon, but we shall briefly present some details of the overall reign of Israel and Judah so as to make an overall evaluation on the role of kings in ancient Israel.

1 Kings 12-2 Kings 13 chapters cover all the events of the divided kingdoms of Israel and Judah, particularly the rule of the kings. The texts focus more on the religious apostasy of the people in the rest of the history following Solomon.

Jeroboam the first newly formed kingdom of north Israel established two religious centers one in Bethel and another in Dan (in far South and far North) in order to break any influence of Jerusalem Temple in his kingdom. He erected golden bull images on these newly constructed shrines. Jeroboam had not intended to be idolatrous by these images, rather meant to be pedestals on which invisible Yahweh was thought to stand, parallel to the Ark of the Covenant in the Jerusalem temple. But in the view of the biblical texts and writers the bull images are symbolic of Canaanite fertility related to god Baal. Prophet Ahijah who anointed Jeroboam as the king of northern Israel was highly critical of the king for his religious apostasy (1 Kings 14:6-16).

Stability in the northern kingdom was brought by Omrides (Omri, Ahab and Ahaziah/Joram). The main move came from king Omri in choosing Samaria as a capital city of northern kingdom and other consolidated efforts brought so much stability to the north Israel. However, the religious judgment on the kings

181 Bruce C. Birch et al., *A Theological Introduction to the Old Testament*, p. 255.

of Omride dynasty were viewed negatively (1 Kings 16:16-28). This was more clearly demonstrated in the case of Omri taking Jezebel as daughter-in-law for his son Ahab. Jezebel, the daughter of Ethbaal, king of Sidonians of Phoenicia. Later Jezebel had played a decisive role in the court of king Ahab by officially sponsoring the prophets of Baal and also planning to exterminate the prophets of Yahweh, particularly Elijah (1 Kings 18-19 chapters) and that plan was of course aborted by Elijah's zealous involvement for Yahweh's cause. On the whole the domestic policy of Omrides, particularly by Ahab and his sons was shaped by the controversy between Yahweh religion and Baal religion.

In the latter years of the northern kingdom anti-Baal campaign was vigorously conducted by the king Jehu who exterminated all the supports of Baal during his reign in Samaria (1 Kings 9-10 chapters). The real aim of Jehu's revolt was 'wiping out Baal from Israel' (1 Kings 10:28).

Jeroboam II's reign was also another important period with high economic boom and recorded to be a period of prosperity although the social upheaval continued resulting in wide gap between the rich and the poor. Prophet Amos appears in this time and offers sharp accusations of social injustices practiced in the northern kingdom.

After the death of Jeroboam II the long drawn stability and continuity in the northern kingdom under the dynasties of Omri and Jehu came to an end. A series of military coups followed in swift succession (2 Kings 15:8-22). The end of northern kingdom appeared soon with the Assyrian advance that made a tremendous impact in the entire region. After a period of unrest in the land in 722 BCE Samaria was captured by the Assyrian king Shalmaneser V made the whole of northern Israel as part of Assyrian province bring a glorious period of northern Israel to an end.

The events of Southern kingdom, Judah were more or less continued with dynastic rule from the time of Rehoboam. Two important kings can be noted for their religious reforms in Judah. One is the reign of Hezekiah who destroyed the high places and other religious worship places (2 Kings 18:4) of stone (*mazzebot*) and wood (*'ašera*) and he also removed the 'brazen serpent' named *Nehushtan.* By these acts it was noted that Hezekiah had removed theomorphic cultic symbols that were practiced from the time of Moses (see Numb 21:4-9).

The reign of Josiah was another significant event in the life of Judah (2 Kings 22:1-30). He was adjudged as the best king after king David in Judah. Josiah also removed all the local cultic worship centers by centralizing the worship in Jerusalem. Josiah's intention was to unite the entire Israel by even uniting what was previously called as northern Israel. Josiah died in an unnecessary involvement in a battle between Egypt and Assyria.

Babylon began to assume its domination in the entire region and that was marked by Egypt being defeated by Babylon in a battle at Carchemish in the year 605. Nebuchadnezzar, the king of Babylon undertook campaign against Judah and in the year 597 he appeared before Jerusalem, where immediately before hand Jehoiachin succeeded his father as king. Jehoiachin seems to have handed over the city voluntarily (2 Kings 24:11f). He was taken as prisoner and deported to Babylon. Nebuchadnezzar appointed his uncle (another son of Josiah) Mattaniah (his name was changed as Zedekiah (2 Kings 24:17), parts of population were deported along with Jehoiachin (2 Kings 24:14). Those included during this deportation were the officials (*sarim*), the well-to-do taxpaying citizens (*gibbore-hayil*) and also particular groups of craftsmen, master-fortress builders. Only the poorer stratum of the population (*dal-am-ha-ares*) were left behind in Judah.

Again in 588 BCE a Babylonian army approached Jerusalem and laid siege to the city (2 Kings 25:1). Apparently the siege was interrupted for a while because of the approach of Egyptian army (Jer 17:5,11 and the dates are mentioned in Ezek 29:1; 39:20). But as part of their deportation in summer 586 BCE the Babylonians first made a breach in the city wall, then finally, about a month later they completely occupied the city, burnt the temple (which they had earlier plundered 2 Kings 25:13-17), the royal palace and the rest of the city, and destroyed the city walls (2 Kings 25:4 and Jer 52:6f). Zedekiah attempted to escape in Jericho, that is, before he could cross the Jordan to safety, but was imprisoned and brought to Nebuchadnezzar's headquarters at Riblah. There he was cruelly punished for his defection. His sons were killed before his eyes, and he himself was blinded and brought to chains to Babylon (2 Kings 25:7) and we hear nothing further about him.

The fall of Jerusalem makes a great division in the history of Israel. With it the rule of the Davidic dynasty, which had more than four hundred years came to an end. For the next four centuries down to the completion of the last book of the Old Testament, Israel (or Judah) lived under the rule of different superpowers.

The above brief historical sketch and the way in which the rulers of both Israel as united kingdom and Israel and Judah as divided kingdoms performed need to be carefully evaluated. The role of the kings in all the affairs of the kingdom is very significant. They either made positive or negative impact on the lives of the people and the future of the kingdom by either being obedient or disobedient to the covenant stipulations in the law of Moses. We shall make few comments on the role of kings in the overall significance of monarchy in ancient Israel.

First, as was noted above in our discussion, the Davidic kingship was crucial and foundational for the entire ideal of monarchy in ancient Israel. 2 Sam 7:12-16 seems to be pivotal reference point for confirming that fact that in and through Davidic kingship Yahweh would make his enabling grace on all the affairs of the kingdom of Israel. The verses are read as follows: *When your days are fulfilled and you lie down with your ancestors, I will raise up your offspring after you, who shall come forth from your body, and I will establish his kingdom. He shall build a house for my name and I will establish the throne of his kingdom forever. I will be a father to him, and he shall be a son to me. When he commits iniquity, I will punish him with a rod such as mortals use, with blows inflicted by human beings. But I will not take my steadfast love from him, as I took it from Saul, whom I put away from before you. Your house and your kingdom shall be made sure forever before me; your throne shall be established forever.*

The above declaration is an indication how God gave priority to Israel through a particular individual without any preconditions. Based on this there is always a claim made that in the Davidic king, Yahweh has made a new and unconditional commitment to protect and prosper Israel. Brueggemann thinks that the above ideological claim "is that in order to receive such peace and prosperity, the well-being, prosperity and authority of the king must be beyond criticism, celebrated in exuberant allegiance. This interpretive claim for what the king signifies alters the way in which Yahweh is understood to be in the midst of Israel."[182]

Second, it looks as if there is an inevitable clash between the torah requirements and the demands made by the king, quite apart from the principles of torah. However, the prophets and others expected that even the kingship is subjected to the very principles of covenant and torah. The Mosaic covenant stipulates that the king must study the torah in order that he must meet the demands of the torah requirements (Deut 17:18-20). The overall requirements for the kings is summarized in 1 Kings 3:14: *If you walk in my ways, keeping my statutes and commandments, as your father David walked, then I will lengthen your life.* "Thus, the tradition that curbs the royal aggrandizement here resituates monarchy in the context of Torah, and it refuses to entertain the notion of an institution that can supersede or transcend Torah obedience. This Torah-insisting "if" occurs in a variety of royal texts, all no doubt derivative from Deuteronomic tradition of Torah"[183] (see for example the texts like: 2 Sam 11: 27b; 12:9-10; 1 Kings 9:4-8; 11:9-11 also cf. Ps 132:11-12).

Third, kingship in Israel (Judah) has to be seen in the light of the Babylonian exile. The debacle in 587 BCE is a clear example when king, temple and city all failed. Among many reasons for the exile, the failure of the monarchy was considered as one prime reason, especially in terms of the practice of justice and righteousness by the kings in all walks of their life. Prophets Jeremiah and Ezekiel links the kingship and exile as follows: *Woe to the shepherds who destroy and scatter the sheep of my pasture! Says the Lord. Therefore thus says the Lord, the God of Israel, concerning the shepherds who shepherd my people; It is you who have scattered my flock and have driven them away, and you have not attended to them* (Jer 23:1-2). It is the kings who "scattered" that symbolically means that they have sent the people to the exile. Same is more forcefully put forth by Ezekiel in 34:3-6 as follows: *You eat the fat, you clothe yourselves with the wool, you slaughter the fatlings; but you do not feed the sheep. You have not strengthened the weak, you have not healed the sick, you have not bound up the injured, you have not brought back the strayed, you have*

182 Walter Brueggemann, *Theology of the Old Testament*, p. 606.

183 Ibid., p. 607.

not sought the lost, but with force and harshness you have ruled over them. So they were scattered, because there was no shepherd; and scattered, they became food for all the wild animals. My sheep were scattered; they wandered over all the mountains and on every high hill; my sheep were scattered over all the face of the earth; with no one to search or seek for them.

There are other places we find similar indictments against the kingship like Jer 22:28-30. In Psalm 89:19-37 it is clearly stated that even by the failure of Davidic dynasty, the very institution of monarchy has failed.

Fourth, despite the above discussed negative side of kingship the interpretive context of kingship is expanded that depicted it with the message of hope. The ideological and earthly power of monarchy as an institution seems to have failed, but the visionary, liturgical, and messianic power of the kingship survived in varied forms and contexts thus making the kingship as a hope to be sustained even after the exile. Prophet Isaiah proclaims the best hope that is to be expected from the "stump of Jesse in Isa 11:3b-5 and the same passage in verses 6-9 talks about the king who will work towards social rehabilitative well-being that will eventually result in well-being of the entire cosmos. Although Jeremiah had no much hope towards the new rule of the king, yet looks a possible hope when the new ruler comes in (Jer 23:5-7; 33:14-16). Same is the case with prophet Ezekiel, who dismissed kingship now awaits in hope for Davidic kingship (Ezek 34:23-24). It was also envisaged by Haggai and Zechariah that this Davidic king is of political kind in which they express their hope (Hag 2:23; Zech 9:9-10).

In the light of the above discussion it is clear that the role of kings in the life of ancient Israel was very significant that took different turns and twists. Each king played a decisive role either in making or unmaking the nature of the people and kingdom and also other institutions like the temple, Jerusalem and the royal ideology of Davidic dynasty on which one part of the Israelite kingdom was built and developed. Even when this has failed to materialize in reality to produce a community of justice and righteousness an ideal kingship and the messianic type was envisaged. Much later the Christian community has seen this promise in the life and work of Jesus Christ in and through the New Testament context.

Leadership in the Indian Christian Church and some Parallel Thinking from Biblical Kingship Examples: It is interesting to note that the leadership models and patterns in the Indian church today, although, envisaged to be derived from the biblical examples and follow their ideals, it is a sad situation that only few selected insights are derived to usurp the power and amass wealth. If we had to emulate Solomonic and Jehoiakim's models of leadership certainly the Bible is very helpful.

Moses, the greatest leader of Israel, after crossing the Red Sea, served as both the legislative and judicial leader. It was usual practice for the people to line up before Moses from morning till late in the evening to have their problems settled, and to know the will of God. When Jethro, Moses' father-in-law, saw what Moses was doing for his people, he said, "What is this you are doing alone for the people? Why do you alone sit as judge, while all those people stand around you from morning till evening?" (Exodus 18:14). Then following Jethro's advice, Moses "chose capable men from all Israel and made them leaders of the people, officials over thousands, hundreds, fifties and tens" (Exodus 18:24). He trained them by instructing them in the precepts and the laws of the Lord, and appointed them to settle problems and disputes within their own jurisdiction. Only more complicated cases were brought before Moses in the event of his attention is needed.

We can say today that Jethro was teaching the art of delegation. When he suggested this principle to Moses, he had two reasons. The first reason was: "you will only wear yourself out." The second reason was: "you cannot handle it alone." It is advisable for any pastor to delegate the responsibility to men of ability, honor, and fear of God. If selection fails, this method will also fail, so select faithful men who are accountable. In this way, the leader can accomplish much work without overly burdening himself. All pastors/leaders must understand that they cannot handle the Lord's work alone, because it is a corporate work. If a pastor is ignorant of this fact, he will ruin himself and the church under his care. While many leaders are ignorant of delegation and accountability there are others who are afraid of delegating any work to anybody. They are not sure about their own ability. So they think that if they entrust responsibility to another person he will do it better and threaten their role. Secondly, they are not sure about their position. They are always afraid of others because they think they will pull them down and take their position. These are clear evidences of the lack of leadership qualities. Jethro's model is the need of the hour in the Indian leadership today.

As was noted above the kingship did function in ancient Israel to mediate between the people and Yahweh. At critical junctures kings participated in battles that brought peace and stability in the nation. The current scenario in the Indian church is filled with many battles like: religious fundamentalism, conservative thinking of all kinds that has ruined the church as a military institution, corruption in the church and so on.

Corruption in the Church scenario-a case of Telugu Baptist Churches in Andhra Pradesh: The church situation in terms of corruption is no different than what is existing in the Indian society. Sometimes the corruption in the church is worse than what exists in the society. For instance, in the Samavesam of Telugu Baptist Churches (STBC), established by the American Baptist Mission in the 19th Century CE had worked so hard to gather millions of converts to the Baptist Church throughout Andhra Pradesh. STBC is a legal body that manages the entire church administration and functions as a liaison between Indian and American Mission station for all administrative purposes. Moreover STBC also acts as a legal Trust with the power of Attorney on all the existing church properties. But by the year of 1975, majority of the prime properties were sold at throw-away price and the pockets of the greedy and selfish leaders were filled with corrupt money. Now virtually all the prime properties belonging to STBC are sold out and all the legal documents were also totally destroyed. The STBC is now split into several factions and in each faction is occupied with corrupt leaders indulged in all kinds of corrupt and illegal activities. The entire organizational structure of STBC is dismantled and still it is under litigation for various allegations. The power hunger leaders with their corrupt practices have totally destroyed the rich resources of the Telugu Baptist Church for quenching their thirst for money and material.[184]

Misuse of political power at the high places and in royal circles: The Old Testament often brings to glaring light the corrupt practices at high places, particularly in terms of political power. The kings and the entire royal house is expected to protect and defend the rights of the poor and ordinary citizens and when that fails to happen the prophets rose against the misuse of political power by the kings. One such classical example is found in the passage of 2 Samuel 11:26-12:13, the account of David's wicked sin against Bathsheba, Uriah's wife. In this story we find even the "man after God's own heart" has been immune to the poisoning of corruption of absolute power. David has not only worked out his evil desire to be fulfilled, but also schemed murder plot against an innocent and yet faithful soldier, Uriah. The narrator in the story at this point remarks: "This thing that David had done was evil in the eyes of Yahweh." (2 Sam 11:27b) is an indication how the readers should evaluate the main character, David. The words of John C. Holbert are appropriate on this:

> Yahweh is painfully disgusted by the Mafioso actions of the man who was presumably "God's favorite." The prophet Nathan is sent to announce God's reactions to David, who is now luxuriating in the presence of his new wife and bouncing son … No greater example may be found of the dire results of the raw abuse of power. To any of us who think that power grants us license, we would all do well to deeply ponder this rich story of warning "To those who are given much, much is expected." The infamy of Israel's second king must never be forgotten.[185]

Jesus' leadership was a servant leadership, which was in direct contrast to the most secular leadership patterns. When there was a dispute among the disciples about who was the greatest among them, Jesus explained His leadership pattern

---

184 For more details on this and related concerns of the STBC see the Telugu writing of Ravela Joseph, *A History of the Telugu Baptist Churches: American Baptist Telugu Mission* (Hyderabad: Andhra Christian Theological College, 2003).

185 John C. Holbert's preaching notes titled: "The Corruption of Power: Reflections on 2 Samuel 11:26-12:13a," in http://www.patheoes.com/Pregressive-Christian/Corruption-of-Power... accessed on 10-11-2012.

by saying, "The kings of the gentiles exercise lordship over them, and those who exercise authority over them are called 'benefactors.' But not so among you; on the contrary, he who is greatest among you, let him be as the younger, and he who governs as he who serves . . . Yet I am among you as the One who serves" (Luke 22: 25-27). What a difference in today's leadership and the leadership of Jesus!

Often we are more attached and faithful to our organizations than the Church of God, the Body of Christ. Even though the Church can be within that organization, that organization is not the Church, for the Church is the assembly of saints!. There is no religious group or church organization in the world that God will not desert and abandon the very hour it ceases to fulfill and carry out God's divine will. Although we need an organization, we must always remember that we are the members of the living Body of Christ. Jesus was very specific about the requirements of discipleship. A disciple must be prepared to forgo home, kindred, and possessions for Christ's sake. He said, "If any man come to me and hate not his father, and mother, and wife, and children, and brethren, and sisters, yea, and his own life also, he cannot be my disciple" (Luke 14:27). Furthermore, a disciple must be willing to carry his cross (Luke 14:2). When a disciple is taught and trained, he will be like his teacher (Matt. 10:24-25).

The Christian tradition appropriated the Old Testament models of kingship in the right perspective by looking at the life and work of Jesus Christ and thus taking it as supreme model of leadership that transcends all other models that the church can evolve from the biblical context. In the midst of the failure of all the earthly monarchs, Jesus stands as an ideal and exemplary king whose leadership model creates a sober ideal for the Christian ministry in the church today.

3.4 Prophets and their Ministry in the Old Testament and its Relevance in the Indian Context

It is virtually impossible to talk about the details of the entire prophetic ministry within the confines of our work. Suffice is to describe a general historical and theological focus of the Hebrew prophets in so far as they describe and inform us the role of mediation between Yahweh and the people.

The term prophecy is an important and theological religious phenomena in the Old Testament is a complex in its origin, history and its scope is so distinct that it cannot be separated from the rest of Israelite socio-political and religio-cultural life. Prophecy also contributes to the dynamic process of the faith of Israel in the Old Testament. Basically there are two approaches to the study of prophecy in the Old Testament. One is to study the theology of each individual prophet at various periods by taking into account the context, message and so on of a particular prophet and another approach may be to study some of the basic underlying concepts that are relevant to one or more prophets within the overall context of the Old Testament. We shall try to use both the approaches in our essay so as to get a comprehensive picture of the theological significance of prophecy and prophets in the Old Testaments.

Historical sketch of prophecy and its theological vitality: Prophecy and prophetic phenomena began in the Old Testament even before monarchy. Moses was called as prophet of God par excellence. At times Moses was called as a fountain-head of Hebrew prophetic tradition. Moses saw God's glorious self-revelation than anyone else in the OT (Exod 3318; 34:29-35). He spoke by God's authority. Israel could find comfort, grace, and blessing because in Moses the role of covenant mediator and intercessor (Exod 32:1-34:10; Numb 14:13-25) came together. Moses prayed for Israel, spoke boldly as their advocate in the presence of the Lord, and encouraged them beyond himself to Yahweh.

In the period of Judges Deborah and Samuel functioned both as prophets and judges. They were charismatic leaders who led the affairs of the people and mediated between Yahweh and the people very effectively. Deborah was available for oracular consultation at "Deborah's Palm." This was the time of severe oppression sponsored by Jabin, king of Canaan reigning at Hazor and executed by his army commander Sisera, who is in-charge of 900 chariots. Deborah combined three functions in her service to the Israelites: legal and military as well as prophetic role. She acted as a key person in a strategic battle between Israelites and Canaanites for Israelite control over central; and northern Palestine.

The prophetic influence is discernable in the life of Samuel at various points in 1 Sam 3:1-21. Especially in the emphasis on the word of the Lord (verse 1,7,19-21). This chapter explains the expansion of Samuel's ministry from mere priestly apprenticeship to full prophetic office. The first oracle he uttered in 1 Sam 3:11-14 was a renunciation of the house of Eli, whose sons had corrupted the cult of Yahweh (1 Sam 2:12-17). This marked the beginning of Samuel's career as a prophet (1 Sam 3:19-4:1). The story of the voice which Samuel mistook for Eli's shows that Samuel had a direct call from God to be a prophet. H. H. Rowley on this prophetic role of Samuel comments that "it is clearly held that what made him a genuine prophet was not parental dedication, but the fact that when he was still a child the word of God came to him by divine initiative."[186]

During the time of Samuel, in the eleventh century BCE a new institution arose in Israel in connection with her spiritual and religious life (1 Sam 10:5-13). Samuel indicated few words after he anointed Saul in 1 Sam 10:5. This is the first mention of such a group of prophets in the Old Testament. It was argued by some scholars that these band of prophets could be the Nazirites and Rechabites. They were also considered as forerunners of the prophets. However, they had no affinity with the prophets as such, but they constantly resisted against the religio-cultural influences of Canaan in the land of Israel (2 Kings 10:1-28; 1 Chr 2:55). The sons of prophets emerged as a result of political conditions of their day and their chief purpose was patriotic. They were bands of religious devotees moving throughout

186 H. H. Rowley, *The Servant of the Lord and Other Essays* p. 112.

Palestine awakening the patriotism of the people. We can see a threefold function and character of these people: (i) they were residing together in common dwellings of religious centers like Gilgal, Bethel, and Jericho; (ii) they were prophesying together (1 Sam 10:5f; 1 Chr 25:1-3); (iii) they also acted as spiritual messengers in important matters pertaining to Israel (1 Kings 20:35-43).

During the time of united monarchy Nathan was considered to be the court prophet who appeared on three critical junctures in the life of David. First, he delivered a dynastic promise to David via classical formula ("Thus, says Yahweh" in 2 Sam 7:5, 8, 17). Second, he confronted David after David's two great sins (2 Sam 12: killing of Uriah and taking his wife Bathsheba). Here he boldly and courageously accused the king of his gross sin. Third, Nathan appeared as Bathsheba's and Solomon's ally in the struggle for succession to David's throne. He helps Bathsheba to plan for a strategy for having Solomon installed (1 Kings 1:11-14).

During ninth century prophetic figures were mainly seen in the affairs related to northern kingdom of Israel as one part of the divided kingdom. The main prophetic warning during this time was: if you ignore your prophets as they did theirs, the same will happen to you (2 Kings 17:7-18, the statement given as a warning to Judah by reminding them of the earlier fate of the northern kingdom). It should be noted that the idea of charismatic leadership, which remained strong in the territory of northern kingdom, acted as a counterforce to hereditary kinship of southern kingdom. This left more room for the involvement of prophets in public affairs.

Prophet Ahijah from Shiloh (1 Kings 11:9) supported Jeroboam's abortive coup against Solomon. He plays a crucial role in the Deuteronomistic historian's depiction of the split between the southern and northern kingdoms during the reign of Rehoboam. Ahijah meets Jeroboam, Solomon's overseer on compulsory labor, outside of Jerusalem and through symbolic action and prophetic utterance provides the theological justification for the division of the kingdom after Solomon's death. The rending of Ahijah's cloak into 12 pieces and giving them of 10 to Jeroboam is reminiscent of Samuel's rejection of Saul in 1 Sam 15. Later when Jeroboam sent his wife to the prophet Ahijah he delivered an oracle of God's rejection of Jeroboam and this seems to be the fulcrum of deuteronomistic rejection of all northern kings. Jeroboam is rejected for his apostasy, particularly for setting up of the rival northern shrines at Bethel and Dan. Robert Wilson[187] rightly comments that Ahijah is a typical peripheral prophet from Ephraim, he represents the view of group outside of and opposed to the royal establishment. His support group is presumably drawn from Ephraimites and probably from the old Shilonite priesthood ousted by Solomon. Ahijah challenged royal establishment in an attempt to redress the balance in this struggle for power.

187 Robert R. Wilson, *Prophecy and Society in Ancient Israel* (Philadelphia: Fortress Press, 1988), pp. 184-187.

Prophet Elijah's stories are found in 1 Kings 17-19, 21 and 2 Kings 1-2 chapters. Elijah has worked as a powerful champion of Yahweh against the royally-patronized worship of Baal. According to 1 Kings 17:1, Elijah not only came from a remote area of Gilead, east of Jordan, but also belonged to the class of small tenant farmers (*tošab*) who owned no land of their own. He shows how people of lowly origin could, through their prophetic activity, come to play a decisive role for the whole society. Elijah also championed the cause of an ordinary citizen of the country for the protection of human rights. In 1 Kings 21 the prophetic response reveals that the socio-economic injustices and land issues are not happening in accident. Elijah's status as a peripheral prophet explains both his authority and message. In an agrarian social context only the representatives of the divine (priests, prophets, and the like) had a source of authority "independent" of the elite governing classes. Here Elijah had come back as the one whose reauthorization from God brought him back to the central stage to offer critique to the royal house. Elijah represents the interests of the marginalized in society and the divine power who stands on their side. Clearly, Jezebel's actions have warranted the attention and condemnation of a God who has been all along represented as demanding righteousness and justice. And Ahab is included in the condemnation since everything was done in his name and by his authority. Elijah threatens with the warning to the royal house that the kingdom of Ahab would be brought to an end by ending the dynasty of Omri. The prophetic response to the injustice meted out to an ordinary citizen is something caused by human greed and the structures created to fulfill the desires of the dominant and privileged socio-economic groups. The dynamic relationship between the religious and covenantal symbols on the one hand and the values of socio-economic institutions created by the rulers on the other hand is at the root of the story of Naboth's vineyard in 1 Kings 21. It is not an exaggeration to state that whenever Elijah appears, there is an eruption like the outbreak of a dynamite. No other prophet of the early period of the monarchy approaches him in effectiveness, or in his readiness for complete involvement in Yahweh's cause.

Elisha, a younger contemporary, the follower, and the designated successor of Elijah appears during the reigns of Ahab, Ahaziah, and Jehu of the northern Israel. Elisha is frequently addressed as "man of God" in addition to his title as a prophet. Even Elisha was considered to be a peripheral prophet and his support group consists of ordinary group of the sons of the prophets removed from the religiously, economically, and politically dominant groups at the center of the Israelite society. They may have had a minimal support from the royal and established court (2 Kings 4:8-17, 42-44). While Elisha's activities are listed as a wonder worker on several occasions (2 Kings 4:1-7, 8-37, 38-41, 42-44; 5:1-19, 20-27; 6:1-7, 8-23; 13:2-21), he was also living in conflict with Omride dynasty and therefore supported Jehu and his rebellion (2 Kings 9:1-10). This changed scenario in the politics of northern kingdom changed the role of Elisha from a peripheral to central prophet. After Jehu's accession to the throne of northern kingdom, Elisha became more closely associated with the royal court, particularly in the military sphere by giving guidance to Jehu (2 Kings 6:8-7:20; 13:14-19).[188]

Micaiah ben Imlah worked amidst the four hundred plus prophets who unanimously declared the wellbeing of the kings Ahab and Jehoshaphat when they inquired and sought after the prophetic advice to wage war against Syria. Broadly speaking we may note that there are two kinds of prophets existed in Israel. They are "well-sayers" and "doom-sayers." Both the kings in 1 Kings 22 preferred to listen to the well-sayers rather than doom-sayers; thus the entire nationalistic structure of Israelite kingdom went into ruins. It is not new that the prophets supported holy war of the Israelite kings if it is in line with Yahweh's plan. However, in this case the dissent voice of Micaiah that differed from the four hundred plus prophets may indicate how the prophets thought of their inspiration, and what they mean when they spoke of standing before Yahweh (1 Kings 17:1; 18:5) or in the council of Yahweh (Jer 23:18-22; Amos 3:7). This means that they don't simply record their dissent voice for the sake of opposing the government, but their dissent is authenticated by the divine plan and purpose. The reward Micaiah received for telling the truth of course is suffering and imprisonment, but his cause is finally vindicated by God.[189]

Prophetic activity during the eighth century is unique than before because of the fact that we now have literary prophets in the sense that their writings are well preserved and collected and presented in the Hebrew Bible. We shall make few general observations on the eighth century prophets: Amos, Hosea, Micah and Isaiah of Jerusalem (1-39 of the book of Isaiah) in relation to their justice concerns. For want of space we will not cover may other issues raised by these prophets.

Hebrew prophets skillfully used interesting metaphors to communicate their powerful message. In fact their metaphorical way of communicating the message of Yahweh has come out so powerfully which is evident all through their oracles. Each prophetic voice became so powerful in that it has certain prophetic speech forms distinctly worked out. It is beyond the scope of this work to deal with the metaphors used by the Hebrew prophets.

The Hebrew prophets do not want to make any compromise on the concerns of socio-economic justice. Their uncompromising fight against the injustices meted out to the marginalized sections of the society even went to the extent of

188 Robert R. Wilson, *Prophecy and Society in Ancient Israel* (Philadelphia: Fortress Press, 1988), pp. 184-187.

189 For more discussion on the dissent voice of Micaiah see, K. Jesurathnam, "Is there not a Prophet of the LORD among You?: Micaiah ben Imlah, Ahab and Jehoshaphat," in Israel Selvanayagam (ed), *Light on Our Dusty Path: Essays for a Bible Lover* (Bangalore: BTESSC/SATHRI, 2008), pp. 156-166.

risking their own lives. We shall make few observations in this regard in relation to each individual prophet, particularly coming from the eighth century BCE.

Amos knew about the murderous oppression of the poor. Amos not only stood against that situation but he also firmly proclaimed that it is diametrically opposed to the will of Yahweh. Amos knew the situation from the older tribal traditions where all the people are protected by the discharge of justice in the local courts. Amos was aware that these traditional laws are faithfully practiced in the small villages like Tekoa, the birth place of Amos. Amos vehemently attacks and systematically analyzes the situation of injustice prevailed during his day by comparing it on the basis of traditional Yahwism practiced at least in some parts of his country.[190]

Hosea was mainly addressing to the generation of leaders who bent on protecting their own narrow interests by seizing every opportunity at the expense of others. In the opinion of these leaders Yahweh had become an awarder of their personal advantages. By means of working out with number of metaphors and similes the prophet communicates his message in a powerful manner.[191]

Micah knows by his firsthand experience that the poor farmers and small landholders are expelled from their traditional livelihood by the dishonest business practices of the rich and landowning ruling minority. Additionally the royal regime also is noted that it connives in the oppression of the poor. Micah is furious that the political and religious leaders of his day are responsible for the deterioration of the old tribal order of communal equity. He is merciless in attacking the rich and powerful who violate the rights of the poor peasants. Moreover the rich bureaucrats manipulate the legal procedures at the expense of their vulnerable fellow citizens.[192] They crush the common people like they crush the bones and make their lives miserable.

Isaiah's basis for the announcement of God's verdict on the people was that both the kingdoms of Judah and Israel, particularly the rulers' rampant violation of the rights of the common people and their approach to amass wealth and power at any cost (1:12-17; 3:13-15; 5:1-7, 8-10).[193] Isaiah's main accusation to the people of Judah is that their external fate in the midst of foreign nations depends on their internal attitude towards their fellow citizens. This attitude is mainly described in terms of maintaining laws of justice and equality right in the midst of their daily living. Additionally Isaiah reminds the people of Judah that the Davidic traditions contain all the necessary ethical and theological standards and political orientations for the leaders to follow the paths of Yahweh and simply trusting in the foreign alliances. Isaiah is firm to warn the rulers of the nation that only by trust and faith they would be saved.

---

190 Norman K. Gottwald, *The Hebrew Bible*, p. 357.

191 Ibid., pp. 357-58.

192 Ibid., p. 375.

193 Ibid., p. 377.

In all the above mentioned examples the consequences of the prophetic speeches is severe. The city and its temple will be flattened, never to build again. The fate of the rich oppressors is such that there is no positive future for them. For the Hebrew prophets the plight of the oppressed poor is the priority and by all possible means they addressed this issue in order to communicate the message that the restoration of human dignity of this vulnerable community is God given mandate for them.

The prophecy during the exilic and post-exilic times is very significant as the people were ready to go to the exile they were once again warned by the prophets to emend their ways and attitude towards God and the marginalized sections of the society. We shall briefly summarize the contribution of some prophets in this regard.

Jeremiah, son of Hilkiah from a place called Anathoth was one of the ancient Hebrew prophets who spoke daringly about the injustices and anomalies of his day in such a straight forward way that he had to pay the heavy price to the extent of risking his own life unto death. In many ways he represented a suffering prophet with full of pathos in his life situation because of his uncompromising words towards justice and peace for his nation. Jeremiah's call, his oracular sayings, his encounter with the royal house and officials, his confrontation with the false prophets all fall in line with his serious dedication to the ministry of his God who has given him a specified task. It is in this light he proclaims and every word he uttered has invited trouble for him virtually from the anemic and self-serving group surrounding him. Jeremiah's words were toughest by all standards of the ancient Hebrew prophets' words of that day. He addresses the rulers and the temple priests who think like robbers in the den as invulnerable and carry out all sorts of evil and exploitative measures against the poor and vulnerable. But such a group Jeremiah addresses, God will soon shatter their false hope and dispel all their wicked schemes. The people who "robbed wives and fields" will lose their own (Jer 8:10).[194] As a Yahwistic prophet Jeremiah had not spared anyone who violated the rights of the poor and oppressed. Jeremiah worked at a very crucial time when the historical nation Judah has had a disastrous end and the fall of the prestigious Jerusalem temple. His words are bittersweet to the rebellious nation which was always adamant to walk in her evil ways even after serious prophetic warnings several centuries prior to Jeremiah's ministry. The consequences of such a committed and whole-hearted involvement invited serious trouble for Jeremiah.

One of the main objectives of Jeremiah's prophetic preaching was to offer an explanation of the catastrophe, which will fall on Judah in 587 B. C. because people have failed to comply with the law and the words of Yahweh mediated

194 For various aspects of Jeremiah's concern for the poor and marginalized communities of his day see an important work on Jeremiah studies in William R. Domeris, "Jeremiah and the Poor," in John Goldingay (ed), *Uprooting and Planting: Essays on Jeremiah for Leslie Allen* (New York/ London: T & T Clark, 2007), pp. 45-58.

to them by the prophets (see, 3:12ff; 11:3ff). Jeremiah charges the nation Judah that her internal order was so corrupt that it will be swept away by the might of Neo-Babylonian power unless she repents and amends her ways. This attach is particularly pointed to the leadership who caused the nation to be in such dismal state. Jeremiah sternly warned the nation that it cannot rely on its so called might of royal Zion traditions of Jerusalem temple traditions nor can it look towards Egypt to escape the wrath of Neo-Babylonian attack. Jeremiah firmly believed that the resurgence of the corrupt nation is possible by submitting to the yoke of Neo-Babylonian. But due to the rebellion of Jehoiakim and Zedekiah and it was suppressed by the Neo-Babylonian power. By now Jeremiah realized that it was too late for an internal reform program to be carried out and thus called on Zedekiah to surrender to the besiegers.[195] Thus, Jeremiah saw the possible future of the nation Judah heavily depend on its unconditional surrender to the Neo-Babylonian power although that situation would only last for few years. After this period the ardent nationalists in Judah wanted to reform its state position but in the process murdered Gedaliah and his supporters (40:13-41:18). After this situation there was a turmoil and utter confusion in the Judahite state and the result was a large party of survivors fled to Egypt to escape Neo-Babylonian reprisals, also carried Jeremiah along with them by force against his will (42:1-43:7).[196]

At the same time Jeremiah affirms that Yahweh will not simply punish the people, but will restore their fortunes and give back their land to them (29:4). Thus, Jeremiah proclaims that the exile is not purposed for punishment, even though it is intended to punish the sins of Judah. It is given as an opportunity to turn to God (29:10-14). The message of hope is impressively presented by Jeremiah in his preaching on the new covenant (chapter 32), also through a symbolic action by purchasing a piece of land (32:17-44). Jeremiah's preaching on the new covenant will be made effective by Yahweh (see 31:31-34; 32:37-41).

Ezekiel's prophetic activity falls right at the time of exile as he was one among the exiles. His words are authentic coming out of his own experience in the exile. The prophet talks about Yahweh and Yahweh's action in a decisive manner. Due to this Ezekiel does not describe the attributes of Yahweh in his message. Only Yahweh's action are depicted at a greater length so that people may realize the greatness of Yahweh ('Know that I am Yahweh' Ezek 6:10; 15:13; 17:21; 37:14). The judgment speeches of the prophet against Israel and other nations are sharp and clearly focused. His threat of the day of Yahweh is put in direct address, threatening the mountains and valleys in Israel with imminent devastation by war. In the regard the prophet replaces the expression "house of Israel" as "house of rebellion" even as the fathers of Israel are rebellious up to this day (Ezek 2:3).

---

195 Norman K. Gottwald, *The Hebrew Bible: A Socio-Literary Introduction* (Philadelphia: Fortress Press, 1985), pp. 396-397.

196 Ibid., p. 397.

Ezekiel also proclaims judgment oracles against 'foreign' nations in chapters 25-32 and 35. In these oracles seven nations are addressed. Speaking against Egypt and its Pharaoh (29:1f and 32:1f) prophet compares the Pharaoh with crocodile of Nile which will be destroyed. Speaking against Tyre (26:1, 28:19), prophet declares that on account of her selfish and calculating gloating over the city of Jerusalem with her rival attitude on Israel it will be destroyed.

Despite the message of judgment, the prophet also speaks of the message of salvation. Yahweh's faithfulness to the house of Israel comes most fully into expression in chapters 34, 36-48. In 37:1f, the creation's language is behind the thought that there is life beyond death. For the sake of his faithfulness, Yahweh will bless the land and make it fruitful in a new way. In this new land, Yahweh will also restore to the house of Israel its original unity. In a symbolic way the prophet demonstrates this message by joining two sticks which carry the inscription: Judah and Israel and Joseph (37:15f). This new salvation envisaged by the prophet consists of two sides: (i) Israel of the period before judgment was shattered by her disobedience and (ii) the act of revival by Yahweh will consequently consists in his creating as an obedient and law-abiding people. The new situation, which Jeremiah 31:31-34 describes as a setting of the commandments on the hearts of the people, is now set out in Ezek 11:9 and 36:26 as the gift of a new heart and a new spirit, the heart of stone replaced by the heart of flesh (Ezek 36:27; 37:14; 39:29). This new salvation that Yahweh is going to grant will be visible where Yahweh will take up his abode in the midst of the hose of Israel (Ezek 48:30-35, the vision of Ezekiel's new temple).

Deutero-Isaiah addresses the second generation of exiles after Jeremiah's and Ezekiel's message did not seem to materialize. Deutero-Isaiah starts his proclamation to the community of remnants who lost hope and lived in utter despondency. They now concluded that God has forsaken and forgotten them. The verses in Isaiah reflect the poignant situation of the book of Lamentations. We need to recall the last verses (20 and 22) of chapter 5 of the book of lamentations in order to see the utter hopelessness of the people of Judah: "Why have you forgotten us completely? Why have you forsaken us these many days? ... you have utterly rejected us, and are angry with us beyond measure." Exactly similar mood is reflected here in Isaiah. Two unexpected facts are related to Zion in verses 19-21 of this passage. First, she has children who were born during the time of her bereavement and that they are so numerous that her concern should shift towards coming to terms with anticipated complaints about crowed conditions. What a shocking news this could be for the bereft Zion whom we encounter in Lamentations. Second, Zion's condition makes even Sarah's look hopeful. A barren widow, cast off, excited, alone has a right to ask where all these children are coming from.

The main socio-historical setting of Deutero-Isaiah must be heard through the metaphor of *Exile*. It is no wonder to say that the Babylonian cultural and religious values in many ways shaped Israelites as they shaped others surrounding them. In as many ways as possible, it was the ideological intent of the empire to talk about the exiles of their perceptions of reality and into Babylonian definitions of reality, to define life in terms of Babylonian values, Babylonian hopes, and Babylonian fears. Jeremiah had judged Babylonian triumph to be the will of Yahweh (Jer. 25:9; 27:6). But in the case of Deutero-Isaiah where the exiles are of new generation, it is Yahweh's will now that the exiles must depart from the alien empire (Isa. 52-11-12). God will gather the displaced (43:5), releasing them from Babylon (43:14). Yahweh will send Cyrus to accomplish the release of this displaced community (45: 1-4), in order that Israel may come home with joy to make a new beginning in restored Jerusalem (54:12-14).

Deutero-Isaiah is talking about in our text. Isaiah 40:1-11 envisions a great procession led by Yahweh as exiled Jews come home. Isaiah 43:5-6 explains that Yahweh will gather into the land of Zion all those who had been scattered in exile. As a result of this homecoming of the exiles the fallen city will be rebuilt (44:28; 54:11-12). Judah had been hopeless but now will be safely at home. Deutero-Isaiah's message of hope is not only a political analysis but more of a liberative imaginative poetry. Through his powerful poetic and imaginative language the poet not only describe a new social reality but evokes a strong hope in the minds of the hopeless exiles.

The exiles were almost certain that they have no other alternative except to accept the Babylonian authority, which is the third metaphor Deutero-Isaiah is using to describe the situation of exiles. The exiles found no immediate alternative to the Babylonian power. This is not simply based on the belief of Israelites but on the basis of the very claims of the Babylonians in Isaiah 47:7, 8, 10. The exiles did not believe Yahweh could counter Babylon. This is why in our passage the tone of despondency dominates (v.14).

Through an imaginative poetic invective the poet subverts the absolute claim of the Babylonian superiority. Both the Babylonian gods as well the empire itself are subjected to humiliation. In 46:1-2 Deutero-Isaiah states: "Bel bows down, Nebo stoops, their idols are on beasts and cattle ... they cannot save the burden, but themselves go into captivity." In 47:1 Isaiah empties the inflated claims of the Babylonian empire: "Come down and sit in the dust, virgin daughter of Babylon! Sit on the ground without a throne, daughter of Chaldea!" The gods of Babylon along with the claims of the empire were eternally taken for granted. That is because no one had raised a serious question to that claim. But now the poet dares to ask the question: "when was the last time a Babylonian god did anything that mattered for our well-being?"

The message of the prophet in Isaiah 49:14-26 is that a God is struggling for the human heart at the center of life. The prophet depicts a God who moves with maternal feelings and committed to the deliverance of those in bondage than to maintain a heroic image as in the case of Babylonian gods. Deutero-Isaiah presents a God in this passage who is passionately opposed to injustice committed by an oppressor against his own covenant people. At the same time this God will see that justice and mercy will prevail at the end and gives an assurance to the entire humanity that "those who wait for the Lord shall not be put to shame," and one day "all flesh shall know he is Yahweh." The prophet concludes his message by presenting two aspects of Yahweh's sovereignty and divinity: Yahweh is the one who wields the imperial and oppressive power of Babylonian domination is at the same time the savior of Israel. Yahweh's liberating and redeeming act speaks of a language that attracts everyone in the world.

During the post-exilic prophecy four prophets were active: Trito-Isaiah, Haggai, Zechariah and Malachi. These prophets again address the returnees of the exile and the new problems they face in the community that was trying to resettle in the land of Palestine. Without delving much into the historical context of this time we shall summarize the message of each prophet briefly.

Trito-Isaiah deals with important themes like: the majesty and omnipotence of Yahweh, the choice of Israel to be Yahweh's people, divine anger over human sin, and the deity's determination to work the divine will in the world. Trito-Isaiah proclaims that Yahweh's glory will be present in the life of the city of Jerusalem (Isa 60:1-2). The city will be a "crown of beauty" and a "royal diadem" to Yahweh (Isa 62:3). All people will respond to the magnificence of the new Jerusalem, both Gentiles (Isa 62:2) and Jews still scattered abroad (Isa 60:4). Great wealth will belong to the city, which will be the place of worship for all people (Isa 60:5-7; 66:23). It will be a time of peace and concord (Isa 65:25) in which Yahweh's presence will provide all the needed light (Isa 60:1).

Trito-Isaiah proclaims that the Gentiles are the participants in the glories of the new age. 'Foreigners' will join themselves to Yahweh (Isa 56:6). They and 'aliens' will serve Yahweh in the age to come but their mental labour is contrasted with the work of the Jews who are to be 'priests of Yahweh' and 'ministers of our God' (Isa 61:5-6). As for the wicked, they are responsible for deadly of the coming of the new age (Isa 59:1-2). The prophet implores Yahweh not to allow these wicked people and thus not to delay any longer the fulfillment of the divine promises, but to institute the judgment with swift and sure ways (Isa 64). In the new age Jerusalem will thrill and rejoice (Isa 60:5).

In Haggai's time the generation that had known of a living temple in which God's glory manifested had now effectively passed away (Hag 2:3), and they found it perfectly possible to survive without temple 9 or without properly restoring the temple). For Haggai, this attitude of the people seems to reflect a perverted sense of priorities. Now a more ambitious work of rebuilding could be embarked upon, that such a plan was possible seems to have been common ground between Haggai and his hearers (Hag 1:2). Haggai supposed that all other blessings would automatically follow upon proper attention to the temple. Just as current troubles were due to its neglect (Hag 2:15-17), so future blessings could be guaranteed if rebuilding was taken seriously in hand (Hag 2:18f). Haggai's intention is not simple rebuilding of the temple, as Peter Ackroyd had rightly pointed out that "the failure to rebuild is much more than a matter of reconstruction of a building. It is reordering of a Temple so that it is a fir place for worship. Rebuilding is therefore linked to the condition of the people for the service of God."[197]

Zechariah's message is sharp and it also compliments Haggai. He too was concerned with the completion of the temple and with the renewal of spiritual life. Haggai emphasized the responsibility of the people in view of the dawning of the new age. Zechariah urged the post-exilic community not to repeat the mistakes of their ancestors, but instead to devote themselves to God (Zech 1:1-6) and to trust him in working out his promised deliverance. Like Haggai, he attached great importance to the future of the temple and Davidic dynasty. But he focused on the presence of God with his people, and in this regard comes closer to Ezekiel. Paul Hanson writes: "Zechariah sees his nation at the point in history prophesied by Ezekiel when Yahweh would return to Zion to dwell in the midst of his people."[198]

Zechariah provided a theological perspective on covenant life with its blessings and threats. He exhorted the people to remember that the prophecies of exile had become a reality (Zech 1:6; 7:7-14). Fearing the recurrence of God's judgment, Zechariah encouraged the new generation to reflect upon the past. They must not repeat the mistakes of their forerunners who had been led into exile and alienation and had received the curse of God (Zech 1:5-6; 7:14). The lessons from the past explain that the former (pre-exilic) prophets had called in vain for repentance (Zech 1:4; 7:11-12), that they had angered the Lord (Zech 1:2; 7:12), that he had stopped listening to their prayers and appeals to his covenant love (Zech 7:13), and that he had unleashed his curse on them.

However, God would restore his people and confirm his promises concerning the people, the land, and by his very presence in blessing, peace, the spiritual metamorphosis (forgiveness, cleansing, and holiness), the inclusion of the nations, and the renewal of creation. The presence of Yahweh in blessing and protection is the present guarantee of the restoration as well as the hope of transformation to come. The focus of the promise is the return of God's presence symbolized by the temple people (Zech 1:16). God's presence will assure the covenant relationship, symbolized in the names associated with the city of God: "Then Jerusalem will be called the city of the truth, and the mountain of the Lord Almighty will be called the Holy Mountain" (Zech 8:3). Yahweh's presence will be experienced in the post-exilic community, as God affirms: "Now I have determined to do good again to Jerusalem and Judah. Do not be afraid" (Zech 8:15). The Lord promised to remove their fear and it gives them reasons to rejoice in his goodness (Zech 2:10-11).

197 Peter R. Ackroyd, *Exile and Restoration*, p. 156.

198 Paul D. Hanson, *The Dawn of the Apocalyptic*, p. 249.

Prophet Malachi is overwhelmingly concerned with religious matters, with the priesthood and the temple, and with the proper way in which God should be worshipped. He also sees this responsibility laid on the religious leaders, on whom he is very much severe than on the community at large. The priests in particular are harshly condemned (Mal 1:6-3:9).

Malachi's words of judgment expressions brings out a strong and positive of God's power. Thus, in Malachi 1:5, the initial condemnation of Edom, which is in some respects very negative and harsh, reaches its climax in an assertion of Yahweh's supernatural power. In Mal 1:11, we note that the prophet talks about the excessive importance given to the sacrificial system in the Jerusalem temple, but God is more concerned about other things than the paraphernalia connected with the ritualistic sacrificial system.

During Malachi's time the Jews had been home from the exile in Babylon about one hundred years. They were cured of their idolatry, but had returned to their former state of indifference and spiritual lethargy. The priests had been lax and degenerate, sacrifices were inferior, tithes and offerings were neglected, divorce and mixed marriages were common (Mal 3:9-11). Still chafing under a foreign yoke, the promises by the prophet concerning Israel's glorious future yet unrealized, many in the nation had begun to ask whether or not God loves Israel (Mal 2:2). What had become of divine justice (Mal 2:17)? Was it profitable to serve God any longer (Mal 3:13-15)? The people complained that as God's chosen people they were left in a low estate while the wicked heathen prosper. If God still loved them, where was the promise of Messiah and his universal kingdom? And where was justice? "Everyone that does evil is good in the sight of Yahweh, and he delights in them ... where is the God of justice?" They cried again and lamented, "It is vain to serve God; and what profit is it that we have kept his charge, and that we have walked mournfully before Yahweh of hosts? And now we call the proud happy; yea, they that work wickedness are built up; yea, they tempt God and escape" (Mal 3:13-15). Many, therefore in the face of disappointments, the lack of prosperity, and unscrupulous nobles and priests, turned to sin, religious indifference and skepticism. Thus, the Jews, impatiently awaited Messiah. Malachi assured them that God would surely come, but his sudden appearance would only issue judgment for such as they except they repented and rendered faithful obedience (Mal 3-4 chapters). In this regard, we can see how the prophet Malachi places considerable emphasis on the "day of the Lord." Six times the prophet announces its approach (Mal 1:11; 3:2, 17; 4:1, 3, 5).

In our long description on the role of prophets and their ministry in ancient Israel it is obvious that they had pivotal role in shaping the nation at all times and certainly their contribution is very vital for the formation of people and nation in ancient Israel. We shall make few observations on their overall ministry in the life and witness of ancient Israel. Then in our next section we shall draw parallels between the life of Hebrew prophets and their relevance in the Indian context.

First, the prophets in Israel were summoned to speak by Yahweh. They were not filled with any personal agenda of their own. They had no vested interest in fulfilling their God-given responsibility. In this regard they fore-warn and caution the rulers and the people of the impending doom so that the people and the rulers might mend their wicked and perverted ways and turn to God in repentance and for God's restoration. In this sense, the prophets whether they in the court or from non-establishment circles cannot be silenced of speaking the truth and the will of Yahweh.

Second, prophets by and large speak of their message in a concrete situation in which they lived. They responded to any crisis situation and advised the people involved to wriggle them out of that situation and only in extreme cases they subject the people to a complete doom and punishment of God. When things went wrong, the prophets even evoked crisis so that the problem may be redressed with utmost seriousness. The pre-exilic prophets like: Elijah (1 Kings 18:1, 17; 21:17), Micaiah (1 Kings 22:8) confronted Ahab on the gross mistakes he has committed in his approach to the religion and other crucial decision making. Amos had direct encounter with Amaziah, priest of Jeroboam (Amos 7:10-17) and Jeremiah had to deal with Zedekiah (Jer 37-38 chapters). Even during the post-exilic period the prophets had to deal with other kind of powers and structures where the crisis was not only present but the prophets evoked crisis.

Third, through poetic invectives and diatribes, the Hebrew prophets communicated the powerful message of Yahweh to the people as and when the situation warranted. By doing this, the prophets reminded the people the acute distress situation. The pain and agony with which the prophets come out clearly on such pathetic situation is moving. For instance, prophets Amos, Zephaniah and Jeremiah envisage such situations: *Fallen, no more to rise, is maiden Israel; forsaken on her land, with no one to raise her up* (Amos 5:2). Zephaniah envisages the disastrous situation in 1:15-16 as follows: *That day will be a day of wrath, a day of distress and anguish, a day of ruin and devastation, a day of darkness and gloom, a day of clouds and thick darkness, a day of trumpet blast and battle cry against the fortified cities and against the lofty battlements.* Jeremiah in 4:31 talks about Jerusalem as being violently assaulted as a woman: *For I heard a cry as of a woman in labor, anguish as of one bringing forth her first child, the cry of daughter Zion gasping for breath, stretching out her hands, 'Woe is me! I am fainting before killers.!"*

Fourth. At the same time the prophets through their poetic and evocative utterances equally generated hope and created a new possibility that God would bring in the midst of present crisis and devastating situation. They, in a courageous manner, talked about a future that will transform the present crisis. Prophets like Micah, Ezekiel, and Zechariah are to taken as examples in this regard: Micah in 5:2, 4-5 proclaims that the Israel's future will be bright that will have a situation to even prevail over Assyria. *But you, O Bethlehem of Ephrathah, who are one of the little clans of Judah, from you hall come forth for me one who is to rule in Israel, whose origin is from of old, from ancient days … And he shall stand and feed his flock in the strength of the Lord, in the majesty of the name of the Lord his God. And they shall live secure, for now he shall be great to the ends of the earth, and he shall be the one of peace.* Prophet Ezekiel through an evocative metaphor of valley of dry bones proclaims a bright and definite future for Israel in 3711-12: *Mortal, these bones are the whole house of Israel. They say, "Our bones are dried up, and our hope is lost, we are cut off completely." Therefore prophesy and say to them, Thus, says the Lord God: I am going to open your graves, and bring you up from your graves, O my people, and I will bring you back to the land of Israel.* Similarly prophet Zechariah talks about a new and sure future for Israel to ignite hope in their minds in 9:9: *Rejoice greatly, O daughter of Zion! Shout aloud, O daughter of Jerusalem! Lo, your king comes to you, triumphant and victorious is he, humble and riding on a donkey, on a colt, the foal of a donkey.*

Fifth, the prophetic ministry in Israel by and large concentrates on the practice of justice in all walks of the people's life in their daily living. No one should discriminate any member of the society. All the sections, particularly the marginalized groups are to be treated with fairness. This is the way in which the practice of justice is to be demonstrated in the Israelite society. Brueggemann is right in saying that "this prophetic accent to be that all members of the community, rich and poor, urban and rural, wise and foolish, powerful and marginalized, are bound to each other in a common historical and social enterprise. Every member, by virtue of membership in the community, has entitlement that cannot be abrogated. Thus, "widow, orphan, alien" are ciphers for those most vulnerable and powerless and marginated in a patriarchal society, who are without legal recourse or economic leverage. They are entitled and must be given their share."[199]

Relevance of the Ministry of the Israelite Prophets in the Indian Context: While several parallels could be drawn between the life and ministry of Hebrew prophets with the Indian socio-economic and religious situation, we shall be very brief in presenting some reflections in this regard. We shall focus our attention of the Dalit discourse and Dalit articulations in this regard. For the sake of clarity, several quotes are taken from Dalit prophetic articulations.

The message and voices of the Hebrew prophets certainly inspire any community that is seeking emancipation and liberation, from the clutches of different kinds of social evils that keep them as slaves. Dalit community in India suffering from the heinous system of caste for more than three thousand years certainly finds the message of the prophets not only relevant but also appropriate to fight against the oppressive system of caste and associated evils. The message of Hebrew prophets also helps us to see the converging points of contacts of certain prophetic figures among Dalits.

199 Walter Brueggemann, *Theology of the Old Testament*, p. 645.

Dalit literature has emerged over the years as a conscious effort to fight against the evils of caste system and other oppressive elements related to it. Through this literature it was also envisaged that it would create a revolution in the mindset of the dejected Dalits, and urge them to work for their emancipation and to build a casteless society. This consciousness is built into the Dalit literature and its goal may be seen as follows:

> [Dalit literature] envisions art that speaks directly to the needs and aspirations of Dalits in India. In order to perform this task, the Dalit Literary movement proposes a radical re-ordering of the Hindu upper caste cultural aesthetic. It proposes a separate symbolism, mythology, critique, and iconology. Dalit literature exposes Brahminism, praises Dalits and supports the lower caste revolution ... Dalit Literature protests against the oppressive Brahminical cultural system which tells lower caste people where they may go and what they may do, where they can live and whom they can marry. What it means to be a dalit in a society which treats people on the basis of inferior or superior birth and what are the real solutions for the emancipation of Dalit world are the major themes of Dalit literature.[200]

Viewed in the above light, Dalit literature aims at providing a prophetic guidance to the millions of Dalits who are oppressed on the basis of caste, and also thereby to gives a stern warning to the oppressors that they no longer accept the social constructs of caste and other derogatory labels given or forced upon them. Before we venture into different areas of Dalit revolutionary prophetic sayings let us see the general tone of such voices of resistance when Dalits were made vulnerable and marginalized.

A Dalit talk to Brahmin about his economic inequality in the following words:

> I carry the dead body to the cemetery. I burn myself attending on it till it gets burnt. You come on the day of death ceremony respected by everyone. And like an eagle grab all things and run away with them.[201]

Dalits always expressed their uneasiness and discomfort towards the dominant caste people for the ill-treatment given to them using caste as the reason for their discrimination. The following words affirm the same situation:

200 G. Lakshmi Narasaiah, *The Essence of Dalit Poetry: A Socio-Philosophic Study of Telugu Dalit Poetry* (Hyderabad: Dalit Sana Publications, 1999), p. 6.

201 Elliah Vemula: *Bahu Vachanam* (Several Voices) ed. S. K. Reddy (Neelagiri Sahiti – Nallagonda, 1996) p. 21. Translated and cited by G. Lakshmi Narasaiah in *The Essence of Dalit Poetry*, p. 11.

> I am still a prohibited human being. Mine is an expelled breath. Tying a brab tree leaf to my waist. And a tiny spittoon to my mouth. Manu made me a wretched human animal among others. The moment he left a mark of prohibition on my face, my race was gradually murdered.[202]

Dalits through their prophetic poetry talk about the history of atrocities forced by upper caste on them in the following words:

> When poured lead into my ears that heard vedas, When chopped my tongue for speaking that some language, When lacerated my head for the thirst quenched by my sperm, Then itself I became a corpse.[203]

Even when Dalits face distressing situations they voice out strong protest against the oppressors and send a clear signal that they will not tolerate any unwanted imposition on them. This comes out in the following words:

> I am an erupting volcano. No one can blow me off. Mine are feet of fire. No ropes can fasten upon my eyes. My head is a proud flag. No one can destroy me. Today mine is a burning face. My hands are thunderbolts. I am walking sward the now. Nobody can touch me. I am awakened tiger.[204]

Dalits portray and protest the situation of bonded slavery imposed on them by the landlords. The words of revolt and revolution are as follows:

> We live as home servants for twelve months. Most of these twelve months we go starving. Both husband and wife have to undertake this task. My son takes care of the cattle of the landlord. Day and night I toiled in vain only lacking sufficient food and adequate clothing. When get into sickness no cure for it. My debts are eternal. I can't stand on this fire and pull my life any more.[205]

Dalit poets vividly employ several daily-life metaphors in order to make their messages of revolt and protest easily understandable to their listeners. This is done for the purpose of evoking a spirit of revolt and protest in the minds of the people. If only the words are heard and listened to with open heart then they

---

202 Sudhakar K. Endluri, *Varthamanam* (The Present) (Manasa Publications: Rajahmundry, 1992), p. 53. Translated and cited by G. Lakshmi Narasaiah in *The Essence of Dalit Poetry*, p. 14.

203 Ibid., pp. 53-54.

204 Ibid., p. 77.

205 Sikhamani, *Smaantara Aadhunika Kavithva Vyasalu* (Hyderabad: Nandini Publications, 2006), p. 73.

will spontaneously respond to the crisis. For instance, a popular poet like Gaddar stirs up the spirit of revolt in the minds of his mala and madiga comrades through his words:

> When the dominant oppressor shoots your blood relatives in the very day light as a hunter shoots the birds and eats their meat why are you simply shedding your tears without any reaction? When the oppressor surrounds your huts and drags your sisters, mothers and your elderly people by trampling them with their feet, and slaughters them with knife and bullets from their guns, why are you crying rather than raising like a sharpened axe? [206]

In another moving description a Dalit poet describes the in-depth nature of Dalit struggle comparable to that of chicken fight that is traditionally conducted in the villages during festivals as competitive celebrations. Yet Dalits affirm that they will not give up their fight and protest. The poet's words are as follows:

> In our fight for justice we pierced each other by our own swords. We are hanging on the cross with the nails. Let our blood flow like a stream up to your wine glasses. Even then you don't take note of it. We fight losing our feathers, shedding our blood until we die like the cocks fight their battle. Even when the skull is broken because of its self-pride the battle is fought by the he goat and in a similar way we continue our fight ... our blood is like a cool water stream for you.[207]

Among the Dalits, women Dalits have a special story to tell in their own and unique way. It is common to see Dalit women working hard to support their family, as they are forced to eat some food that is available to them. Often they have to be satisfied with the stale food available to them. Karra Vijayakumari presents the case of a woman who does cobbling to get some stale food for the work done:

> Skinning the bull applying lime all over it till my hands become sore filling the mossy tank with potful of water drying the skin till it becomes tough. Saying I would make him a pair of tiny slippers. I've taken my little one along in the sun to watch over the skin. I've been ordered to make three pairs for the master mistress and the brother in the remaining skin if at all I see the pitiful face of my young one. Hoping they may give at least some *sombuvva* straining my back

206 Gaddar, "Rajyadhikaaraniki Maadiganna," in K. Lakshminarayana (ed), *Dalta Kavithvam – 2* (Anantapur: Ramaa Publications, 2003), p. 42.

207 Saginaala Prakash, "Vivakshala Chhekati," in K. Lakshminarayana (ed), *Dalta Kavithvam – 2* (Anantapur: Ramaa Publications, 2003), p. 151.

> beating with an iron pestle till my hands ache collecting all my drained strength to make holes with an awl and stitch the slippers. When I carry the slippers in a pewter vessel apply castor oil on your soles and put the slippers on the master says throw her some food. For my hardship the mistress brings and throws into my pewter vessel some stale *sombuvva.*[208]

This story illustrates in a moving way how Dalit women make slippers and the irony is that their own children are not provided with a pair of tiny slippers. While the dominant caste children enjoy the outcome of Dalit women's labor, Dalit children have to remain with 'pitiful' faces. However, the Dalit women do not silently suffer their fate, rather they question and at times demand their rights. Two things are clearly known to them: first, dominant caste women never hesitate to look down on them. Gender solidarity, in this connection, cannot exert influence on them; second, Dalit men exercise their authority on their women irrespective of their caste consciousness. Thus, they warn the dominant caste women for being part of their oppression. The following words reveal the same:

> You have done nothing to me. Even my man has never treated me as human I know. Your man too has never stood for you. At last the one that is fully damaged is me.[209]

Dalit women are very vociferous in arguing against the caste system and untouchability and they express it with anger in powerful words like the words of Teresa Devadanam:

> Untouchability is worse than leprosy in terms of its stigma if it doesn't change there is no scope for progress. We were called Adiandhras then and Harijans now. We were called male and Madigas now by stigmatizing us as untouchables. Though we are untouchables we were made to work as slaves and our work has no untouchability ... even though several laws were made and announced against the evil practice of untouchability it still continues in different forms. At the time of elections politicians come and hug us by saying that we are their friends. For them our vote is not untouchable. Therefore teach them a lesson who belittled us in all possible ways. We no longer tolerate intimidation and insult from our oppressor. O Ambedkaraa, our voice has begun to go out today.[210]

---

208 Karra Vijayakumari, 'Sombuvva' from Mogi (Nalgonda: Gosangi, 1998), p. 23.

209 Darsie Sasi Nirmala, Note 38 cited in G. Lakshmi Narasaiah, *The Essence of Dalit Poetry*, p. 58.

210 Teresa Devadanam, "Antaraanitanamu Nirmoolana," in Gogu Shyamala (ed), *Nallapodhu: Dalita Streela Saahityam, 1921-2002* (Hyderabad: Hyderabad Book Trust, 2004), pp. 106-110.

Dalits are very optimistic about their future hope and this is once again symbolically expressed in the heart and soul of Dalit poetry in the following words:

> These clouds must be vanished. These walls must be ruined. This silence must be bursted. This gum must be dried up. O man, I want real citizenship, Will you give? What do I want, I want you, I want a place in your heart. I must wash my hands at your home. You must come to my hut and ask our girl for marriage. We must become relative's friend! This country becomes ours as we walk hand in hand this uneven earth become smooth will you come?[211]

The following words of Namdev Dhasal will tell the future aspirations of Dalits in a metaphorical way:

> Our blood was spilled for this glorious city and what we got was the right to eat stones. Now, now, we must explode the building which kisses the sky. After a thousand years we were blessed with a sunflower. Now, now we must, like sunflowers, turn our faces to the sun.[212]

As we noted above, the voices of both the Hebrew and Dalit prophets echo voices of protest very strongly in their socio-political and economic milieu. Even though they faced severe opposition, and reprisal at times, they never lost their vigor for voicing out their strong concerns. 'You can kill everything but not the voice,' says Gaddar as he extols the virtues of the songs and music that are capable of bringing about a revolution. His prophetic voice is geared towards emancipating the millions of Dalits who are crushed under the feet of the oppressor in the name of the caste system. His attire and costume reminds the audience that unquenching thirst for revolution. His voice is like the voices of Bhimrao Ambedkar and Jyotirao Phule who fought against the oppression of caste and untouchability. His voice also reminds us the voices of several Dalit martyrs whose sweat and blood brought the Dalit cause thus far.

The unified voice of the Dalit and Hebrew prophets is somewhat like as put it beautifully in the words of Walter Brueggemann:

> They are (the prophets *per se*) are simply the vehicles of undomesticated utterance, who utter what the present order regards as outrageous, obscene, treasured, crazy—and sometimes true... They mediate Yahweh, make Yahweh palpably available, as threat and as possibility. They

211 Madduri Nagesh Babu, "What is Your Caste," in *What is Your Caste* (Narsarao Peta: Sreeja Publications, 1998), pp. 60-61.

212 Namdev Dhasal, *An anthology of Dalit Literature,* ed. Mulkraj Anand and Eleanor Zelliot (New Delhi: Gyan Publishing House, 1992), p. 60.

> demand a hearing. In their memorable utterances, the prophets leave images and metaphors so ringing in the ears of Israel (contemporary listeners) that life is never again thinkable or livable without reference to the "Wild One" who lives at the center of Israel's life (our life), who in sovereign severity will dispense with Israel (us) and who with impervious resolve will begin again.[213]

We began our discussion on the nature of Hebrew and Dalit prophetic discourse and their possible resonance in the light of their respective socio-political contexts. We have demonstrated that in both the biblical and Dalit contexts the voices of the prophetic discourse had tremendous potential that would directly hit the anemic, cowardly, self-serving and hegemonic forces of power that may in subtle ways try to thwart the power of these utterances. When such devastating forces thwart strong and uncompromising voices of justice they can only ruin the external forces of flesh not the inner voice of protest that can never be stopped. Both the Hebrew and Dalit prophets never gave up their fight till the last drop of blood is shed from their bodies. Their voices of protest continued untiringly despite the hard circumstances. The Hebrew and Dalit prophets had special favor towards the suffering and disadvantaged communities to which they belong to. They are not brainwashed by the changes that prompted the rulers and administrators to manipulate the lives of those marginated in the society. Rather they called their oppressors to truly repent for their sin towards their fellow human beings. Their voices create a hope, in a genuine way for the kairos to be broken in the history. To discern that time and to seize that opportunity, the oppressed and disinherited in the world of Dalits and Hebrew prophets today have stood up as it was in the ancient times.[214] The marginated communities in every kairotic moment rise up to the occasion to express their solidarity and claim their unique space in the God given created order. It was with that hope Hebrew prophets pronounced their oracles and with the same hope the Dalit prophets work towards the emancipation of millions of Dalits in India. It is with the same goal the Dalit Prophetic voices emerged against their oppressors in order to show them that God is on their side.

---

213 Walter Brueggemann, *Theology of the Old Testament*, p. 649. Words placed in brackets are mine for emphasis.

214 For a detailed discussion on the importance of Kairos for the marginated communities like Dalits see, Choan-Seng Song, "Ecclesiastes 3:1-8 an Asian Perspective," in Priscilla Pope-Levison and John R. Levison (eds.) in *Return to Babel: Global Perspectives on the Bible* (Louisville: Westminster John Knox Press, 1999), pp. 87-92.

3.5 Ministry of the Old Testament Sages and Apocalyptic Thinkers and their Relevance in the Indian Context

"The fear of the Lord is the beginning of all wisdom" is the dictum by which Israelites reworked their God's great deeds, unique and vital to her own context in the midst of several international wisdom propositions. The entire creation is praised, because by wisdom Yahweh created it. God established the foundations of the earth, by his wisdom and might he has caused everything to come into the earth and to play its active part. Yahweh is not only the creator but also the sustainer of his beautiful creation. By wisdom and insight human beings can learn to live in right relationship with God and his creation. Hebrew wisdom presented to us in the three canonical books of the Old Testament.[215] These books are concerned with informed observations regarding life and its challenges, rather than formal instructions by scribes or others. Hebrew wisdom encourages readers not to limit themselves to mere study, but to practice discretion. This leads to equating wisdom with righteousness and with religiosity. In distinction from their neighbors Israel's wisdom literature: (a) granted less priority to the privileged classes, (b) remembered familial obligations in connection with its tribal roots, and (c) understood itself in terms of Yahweh's demands. The wisdom teaches on the whole express the value of worth living by means of practical observation and gained prudence by taking insight out of that lived experience. Although there is a general complaint that wisdom writers, unlike the prophetic utterances, do not talk much about social justice concerns it is not altogether true that they are indifferent to the social concerns. In fact their class ethic comes very strongly that they share in the pain and oppression of the marginalized and oppressed communities in the Hebrew society. They in fact trained their students to take a strong note of the disparity existing in the society between rich and poor and thus be concerned about the social structures that promote the disparity.[216]

In the realm of education in the ancient Israel this aspect comes very sharp and clear. the main pedagogical goal in teaching in the ancient Israel was to promote order and continuity on society by character building of the learners. In this direction it is stressed that the fear of the deity is considered to be the

---

215 By canonical we mean the books of the wisdom literature proper like: Job, Proverbs and Ecclesiastes accepted by the protestant canon. At the purely literary level, the designation 'wisdom writings' is not an adequate term because of the wide variety of wisdom material found in other parts of the Hebrew Bible. Very few books like the books of Job, Proverbs and Ecclesiastes can be called sapiential in the sense of imparting instruction or addressing themselves to broad issues of a philosophical or theological nature. For some details on this point see, Joseph Blenkinsopp, *Wisdom and Law in the Old Testament: The Ordering of Life in Israel and Early Judaism* (Oxford: Oxford University Press, 1995).

216 For a more detailed discussion on this point of view see, Bruce V. Malchow, "Social Justice in the Wisdom Literature," *Biblical Theology Bulletin* 12 (1982), pp. 120-124.

beginning of all knowledge and wisdom (Prov 1:7). James Crenshaw summarizes the overall goal of education in ancient Israel as follows:

> In brief, human conduct determined one's to life's good things, and education assisted young people in their pursuit of those blessings ... Central to sages was the acquisition of four virtues: self-control, restraint, eloquence, and honesty. The first virtue recognizes the enormous power of passion [fear, anxiety, and lust]. The second virtue, restraint, provided a necessary balance in a culture given to rhetorical excess, elevating modesty and reticence as a desideration to crowds in danger of losing perspective. The third, eloquence, acknowledges the persuasive power of speech for both good and evil. The fourth virtue guaranteed integrity, the tongue's use in communicating truth, especially in judicial contexts.[217]

Thus, this presentation takes seriously the importance of wisdom writers in the light of their overall concerns for the issues of the society, the way in which God's set order is functioning etc. In this light we shall discuss various issues connected with the contribution of wisdom writers and their relevance in the Indian context. Again few aspects of Indian context are highlighted in order to be more focused.

Wisdom is the ability to "cope" with everyday life; wisdom is quest for understanding (self-understanding) and for the mastery of the world. Wisdom asks for what is good for the people, believes that all the essential answers can be learned in experience pregnant with signs about reality itself. The human responsibility is to search for that insight and then to learn to live in harmony with the cosmos. Israel's wisdom teachers were first and foremost students of the universe. They studied Yahweh's creation to determine order and command human conduct which would sustain that order socially and cosmologically. Wisdom teachers understood and lived very close to "concrete, daily reality and give to Israel a sense that Yahweh is present in, with, and under daily, lived experience." The sages also preset to us a new understanding of the involvement of Yahweh that is hitherto not known to us. "They were secularists in ancient Israel, but their secular ways of discernment and speech continued to reflect on lived reality as the carrier of Yahweh in the world."[218] The sages are of the firm view that Yahweh is reliable and the name to be trusted, because Yahweh is the one who created orderly and coherent and ethically reliable creation and continues to protect that order despite changing circumstances. It is because of this precise reason the sages

217 James L. Crenshaw, "Education, OT," in Katherine Doob Sakenfeld (ed), *The New Interpreter's Dictionary of the Bible*, Vol. 2 (Nashville: Abingdon Press, 2007), p. 201.

218 Walter Brueggemann, *Theology of the Old Testament: Testimony, Dispute, Advocacy* (Minneapolis: Fortress Press, 1997), p. 688.

believe that Yahweh guarantees the order that is reliable and that is the insight that the sages are teaching us.[219]

Wisdom is the ability to "cope" with everyday life; wisdom is quest for understanding (self-understanding) and for the mastery of the world. Wisdom asks for what is good for the people, believes that all the essential answers can be learned in experience pregnant with signs about reality itself. The human responsibility is to search for that insight and then to learn to live in harmony with the cosmos. Israel's wisdom teachers were first and foremost students of the universe. They studied Yahweh's creation to determine order and command human conduct which would sustain that order socially and cosmologically. Wisdom teachers understood and lived very close to "concrete, daily reality and give to Israel a sense that Yahweh is present in, with, and under daily, lived experience." The sages also preset to us a new understanding of the involvement of Yahweh that is hitherto not known to us. "They were secularists in ancient Israel, but their secular ways of discernment and speech continued to reflect on lived reality as the carrier of Yahweh in the world."[220] The sages are of the firm view that Yahweh is reliable and the name to be trusted, because Yahweh is the one who created orderly and coherent and ethically reliable creation and continues to protect that order despite changing circumstances. It is because of this precise reason the sages believe that Yahweh guarantees the order that is reliable and that is the insight that the sages are teaching us.[221]

With regard to the identity and setting of wisdom Norman K. Gottwald[222] suggests the following stages based on its historical epochs: First, the wise were parents in families or elders and counselors in clans and tribes. Second, the wise were government officials, scribes and possibly priests who kept the records of the state, counseled kings and trained future political leaders. Third, the wise were non-priestly authorities in the collected and venerated law of Moses who interpreted its meaning and present application and who passed on their skills in legal scribal schools. While some hold on to the older view that wisdom had its origin in the Jerusalem court, it is no longer a tenable argument.[223] Obviously Israel did not wait until Solomon to have its share of experiential wisdom.

With regard to the sociological setting of Hebrew wisdom we have hardly any evidence to argue for its clarity. It is more difficult question to argue how the wisdom is connected to the society at large in Israelite context. Leo Perdue

---

219 Walter Brueggemann, *Theology of the Old Testament: Testimony, Dispute, Advocacy* (Minneapolis: Fortress Press, 1997), p. 688.

220 Ibid.

221 Ibid.

222 Norman K. Gottwald, *The Hebrew Bible: A Socio-literary Introduction* (Philadelphia: Fortress Press, 1985), p. 564.

223 Roland E. Murphy, "Wisdom Theses and Hypothesis," in eds. J. G. Gammie, et. al, *Israel's Wisdom: Samuel Terrien Festschrift* (New York; Scholar's Press, 1978), pp. 35-42.

postulates two paradigms in relation to wisdom to Hebrew society at large.[224] First, order and conflict. The book of Ecclesiastes, with its pronouncements to submit to God and king, followed the model of order, as did Proverbs, with its emphasis on righteousness and discipline. By contrast the book of Job presents God's creative forces in struggle with nihilistic forces. Proverbs, Psalms, Sirach and the Wisdom of Solomon endorse ideas of prosperity for the righteous and punishment for the wicked. This represents the orthodox view of wisdom. Job and Ecclesiastes are critical about such common assumptions regarding the basis of divine reward and punishment and so question human capacity to predict or induce God's favor. The critical question thus arises: Does wisdom teachings primarily enforce or challenge prevailing cultural and religious attitudes? Interpreters remain divided on the issue. Central to the question is the interpreters' choice of Proverbs/Job/Ecclesiastes as normative wisdom. The direct opposition of the claims (the righteous do/do not suffer: the wicked do/do not prosper) makes such divisions inevitable. Second, The perspective on social setting of wisdom is analyzed in terms of ethics. Ecclesiastes shows little concern for the poor as in the case of Job. Rather than emerging with compassion, Ecclesiastes suggests a few relatively rigid patterns for behavior in what approximates a "least resistance" philosophy. The book advises the reader to find the measure of enjoyment amid life's confusion. Proverbs mixes concern for following rules and showing human concern. Wisdom serves as a tool which could used either to reinforce or challenge the consensus depending on the perspective of the thinker and the situation of community. R. N. Whybray[225] shows that no one has succeeded in positioning the sages in any distinct social group except some general observations made on the social setting as done above. Scholars used several phrases to refer to the sages like: "elite class", "intellectuals", "urban owners of landed estates", "countries", and "professional counselors or teachers." In addition interpreters usually acknowledge an early period when wisdom's origin and transmission occurred within family units and a late epoch during which teachers administered their own private schools, with a possible intermediate stage associated with the royal court. Andre Lemaire[226] analyzes the complex system of education during the monarchy embracing most cities in Israel and extending to many remote villages.

Therefore it would be appropriate to conclude that the wisdom tradition has a way of explaining the contradictions in one's life by means of practical

224 Leo G. Perdue, "Cosmology and Social Order in the Wisdom Tradition," in John G. Gammie and Leo G. Perdue (eds.), *The Sage in Israel and the Ancient Near East* (Winona Lake: Eisenbrauns, 1990), pp. 457-478.

225 R. N. Whybray, "The Social World of Wisdom Writers," in ed. R. E. Clements, *The World of Ancient Israel* (Cambridge: Cambridge University Press, 1989,), pp. 227-250.

226 Andre Lemaire "The Sage in School and Temple," in John G. Gammie and Leo G. Perdue (eds.), *The Sage in Israel and the Ancient Near East* (Winona Lake: Eisenbrauns, 1990), pp. 165-181.

observations. What can be learned is only possible by way of firsthand experience and no other way it is possible. Practical living is the only option available in order to live and cope with the life in this world. The sages are of the view that the experience lived as reality of the people is indeed an experience of Yahweh and there should be no distraction from this dictum.

With regard to the vocabulary and the ethos of wisdom writers and their support to the underprivileged groups in the Israelite society, it would be appropriate for us to capture their concerns as reflected in each of the books.[227] Before venturing into that task we shall make few general observations in general. We must take a general note that for wisdom the sphere of the world is very broad ranging from "natural environment, historical events, social relations, political order, family affairs, daily work, and religious belief and practice."[228] In this sense wisdom tries to learn from all walks of life and for that purpose human beings are at the center of wisdom learning. The ultimate goal of this exercise is to develop a practical and comprehensive ethic and behavioral style which is necessary and adequate to all the hard situations that life moves along. It will also help to interact with one another with the necessary shrewdness and skill to live up to any situation. Moreover, wisdom tradition is firmly anchored in the royal court and its associated institutions. Gottwald points out two major and important lines of thinking that is pursued by the wisdom writers:

> Some of the wisdom literature … focused … on the cultivation of a pedestrian ethic of obedience to superiors and the refinement of proper court manners which were highly self-protective of the precarious position of lesser officials under arbitrary rulers. On the other hand, the wise officials has family and tribal ties, as well as wider socioreligious concerns, and their literature also reflects a pronounced concern to preserve the integrity of rural communities against predatory wealth and suborned legal institutions.[229]

It was also believed that some of the wise men who had concern for the just social order had contact with prophets, priests and elders who had similar concerns. It is possible that like-minded people formed a "wisdom circle" and that circle consists of all the categories of people as mentioned above.

With regard to the class and social ethic of the wisdom writers Crenshaw has the following to say:

227 We limit our discussion to the three canonical books of wisdom viz., Proverbs, Job and Ecclesiastes.

228 Gottwald, *The Hebrew Bible*, p. 566.

229 Ibid., p. 570.

> Observation about the intrinsic relationship between human and divine truth marks the arrival of the third facet of wisdom's legacy which will be emphasized: wisdom enabled people to cope. The secret of Wisdom's appeal lay in the reward which she bestowed upon those who followed her path. No situation arose in which sages found themselves unprepared, for they addressed every eventuality. Their goal was to know what to do or say on any given occasion. To this end they gathered information and perfected their powers of drawing analogies between different realms and categories. Through centuries of experience the sages acquired valuable insight into personal and human character.[230]

The sages instead of launching an attack on the social order that is lying in corruption always take up the view that its inner dynamics are observed in such a way that it will teach us a lesson for us to live wisely in any skewed situation. Gerhard von Rad rightly states on this point:

> All the more important and all the more interesting to the teachers is *what* happens in this given, social sphere and *how* it happens. Their observation of men's activities, of their behaviour in the most varies situations, of their peculiarities and of everything paradoxical, is acute in spite of a marked tendency to didactic standardization. Their judgments are on the side of extreme sobriety, often strongly accentuated, in form often solemn. If one must mention something which appears to be characteristic of the concept of life in many didactic sentences and which is definitely also to a certain extent sociologically determined, then it is a tendency towards caution, towards wariness. Here, reticence, caution in action, is esteemed more highly than overzealous enthusiasm. Everything hasty, anything that is acquired quickly, such as 'hastily won wealth', hasty speech, is suspicious from the outset.[231]

The sages warn their readers the lapse that can happen due to their sin. The word for sin is *peša* which does not mean sin in terms of moral default; rather it was always meant a violation of property or an offence against one's fellow human being. Among the twelve occurrences[232] in the book of Proverbs none of them talk about "crime" as a sin of man against God, but as a failure of relationship

230 James L. Crenshaw, *Old Testament Wisdom: An Introduction* (Atlanta: John Knox Press, 1981), p. 210.

231 12 Gerhard von Rad, *Wisdom in Israel* (London: SCM Press, 1972), p. 85.

232 Proverbs 10:12, 19; 12:13; 17:9, 19; 19:11; 28:2, 13, 24; 29:6, 16, 22.

between one human and another.[233] The social order that all the books of wisdom literature take up has some legal basis from the torah. Since each book approaches this problem in a particular way although the wisdom writers base their arguments depending heavily on the torah principles.[234]

The importance of the role of women in the wisdom writings and the opinion of the sages on different roles of the women is another matter to be examined how the patriarchal values have been perpetuated by the wisdom writers. At the same time the sages are very creative in portraying the positive and potential role of women in the Hebrew society.[235]

Proverbs: The book of Proverbs seriously takes note of the major concern that Yahweh is the creator or maker of the poor and therefore they should not be despised or oppressed. As noted earlier in this presentation the book of Proverbs, in spite of its strong ties with royal elite schools do "preserve the integrity of rural communities against predatory wealth and suborned legal institutions."[236] The process of transferring wealth from many to few is noted in the book of Proverbs in the form of admonitions. For instance, one admonition warns the people that they should not move the boundary marks of the fields of orphans and widows (23:10-11). This makes it clear that the book of Proverbs is concerned about the rural and poor populace who are under constant threat of their survival. During the post monarchic period the absence of king created a great vacuum in sustaining the ideas as mentioned above. But the book of Proverbs begins to note the change that took place with the emerging family and society as stronger than before. The idea of God as creator and the one who maintains the order in the community began to reemerge.[237] The author of Proverbs no longer satisfied with the status quo that rampantly creates a division among the rich and poor, thus moves on to offer his critique against the system and admonished the heavens to respond to God, who maintains order in the society. In Proverbs 14:31 the author advanced his argument by making use of earlier traditions in Old Testament concern for the poor The word *dāl* is used in relation to the word *'śh* means "maker", creator who has special concern for the poor. While the concern for the poor is an earlier concern even in the pre-exilic period, the term maker could be a later word used

233 von Rad, *Wisdom,* p. 88.

234 For a more detailed discussion on this point see Claus Westermann, *Roots of Wisdom: The Oldest Proverbs of Israel and Other Peoples*, trans. J. Daryl Charles (Louisville: Westminster John Knox Press, 1995).

235 It is beyond the scope of this book to discuss the details of this issue. For an elaborate discussion on this and related issues see, Carole Fontaine, *Smooth Words: Women, Proverbs, and Performance in Biblical Wisdom* (London: Sheffield Academic Press, 2002).

236 See note 12 above for the same quotation. See Proverbs 14:21, 31; 17:5; 23:10-11 for the explanation of this view by the author of Proverbs.

237 For more details on this point see Claudia Camp, *Wisdom and the Feminine in the Book of Proverbs* (Sheffield: JSOT Press, 1985), pp. 244-248.

for the creator as in Job 4:17; 35:10; Isa 51:13; 54:15 and Psalm 95:6.[238] Thus, the creator and the poor are closer to each other and everyone who hears the wisdom admonition is expected to take heed to this instruction. In this regard, Ceresko summarizes the position of the book of Proverbs as follows:

> The book of Proverbs describes, often in vivid terms, the disorder and unjust socio-economic conditions during this (post-exilic) period. These conditions resulted both from the exploitative demands imposed by the successive imperial regimes and from self-serving practices of those Jews who collaborated with the foreign rulers and/or took advantage of the disorder for their own selfish purposes.[239]

Another proverbial admonition mentioned in Prov. 23:10-11 is intended to protect the rights of the oppressed or underprivileged or those whose rights are violated by the greedy and wealthy people. The concerns expressed by the poet in these two verses once again reflect an order (social order) to be maintained among the human relations, which is also intended by God. Since God is the one who intends such an order, God hates the violation of legal rights of the community in which the rights of the poor and underprivileged are protected in particular. The removal of the boundary stones of the poor widows is one such legal violation, to which God files the suit against those who were involved in violating regulations set by God. The intervention by Yahweh is explained here by means of the word *gō'el* when the rights of the poor are denied, and this *gō'el* strengthens the weak who can be exploited with wrong accusations.[240] The intervention by Yahweh as a *gō'el* is explained by legal terms is further attested by the word *rîb* here. This word is generally used as Yahweh's adjudication on behalf of his people which is carried out in legal terms (Pss. 68:6; 146:9; Isa. 1:17; Jer. 7:6; 22:3).[241] In the prophetic rib pattern we find somewhat different kind of structure, wherein the prophets act as a summoner to the rib of Yahweh, in the process of rib the mountains and the foundations of the earth are summoned as witnesses (cf. Micah 6:1-8). But here Yahweh directly intervenes and that no witnesses are summoned, but the adversaries are called "my adversaries" (for similar expression in 1Sam. 2:10 and Jer. 18:19) for the direct confrontation. There is no mediation here as in the prophetic lawsuit, but Yahweh acts as a powerful advocate who will fight the case

---

238 C. T. Fritsch and R. W. Schloreb, "The Book of Proverbs," in *The Interpreters Bible*, Vol. 4 (New York: Abingdon Press, 1955), pp. 867-868.

239 Anthony R. Ceresko, "The function of 'Order' (SEDEQ) and 'creation' in the book of Proverbs, with some implications for today," *Indian Theological Studies* 32 (1995), p. 228.

240 Here, the word *gō'el* would appear as a helper in a lawsuit to see that justice was done to his protégé. For more details on this point see Helmer Ringgren, "gā'al, gō'el, ge'ullah," *Theological Dictionary of the Old Testament*, Vol. 2 (Grand Rapids, MI: William B. Eerdmans Publishing Company, 1977), pp. 350-355.

241 Otto Plöger, *Spruche Salamos* (Neukirchen Vluyn: Neukirchener Verlag, 1984), p. 272.

of the poor and orphans and take a legal action on those who violate the laws set by God. The motivation *kî* in verse 11 refers to the result of behaviour mentioned in verse 10; therefore God would want to take the case by himself. Since God maintains the order in the society, God will act as the patron of those whose rights are denied. When the rights of the underprivileged are denied, the created order is disturbed, thus God intervenes as a judge in the law court and restores the order again.[242]

Since this admonition from the wise men consists for an appeal to order, it may have a reference to the cosmic order "which interpenetrates the entire world of all life and which joins behaviour and consequences with the sanction of the creator's unsearchable wisdom."[243] Therefore the practice of injustice is the result of disorder, foolishness and also sin against Yahweh.[244] The overall concern of the wisdom writers expressed in the book of Proverbs is well summarized by Pleins:

> Assisting the poor through giving—charity-was an important concern to the wise. The student is warned against neglecting the poor (*dal* Prov. 21.13). It may be that one day the student might be in distress and the neglect of others would rebound to leave the student naked before disaster, with no one to assist The wise person shares food with the poor (*dal*, Prov. 22.9). The defining feature of just rulers is their treatment of the poor (*dal*) in legal contexts (Pro. 29.14) ... to the wise the just treatment of the poor is a mark of righteousness.[245]

These texts express God's immediacy to the poor in creation and redemption and thus the wise men are expected to show similar concern towards the poor as they are responsible to their creator in their dealing with the poor and underprivileged.

Job: Job overlaps more with the prophetic materials in terms of dealing with the concern for the poor. By the use of choice words like: *'ebyôn*, *dal*, and *'ānî* Job understands poverty as a condition resulting from social injustice (see, Job 24:4, 9, 14; 29:12; 30:25; 31:16; 34:28; 36:6, 15).[246]

The term'*ebyôn* is translated as "powerless" an it is found in many places in the book of Job (5:15; 24:4, 14; 29:16; 30:25; 31:19). In these verses there is twofold concern of the author of Job in using this term. It talks about the relationship of the powerless to the wicked and also Job's relation with the powerless. Job as the

242 Philip Johannes Nel, *The Structure and Ethos of Wisdom Admonitions in Proverbs* (Berlin: Walter de Gruyter, 1982), pp. 33-34.

243 Brian W. Kovacs, "Is there a Class-ethic in Proverbs?" in J. L. Crenshaw and J. T. Willis (eds.), *Essays in the Old Testament Ethics* (New York: Ktav Publishing House, 1974), p. 185.

244 Gottwald, *The Hebrew Bible*, p. 574.

245 J. David Pleins, "Poverty in the Social World of the Wise," *JSOT* 37 (1987), p. 70.

246 Ibid.

representative of the oppressed and the powerless laments bitterly for his pathetic condition. Job's friend Eliphaz portrays God as the champion of social justice and the same God also created the foundations of the earth with the same principle. God is directly involved in executing his justice as the creator of the earth on behalf of the poor and powerless in the society.[247]

In another passage of Job 24:2-12 and 13-17 the author speaks of exploitation of the downtrodden and the reign of miscreants. Job points out the widespread exploitation in the world during his time, caused by many evil and wicked deeds. The removal of landmarks as a means of appropriating a portion of the weaker neighbor's property. Maintenance of landmarks was necessary to preserve one's inheritance as a trust from God clearly mentioned in Deut. 19:14; 27:17. Whenever the property and possessions of the poor and underprivileged are appropriated illegally, they are compelled to leave the main stream of the society and go to hidden corners and strive for their sustenance like wild asses. Their only source of food material is barren wilderness (Job 24:4-5).[248] The misery of the hungry poor is further intensified by their lack of clothing and shelter and they cling on to their only source of help, God. Thus, the intention of Job in using the term *'ebyôn* is very clear that these are the underprivileged and marginalized of his society who are the victims of economic and political injustice. Also by using this term Job wants to communicate that he had to fight against the institutional evils like judiciary, political and economic system in order to safeguard the rights of *'ebyôn*. The evil forces who oppress this powerless community are greedy influential people existing in his day in the Israelite society.[249] Job here takes the position of an advocate of the underprivileged class of his society and Job takes a clear position to defend them at any cost.

Use of the term *dal* is very important in the context of the book of Job and it further intensifies Job's concern for the marginalized sections of his society. This word is used six times in the book of Job in 5:16; 20:10, 19; 34:19, 28; 31:16. In most cases the word is used in the context of how the poor are treated in different spheres of societal life. Job used this term with the sense that the *dal* are the vulnerable, although they are the better than the *'ebyôn* they are still subjected to exploitation and oppression. Because of their vulnerability they are always helpless people In 22:5-9 Eliphaz accuses Job of exploiting the *dal* and Job spends lot of time in his final testimony speech to refute the allegation made by Eliphaz. Job's friends by defending this class of people affirm that God is the righteous ruler who will bring justice to the *dal* and punish miscreants that are working against this helpless people is the main conclusion of Job.[250]

247 Norman C. Habel, *The Book of Job* (Philadelphia: Westminster Press, 1985), p. 133.

248 Francis Madanu, *Understanding of the Poor in Job: In the Context of Biblical Wisdom Literature* (Hyderabad: St. John's Regional Seminary, 1997), p. 113.

249 Ibid., p. 144.

250 Ibid., p. 168.

The use of the term *'ānî* which is translated as "needy" needs some discussion in relation to Job. This group consists of those who has basic needs like food, shelter, need of social and political protection. This word is used seven times in the book of Job. The needy are described in the context that: they are forced into hiding (24:4), their children are seized as a pledge (24:9), and they are murdered (24:14). Job talks about the condition of the needy in two levels. First, the needy are exploited as described in 24:2-11. The rich oppressors are very shrewd to remove the boundaries of the needy. The miscreants are so powerful they pasture the stolen herd, on the land of the needy gained by the miscreants by illegal means. The miscreants take the children of the needy by payment or in a pledge. This is done with the view to get maximum profits with minimum costs paid to the children. Second, the unrequited criminal acts are conducted by the miscreants on the part of the needy. Misery and abuse are rampant in the city and urban contexts. The victims groan and cry out for help against their oppressors. The victims of the murderous miscreants are powerless and needy, the innocent citizens who are unable to muster any resistance. Since, they come from lowest rung of the society, no one cares about their problems. The murderous miscreant has no fear of being caught for his criminal acts. They walk like a thief coming at night to rob. After achieving the target, he digs through the mud-brick wall to get an undetected entrance. Then they watch for dusk in order to get a victim. Thus, the author describes to depict the criminal act of the miscreant on the part of the needy person.[251]

In all this vocabulary Job clearly argues that Yahweh is the one who maintains order and justice in his created order and that nothing could go wrong against that created order. However, Job is also of the view that "God does not have evil and suffering totally under control and thus God also suffers."[252]

Ecclesiastes: The book of Ecclesiastes is very interesting in terms of its radical propositions that question the traditional patterns of wisdom thinking. The author is popularly called as Qoheleth or the preacher has some interesting things to say about the poor and needy and the underprivileged classes of Israelite society in comparison with other wisdom writers. The preacher while affirming the older traditions of wisdom questions them as well. For example, in chapter 6:7-8, it is written in verse 7 that "all human toil is for mouth, yet the appetite is not satisfied' is a traditional wisdom saying. But verse 8 reads: "for what advantage have the wise over the fools? And what do the poor who know how to conduct themselves before the living?" This saying is an innovation of the preacher that departs from the traditional understanding. Although the book of Ecclesiastes does not deal with poor and underprivileged directly like other wisdom books, yet there are some texts that describe the poor and powerless reflecting the

251 Francis Madanu, *Understanding of the Poor in Job: In the Context of Biblical Wisdom Literature* (Hyderabad: St. John's Regional Seminary, 1997), p. 172.

252 Gottwald, *The Hebrew Bible*, p. 578.

biblical tradition. The preacher was very much aware of the existence of the poor, oppression, injustice, and discrimination meted out to poor in the world. And refers to this in several passages like: 3:16-4:3; 5:7; 7:15; 8:9-14; 9:14-16.

The preacher talks about the life that is not worth living due to the following reasons. That which is, already has been; that which is to be, already is; and God seeks out what has gone by. According to the Stoic teachers, the wise would discern good times either to act or abstain from acting. This act is also determined by the specific circumstances. These timely acts would therefore be available to wise people to act accordingly. While Qoheleth may agree with this view in principle, the only problem, as he sees it, is that the knowledge which would enable us to bring our actions into coincidence with what is predestined to happen is just not available to us. Even to make it more clear Qoheleth goes a step further in his thesis that: whatever occurs has already happened; what is to happen in the future has already happened in the past; God seeks out what has been driven away, i.e., God recalls occurrences which have moved from the future into the present and then into the past so that they may be recycled eventually in a new present, the circle is closed; there is no room for novelty, the time spoken by Qoheleth is present on this circuit knowledge, however, is denied to the human agent. The 'circle of destiny' and 'ideal living' according to the times and seasons are well within the teachings of Stoics. Qoheleth is well aware of this but departs from this by proposing: God has an all-encompassing temporal perspective within every human mind. Human beings have the capacity to transcend and transient moments of their absurd lives, although there is some ceiling on it that no one can breach. In this sense, Qoheleth is cognizant of the enduring permanence of divine providential involvement.

For the preacher power belonged to the wicked and they wield it ruthlessly to oppress the powerless. The twin problems of corruption of justice and the oppression of the helpless lead Qoheleth to conclude that the dead are better than the living, and that the unborn are more fortunate yet, to have been spared from the undeserved suffering (4:2-3). For Qoheleth life is hardly worth living because of the wretchedness of the poor. The preacher brings about a straight forward attribution of ubiquitous oppression and injustice to the hierarchic organization of the state.[253] The words of the preacher is a clear indication that the corruption prevailed from top to bottom in the hierarchical structure. This is reflected in Qoheleth 5:7:

> If you see in the province the oppression of the poor and violation of justice and the right, do not be amazed at the matter, because an official watches over another official, and there are higher officials over them.

253 Frank Crüsemann, "The unchangeable World: The Crisis of Wisdom in Koheleth," in Willy Scottroff, et. al, (eds.), *God of the Lowly* (New York: Orbis Books, 1984), p. 70.

It is normally expected in ancient Israel that the judicial system is to be kept without any corruption and that in turn would help to maintain an uncorrupt system where the poor and their rights are safe-guarded. Instead the entire judicial and bureaucratic system was corrupt that works for the disadvantage of the poor and underprivileged in the society. The higher officers extract as much revenue as possible from the lesser officers, who in turn extract from the common poor in the form of taxes. The preacher observes that the way authorities exercise their power to hurt others (8:9). The wicked went about in holy places unquestioned. Punishment for evildoers was delayed. This encouraged them to commit more atrocities against the poor (8:10-11). This perversion of justice is so dreadful that it made the preacher to challenge the traditional doctrine of retributive justice mentioned in Deuteronomy and later supported by the prophets.[254]

Through another parable in 9:14-16 the preacher reflects and depicts the discrimination and disparity existing in the society. The predicament of the poor man, even if he is wise is explained here as against the dominant in the society. Even the wise man who lacked wealth was despised, if so what would have been the condition of the poor man?

If we agree for a later date of the book of Ecclesiastes then what was described above in 5:7-9 depicts the situation of Ptolemaic administration in Palestine. By presenting a ubiquitous situation of corruption and by offering a strong critique against the corrupt system the preacher radically questions the remoteness of God and his protection to the poor and underprivileged in the society. Gottwald conveys this idea clearly:

> The socio-religious situation of this astute sage is a setting where *God and government are distanced from the people.* He presupposes the reality and absolute power of God and state, though the former is vaster than the latter. Both the divine and secular authorities work in unfathomable ways that cannot be contested. Their decisions and deeds are consequential for human life, but they are not approachable or swayable in their doings, except perhaps through what modest voice the sage might have in his writings and in the counsels of state when he is consulted for his views.[255]

Thus, the wisdom writers captivated by the wonders of nature, believed that their God who was responsible for the order in creation and order in the socio-economic realms of life. Dianne Bergant captures this idea beautifully:

> This creator was not only the primeval architect of the universe and provident sustainer of reality but also the demanding judge who

254 Francis Madanu, *Understanding of the Poor in Job*, p. 73.

255 Gottwald, *The Hebrew Bible*, p. 582.

> preserved established order. Since Israel believed that social order was but a reflection of the natural order of the universe, creation theology quite possibly played a more significant role in its worldview than was previously thought.[256]

Thus, the wisdom writers in the Hebrew Bible are very much in tune with the affairs of the nation and they guided the people in all matters of life and death in their day-to-day living.

Relevance of the Hebrew wisdom thinking to the present day Indian context: we shall make few comments on the relevance of wisdom ethic and its significance in the Indian context.

Wisdom ethic of the social order: As noted above the sages are concerned about the orderliness of the society on daily matters and that order is something derived from God's creation itself. The sages always affirm that there is inherent order in everything that is created by God. Whenever relationships are skewed among the human communities this established and creative order of God is something that is concretely discussed by the sages. It is expected that no one has the right to go against that created order. If anyone transgresses it that is a blatant sin against God, the creator. Every human being is thus treated equal in the sight of God and there is no possibility for any discrimination. In the ancient Near East the deities like *šamaš* are expected to maintain order in the creation, the failure to maintain it will result in chaos and disorder. Whereas in the ancient Israel the order is not divinized. Every citizen is expected to maintain order of creation by maintaining right relationship with his or her neighbour. In this respect it is affirmed that all are equal in this order created by Yahweh. There is no disparity among different classes of people. This is precisely the point that we need to affirm in relation to Dalits in India. Dalits are discriminated in the name of their low caste origin which also dehumanizes them. The Hebrew sages are of the firm view that anyone who mistreats his or her neighbour is violating the order set by the creator, that disrupts the social, political and religious order, that will result in chaos. In the New Testament we see Jesus' mission to the Samaritans is just the fulfillment of Hebrew sages' expectation. Raj Irudaya makes this point clear:

> Jesus' mission with the Samaritans as a marginalized people has been a life-giving one in order to make them all the children of God. The Samaritan woman as a marginalized person has experienced the liberative, revelatory, missionary and testimonial facets of the Samaritan mission of Jesus. In the backdrop of the hatred-filled, divided and intolerant socio-religious context of the Jews and Samaritans, Jesus' singular mission has opened up a new epoch of

256 Dianne Bergant, *Israel's Wisdom Literature: A Liberation-Critical Reading* (Minneapolis: Fortress Press, 1997), p. 12.

> respect, dignity and unity for the Samaritans and Jews as the children of God and has ushered in a ground-breaking mission of universal fellowship of all peoples and nations. ... Even in the twenty-first century India continues to be confronted with the problem of casteism and untouchability. The Dalits are caught up in the throttling tentacles of this dehumanizing problem and so they are oppressed and marginalized economically, socially, politically and culturally. ... Therefore all Christians should endeavour wholeheartedly to work relentlessly for the eradication of untouchability still existing in and among us in several forms overt and covert. Jesus, who reached out with his life-giving mission to the marginalized and untouchable Samaritans, transcending the ethnic and religious barriers to include them in his wider community of New Israel, is an ever challenging model to us all. ... The Samaritan mission of Jesus to the marginalized has shown us the way par excellence. Therefore the deep-rooted and well perpetuated casteism demands of the Churches today ongoing concerted, sincere and indefatigable efforts to rid themselves of this age-old problem so that they may continue to be a witness to the Body of Christ in whom there is neither Dalit nor caste, neither slave nor marginalized but in whom all are the children of God.[257]

The mission of Jesus to the marginalized communities of his own time is the need of the time in our contemporary predicament which Dalits are facing now. If we take seriously the dictum of the Hebrew sages that God's creative order is to protect all people in the community irrespective their class and caste, then there is a hope for Dalit communities in India to live as worthy human beings.

Powerless, needy, helpless and underprivileged: As was noted earlier the wisdom writers used several terms to describe the underprivileged sections of the society. The prophetic insight is further strengthened by the wisdom writers by upholding the lost dignity of the underprivileged sections of the society. Dalits in India are always made powerless and treated brutally if they claim their rightful place in the society. Like many other international for a of the Christian church the Vatican II of the Roman Catholic Church has redefined the mission of the church as preferential option for the poor and marginalized communities. The following statement affirms the same holistic mission:

> The holistic mission of the Church consists of proclamation of the good news to all strata of people, evangelization of culture, dialogue, option for the poor, solidarity with others, commitment to God and man and concern. The challenge to the holistic mission of the Church

257 Raj Irudaya, *Mission to the Marginalized: A Subaltern, Feminist and Interreligious Reading of John 4:1-42* (Bangalore: Asian Trading Corporation, 2007), pp. 248-249.

> is to create an atmosphere of a just community (a kingdom of God) where the Dalit Christians and other Dalits can feel human persons and everyone can relate and live with fraternity and fellowship (as in the first Christian community) without impact of caste system and the discrimination from the Government and the traditional Church.[258]

The underprivileged classes are in particular addressed by the Hebrew sages are already well protected according to the covenant and other legal codes. There is nothing new that the sages are adding in their concern towards the marginalized communities. The use of significant words relating to the poor and powerless is an indication that the sages are concerned about the pain and pathos of the majority of the oppressed groups in the Hebrew society. These vulnerable groups are particularly favored by the creator God according to sages. Dalits are in particular made powerless and are reduced to depend on the mercy of the dominant caste groups who control all the resources. The biblical paradigms for liberation consists of God leading the powerful and marginalized community of oppressed people Israel out of the bondage by seeing their misery and giving ear to their cries. They are the Dalits of the Bible who were once non-people made God's people. Dalits need freedom from oppressive and dehumanizing caste system so that they can live with self-respect and human dignity. Thus, all the terms employed by the Hebrew sages are appropriate to the Dalit situation in the contemporary Indian situation. The sages remind us that God has special concern for these marginalized communities and the Christian church should take this mission God seriously in its talk and walk.

Wisdom life based on observations of misery and oppression: God is the God of universe and everything is brought under his control. While this is the general understanding of the sages, there are certain matters that are beyond the purview of human observation and knowledge. However, no fatalism operates in the wisdom thinking. The preacher teaches how to make the best of a bad situation, how to look inward to fell the pleasures that come to us and to exercise whatever wisdom we are granted. By realizing our slender faltering powers we become most fully human and, perhaps, happy, is the message of Qoheleth (11:7f). Qoheleth calls us to take up variety of good things and recommends them in various maxims: being young and smart (4:9), peaceful sleep (5:11), companionship (4:9), reputation (7:1) etc. Though for Qoheleth justice is often violated, it is unquestionably the way things should be; Righteousness, which is the foundation of justice, is indisputably good. It is within this area of concern the preacher posits a very optimistic future that is not subjected to fatalism. But human beings can't have direct access to it; it is God who is in control of it.

258 Francis Paravila, "The Holistic Mission of the Church among the Dalit Christians," in Selvister Ponnumuthan and Shaji Jerman (eds.), *Mission and Conversion: Towards a New Ecclesiology* (Bangalore: Asian Trading Corporation, 2008), p. 444.

Nevertheless human beings can learn from the misery and oppression that is carried out in the present life.

Karma and caste are the twin principles that operate in a Hindu and Indian context as resources to keep Dalit Christians under the banner of untouchables and inculcate an "inferiority complex." Dalit Christians along with their Dalit partners in general are made to think that it is their karma to suffer in this world and their birth is nothing but the result of their past karma coming from their previous births. The Hebrew sages, particularly the preacher is clearly against this view. No human agent have any control to impose fatalism on any other human neighbor, that too the vulnerable and marginalized sections of the community. It is God who is in control of every human destiny and his uncompromising side with the oppressed and underprivileged communities is the message of the Hebrew sages.

Tsedeqah as a cardinal virtue of the wise: Wisdom writers talk about the righteousness of God as a cardinal virtue that the wise can posses. The righteousness is also defined as something inherent in the created order of God that is responsible for the order of all things and that no human force should attempt to skew this order. Already the prophets in their message of justice and righteousness affirm the importance of *Tsedeqah*. Concerning *ṣedāqā* and its dynamism James L. Mays states:

> *ṣedāqā* is the quality of life displayed by those who live up to the norms inherent in a given relationship and thereby do right by the other person or persons involved. The two most important spheres for righteousness were the relationship between Yahweh and Israel defined in the covenant and expressed in the cult, and the relationship of man in the social order of the folk ... In Amos *ṣedāqā* applies to the relational life of the social partners in the people of Israel. Of course Yahweh is regarded as the patron and enforcer of the social order, but what is in view is the righteousness of Israelites in relation to each other.[259]

The Hebrew sages not only affirm what is stated by the prophets but also go one step forward to describe why there is a need to defend the marginalized sections of the society. Since Yahweh is the patron of the weak in the idea of Hebrew sages no one can oppress his people. This is what we need to affirm in Dalit situation in India today.

Retributive justice: Wisdom deals with very important concern of retributive justice of God, theodicy of God that is most prominent for our contemporary application of Dalit situation in India. The wisdom writers, particularly Job questions the retributive justice of God presented by the traditional writers: God

259 James Luther Mays, Amos*: A Commentary* (London: SCM Press, 1969), pp. 92-93.

rewards the just and punishes the wicked. Job vehemently protests against the blind acceptance of such affirmation.[260] The preacher also questions the mechanical operation of retribution unless wisdom can clarify the ever-changing present.[261] Speaking on the demythologization of karma theory based on the Book of Job, Devasahayam argues that in the story of Job the myth of karma theory is exploded when God finally answers Job quashing the judgment of Job's friends, whose main contention with Job was that Job is suffering because of his guilt or sins. Job becomes very frustrated when his friends maintained that God is a just God and that God rewards or punishes according to merit. Reward is symbolized in riches and health, and punishment in poverty and sickness. But towards the end Job's friends are proved to be wrong when the accusers become the accused and the accused is acquitted. The myth that God punished Job for his sins is totally shattered.[262] As was noted earlier Dalits are made to suffer using and imposing the Hindu doctrine of Karma. But it is very clear that the wisdom writers of the Hebrew Bible squash such a traditional and mechanical understanding of retributive justice and point out that God indeed will heed to the innocent sufferers like Job and Dalits.

Apocalyptic thinkers in the Old Testament and their significance: God never permitted security in the present for the people of Israel. They never found "rest" in the sense that they could find answers and settle with all their mundane and spiritual issues in their present journey. They always lived in anticipation without any consummation. Their every present is stamped with the seal of "not yet" theological discourse. Israel's existence was always tentative and preliminary to what was still to come. The Old Testament understanding of this "not yet" is not an expectation of merely a return to paradise, Eden, or the primeval age in which there was a complete shalom in the world, but it is a new beginning, a beginning marked by the idea that something vital has occurred between the beginning and the end.

The apocalyptic literature in the Bible can be viewed in the above light. It offers a new depth of theological vision in Judaism. The word *apocalyptic* seen as an adjective refer to both a specific type of literature and a theological perspective. In the first instance an apocalypse is a narrative "describing the disclosure of otherwise inaccessible secrets to a human seer by a heavenly being."[263] Another definition of apocalypse runs as follows: "'Apocalypse' is a genre of revelatory literature with a narrative framework, in which revelation is mediated by an otherworldly being

---

260 For some discussion on this point see, R. De Smet, "Job's 'Insufferable Comforters' and the Law of Karma," *Vidyajyoti Journal of Theological Reflection* 58 (1994), pp. 308-318.

261 Richard J. Clifford, *The Wisdom Literature* (Nashville: Abingdon Press, 1998), p. 20.

262 V. Devasahayam, "Job: Demythologization of Karma Theory," in V. Devasahayam (ed.), *Dalits and Women: Quest for Humanity* (Madras: Gurukul, 1992), pp. 227-31.

263 F. Murphy, "Introduction to Apocalyptic Literature," *New Interpreter's Bible,* Vol. 7 (Nashville: Abingdon, 1996), p. 2.

to a human recipient, disclosing a transcendent reality which is both temporal, insofar as it envisages eschatological salvation, and spatial insofar as it involves another supernatural world."[264]

If these definitions are strictly applied then there are two apocalypses in the Bible, Daniel and Revelation. Fourth Ezra in the Apocrypha and *1 Enoch* and *2 Baruch* from Pseudepigrapha, also exemplify apocalyptic literature. Despite the diversity in the content and ideas appear in this literature they share some common theological perspective. The cosmic perspective on the world can be noted in this literature as follows: God, although in control of the existing order and situation, often stands in conflict with destructive forces, whether human or divine. In this connection there appears a dualism that manifests itself in the human realm, sons of light versus sons of darkness. Conflict between these varied opposing elements will culminate in an eschatological cataclysm ('the end' according to Daniel 12:1-4), after which a new age will dawn. Many apocalypses present the idea that the appearance of this new age is imminent. The nature of the conflict and its outcome are revealed by a seer to righteous individuals and such knowledge remain guarded (Daniel 12:9), available only to the elect. In the new age beyond death, those who have suffered will be rewarded, whereas who have been oppressors will suffer.

The overarching theme of the apocalyptic literature can be summed up under the title: "living under God's sovereignty." This theme unfolds in different ways as a life-style of the people lived based on faithfulness to God in the face of competing claims of loyalty. The literature as a whole is produced and concentrates on times of crisis, times of great trauma, times of great stress, and times when the foundations of the faith are being shaken of course the whole Bible presents such problems in many other places. However, the interesting thing about the apocalyptic literature is this: *apocalyptic literature tends to be most popular among persecuted and oppressed and harassed Christian communities in the present day context. It tends to be unpopular among Western, middle-class Christians.* And indeed many people have lost their nerve about apocalyptic literature - we feel that it is something that does not speak easily into our world. But I think of the kind of threatening world we live in is making apocalyptic literature once again, as it always should have been, tremendously relevant to us. In a world threatened with terrorism, fragmentation and division based on class, caste, creed and color the search for peace has become a compelling task.

The Babylonian exile was one of the most decisive events in the history of Israel. It was also most traumatic, not only because of the fate of the people in exile, but more because of the events that led to the destruction and deportation. The fundamental question posed by the people of this age was: Yahweh as God of Israel, was he still in control of the events in the history in the midst of the events

264 As cited by J. J. Collins, "Introduction: Towards the Morphology of a Genre," in *Apocalypse: The Morphology of a Genre*, ed. J. J. Collins, Semeia 14 (Missoula: Scholars Press, 1979), p. 9.

that had occurred one after another, finally shattered the nation in this exilic age? What's happened to the covenant? God had said that he had made his covenant with his people and he wouldn't withdraw it. What had happened to the Davidic king? What had happened to the covenant with David that one of his descendants will reign for ever on the throne in Zion? What had happened to their whole worship system? They could still worship their God in Babylon, but they didn't have the whole system of priests, of prophets, and of sacrifices to help them. So the exile is a time which calls into question everything about Israel's faith.

Now that means something very important. Since this is such an unprecedented event, God sends massive preparation for it. God sends prophets to prepare them for exile. Isaiah, for example, prophecies in 8th century Jerusalem that the nation will be taken into exile; and he prophecies their return. And in effect what prophets and apocalyptic writers are giving is a whole theology of history. You could put it in this way: God will be God, and the world will know it. Now God is God at the moment, whether the world knows it or not. But the apocalyptic writers are saying God will be God and the world will know it. Daniel 4:34b-35 confirms this idea: *His dominion is an eternal dominion; his kingdom endures from generation to generation. All the peoples of the earth are regarded as nothing. He does as he pleases with the powers of heaven and the peoples of the earth. No one can hold back his hand or say to him: "What have you done?"* These are not the words of Daniel, but the words of Nebuchadnezzar. He has been humbled, restored and now comes to make this astonishing confession that this is the God who controls history. And not only controls history, but reveals history to his servants, the prophets. The exilic writers, Daniel and Ezekiel in particular, strengthen the people during that time. And, of course, the post-exilic prophets call people back to God and say, "Look- you are in danger of slipping back into old ways." So apocalyptic literature is particularly given to help people during a time of exile, which is a time when God seems to be absent. It's not difficult to see the relevance of that to our own society. We do not look out on a society in which God is acknowledged to be God. And so this is a message we need to proclaim- "God will be God and the world will know it".

According to Hanson, *apocalypticism* refers to a social and religious movement in which adherents perceive life through the apocalyptic eschatological lens. In the past, it has been argued that such movements sprout and flourish among groups who feel powerless and alienated from institutional structures. These groups respond to this alienation by constructing alternative symbolic universes in which the deity ensures the ultimate triumph of the group.[265]

As stated above it is generally agreed that apocalyptic texts tend to share a series of common features: 1. Temporal dualism: the distinction of the present age from the age to come. 2. Pessimism regarding the present and optimism

265 Paul D. Hanson, *Old Testament Apocalyptic*, Interpreting Biblical Texts (Nashville: Abingdon Press, 1987), pp. 25-43.

concerning the future. The solution to the problems of the present age is found in the hope of a new future order. 3. The periodization of history. The division of history into eons/segments (usually four, but also seven or twelve) reflects the predetermined divine plan. 4. The imminent arrival of the reign of God. The divine intervention will spell the doom of existing earthly powers. 5. A cosmic perspective. The events of the future are not focused on an individual, or the nation of Israel, or the people of God, but are cosmic in scope. 6. The vindication of the righteous. In the future order, which will involve a restoration of Edenic conditions, the righteous will be vindicated and the wicked condemned. 7. The involvement of supernatural beings. Angels and demons are involved not only in the revelation of the future, but are actively engaged in eschatological events. 8. A messianic element. God designates a royal figure as a symbol and executor of his rule.

For the Israelite community living under the shadow of foreign rulers shalom means nothing more than how to organize itself, particularly in political and religious terms. This question in complicated since Israel understood the previous polity, monarchy as given by God. Series of questions[266] are raised by them in this regards to appropriate the understanding of shalom in this context: Must Israel remain a political entity under Persian Empire? Must the civil authority be a Yahwist? What role should the priests have in a new polity? What import did the promises for an everlasting covenant with David as king offer in such circumstances? What was the relationship of those Yahwists living outside the land to those who resided in or around Jerusalem? All these questions are political as well as religious in nature. Prophet Ezekiel in chapters 40-48 deal with the above mentioned questions by means of a dense but provocative description of life after the temple has been rebuilt. In this vision the prophet envisions a rebuilt temple as God's return to it. The vision also offers a description of the land and of priestly responsibilities and prerogatives. There is no place for a king, only for a price or a leader. This vision of Ezekiel puts emphasis on hierocracy, a nation ruled by priests.

Prophet Haggai as a political strategist advocates for the rebuilding of the temple as a means of achieving shalom of the entire community. He believes the importance of restoring Davidic monarchy (Hag 2:20-23). In order to achieve the lost shalom the community must not only have the temple but also a king of the Davidic line.

Prophet Zechariah gives a third option to build up the shalom community that he proposes a dyarchic model of leadership where the responsibilities are shared by a political and a religious leader by suggesting "the two anointed ones" who are identified as Zerubbabel, the governor and Joshua, the high priest (Zech 4:14).

---

266 For details on this discussion see, Bruce C. Birch, et al., *A Theological Introduction to the Old Testament* 2nd edition (Nashville: Abingdon Press, 2005), 431-32.

All the above three visions envisaged by the prophets indicate the conflicted situation that the Yahwists were confronting at the end of the sixth century BCE where there was so much of desire was present to go back to the days of shalom community as of Davidic kingdom. Although in the ensuing centuries none of these options saw their development in pure form the so called prophetic apocalyptic visions made their impact upon the exilic community.

Issues of identity that were crept and solidified in the community of Judaism during the Persian period were raised again as the cultural force of Hellenism impinged upon Jews, both in diaspora and in homeland. The book of Daniel is widely influenced by this trend apart from other complex issues. We shall point out few crucial issues in this regard as factors that are responsible for building up a community of shalom in the midst of their complex socio-religious and political situation.

In the book of Daniel, the designations for God (the Lord, God of heaven, Most high God) are chosen to reinforce the ambiguous relationship between God, Jews and Gentile king. It is often stated that paganism is a major target of the book of Daniel. While the heroes bear Babylonian names compounded with Bel, Nebo and Marduk, these gods themselves play no part in the action. As many have suggested that idolatry is the main theme of the book, but it is doubtful whether it is true. The incompetence of the Babylonian wise men in chapter 2 is said to be a symptom, not of the impotence of their gods, but of their inaccessibility to the wise men (2:11). In chapter 6 we find that there are no pagan gods mentioned. The Jew is victimized as disobedient subject of the king, not as one who impiously rejects the local deities. The Jews' God, and his power, are being opposed not to other gods, but to political powers, be they kings or courtiers.

The sober view of God of Israel is present throughout the book. God is represented as showing to the king that "there is a God in heaven who reveals mysteries, and he has made known to King Nebuchadnezzar what will be in the latter days." (2:28). God also reveals, for the benefit of the king, the interpretation in 2:30: "not because of any wisdom that I have than all the living has this mystery been revealed to me, but in order that the interpretation may be made known to the king, and that you may know the thoughts of your mind."

In the vision stories, the Jewish-Gentile relationship has undergone a drastic transformation. In the midst of the conflicting situation there is a positive affirmation that God would heal and establish this relationship as sign of his shalom in the future kingdom. There is an emphasis on the Jewish people as a nation. In chapter 7 they are the 'holy ones of the Most High' who will succeed all other earthly kingdoms; in chapters 10-12 we find constant reference to the 'people' (10:14; 11:14, 32, 33 and 12:1) and to the prince who 'stands for them', Michael (10:13, 21; 12:1). In these stories the idea of exemplary Jew in the stories is replaced in the visions by the suffering, but soon to be vindicated, nation. Correspondingly, the Gentile kings and kingdoms are destined for destruction. In chapter 2 we are given a picture of successively degenerate kingdoms; in chapter 7 they are successively more brutal, and instead of the Gentile king who needs enlightenment and correction, as in the stories, we are shown a procession of beasts whose destiny is perdition. To sum up the stories in the book in chapters 1-6 are about the harmony between Jew and Gentile, overseen by a providential God, whereas the visions are about a definitive confrontation between Gentile and Jew, or, more accurately, Gentile king and God. Here God is the final destroyer of all Gentile kingdoms, and the only immediate resolution to the present crisis is the advent of a Jewish kingdom. The challenge to God comes not from other gods, but from human kings.

Not only does God acts as defender of his people and nation, the book of Daniel also present God as God of history. God *knows* all, he *controls* all, and he *rescues* as 2:21 and 6:27 affirms: "He changes times and seasons; he removes kings and sets up kings; he gives wisdom to the wise and knowledge to those who have understanding." "He delivers and rescues, he works signs and wonders in heaven and on earth." In this chapter the issue is omniscience of God. It is not simply what God has provided to Nebuchadnezzar the interpretation of his dream but *what has been revealed is the future, and only the God who controls the future can reveal it. The God who has revealed the dream is the same God who will fulfill it* (v.44). In other words what this leads is to the claim that the succession of the kingdoms is in control of this God, and the interpretation is a demonstration *not so much of the mantic power derived from God, but of his control over history*. This control of God is made very clear in a more concrete manner in chapter 4:17 as follows: "The sentence is by the decree of the watchers, the decision by the word of the holy ones, to the end that the living may know that the Most High rules in the kingdom of men, and gives it to whom he will, and sets over it the lowest of men."

In the visions, the sequence of world events is at a greater remove from the time of Daniel than in the stories, and in chapters 10-12 we see that the course of history has been ordained in the minutest degree. This gives an assurance to those suffering persecution. Even their own misery has been foreseen, yet its end will not be delayed, for it can be measured in days. This is exemplified in some verses as follows: 10:19: "He said, do not fear, greatly beloved, you are safe. Be strong and courageous! When he spoke to me, I was strengthened and said, let my lord speak, for you have strengthened me." 11:43: "He shall become ruler of the treasures of gold and silver, and all the riches of Egypt; and the Libyans and the Ethiopians shall follow in his train." 12:1-2: "There shall be a time of anguish, such as has never occurred since nation first came into existence. But at that time your people shall be delivered, everyone who is found written in the book. Many of those who sleep in the dust of the earth shall awake, some to everlasting life, and some to shame and everlasting contempt."

Unlike the stories in 1-6 chapters we do not find in the visions that there is a little or no place for divine intervention in history. The historical process unfolds as planned, and the God behind it all becomes visible only at the last. Providence consists in God's foreknowledge from the beginning and at his final intervention, but between these two extremes of history there is no room for divine action. God as God of history is demonstrated in the culmination of the royal confessional statement in 3:29 as follows: "There is no other god who is able to deliver in this way ... His dominion shall be to the end. He delivers and rescues, he works signs and wonders in heaven and on earth." This statement indicates that the Jew looks for his God to rescue him 'on earth', here and now. The idea of shalom in the book remains in the Jewish belief that God *will* deliver, because he is the God of the Jews, he is just, and he is the lord of history.

Contemporary Relevance of the Apocalyptic Understanding of Peace: The understanding of the message of peace or shalom in the apocalyptic thinking of the biblical books like earlier apocalyptic prophets, Daniel and revelation has the following hallmarks of its theological implications:

The apocalyptic message provides a template by means of which people in many periods can understand what is going on around them. It allows individuals, particularly if they are part of a group that suffers, or thinks they have been marginalized, to comprehend the source of their plight. Moreover, they understand that God is in control of their fates and that, ultimately, they will be victorious. The dualistic elements will enable them to distinguish their own situation from that of others, whom they may perceive as their oppressors, creating an "us/them" mentality.

The apocalyptic thought creates an opportunity of thinking newness even when such a possibility seems beyond the present life. For instance the Dalit Christians in India to *embrace cross as the central symbol of shalom*. This becomes for Dalit Christians a major identifying symbol, an ugly embodiment of rejection and hostility. Walter Brueggemann[267] explains how cross expresses old age/new age imagery:

The cross is about the abandonment of the old and it is about embrace of the new, in all its terror and precariousness. The cross is about repentance, of departing from the old but entering into a new experience of shalom. In the cross all the life negating forces that thwart the establishment of shalom is to be abandoned. This abandonment is articulated in terms of building walls that secure our own existence, to control our neighbors, and to be filled with greed that we should posses at the expense of others. At the same time the cross leads us to embrace the gift of life and security that is freely given to those who affirm life renewing realities. It leads us to work towards a society where equality and justice reign as marks of shalom society. The books of Daniel and Revelation talks about

267 See chapter 11 in Walter Brueggemann, *Living Toward a Vision: Biblical Reflections on Shalom* (Philadelphia: United Church Press, 1976).

the new age where the life is handed back to us, after it is broken and after it is established under God's rule. This kind of thinking of newness requires hope that the prophetic verses of Daniel proclaims and the vitality of the poet of Revelation to know that everything has happened. These writings arose in contexts of great spiritual crisis, when God's people were tempted to despair and wonder who was in control of history or if they would survive the present distress. The apocalyptic message thus reiterates the fundamental assertion that life has been given up and it has been received again. The intention of apocalyptic is not to chart out God's plan for the future so future generations may draw up calendars but to assure the present generation that—perhaps contrary to appearance—God is still on the throne (cf. Dan. 7:18, 21-22, 27; 8:25; 12:1-4), and that the future is firmly in his hands. All things are envisaged under God's rule towards building of shalom society in which all things are new.

Chapter 4

Select Themes of the Old Testament and their Theological Significance

4.1 Creation and Ecology in the Old Testament and its Relevance to the Present Ecological Crisis in India Today

The world is heading towards an ecological death. The biosphere is rapidly diminishing. Thousands of species of plants and animals, may not yet known to us, are becoming extinct. According to 1980s estimate in the Indian sub-continent satellite data confirm that India is losing 1.3 million hectare of forests a year.[268] The depletion of forests is directly related to the disappearance of the animals. According to the zoological survey of India red-data book which "categorizes the status of 153 animal species—77 among mammals, 55 among birds, 20 among reptiles and an amphibian species—as extinct, critical, endangered, vulnerable."[269]

The above examples show how human beings have misused and abused the natural resources and the most vulnerable species of plants and animals in order to sustain their selfish ends in the name of development. The ecological crisis created due to human unlimited plundering of God's creation can no more be regarded as only scientific, technical and political problem, but it should be looked as an ethical issue that could be addressed from the point of view of religious dimension.[270]

268 *The State of India's Environment, 1984-85, The Second Citizen's Report*, New Delhi, 1986, p. 49.

269 Soutic Biswas, "Preservation: Wildlife Warning," *India Today*, Vol. 19, Oct. 16-31, (1994), p. 211.

270 James A. Nash, *Loving Nature* (Nashville: Abingdon Press, 1991), p. 23.

There had been a wide discussion about God's creation, the role of human beings, and their relation and responsibility to the environment and ecology. From the past several decades the concern for eco-theology and eco-justice has been considered a vital theological mandate for the Christian theologians and biblical scholars. The World Council of Churches recognized the fact that the whole creation and its integrity with human beings and God's intimate relationship with human and other living and non-living beings is considered to be a vital theological agenda of the church.

Actually why should we consider the motif of ecological awareness in the creation theme? What is the necessity to talk about the human responsibility towards creation? These questions can only be addressed when we realize the actual problem nd its acuteness. It has been realized that human greed is responsible for the destruction of nature and all living beings on earth. Some of the problems in this regard include: modernization, scientific advancement by means of new inventions, large-scale technology for mass agricultural production are some of the causes of plundering the earth's resources, even to the extent of destroying the natural ecosystems. While it is necessary to make use of natural resources for human living, human beings had gone to the extent of permanently destroying the natural resources. In this context both the biblical and extra-biblical sources are helpful to guide us and help us to see how to be responsible stewards of God's creation. Additionally the religious texts of Hinduism, Islam, Buddhism and Jainism also help us to derive insights for ecological awareness and responsibility. We shall use these resources along with the biblical texts for the above mentioned purpose.

Creation and ecology motif in the Hindu religious and wisdom texts: Hinduism believes that human beings are none other than partners and participants in the grandeur of God's creation. "In fact, every worm, every soil bacterium, every herb, every tree, every bush, plays a more impressive role in this participatory universe than man."[271] Only in relationship and partnership with the nature every other creature can exist in good relationship. If that relationship is disturbed everything disintegrates and the ecological imbalance occurs.

Hindu wisdom teaches the integral relationship exists between human beings and everything else in the nature. The following list[272] illustrates this point clearly:

- One should not destroy the trees (Rig Veda Samhita vi-48-17)

271 G. Naganathan, *Ecological Spirituality: Hindu Scriptural Perspectives* (Delhi: New Age Books, 2004), p. 19.

272 For this concise list of ecological concerns in Hinduism I am indebted to the unpublished paper of Sriranjini Sivasubramanian, "Incompatability of Hindu ecofemiism with modern temples in India," Paper presented at the National Conference on "Natural resources – a multi religious approach," 14-16 October, 2009, organized by Centre for Cross-Cultural Studies, Chennai, South India.

- Plants are mothers and Goddesses (Rig Veda Samhita x-97-4)
- Sacred grass has to be protected from man's exploitation (Rig Veda Samhita vii-75-8)
- Plants and waters are treasures for generations (Rig Veda Samhita vii-70-4)
- One shall take care of quadrupeds (Taittiriya Samhita iv-4-10)
- One shall not find fault with animals (Chandogya Upanishad ii-18-2)
- Whoever injures the essence of food, kine or steeds is a robber who sinks both himself and his offspring into destruction (Rig Veda Samhita vii-104-10)

A Hindu believes that the unity between human beings and nature will only save the humanity from the present eco-crisis. The earth becomes full of sweetness with all its natural resources and the heaven can be experienced on earth. The Vedic seers and sages in Rig Veda unambiguously affirm the positive relationship that exists between the human and nature is portrayed beautifully in the form of a prayer as follows:

> For one who lives by eternal law the winds are full of sweetness; the rivers pour sweets; so may plants be full of sweetness for us. Sweet be the night and sweet the dawns; sweet be our Father Heaven to us. For us may the forest tree be full of sweetness, full of sweetness of the sun, And full of sweetness the kine for us.[273]

In some texts of Hindu religious tradition it is clearly portrayed that the creation is beautifully made by gods and it is created with a variety and for the good of the human beings. The responsibility of the human beings is to enjoy the good of god's creation and the five elements in it: sky, water, air, fire and earth which are interconnected to one another. They all bring goodness and welfare for the peace and tranquility of human beings. It is the responsibility of the human beings to appreciate these elements of nature and live in right relationship with them. For instance it is depicted about the earth (Prithvī) as the source of all life and humans have to respect it. Because Pṛthvī is considered to be the bestower of water, foodgrains and all other requirements for the survival of human beings, the prayer is offered in respect to it as follows:

> The earth which possesses oceans, rivers, and other bodies of water, and which gives us land to produce foodgrains and on which human

273 Rig Veda 1.90. 6-8. The translation of this text is taken from O. P. Dwivedi and B. N. Tiwari, *Environmental Crisis and Hindu Religion* (New Delhi: Gitanjali Publishing House, 1987), p. 86.

> beings depend for their survival, continue to possess these for all of us.[274]

In the same vein, the Vedic sage and seer offers prayer to Prithvī with high regard and respect asking:

> May she, our mother land, on whom grow wheat, rice and barley, on whom are born five races of mankind, homage to her, nourished by the cloud, and loved by the rain, whose castles and fortresses have been constructed by efficient engineers, in each province of whose men work hard for advancement, may God, the lord of life make our motherland, who beareth all precious things in her womb, pleasant to us on every side.[275]

Similar texts in the Vedic period depict the importance of all the five elements of nature. They belong to everyone and no one individual or a group can monopolize the rich natural resources available. The sages therefore advised everyone to see its richness:

> May the earth that bears people speaking varied languages, With various religious rights according to the places of abode, Enrich me with wealth in a thousand streams, Like a milk-cow that never fails.[276]

The above discussion clearly demonstrates the value of one of the five elements of the nature and how human life is integrally connected with it. Hinduism holds deep respect and worship to the nature so as to maintain ecological balance between human life and nature. The positive attitude towards nature and all its elements is what the Hinduism basically affirms. The crises occurred as long as scientific prowess and technological control over the nature is exercised in the name of progress and development.

Kautilya's Arthashastra (c. fourth century BCE.), a classical wisdom piece prescribes varying levels of fines for those who destroy trees, groves, and forests. Kautilya says:

> For cutting off the tender sprouts of fruit trees, flower trees or shady trees in the parks near a city, a fine of 6 panas shall be imposed; for cutting off the minor branches of the same trees, 12 panas, and for cutting off the big branches, 24 panas shall be levied. Cutting off

274 *Atharvaveda,* 12.1.3. This text is taken from O. P. Dwivedi and B. N. Tiwari, *Environmental Crisis and Hindu Religion* (New Delhi: Gitanjali Publishing House, 1987), p. 35.

275 The text cited above is *Atharvaveda,* 12.1. 42-43 taken from Ibid.

276 The text cited above is *Atharvaveda,* 12.1.45 taken from Ibid.

> the trunks of the same shall be punished [with a fine between 48-96 panas]; and felling of the same shall be punished with [a fine between 200-500 panas] ... For similar offenses committed in connection with the trees which mark boundaries, or which are worshipped ... double the above fines shall be levied.[277]

The kings and rulers in the ancient times primarily worked with the attitude of exploiting and plundering the vast riches of the forests. For them forests are the source of consumption and hunting. Thus, large portions of forest lands are annexed by the kings for these purposes. Contrary to this the sages in the ancient world maintained "conservation strategy" in their approach towards forests and all their rich natural resources. In fact they chose to reside in the forests and practiced an attitude of nonviolence and transformed their surroundings like "earthly paradise."[278] As the sages and hermits dwell and involved in deep devotion it was expected that there in the forests gods most often descend and communicate with human beings in a most intimate way.

In the great epic of Vālmīki *Rāmāyana* in *Aranyakānda* 1:1-5 it is depicted beautifully how Rāma, the prince of Ayodhya was astonished by the beauty and natural environment of the forest:

> Soon after entering the vast wilderness, the wilderness of Dandaka, Rāma, the self-disciplined and invincible prince, saw a circle of ashrams, where ascetics dwelt.*Kuśa* grass and bark garments were strewn about it, and, flooded with Brahminical splendor, it was as luminous and blinding to the eye as the sun's circle in heaven. It was a place of refuge for all creatures; its grounds were always kept immaculate, and troupes of *apsarases* ever paid homage there and danced. Spacious fire-sanctuaries made it beautiful, so too the sacrificial implements, the ladles and all, hide garments and *kuśa* grass, bundles of kindling, pitchers of water, and roots and fruit. Tall forest trees encircled it, holy trees that bore sweet fruit.[279]

---

277 This text is taken from Shamasastry, trans., Kautilya's Arthasastra (Mysore: Mysore Printing and Publishing House, 1967), p. 225, cited by Vasudha Narayanan, "Water, Wood, and Wisdom: Ecological Perspectives from Hindu Traditions," *Daedalus* 130:4 (2001), p. 188.

278 For more details on this point see Philip Lutgendorf, "City, forest, and Cosmos: Ecological Perspectives from the Sanskrit Epics," in Christopher Key Chapple and Mary Evelyn Tucker (eds.), *Hinduism and Ecology: The Intersection of Earth, Sky, and Water* (New Delhi: Oxford University Press, 2000), pp. 269-289.

279 This text is cited from Sheldon I. Pollock, *The Rāmāyana of* Vālmīki, Vol. 3, *Aranyakānda* (Princeton: Princeton University Press, 1986), p. 87, cited by David Lee "The Natural History of the Rāmāyaṇa," in Christopher Key Chapple and Mary Evelyn Tucker (eds.), *Hinduism and Ecology: The Intersection of Earth, Sky, and Water* (New Delhi: Oxford University Press, 2000), p. 254.

Swarnalatha Rangarajan analyses the subversive character of Ramayana by the subalterns in many folk versions. These versions not only subvert the patriarchal thrust of the traditional Valmiki Ramayana but also highlight the importance of the ecological concerns. She analyses Sitayanas where the traditional story of Ramayana was retold with the above focus. Rangarajan talks about the eco-centric value of the Sitayanas that are retold in order to highlight the integral relationship, what she calls as 'partnership model,' between men and women and nature. She writes:

> These eco-centric Sitayanas not only break down the Cartesian binaries of intellect/emotion, civilization/wilderness, becoming/being but they also conceive the feminine as a holistic ecosystem in which everything is connected to everything else. Various retellings of the epic celebrate not merely the feminine principle, but also its relationship to the biotic and the a-biotic. Rocks, deer and flowers are integrated in a synergetic relationship with feminine principle, *prakriti* which complements and nourishes the male principle, p*urusha*.[280]

Thus, the Hindu wisdom recognizes the relationship that human beings shared with all the important elements of nature that include animals, flora, fauna and other micro organisms. Every creature including human beings is related to every other creature and integrally they are connected to the cosmos. Thus, the entire creation is depicted in relational terms and everything functions in a complimentary way without any superior or inferior status.

Creation and ecology motif in the Islamic religious and wisdom texts: In Islam ecological concerns are sporadically present yet emphatically mentioned in those places. The broad principles of environmental ethics can be drawn from some verses that are stated from Qur'an. The Qur'an speaks of the existence of a cosmic balance (*mīzān*) and declares that everything except God is "measured out" (*qadar, qadr, taqdīr*)—that is, everything is given its natural principle of being and its place in the larger cosmic whole—and this is precisely the meaning of the *amr* (command) of an entity. The same message is expressed in a moral language: "God intends no injustice to any of His creatures. To Him belongs all that is in the heavens and the earth."[281]

"Created with divine deliberation, nature is so coherently interconnected and integrated, and works with such regularity and order, that it is God's prime miracle: if good is done to it or in it, good will return; if evil is wrought to it or in

280 Swarnalatha Rangarajan, "Forest Discourses by Women: Earth-centric Retellings of the Ramayana," in *Jeevadhara* XL: 235 (2010), p. 68.

281 S. Nomanul Haq, "Islam and Ecology: Towards Retrieval and Reconstruction," *Daedalus* 130:4 (2001), p. 153.

it, what accrues is sheer terror"[282] In the same light following words from Quran affirm:

> And you see mountains and think them solid [and stationary] but they are fleeting like clouds—such is the artistry of God who has well-completed [the creation] of everything. He is well acquainted with all that you do. If any do good, good will accrue to them therefrom; and they will be secure from the terror of the Doom. And if any do evil, their faces will be thrown headlong into the Fire.[283]

In a more clear and intensive text the verdict, handed down by a nonhuman creature, reads as follows:

> Let man not imagine . . . that just because he is superior to the animals they are his slaves. Rather it is that we are all slaves of the Almighty and must obey His commands . . . Let man not forget that he is accountable to his Maker for the way in which he treats all animals, just as he is accountable for his behavior towards his fellow human beings. Man bears a heavy responsibility.[284]

There exists the rule of equal sharing of water, and this rule makes no distinction between human beings and animals. Thus, for example, in the "Book of Ablution" of the Bukhari corpus, as well as in other corpora, there is the account of a man that runs as follows:

> who was walking along a road and felt thirsty. Finding a well, he lowered himself into it and drank. When he came out he found a dog painting from thirst and licking at the earth. He therefore went down again into the well and filled his shoe with water and gave it to the dog. For this act God Almighty forgave him his sins. The Prophet was then asked whether man had a reward through animals, and he replied: "In everything that lives there is a reward."[285]

---

282 S. Nomanul Haq, "Islam and Ecology: Towards Retrieval and Reconstruction," *Daedalus* 130:4 (2001), p. 153.

283 Translations of the Qur'an used for this article are The Holy Qur'an, trans. Abdullah Y. Ali (Brentwood, Md.: Amana Corporation, 1989); and The Qur'an Interpreted, trans. Arthur J. Arberry (New York: Macmillan Publishing Company, 1955). For this quotation is cited from Qur'an Surah 27:88-90 cited by S. Nomanul Haq, "Islam and Ecology: Towards Retrieval and reconstruction," *Daedalus* 130:4 (2001), p. 153.

284 Denys Johnson-Davies, *The Island of Animals, Adapted from an Arabic Fable* (Austin: University of Texas Press, 1994), p. 75.

285 Ibid., p. ix.

"In everything that lives there is a reward" may be considered a broad central principle of Islam's environmental ethics. The interdependence between human beings and the other nonhuman creation is the broader emphasis of environmental concern in the Islamic wisdom tradition. Human beings therefore, cannot claim any superior status over against the rest of creation.

Creation and ecology motif in the Buddhist religious and wisdom tradition: Buddhism although heavily rests on karma and rebirth theories as functional aspects of life, also lays emphasis on the individual's action and responsibility in relation to the environmental and ecological crises. Theravada Buddhism emphasizes that the environmental crises occurs due to human greed and selfishness.

In the Buddhist cosmological model, individual entities are by their very nature relational. There is no autonomous self that is set against the "other," be that other human, animal, or plant. Buddhist environmentalists reject the domination of one human over another and the human domination of nature, instead promote an ethic of compassion that respects biodiversity. In the view of the Thai monk Buddhadasa Bhikkhu,

> The entire cosmos is a cooperative. The sun, the moon, and the stars live together as a cooperative. The same is true for humans and animals, trees, and the earth. When we realize that the world is a mutual, interdependent, cooperative enterprise . . . then we can build a noble environment. If our lives are not based on this truth, then we shall perish.[286]

For contemporary engaged Buddhists most notably the Dalai Lama's sense of responsibility rooted in compassion lies at the heart of an ecological ethic. Nash summarizes the main emphasis of Dalai Lama's idea as follows:

> The world grows smaller and smaller more and more interdependent ... today more than ever before life must be characterized by a sense of universal responsibility, not only . . . human to human but also human to other forms of life.[287]

For many Buddhist environmentalists, compassion necessarily is the consequence of an understanding of all life forms as mutually interdependent.

---

286 Buddhadasa Bhikkhu, *Phutasasanik Kap Kan Anurak Thamachat* (Buddhists and the Care for Nature) (Bangkok: Komol Thimthong Foundation, 1990), p. 35; This reference is cited and translated by Donald K. Swearer, "Principles and Poetry, Places and Stories: The Resources of Buddhist Ecology," *Daedalus* 130:4 (2001), p. 229.

287 Nancy Nash, "The Buddhist Perception of Nature Project," in Buddhist Perspectives on the Ecocrisis, ed. Klas Sandell, in The Wheel, Vol. 18 (Kandy, Sri Lanka: Buddhist Publication Society, 1987), p. 73, cited by Donald K. Swearer, "Principles and Poetry, Places and Stories: The Resources of Buddhist Ecology," *Daedalus* 130:4 (2001), p. 234.

Others argue that a mere cognitive recognition of interdependence is a necessary but not a sufficient condition for an ecological ethic. These critics emphasize the centrality of practice in Buddhism and uphold the tradition's insistence on training in virtue and the threefold path to moral and spiritual excellence, morality, mindful awareness, wisdom. Among contemporary Buddhists, the Vietnamese monk Thich Nhat Hanh is the most insistent on the practice of mindful awareness in the development of a peaceful and sustainable world where one perceives the fundamental interconnectedness of life and a feeling of identification with all life forms. He writes:

> Look deeply: I arrive in every second to be a bud on a spring branch to be a tiny bird, with wings still fragile learning to sing in my new nest to be a caterpillar in the heart of a flower to be a jewel hiding itself in a stone. I am the mayfly metamorphosing on the surface of the river and I am the bird which, when spring comes arrives in time to eat the mayfly. I am the child in Uganda, all skin and bones my legs as thin as bamboo sticks and I am the arms merchant selling deadly weapons to Uganda. I am the twelve-year-old girl, refugee on a small boat who throws herself into the ocean after being raped by a sea pirate and I am the pirate, my heart not yet capable of seeing and loving Please call me by my true names so I can wake up and so the door of my heart can be left open, the door of compassion.[288]

Interrelatedness and interdependence between human and nonhuman in the cosmic order is once again the major emphasis of environmental concern found in Buddhism. This will enable for everyone and all forms of life in the cosmic order to live in harmony and peace.

Creation and ecology motif in the Jaina religious and wisdom tradition: Non–violence (ahimsa), non-possession (aparigraha), vows (vrata), and self-restraint (samyama) are the major ideas found in the Jaina environmental concerns. Jainism emphasizes a right conduct and attitude towards life. This attitude will enable every individual and community to live in right relationship with the environment. While there are number of vows that different individuals are expected to practice we shall mention few important ones[289] for our purpose in line with the wisdom tradition of Jaina religion.

288 Thich Nhat Hanh, "Please Call Me By My True Names," in *Hanh, Being Peace* (Berkeley: Parallax Press, 1984), pp. 63-64, cited by Donald K. Swearer, "Principles and Poetry, Places and Stories: The Resources of Buddhist Ecology," *Daedalus* 130:4 (2001), p. 235.

289 For the list of few vows and other vows I am indebted to the unpublished paper of Priyadarshana Jain in her paper entitled: "Environmental Awareness in Jainism and Buddhism," Paper presented at the National Conference on "Natural Resources – a Multi Religious Approach," 14-16 October, 2009, organized by Centre for Cross-Cultural Studies, Chennai, South India.

The four disciplinary vows are to be practiced in order to maintain the right attitude, thoughts and deeds to ones inner as well as outer environment. They also help to cleanse the soul of karmas, to maintain social harmony and environmental balance. They are four disciplinary vows:

(i) Practice equanimity
(ii) Practicing further restraint in limiting movements to gain self discipline
(iii) Advance spiritual exercise – to live like an ascetic for a limited period
(iv) Taking food only after serving someone needy and hungry

A true Jaina will judiciously avoid the following trades by not exploiting and burdening the environment:

(i) Livelihood from charcoal
(ii) Livelihood from destroying plants
(iii) Trade in ivory
(iv) Trade in fur, etc.
(v) Trade in alcohol and forbidden food stuffs
(vi) Trade in human beings and animals
(vii) Trade in destructive things like drugs, weapons, etc.
(viii) Works involving milling and mutilation
(ix) Work involving destruction of water resources
(x) Work involving breeding and rearing

Mahavira laid out a series of rules to assist everyone along the path to liberation. These rules were designed to minimize and eliminate karma through a careful observance of nonviolent behavior. Mahavira instructs his monks and nuns to avoid harming life in its myriad forms through various methods. These include explicit instructions for when and what and how to eat; when and how to travel; where and when to defecate; and from whom to accept food, as well as lists of various activities, including attendance at wedding ceremonies, to be avoided.[290]

All these rules, as well as the various preferred professions for laypersons, are to be observed in order to prevent harm to living beings. In fact, Mahavira even exhorts his monks and nuns not to gesture or point because "the deer, cattle, birds, snakes, animals living in water, on land, in the air might be disturbed or frightened, and strive to get to a fold or refuge, thinking 'the Sramana [monk] will harm me.'"[291] This profound respect for the natural world distinguishes Jainism among the world's religious traditions as potentially the most eco-friendly.

290 For more details on this point see, R. Williams, *Jaina Yoga: A Survey of the Mediaeval Sravakacaras* (London: Oxford University Press, 1964).

291 *Acharanga Sutra*, II:3.III.3 cited in Christopher Key Chapple, "A Traditional Science Grounded in Environmental Ethics," *Daedalus* 130:4 (2001), p. 215.

Right attitude, right knowledge and right conduct are the triple jewels of Jainism. This is not exclusively for Jaina but for all and at all times. Mahavira emphasized that all life is divine and sacred and it should be sustained by all means, therefore do not injure, abuse, oppress, enslave, insult, torment, torture or kill any creature or living beings. In this way Mahavira said that you are that which you intend to hit, injure, insult, torment, persecute, fortune, enslave and kill. In this way one who neglects and disregards the existence of earth, air, fire, water and vegetation disregards their own existence which is entangled with them.[292]

Creation and ecology motif in the ancient West Asian Texts: In the creation parallel stories of ancient West Asia we often come across significant allusions and motifs for ecological and environmental concerns. Few examples can be mentioned as follows:

Egyptian texts of creation: In Egypt, in the beginning life was not possible for human settlement because of continuous flowing of river water, and also due to the process on inundation. Only gradually by about 3000 BCE human settlement was possible; the flossing river was controlled and conserved. This is an evident factor of conservation of natural resources, that is, water, which was prominent in the Egyptian creation stories.[293] In one of the Egyptian texts we find that God created wind for everyone, for every creature to breathe. And also created great river (Nile) in order that poor might have equal right as rich people.[294]

Mesopotamian texts of creation: In one of the texts of Mesopotamian creation legends there is an expression of ecological concern. It reads as follows: "The land of Dilmun is clean ... the lion kills not, the wolf snatches not the lamb..."[295] This is a clear indication that there was a high regard and value for the creation and living beings and their harmony in creation. Even the naming of animals by Enkidu and his communion with animals is an important factor that human being are supposed to be the responsible stewards of God's creation.[296]

Babylonian texts of creation: In the Babylonian creation story *Enuma Elish*, when the creation is enacted and recited every year in the Babylonian festival of *akîtu*, which symbolizes seeking God's favor for the renewal of the entire creation and all its creatures thereby maintain peace and harmony with each other.[297]

---

292 The words are from *Acharanga Sutra,* cited by Priyadarshana Jain, "Environmental Awareness in Jainism and Buddhism," pp. 13-14.

293 S. G. F. Brandon, *Creation Legends of Ancient Near East* (London: Hodder and Stoughton, 1963), p. 15.

294 Hellmut Brunner, "Egyptian Texts," *Near Eastern Texts Relating to the Old Testament* (Philadelphia: Westminster Press, 1978), p. 7.

295 J. B. Pritchard (ed), *Ancient Near Eastern Texts* (Princeton: Princeton University Press, 1955), p. 38.

296 S. G. F. Brandon, *Creation Legends*, p. 126.

297 Ibid., p. 91.

Creation and ecology motif in the Biblical Texts: In the recent years there has been a great emphasis on rereading the Bible, particularly the creation account with ecotheological motif. The encounters of ecojustice are very much felt in reading the biblical texts. This was realized because of the awareness that human beings have broken their relationship with creation and consequently with God by plundering the natural resources. In the following paragraphs we shall present a brief overview of the OT and NT texts for a comprehensive understanding of ecological concerns in the Bible in the context of creation.

Genesis accounts of creation: There has been two accounts of creation, one belonging to P and another to J where we can recognize profound theological insights regarding ecotheology.

P narrative in Genesis 1:1-2:4a: In P account of creation in the book of Genesis God's creative activity is emphasized. God's creation is understood as positive and good.[298] But the problem continues due to the misinterpretation of Gen 1:26-28, which was always understood as a text for divine sanction for domination or exploitation to be carried out by human beings over the rest of creation.

The word 'dominion' or 'to rule' according to P's intention, certainly do not mean the plant and animal world on the part of human beings. According P human beings were not given automatic power either to misuse or to exploit God's creation or creatures. However, in contrast to God's intention human beings always misused the available resources in God's creation with a deliberate attempt.[299] In Gen 1:26b in the phrase: "And let them have dominion over…", the verb used here for dominion is *rādā*, literally means "to tread the wine press," which is also translated as 'dominion' and 'subdue'. Here the motif of domination is originated from the ancient West Asian (Babylonian and Egyptian) royal ideology according to Hans Wildberger and Werner Schmidt says Claus Westermann.[300] Moreover P's attitude here means not the one of exploitation of human beings over other creatures and creation, but it only means a positive sense of stewardship. This is the obvious intention of the author in the text of Genesis because, Israel, basically comes from a semi-nomadic context was always positive about their relationship with creation and environment.[301] The use of the word *kābaš* in Gen 1:28b also

298 Odil Hannes Steck, *World and Environment* (Nashville: Abingdon Press, 1980), p. 105.

299 Arthur McCormick, 'Subduing the Earth," *Frontline* 15:1 (March 1972), pp. 35-38.

300 Claus Westermann, *Genesis 1-11: A Commentary* (Minneapolis: Augsburg, 1984), p. 158.

301 Odil Hannes Steck, *World and Environment*, p. 62. The food habits of the ancient Hebrews were connected with nature. As it was mentioned in Deuteronomy 32:13-14 it was clearly affirmed about various kinds of food that comes to them from the nature by the bountiful hand and grace of Yahweh. First, what is stated as "increase of the hills" and "honey from the crag", which is usually the common food of the hunting people who would normally be involved in stalking their game upon the mountains, and securing their sweets from honey-combs found in the crags of the rocks. Second, "butter of the herd and milk of the flock, with fat of lambs and rams and goats" which seems to be the realistic food of the nomadic community as they

agrees with the word *rādā* in Gen 1:26b which was already discussed. The word *kābaš* is translated as "stamp", which does not confer the meaning of purposeful exploitation of the creatures, rather there is a limitation in human act of dominion in the sense of human responsibility to creatures.[302]

Yahwist accounts of creation: We find some important references in Gen 2:4b-3:24, where Yahwist was concerned about creation-ecological awareness. In Gen 2:9, the planting of garden and all kinds of trees with it is an indication that God as creator is very much concerned about the entire creation. In Gen 2:15 God commanded Adam to "till" and "keep" the earth so as to preserve its rich natural resources. In this context the J writer wants the human beings to be the responsible stewards of the God given natural resources of the earth so that all those available resources could be preserved for the future generations. Human beings, in this sense are not supposed to master over the creation in the sense of domination and exploitation, but to take care of it in a responsible manner.[303]

Creation accounts in Psalms and other Wisdom Literature: In the book of Psalms, particularly in Psalm 8 and 104, the psalmist calls the readers to be attentive to creation-ecological concerns. In Psalm 8 human beings are created and appointed to manage God's creation, but again here there is an emphasis of the positive role of human beings in caring God's creation as responsible representatives of God (Psalm 8:6ff).[304] In Psalm 104 care for God's creation and environment is very evident. Equal rights are given to both human and non-human creation and this idea is reflected throughout the psalm. It is also stressed in this psalm that God has special plan and design for each of the non-human creatures that are created and God's glory is to be manifested in and through each of the beings (both human and non-human) in the entire creation. In Psalms 148:7-14 and 65:12ff it is further confirmed that there exists a blessedness in the interrelationships and interconnection between God (creator) and humans, between human and non-human creation. Equal value for both human and non-human is stressed without undermining the value of human responsibility and position in the creation. Human beings are supposed to be aware that they are no more than responsible stewards of God's creation.[305]

---

get these products from their flocks and herds. Third and final, there are provisions of a settled agricultural people, who raise wheat and other grains, cultivate vineyards and make wine. For more discussion on this and related points see John W. Flight, "Nomadic Idea and Ideal in the Old Testament," *Journal of Biblical Literature* 42:3/4 (1923), pp. 159-207.

302 Gerhard von Rad, *Genesis* (London; SCM Press, 1972), p. 61.

303 Odil Hannes Steck, *World and Environment*, p. 67.

304 B. W. Anderson (ed), *Creation in the Old Testament* (Philadelphia: Fortress Press, 1984), p. 163.

305 William E. Gibson, "Eco-justice, New Perspective for a Time of Turning," in *For Creation's Sake* (Philadelphia: The Geneva Press, 1985), p. 15.

In the wisdom Literature we find several significant concerns on the idea of creation-ecology concerns. **Command to learn wisdom from the ant and its ways (Proverbs 6:6-8):** This is a didactic poem teaching the lesson that despite the physical weakness and insignificance an ant is able to impart some lesson to human beings. It is also an admonition and a warning against laziness of human beings taught by the wisdom teacher with the lesson being derived from an ant. This type of drawing lessons from the nature and the behaviour of animals was common in the ancient wisdom instruction imparted to the students by their teachers. **Wisdom of small creatures (Proverbs 30:24-28):** Proverbs 30:24-28 is part of larger unit of numerical sayings of 30:15-33. It is argued that the main purpose of this section is for instruction from the nature. This ungraded and simple numerical saying is intended for keen observation on the behavioral pattern of the animal world so as to derive lessons for human conduct. It talks about the fact in real life, success is not confined to bigness, but success is bestowed to the wise. If this is the focus of this passage then it envisages a strong and intrinsic relationship that exists between human and non-human world (animals, plants, birds and natural world). The animal behaviour in this passage illuminates that fact how human beings through simple observation should derive benefit from the animal life and behaviour.[306] The four creatures mentioned in this passage are unique and wise despite their tiny and feeble physical structure. They all live in harmonious life that human beings should learn from such animal behaviour.

In this way, human beings are to be in constant dialogue with the natural environment and thus the insights of wisdom could be learned from the so called small and "insignificant" creatures. This brings out the basic dynamics involved in the human and non-human struggle for survival. It is the question of our survival along with the creatures on this planet at this moment of serious disturbance in the eco system. The question of interdependence and inter-relatedness between human beings and other living beings in creation brings harmony and peace in the entire eco system.[307]

God is the source of all life on earth (Job 12:7-10): This text according to some scholars represents "wisdom instruction genre." This can be noticed by the words like: "ask," "speak" (as imperatives) in vv 7-8 and rhetorical question in vv 9 & 11 and a proverb in vv 11, 12. Here the poet is interested in teaching of animal wisdom, the teaching from the natural order of creation. Job, in this passage is giving a biting response to the friend's sarcastic speeches. In response to his friend's advise that Job better learn from the wise people, Job is arguing that all earthly creatures are able to instruct human beings. Norman C. Habel observes that many traditional and ancient proverbs discerned a relationship between patterns in nature and human behaviour (see, Prov 27:3, 8, 15, 17, 21).

306 Katharine J. Dell, "'Green' Ideas in the Wisdom Tradition," *Scottish Journal of Theology*, Vol. 47 (1994), p. 438.

307 P. G. George, "Ecological Agenda of the Wisdom," pp. 170, 174-175.

The nature and the behaviour of animals/plants were sometimes considered as mysterious not only make human beings to wonder but also to educate them to live in harmony with nature. Wisdom is seen as governing principle behind such mysteries of natural world.[308] Thus, vv 7-8 teach us that animals and plants are able to impart wisdom to human beings. But the question is what do they teach to human beings? The answer is given in vv 9-10. These creatures know that the "hand of Yahweh" has done this. This means that plants and animals do recognize the fact that God is the source of everything. David Clines observes that it is this sort of *mute testimony* that the creatures are giving about their own existence, and God's control of everything in the creation.[309]

Since God created the whole life on earth including human beings, God sustains everything upon the earth, and there is nothing beyond God's governing control. The language and tone in this passage reflect that God is at the centre of the quest for wisdom. Order can be observed in the creation. Since God is in control God sustains every human as well as non-human life on earth.[310] Since God is the creator and governor of all life on earth, human beings in particular depend on non-human creation for sustenance, life and even for wisdom.[311]

The entire speech of Yahweh in Job 38:1-40:5 reveals that God is the author and sustainer of the creation. The entire creation, both God's cosmic design and the design of the animal and bird kingdoms reflects the glory and might of God. God makes everything perfect and orderly and there is no question of confusion in this created order. In this regard, James Barr comments that the creation is viewed as God's "a part which extends out into far vistas of mystery which men of that time (Job in our context) could not penetrate."[312] The case of Job at the end of the Yahweh's speech is nothing but his recognition of the marvels of God's care and God's mysterious ways of ordering the creation. Since, God is the creator of this universe, God sustains it by love and with deep concern. On the one hand human beings are expected to learn and live in interaction and interdependence with the non-human creation, and on the other hand human beings need to acknowledge God's design and plan for the entire creation that includes animals, birds, and rest of the elements in the entire cosmos (Job 38:4-39:30). As much as God created human beings and sustains them with care and concern, the same can be applied to other non-human creation. Everything in the universe is purposefully designed by God and each creature and element in the creation has God's personal care and attention. This insight from the Yahweh speech of the book of Job gives us sufficient mandate for our interdependence upon the nature and use its resources

308 Norman C. Habel, *The Book of Job* (London: SCM Press, 1985), p. 219.

309 David J. A. Clines, *Job 1-20* (Dallas/ Texas: Word Books, 1989), pp. 293-294.

310 Katharine J. Dell, "'Green' Ideas in the Wisdom Tradition," pp. 446-451.

311 J. B. Curtis, "On Job's Witness in Heaven," *Journal of Biblical Literature* 102 (1983), p. 562.

312 James Barr, "Man and Nature: The Ecological Controversy and the Old Testament," *Bulletin of John Rylands Library* 55 (1972), p. 32.

in a responsible manner. Since everything is under God's control human beings can in no way claim their right and superiority over the rest of creation.

Creation and Ecology: A Theological and Ethical Appraisal: In the light of the foregoing discussion it is important that we make the following theological and ethical response in order to see the urgency of the situation in the Indian and global context.

First, it is necessary to create an awareness and consciousness about eco-theological imperative in the church and society at large. We must proclaim that the Israelite view on creation and ecology is very positive as she always maintained a right relationship with God's creation. Some activists on environment propose that in order to maintain the future eco-systems we need to think in terms of using earth resources without creating any harm to the life in the future.[313] This is a great realization that everyone should have.

Second, Bible gives us a clear mandate that there can be no compromise with human greed and thus exploitation of God's creation and its resources. The concept of love is very much applicable here in our understanding of care for God's creation. If we want to maintain our right relationship with God, we ought to that first in maintaining right relationship with God's creation, by demonstrating our love for all the creatures in God's creation. This could be like covenant relationship between God and human beings, and between human beings and other creatures. Our love towards creation can lead us out towards God and vice versa.

Third, if we are concerned about seeking justice it should be the eco-justice and before seeking his we should be aware of what is eco-justice. The theology of liberation is not only to care and express our solidarity with the oppressed in human community, but also liberate the oppression that the whole of our eco-systems are facing through due to the technological advancement and large-scale production. This does not mean to reduce the human dependency on natural resources, but only to seek the mutual support and benefit from God's creation. If we follow the principle of conservation, we might not do any harm to the long-existing eco-systems.

Fourth, the idea of companionship, partnership is very much needed in our understanding of ecotheology in God's creation. God has given us the responsibility to be care-takers and faithful stewards of his creation. This is a high ethical demand to which human beings are obliged to respond in order to take care and preserve the earth and its rich natural resources.

Fifth, new ways and means should be evolved as a result of our consciousness and awareness to the ecological crisis. Schumacher in his book entitled: *Small is Beautiful* in pages 134f suggests that it is better to go for the traditional and ancient patterns of cultivation, production and so on instead of destroying and plundering rare natural resources in the name of mass, large-scale production.

313 Vandana Shiva, "Anticipating the Future Eco-Systems," *Bangalore Theological Forum* 17 (1988), p. 46.

In the light of the above discussion and biblical mandate given to us, Christians should respond to the environmental crisis and contribute positively to the ever-increasing attempt to renew and replenish God's creation.

4.2 Creation in the Old Testament and the Scientific Theories on Evolution and Creation of the World

When was the world created? How was it created? Who created the world? Why was it created? Are usual and common questions people always ask and struggle to find satisfactory answers to such complex questions. Christianity with its religious background of Judaism, it is clearly affirmed that God created the world. Some conservative Christians show lot of interest in literally calculating the age of the world from the biblical years and tried to answer that the world came into existence a few thousand years ago. These views were propagated by several preachers in many Christian conventional meetings and church meetings. But these traditional views on the creation of the world were challenged and even questioned once the scientific discoveries on the origin of the world began to appear. The scientists began to claim that the world came into existence before billions of years. These scientific discoveries maintained the view that both the matter and the living creatures have been evolved from one form to another in a gradual process of development. At this juncture, the theologians and Christians struggled to make meaning out of the biblical accounts of creation. In the light of the above discussion, this presentation aims to first of all talk about the biblical accounts of creation and its distinct claims on the creation of the world, creatures and other elements of creation. Secondly, to present some popular scientific theories on creation and their distinct claims. Thirdly, to make some evaluatory comments on the possible reconciliation between the scientific claims and biblical faith.

Creation of the world in the Old Testament: In the Old Testament, we have the creation of the world story narrated in two different places and by two different traditions namely: Priestly account in Gen1:1-2:4a and Yahwistic account in Gen 2:4b-25. According to the priestly account of creation story the event of entire creation by God occurred in six days by succession. First day light, second day sky, third day land and vegetation, fourth day sun, moon and stars, fifth day birds, sixth day animals and man. On the seventh day God completed all the work and rested. Important question in this seven day sequence of creation is, what was there before the first day? Or before God said: 'Let there be light.' The church fathers understood this as *creatio ex nihilo* (creation out of nothing). The first church father who upheld this position was Theophilus of Antioch. He argued that matter were eternal, then it would mean God is on par with the matter. He said even though the biblical writers had not said explicitly that creation was formed from nothing, they certainly would have made it clear if God had used preexisting matter, now this interpretations are almost abandoned.[314] Some others argue that, verse 1 and verse 2 in Genesis 1 are two different accounts of creation story. Such proposals contended that there was a primeval universe before the existing one. God destroyed that primeval universe.[315] But now verse 2 is generally accepted as a description of the condition or a state before the act of creation. From the foregoing discussion we can conclude that the words of human beings are limited in expressing the unique idea of the beginning other than what is explained by the priestly writer in Genesis 1;1.

Yahwistic account of creation story seems to be older than the priestly account. The author in this story, in an interesting way brings the picture of creation events before its readers. The author fist depicts a situation where there are no plants, streams and human beings. Man is formed first out of dust which is in contrast to priestly account, where man and woman are created by the creative word of God. According to Yahwistic account, woman is formed out of the rib of Adam. God plants garden and trees. Then the author describes the rivers watering the garden. God formed animals and birds out of dust is another difference in J narrative than P account. In J, God first created man and all other things are created for man. Whereas for the priestly writer, God created everything first and at last human beings are created as a crown of creation. Yahwist's story also talks about the primeval state of man, and man's separation and the result of that separation from God.

Church's understanding about the creation of the world: The church inherited its belief on the creation of the world from Judaism. Jewish idea was a belief in a three-story universe. The heaven was believed to be a great vault arching over the earth. The earth itself was seen as a flat disc resting on pillar with waters above heaven.[316] The statements in the Apostolic Creed are implicit betrayal of this type of understanding. It could be said that the belief of time was given a biblical interpretation and dogmatic sanction. The geo-centric Aristotelian universe idea came up widely in the 4th century BCE. It consisted of a central earth surrounded by revolving, translucent spheres in which sun and other planets are attached. During 13th century CE this Aristotelian idea of universe was adopted by a Christian theologian Thomas Aquinas. Regarding the question of the relationship between creation and time, Augustine is of the view that the time was created with the world so that the creation did not begin in time but at the beginning of the time.[317]

314 Richard H. Overmann, *Evolution and Christian Doctrine of Creation* (Philadelphia: Westminster Press, 1952,), p. 240.

315 Clyde T. Francisco, "Genesis," *The Broadman Bible Commentary* (Tennessee: Broadmann and Holmann, 1955), p. 121.

316 Richard H. Overmann, *Evolution and Christian Doctrine of Creation*, (Philadelphia: Westminster Press, 1952) p. 238.

317 Robert McHenry, "Cosmology," *The New Encyclopedia Britannica,* Vol. 3, p. 661.

Scientific theories on the origin of the world: Among any available theories of science on the origin of the world, we shall concentrate on only few important ones.

Big-Bang model: This was a widely popular theory for the evolution of the universe. It's essential feature is the emergence of the universe from a state of extremely high temperature and density. The so-called big-bang occurred at least 10 billion years ago. Although this type of the origin of the universe was presented by Friedmann and Abbe George Lemaitre in 1920s, the modern version was developed by George Gamoro and his colleagues in 1940s. According to the bi-bang model, the universe expanded rapidly from a highly compressed primordial state, which resulted in a significant decrease in density and temperature. Soon afterwards, the dominance of matter over anti-matter may have been established by the process that also predict proton decay. During this stage many types of elementary particles may have been present. After a few seconds, the universe cooled enough to allow the formation of certain nuclei. The theory predicts that definite amounts of hydrogen, helium, and lithium were produced. Their abundance agree with what is observed today. About 1,000,000 years later the universe was sufficiently cool for atoms to form. The radiation that also filled the universe was then free to travel through the space.[318] This model presents the formation of universe from a compressed primordial state, then formation of matter, nuclei organic and inorganic elements, and radiations.

Evolution theory in Biology: According to this theory, various types of animals and plants have their origin in other preexisting types and that the distinguishable differences are due to modifications in successive generations. It was Charles Darwin the treatise on evolution that would revolutionize all later biological study. The heart of Darwinian evolution is the mechanism of natural selection. It proceeds from the past that there are a greater number of offspring produced by most organisms than can survive to maturity. A high rate of mortality through starvation, predation, disease and accidents reduces the population. The survival individual which may have the smaller variation that enables them to live longer and reproduce, pass on their advantage to succeeding generations, which may evolve superior means of adaptation. Part of the proof of evolution is provided by the fossil record which shows a succession of gradually changed forms leading up to the present structural similarities among living forms also point to common ancestry, as do similarities in the embryonic development of different species.[319] In 1871, Darwin published a work entitled: *The Descent of Man* where he extended the above discussed theory to human beings. Darwin wanted "to show how human characteristics might be accounted for in terms of the gradual modification of anthropoid ancestors by the process of natural

---

318 Robert McHenry, "Big Bang model," *The New Encyclopedia Britannica,* Vol. 2, p. 205.

319 Ibid., p. 623.

selection."[320] Further it is understood that the Darwin's theory of evolution totally changed and challenged our understanding of God's creation of human beings in the Bible. Sarojini Henry comments: "Human existence hitherto considered to be sacrosanct was brought within the sphere of natural law and explained using the same categories applied to non-human animals. In short, the theory of evolution has changed our understanding of nature and thereby challenged our views of humanity and also our concept of God's relation to the universe."[321]

Both the above mentioned theories bring forth significant clues of origin and the existence of the world. This can be summarized as follows: (i) The universe came into existence before billion of years; (ii) The present form of the universe and creation are the result of evolution by natural selection; (iii) Human beings, animals, birds, plants etc, all developed from similar forms of species to more sophisticated form.

Science versus Scripture: For several centuries, Christians believed that creation account in the Bible is the correct description of the creation of the world. The location of Eden has been the object of geographical speculation with a variety of sites proposed for its trees and rivers. The time of Adam and Eve has been given careful historical scrutiny and assigned to variety of periods from 4000 BCE. Christians claimed that without doubt God created heaven and earth and all the creatures. But with the discovery of scientific theories, the Christian claims on the origin of the universe is seriously threatened. The Christian church became alert and began to think seriously the questions raised by the scientists on the origin of the world and human beings. The controversy between Christian view and scientific origin of the world has been looked in different ways. We shall summarize these ways briefly in the paragraphs that follow.

Reaffirming Approach: This is a type of approach in which scriptural details are presented and reaffirmed against modern scientific theories. Here scientific theories are treated as enemies to scriptural beliefs. The basic presupposition of this theory is that the Bible is infallible word of God and it contains the truth ever known about the creation. So any theory which seems to be different is opposed. The flaws in the scientific theories are printed out. For example, Charles Hodge, who lived in the late nineteenth century pointed out that the Darwin's theory as "anti-scriptural theory of the universe." The most important flaw that he found in Darwin's theory was that it was a mere hypothesis, incapable of showing any proof. He also noted its failure to take seriously the distinction between natural and artificial species that is, between genuinely different species and sample varieties within species.[322]

---

320 Sarojini Henry, *Science Meets Faith: An Interdisciplinary Conversation* (Mumbai: St. Paul's Publication, 2009), p. 88.

321 Ibid.

322 David N. Livingstone, *Darwin's Forgotten Defenders: The Encounter Between Evangelical Theology and Evolutionary Thought* (Grand Rapids, MI: William B. Eerdmans Publishing

Relating Approach: This is another type of approach where the modern scientific theories are seen in relation to biblical creation account. Many different terms are used in relation to this: Theistic evolution, scientific creationism, scientific materialism etc. Here, the scripture is reinterpreted on the basis of the modern scientific theories.

In the case of *theistic evolution* the following important points are shared between science and the Bible. The design argument is primarily put forward here in this context. There is a designer, may be God who had created the world according to some definite purpose. Nature exhibits such beauty and intelligibility that theologians often wonder if the physical universe reflects the purpose of a pre-existent mind. The argument for design was particularly made popular in early nineteenth century by William Paley in his book entitled as: *Natural Theology* (1802). Paley argues that anybody who finds a watch the field would be overwhelmed by the intricate and delicate organization and would assume that the watch was designed. Paley further argues that it is unlikely that such an object would arise by chance. This argument is not weak if the person had not seen the watch before or if the watch did not function properly. Since the universe resembles a watch in its organization, Paley argued that there must be a cosmic designer who had arranged the world with a definite purpose.[323]

As a rival theory against Darwin's theory of evolution, creationism (theistic evolution) was constructed which posited creation of species by a supernatural being did not appeal to these scholars partly because such an assumption meant the existence of a putative creator who must have worked on intricate details, a proposition seemed to be beneath his dignity. But, these biologists were also aware that Darwin's explanation of evolution by natural selection had not solved every problem. Some problems like the origin of life, or the origin of faculty of vision and some complex biochemical systems remained unexplained. These were like a black box, namely, something whose general functions were known, but whose inner working remained hidden in darkness.[324]

In the case of *scientific creationism* it all started with the banning of teaching of Darwin's theory in the schools in 1925 by means of a Butler Act. With further developments of defying this act, the creationists of Christian tradition have opposed all along the evolutionary theory of Charles Darwin. This was due to the reason that acceptance of evolution is incompatible with their religious faith. Stating the stand of creationists John Haught argues, "These are Christian theists who agree with skeptics that Darwinian evolution, if true, would logically ride out the idea of God and a purposeful Universe." Then he continues, "To Creationists, contemporary evolutionary biology is much more than an innocuous act of

Company, 1953), p. 102.

323 Sarojini Henry, *Science Meets Faith*, p. 198.

324 Ibid.

scientific ideas devoid of theological implications."[325] According to scientific creationism then creation is generally understood to indicate instantaneous origin of all things in the universe through the action of some supernatural process, so that things are assumed to have been created as they are now, except for some minor changes. Christian creationism started as a vague notion of the literal reading of the creation story given in the book of Genesis. When Darwin's theory of evolution began to propose that life on earth including human life is the result of chance mutation and natural selection, it meant that human persons, in common with animals, were products of blind chance. For the creationists, these factors were totally contrary to biblical claims. Hence their main attack was on Darwin's theory of evolution which was already taught in public schools. It is because of this reason the creationists wanted to uphold the inerrancy of the Bible and its content on creation. Moreover these creationists argue for a presence of scientific order in the Genesis creation story itself in order that it is placed alongside evolutionary theory as a competing set of scientific ideas.[326]

In the case of *scientific materialism*, it is believed that the matter is the fundamental reality in the universe. The materialist believes that all phenomena will eventually be explained in terms of matter, energy and their reactions. Scientific materialism implies that science and materialism provide the key to comprehend the world and its constituents. Thus, scientific materialism includes the assumption, known as scientism, that the scientific method is the only reliable way of gaining any understanding of reality. This view certainly be seen in conflict with any religious idea which focuses on the metaphysical ingredients, let alone with claims to supernatural revelation. To explain this process of scientific materialism we would cite a couple of scholars' views in the following paragraph.

Richard Dawkin in his work entitled: *The Blind Watchmaker: Why the Evidence of Evolution Reveals a Universe Without Design* supports Darwin's theory of evolution of the origin of species. He writes to state his view as follows:

> Natural selection, the blind, unconscious, automatic process which Darwin discovered and which we now know is the explanation for the existence and apparently purposeful form of all life, has no purpose in mind. It has no mind, and no mind's eye. It does not plan for the future. It has no vision, no foresight, no sight at all. It can be said to play the role of a watchmaker in name, it is the blind watchmaker.[327]

In the above discussion it is clear how Dawkin out rightly defends Darwin's theory of natural selection and evolutionary theory. However, Dawkin's criticism

325 John Haught, *God After Darwin*, pp. 26-27.

326 Sarojini Henry, *Science Meets Faith*, p. 194.

327 Richard Dawkin, *The Blind Watchmaker: Why the Evidence of Evolution Reveals a Universe without Design* (New York: W.W. Norton & Company, 1961), p. 5.

comes very sharp on the role of religion in explaining the origin of the world. He writes:

> I think a case can be made that faith is one of the world's great evils, comparable to smallpox virus but harder to eradicate. Faith, being belief that isn't based on evidence, is the principle vice of religion … Don't fall for the argument that religion and science operate on separate dimensions or are connected with quite separate sorts of questions. Religions have historically always attempted to answer questions properly belonging to science.[328]

On the basis of the above discussion it is claimed that the science is the answer for all problems and processes that are operative in this universe and religious claims in this direction cannot be proved with substantial evidence. All the three stands like theistic evolution, scientific creationism and scientific materialism have somehow tried to come closer with the Biblical claims of creation often ended up in contradictory views.

In relating approach on the whole there was an attempt made to seek scientific explanations from the biblical accounts of creation of the world and human beings. In the first creation story of the Priestly writer in Genesis 1 the words like **kind** (min) and **day** (yom) are given meaning in relation to evolutionary theory. Some type of evolution is observed where the Priestly writer develops the creation story from lower form of creatures up to the higher form, that is, the human beings. But the major difference in this comparison is that here in the biblical story the evolution is not by natural selection but by God's creation.

Recognizing Approach: In this type the basic purpose and literary types of scientific theories and scripture are to be recognized as interdependent. Here, the theologians recognize biblical account and scientific theory serving as different purposes. In the words of Conrad Hyers: "Scientific and religious languages, correspondingly, serve different function operate out of different assumptions, draw upon different experiences, use different methods, and deal with different type of truth. To use a game analogy, they are playing very different types of games according to different rules, with different goals, and on different playing fields. They come in conflict when we try to play one game by the rules of the other or presume that they are really one and the same game."[329] In the light of this discussion science and scripture are taken as different type of studies, having different aims and participations in human life. Their purpose and method of investigation are different.

---

328 Richard Dawkin, "Is Science Religion?" in Ian Barbour, *When Science Meets Religion*, p. 155.

329 Conrad Hyers, *The Meaning of Creation: Genesis and Modern Science* (Atlanta: John Knox Press, 1984), p. 33.

Owen C. Thomas quotes Paul Tillich in his book *Introduction to Theology* as follows: "Theology has no right and no obligation to prejudice a physical or historical, sociological or psychological inquiry. And no result of such an inquiry can be directly productive or disastrous for theology." And he also concludes, "Theology cannot interfere or intervene with any of the area of the special sciences or prejudice any of their investigations, nor can any scientific conclusion be decisive for theology."[330] So, while describing the theology of creation, Thomas says when scientists talk about the origin of the universe they are referring to the earliest state of affairs in the history of universe, but theologians speak of why there is universe at all and not simply nothing. Thus, in the recognizing approach the difference that exist between scientific theories and Christian scripture and doctrines are very much taken seriously.

Evaluation on different approaches: The above mentioned approaches are not completely satisfactory. The problems are inherent in each of the approach we discussed above. The reaffirming approach has the presupposition that the Bible is infallible word of God. It means to us, not just the Bible as the word of God but the Bible as it is understood in the word of God. So, those who support reaffirming approach can't accept anything which is in opposition to their understanding of the Bible. Let us take this point seriously that the Bible is infallible word of God and all that it contains is true to believe. Then how do we account for different creation stories in the Bible? Which account of creation in the Bible should be equated with the scientific theories? Those who argue against the evolutionary theory of creation only sought to defend the Bible without providing substantial proof to the creation stories and the origin of the universe in the Bible itself.

Relating approach presupposes the infallibility of the word of God. Here the older understanding of the scripture is reinterpreted and the new interpretation is given as the basis of new scientific theories. In one way reinterpretation of the scripture means that old interpretation is wrong. Additionally it implies that there is enough ambiguity to interpret the biblical account of creation. So there is no constant and basic truth that one can affirm in this matter. In another way, the scripture becomes the handmaid of science. In this interpretation the major criterion is the new scientific invention that accommodates scripture. Nevertheless, after some decades, scientists may propose another theory with much concrete evidence which is against the present theory, then once more we may need to say what we said once is wrong now.

Recognizing approach accepts that both science and religion are two different areas of life and they deal with different aspects of life. This approach tries to avoid many problems and questions raised science against the scripture. In this light we may now ask the following questions: what is the relationship between scientific theories and biblical stories on creation of the world and human beings?

330 Owen C. Thomas, *Introduction to Theology* (Serampore: Indian Theological Library, 1989), p. 6.

What is the relationship on the whole between science and religion? Where do science and religion interacts each other? In this regard John Macquarie argues: Is there indeed a dimension which science misses, and which religion or theology perceives? When the theologian renounces the world of empirical fact to scientist, has he himself anything else to talk about?[331] Macquarie's question are raised in the context of human understanding that the universe as a self-regulating mechanism, where each event that takes place is adequately accounted for in terms of other events within the system without much appeal to supernatural force. While recognizing approach helps to avoid many complications and contradictions within the science and religion debate, at times it tends to be also indifferent to each other as if they are not at all connected to one another and that they are two separate entities of human life.

Conclusion: The biblical account on creation can't be taken either as chronologically correct or as scientific account concerning the origin of the world and human beings. Trying to read the Bible through the lens of scientific theories will not help the biblical reader to understand its purpose. As was argued earlier, even though it is better to recognize the difference between the scientific theories and the Bible to some extent, can we simply leave them apart without seeking a meaningful dialogue? What does the creation account in the Bible mean to modern human beings who are fully aware of scientific theories on creation? Does the creation account in the Bible has more to say than simply confessing God as the creator? Should not a biblical scholar or a theologian make sense out of creation stories in the Bible that would be meaningful in the modern age of scientific developments? Is it not necessary to talk about the dialogue and meaningful partnership between science and religion, in our case the scientific theories and biblical accounts on creation of the world and human and as well as non-human beings.[332]

4.3 Yahweh in Relation to the Old Testament and its Implication for God's Revelation in and through Jesus Christ and the Ongoing Revelation of God in Today's World

In the Old Testament in every stage and in every book God becomes central religious thought who was depicted as the one who determines and controls the events of human beings.[333] In the midst of several names used for God in the OT, the proper name for God used in Tetragrammaton YHWH carries more definite and concrete meaning in the context of Israelite faith. Perhaps Yahweh as an

331 John Macquarie, *Principles of Christian Theology* (New York: Charles Scribner's Sons, 1986), pp. 19, 28-29.

332 For a detailed discussion on this are related area see Sarojini Henry, *Science Meets Faith*, pp. 229-252.

333 J. Stanly Chestnut, *The Old Testament Understanding of God* (Philadelphia: The Westminster Press, 1968), p. 13.

important theme of Old Testament theology is presented in the variety of material contained in the Old Testament. Some OT theologians use the theme Yahweh as the very center of their theological discussion, presumably because everything in the OT refers to this God, Yahweh. The very name Yahweh, its origin, and history has been subjected to variety of disputed views, perhaps, there is no consensus among the scholars on these issues.[334] Some scholars argue that it is not important for OT theology to consider the origin of the name and related issues. But, what needs to be concentrated is that the confession of the name on the basis of divine revelation, and the monotheistic practices of Yahwism in the context of Israelite worship.[335] Eichrodt is of the view that "it may by no means pointless to inquire what meaning originally lay behind the name Yahweh."[336]

When considering the center of OT theology in the midst of variety of centers offered by different OT theologians, some scholars would prefer God as Yahweh, the dynamic and unifying center of OT theology. The reason for doing this is not to make Yahweh as static thematic concept, but Yahweh as all pervading and dynamic throughout the Old Testament, in order that they may arrive at some systematic presentation of the entire material of the Old Testament. According to Werner H. Schmidt, on the basis of the first commandment in the Decalogue, and on the claim that Yahweh as the unique and perhaps the only God could become an answer in the unifying principle of the OT in the midst of its multiple testimonies. For Walther Zimmerli, it is the same Lord, Yahweh from the creation of the world till the post-exilic time, who is operative in the OT and that should be the commitment of the theological work of the Old Testament.[337]

Origin and meaning of the name Yahweh: On the basis of whatever the historical records available from Egypt the name YHWH was not present. Therefore the name YHWH was probably unknown in Israel during the Egyptian bondage.[338] G. R. Driver, however, argues that the name *Yāh* perhaps an equivalent to YHWH has the origins even before the Egyptian bondage of Israelites.[339] The philological and historical scholarship in this regard has not yet reached to any common agreement. The extrabiblical evidence also reflects how this name was used in complex forms even before it is revealed to Moses in Exodus.

As per the traditional understanding, the name Yahweh has the origin from the Midianites, according to Kenite hypothesis; a tern borrowed from Moses'

334 Raymond Abba, "The Divine Name Yahweh," *Journal of Biblical Literature* 80 (1961), p. 320.

335 Ludwig Köhler, *Old Testament Theology* (Philadelphia: The Westminster Press, 1957), p. 40.

336 Walther Eichrodt, *Theology of the Old Testament,* Vol. 1, p. 187.

337 Walther Zimmerli, *Old Testament Theology in Outline* (Atlanta: John Knox Press, 1978).

338 E. C. B. MacLaurin, "YHWH the Origin of Tetragrammaton," *Vetus Testamentum* 12 (1962), p. 439.

339 G. R. Driver, "The Original Form of the Name 'Yahweh': Evidence and Conclusions," *ZAW* 46 (1928), p 24.

father-in-law, Jethro.[340] However, there are several possibilities proposed by different scholars. We shall consider few of them at this juncture. W. F. Albright thinks that thc name *yāhu* could be older than the tern YHWH and its occurrence is certain as an abbreviated form of Tetragrammaton known from the time of Moses. Further Albright brings out the validity or importance of Yahweh in the OT as distinct than the so-called equivalent forms present in the ancient West Asian texts. Picking up an example from Anthropomorphic presentation of Yahweh in the OT, Albright[341] argues that, in the West Asian context God's are shifted from astral forms to zoomorphic, dedromorphic etc, but in the OT Yahweh, whose human form was always manifested behind and in and through his glory (*kabodh* in Exod 33:23). Albrecht Alt strongly holds the view that the very existence of people of Israel as tribes is due to their union in the worship of God Yahweh, it is only within this framework of worship of Yahweh, can we talk about history of Israelites as a nation and people of God in their own right.[342] However, Alt thinks that due to the nature of sagas present in the OT, we cannot ascertain the process by which Israelite tribes were united in the worship of Yahweh.

Yahwist mentions in Gen 4:26b, the worship of Yahweh began with Enosh or from his time. But there is hardly any evidence regarding the name Enosh; perhaps the idea here is not to begin the worship of Yahweh with murderer Cain but with innocent Enosh.[343] The use of proper name Yahweh by the Yahwist is very remarkable in time with his theological framework. Vriezen argues that for J, Yahweh is the Lord of Israel in their historical realm, and moreover Yahweh is not only God of Israel but also the God of the whole world.[344] These ideas of J however do not answer the question of how old was the worship of Yahweh before the time of Moses and in what form. There is no genuine records to answer these questions.

In the book of Exodus, there are two places where the revelation of divine name Yahweh is mentioned: Exod 3:14-15 belongs to E source and Exod 6:2-3 belongs to P source. According to the first text, there is a claim in the text for the religion of Patriarchs and Yahwistic faith of later Israel that is, from Moses' time, but at the same time the text identifies Yahweh as the God of Fathers, who were the ancestors of Israel, that is, the patriarchs.[345] Alt places Exod 3:24 in relation to 3:14-15 where in the former text Yahweh and God of Fathers are clubbed together. Even though the sagas of Patriarchs and Moses are different, they are brought

340 Raymond Abba, "The Divine Name Yahweh," p. 320.

341 W. F. Albright, *From Stone Age to Christianity* (Baltimore: John Hopkins Press, 1946), p. 198.

342 Albrecht Alt, *Essays on OT History and Religion* (Oxford: Basil Blackwell, 1966), p. 3.

343 I. Lewy, "The Beginnings of Worship of Yahweh. Conflicting Biblical Views," *Vetus Testamentum* 6 (1956), p. 430.

344 Th. C. Vriezen, *An Outline of OT Theology* (Oxford: Basil Blackwell, 1970), pp. 56-58.

345 F. M. Cross Jr., "Yahweh and the God of the Patriarchs," *Harvard Theological Review* 55 (1962), p. 227.

together in close relationship to one another. When we read the phrase in 3:14: *I will be that I will be,* many interpretations surround this statement. According to Goitein, the name YHWH came into existence from YH, YW, YHW, later Yahweh is derived. If we accept Yāh as the abbreviated form of YHWH then this name took forms like Yahwā then it took the form Yahweh and this must have happened in the midst of monotheistic and exclusive claims that Yahweh alone is the God of Israelites. Perhaps, Moses would have initiated this so-called new name in the context of Egyptian bondage of the people of Israel.[346] Walther Zimmerli argues that the verb *hyh* should be understood in the light of Exod 33:19 where the sovereign freedom of Yahweh is manifested, that is, even in relation to his name, Yahweh can at times reveal his name, at times refuses to do so, thereby allowing human beings to comprehend him.[347] The idea that the name Yahweh was revealed to Moses for the first time here in this text of Exod 3:14 is disputed because, people in bandage would not have accepted Moses as their speaker in the hitherto unknown name of God People of Israel accepted Moses only because he was a messenger of God of Fathers already known to them.[348]

In another passage, Exod 6:2-3 where revelation of God's name is mentioned stands distinct with the occurrence of the phrase: "I am Yahweh." Form critical analysis shows that this text does not speak of an unknown name, but the very known name. Priestly writer points out to various traditions, that God revealed himself in different forms in different times. To the patriarchs as El Shaddai, but to Moses the new name Yahweh was made known.[349]

Yahweh in relation to "El" and 'Baal": The divine name Yahweh is often used in relation to El and Baal. In the former name as equivalent or patron deity and in the latter case as an opposite deity in the cultic setup. A brief discussion on each of these deities in relation to Yahweh would be helpful at this point.

El is the most prominent deities of Canaanite religion. Often the name El is identified with Yahweh of Israel, especially during the time of patriarchs and their worship of God's in epithets of El (El-Elyon in Gen 14:18; El-Roi in Gen 22:14 and El-Shaddai in Gen 17:1).[350] Perhaps El was venerated as chief deity during pre-Israelite time in the land of Canaan, but to determine with certainty how this could have been done is very difficult. Zimmerli argues convincingly how the term El has gradually become Yahweh on the basis of Gen 14:18-20. Here in this text, the high priest Melchizedek called as the priest of "the most high God/ El"—El Elyon (verse 19). However, in 14:22 Abram speaks of Yahweh, as God

346 S. D. Goitein, "Yahweh the Passionate. The Monotheistic Meaning and Origin of the Name YHWH," *Vetus Testamentum* 6 (1956), pp. 1-9.

347 Walther Zimmerli, *Old Testament Theology*, p. 20.

348 J. P. Hyatt, "Yahweh as the God of My Father," *Vetus Testamentum* 5 (1955), p. 136.

349 Brevard S. Childs, *Exodus: A Commentary* (London: SCM Press, 1979), p. 112.

350 Ronald E. Clements, *Old Testament Theology* (England: Marshall, Morgan and Scott, 1978), p. 64.

of most high that is, El. In this sense El can be none other than Yahweh.[351] In Psalm 19 and in Pss 29:10; 104:3, we find a sequence of El identified with God of Israel's patriarchs with the God of Yahweh of Exodus. In Psalm 19, Yahweh is called as El related to sun-God whose tent is set in the waters (Ps 19:4).[352] Otto Eissfeldt argues that El is the God of Canaan, when Israelites invaded Canaan, later Israelites fused El with Yahweh. Further Eissfeldt noticed that there is no obvious tension between El and Yahweh as in the case of Yahweh and Baal. On the basis of certain other texts (Deut 32:8-9; Psalm 72), El is considered to be the highest God, but the name Yahweh in the context of the creator of the world (and the king of the Gods) has already developed fully with the invasion of Israelites into Canaan, and Yahweh assuming superior status, as highest, even the sole God.[353]

Yahweh in relation Baal is also used widely in different contexts of the OT material; but unlike El, Baal is used as a contrasting deity to Yahweh. F. M. Cross comments that Yahwism on the whole is highly indebted to the myths of Baal, especially in the hymns depicting Yahweh as divine warrior, borrowed directly from Canaanite description on Baal as storm god.[354] Some scholars argue that Psalm 29 was originally an ancient hymn of Baal with little modifications used in the cultus of Yahweh. In this Psalm, God (Yahweh) is depicted as the warrior king would even shatter the mountains and the whole nature trembles before him.[355] When Israelites lived side by side with Canaanites there was always a possibility of overlap and exchange between the worshippers of Yahweh with the worshippers of Baal. For instance, in the family names of Saul and David we find this evident as we see in 2 Sam 2-4 chapters and 1 Chr 8:34. However, during the time of national consciousness of organization of the nation under monarchy, worship of Baal was considered as against the worship of Yahweh.[356] This was evidently seen in the ninth century prophets especially in Elijah, with striking phrase: "Yahweh versus Baal." During this time, it was felt that there was a serious threat to Yahwism due to the influence of Baalism to the extent that the name Yahweh seems to have been forgotten.

Theological articulation on the theme of Yahweh: In the above discussion, we considered few issues related to the name Yahweh in its historical context along with some details on the very term itself. In the following paragraphs we look at the claims of Israel in their faith journey on the name Yahweh and its significance will be seen later in the light of revelation of God in and through Jesus Christ.

351 Walther Zimmerli, *Old Testament Theology*, p. 32.

352 Walter Witfall, "El Shaddai or El of Fields," *ZAW* 92 (1980), p. 30.

353 Otto Eissfeldt, "El and Yahweh," *Journal of Semitic Studies* 1 (1956), pp. 25-37.

354 F. M. Cross, *Canaanite Myth and Hebrew Epic* (Cambridge: Harvard University Press, 1978), p. 147.

355 Ibid., p. 160.

356 Walther Eichrodt, *Theology of the OT I*, pp. 201-202.

Yahweh as warrior God: Old Testament contains ample number of wars fought by Israel with other nations. At the very first sight if one looks at the wars there seems to be full of violence and bloodshed at least for a long time among the Israelites, in the context of wars. In fact, Yahweh remained as war-God for the people of Israel before and after their settlement in the land of Canaan. However, Yahweh fought for Israel with their enemies not so much be means of armies (although armies are part of the war strategy) but by means of a miracle (Joshua 24:12).[357] At the time of danger and defeat Israel solely depended on the miraculous power of Yahweh, so that they looked forward Yahweh's miraculous saving act at that time. At the same time Yahweh considered the enemies of Israel as his enemies and wars of Israel as his wars (Judg 5:23-31; 1 Sam 18:17). Furthermore Yahweh gives strength to the warriors. Yahweh inspires the heroes and warriors fight before the presence of Yahweh by deriving strength from him 9 Num 32: 22, 27, 32). All through the wars of Israel Yahweh is active and is the one who bestows victory to them. On this concern some would argue for the presence of the concept of holy war. It was perhaps Isaiah of 8th century who makes first attempt in the lines of holy war by calling king Hezekiah to entirely depend upon Yahweh's miraculous power (Isa 7:4-8). It is in the context of holy war the prophets of Israel confronted with the kings, when the kings secularized the institution of war for their selfish motives.[358]

At the same time, it should be noted that Yahweh not only defended Israel in their wars, but even subjected them to the threats of dreadful wars as a kind of punishment whenever Israel rebelled or sinned against Yahweh. Even at those crisis points, Yahweh continued to show his compassion on his people by promising a continuous kingdom and the nation. In this sense Yahweh was unique and compassionate God, ever loving his people despite their attitude of rebellion towards Yahweh. This act of God seems to be totally different in Israel when compared to other nations.[359]

At certain other times, Yahweh even grants victory to other nations over against Israel as a sign of God's own freedom and choice (1 Sam 4; 1 Kings 14:15; 2 Kings 8:12-13)[360] Despite the fact that Yahweh as God of Israel, the latter was defeated utterly in the hands of their enemies. At times, Yahweh himself deserts Israel and give them to the hands of their enemies (Josh 7:7-8 and 1 Sam 4: 3,8). Whenever Yahweh's presence was absent, Israel was defeated in the war. However, after the defeat Yahweh will show compassion on his people (Deut 32:39) in terms of initiating covenant with them. Even before the exile when Israel was utterly

357 M. C. Lind, *Yahweh is a Warrior* (Scottsdale: Herald Press, 1980), p. 23.

358 Ibid., pp. 26, 50.

359 Ibid., pp. 167-168.

360 Walther Zimmerli, *Old Testament Theology*, p. 63.

defeated, Yahweh as warrior God intervened in their history and led them to the new avenues of life by sustaining Israel and leading them unto a new future.[361]

Yahweh, the covenant God: The Old Testament talk on Yahweh can be better understood in terms of Yahweh as covenant God. Perhaps, this covenant idea is present throughout the history of Israel. In all the events of Israel there are covenant expressions to show how Yahweh was active in the history of people of Israel. Walther Eichrodt who basically follows the covenant scheme in analyzing the materials of the Old Testament points out that, Israel was less interested in the etymological significance of the divine name Yahweh, rather how that divine name is concretely manifested within their context that is, the real presence of Yahweh, as the covenant God.[362] Eichrodt suggests three things through which Yahweh as the covenant God was known in Israel. First, Israelites can experience "the factual nature of divine revelation" in the covenant. Second, "a clear divine will" and "an atmosphere of trust and security" is created through the covenant. Third, Yahweh is known as unique God by giving the covenant to Israel. It is in this name Yahweh as covenant God, Israel as people of Yahweh are unified as a tribal nation.[363]

It is customary for us think that Yahweh should naturally reward or obliged to bless those who are faithful. But Yahweh has his own choices that are beyond human comprehension. Walter Brueggemann clarifies that by liberating the oppressed community of Israel from the Egyptian bondage Yahweh redefined the traditional understanding of God's justice and affirmed that Yahweh chooses the vulnerable for his act of salvation. Brueggemann writes:

> In place of the gods of Egypt, creatures of the imperial consciousness, Moses discloses Yahweh, the sovereign one who acts in his lordly freedom, is extrapolated from no social reality, and is captive to no social perception but acts from his own person toward his own purposes. At the same time, Moses dismantles the politics of justice and compassion … The participants in the Exodus found themselves … involved in the intentional formation of a new social community to match the vision of God's freedom.[364]

This freedom of God in choosing the communities of God's desire is not simply for the sake of freedom alone. God by opting for God's own communities also become vulnerable to human experience. This vulnerability is seen in God's participation and liberation of Israelites from the oppressive regime of Egypt. The

361 M. C. Lind, *Yahweh is a Warrior*, p. 174.

362 Walther Eichrodt, *Theology I*, p. 187.

363 Ibid., pp. 37-39.

364 Walter Brueggemann, *The Prophetic Imagination* (Philadelphia: Fortress Press, 1978), pp. 16-17.

covenanting God Yahweh all through the history of the nation Israel became the caring and compassionate God. This idea is concretely found in the use of certain Hebrew terms. Bruce Birch captures this idea beautifully. He writes:

> God is not only free from but free for, choosing freely to become vulnerable to the world's pain and suffering. God says to Moses. "I know [experience] their suffering" (Exod. 3:7). Thus, the God of covenant is especially present in the midst of human need and especially caring of the poor, the oppressed and the hurting. The quality of God frequently used to describe this divinely chosen vulnerability is compassion (*rehem*), a word derived from the Hebrew word for womb or uterus. God's compassion is a metaphor of the womb, expressive of the tender oneness yet separateness shared between a mother and the child she is carrying.[365]

This God of the covenant is also faithful to the promise made as a faithful covenant partner despite the changing circumstances. It is this fidelity of God that marks uncompromising covenanted God for building an alternate community in and around the people of Israel. In spite of Israel's infidelity God's unfailing covenant guarantees God's sustained compassion on the part of the people of Israel. The covenant also guarantees legal security and peace as opposed to caprice, uncertainty and animosity. It goes beyond fluctuating human emotions and thus stands as stable divine-human relationship and fellowship. It is a two-way traffic that demands active and firm relationship not only on the part of humans but also on the part of God. John Goldingay explains this process of mutual relationship between divine and human as in dynamic tension:

> The key theological issue that covenant raises is the relationship between divine commitment and human obligation. Covenant can put the stress on divine initiative and commitment, though it will then regard human obedience as absolutely required. Or it can put the stress on human commitment to obedience to an obligation set forth by God, though it will assume that this commitment is offered in the context of the framework of the divine grace. Or it can hold these two in balance in the marriage does; Yahweh initiates the covenant but it becomes properly operative only when humanity responds to "Yahweh's covenant." The dynamic tension between these ways of looking at the matter means God can never be taken for granted but can always be appealed to.[366]

365 Bruce C. Birch, "Old Testament Foundations for Peacemaking in the Nuclear Era," *The Christian Century*, December 4, (1985), pp. 1115-1119.

366 John Goldingay, "Covenant, OT and NT," in Katherine Doob Sakenfeld (ed), *The New Interpreter's Dictionary of the Bible*, Vol. 1. A-C. Nashville: Abingdon Press, 2006, p. 772.

Thus, the God the covenant in the Old Testament stand as the only hope that the people can count on in all circumstances of their life including the testing times of their slavery and oppression in Egypt and in similar situations. Hope was possible in such situations because the covenant God in whom they believed was also God of justice faithful towards the people of Israel in all situations. That is why the prophets could speak and announce about God's judgment and salvation at the same time. The same God although punishes the people for their failures will nevertheless remain faithful to save them from any distress and disastrous situation. The God who cares is firmly upheld when the people are pushed to the brink of hopelessness so that they can surely count on the impending hope and salvation that will outbreak in the covenant community. God who led and initiated this covenant will see that the covenant people will remain different than all of their surrounding nations.

Yahweh in the saving acts of Israel: Yahweh, as God of Israel is concretely manifested in the very saving acts of the people of Israel. In the context of cult Yahweh's presence is realized by his very name. It is this name which is fundamental and normative factor for the people of Israel in this saving acts that is, in every act Israel realized her God Yahweh; and these acts are continuous acts present in different places. Further it has been understood the name Yahweh as a God who protects and keeps Israel is called for particularly during the time of religious syncretism: pure Yahwism at these times was strictly called into practice.[367]

Claus Westermann points out that Yahweh in the Old Testament is basically known in the saving acts of Israel. It is in the little historical creed in Deut 26, which is the encounter between Yahweh and his people, transcending the history of Israel and recalling the saving acts of God in the life of Israel. In fact, all through the OT Yahweh as saving God was encountered by the people of Israel except that is not very explicitly found in the wisdom literature.[368] The very name Yahweh points out von Rad, is not to be simply reduced to a mystery or to a mere speculation but to be realized in every historical experience of the people of Israel. As was pointed out earlier, in every aspect of cult this saving act of Yahweh was recalled in fresh and concentrated way. In other words, this name Yahweh is available to every Israelite who realized his or her saving act of Yahweh and it should be made known among other nations.[369]

Yahweh as king: In the OT Yahweh as God of Israel further manifested concretely in the image of king or kingship. The Royal psalms mention the key phrase *Yahweh malak* which is translated as "Yahweh (none other) is king"[370] On the other hand according to Sigmund Mowinckel, *Yahweh malak* is to be translated as "Yahweh has become king" (Pss 93:1; 96:10) in the context of the

367 Gerhard von Rad, *OT Theology I,* pp. 181-184.

368 Claus Westermann, *What Does OT Says About God* (Atlanta: John Knox Press, 1979), p. 26.

369 Gerhard von Rad, *OT Theology I,* p. 184.

370 Walther Zimmerli, *Old Testament Theology*, p. 40.

enthronement of Yahweh as king in a new year festival celebrated annually by the people of Israel.[371] The word *melek* is also compounded with a large number of personal names as a common practice in the Semitic world. Moreover, this word is also understood as the word for guide, counselor, without any reference as such to the institution of kingship.[372] This image of Yahweh as king is very significant for the marginalized communities in a given context. Daniel Jones Muthunayagom rightly affirms that,

> When the theocratic vision of God's rule permeated among all members of the community of Yahweh was replaced by royal hierarchy through the perversion of justice and righteousness, the Psalmist envisions a new hope that Yahweh Himself shall establish his reign *(malkut)*. In Psalm 145, the Psalmist instructs the members of the congregation with the assurance that Yahweh upholds all who are falling and raises up all who are bowed down (cf. 1 Sam 2:8. Ps.113:7-8, Ps.146:8). Yahweh's greatness is extolled not because He is Lord of history who protects the life of His people from generation to generation, but because of His benevolent care and compassionate deeds (Ps.145:17). The Psalmist says that the Lord is just in all his ways and kind in all his doings. In Psalm 146, Yahweh as king and creator is praised for his reliability and fidelity. He is praised for his care and concern for the poor, exploited and deficient and socially ostracized and disadvantaged. The Psalmist lists seven different groups who are brought under the category of the "oppressed ones" *(ashuqim)* in Psalm 146:7-9. They are the "hungry ones" (*reēbim* cf. Ps. 7-5, 9, 36), the "bound ones" who are the socially hurt and underprivileged, "the blind ones" and the "bent ones." The blind and the bent are the physically challenged people. Metaphorically they are the marginalised section of our society who have been treated harshly by unjust laws (cf. Lev.19:14, Is.29:18; 35:5; 42:7).[373]

With the introduction of monarchy, the title of king for Yahweh has become obvious. For example, Ps 24:7-10, this is taken as a poem from the early monarchy gives more emphasis on the use of the title king for Yahweh. Deutero-Isaiah makes use of the title king for Yahweh in terms of Yahweh's eschatological act of salvation (Isa 52:7, 10). The title of Yahweh as king is further developed as something of Yahweh's universal kingdom is also seen in conformity with Deutero-Isaiah's thought (see also Mal 1:4; Pss 103:19, 145:11-13). In all these passages there is a

371 S. Mowinckel, *The Psalms in Israel's Worship*, Vol. 1: (Oxford: Basil Blackwell, 1962), p. 102.

372 Walther Eichrodt, *Theology I*, p. 194.

373 Daniel Jones Muthunayagom, "The Image of God as King and the Nature of his Power in the Old Testament," *Bangalore Theological Forum* 41:2 (2009), p. 41.

strong note of God's dominion as king in the future, with the present reality here and now.[374]

Another important factor of Yahweh as king is associated with Royal Zion theology. It is in Zion, Yahweh the king lives forever (2 Kings 20:5). Yahweh was worshipped throughout the monarchial period as king who dwells in Zion. In the process of establishing the cult of Yahwism, Yahweh as king tended to become more and more victorious ruler.[375] Furthermore Yahweh as king is manifested in the OT understanding of the kingdom of God. This kingdom of God is understood as God's sovereign rule over all things, the entire universe. It is this sovereign power with which Yahweh reigns as king of the entire universe and his dominion in the entire world as king (Pss 92:28; 97:1). But this dominion as was discussed above is to protect the marginalized and control the hegemonic forces who oppress and even harass the marginalized and there Yahweh come to the rescue of these depressed communities or even as a king his power is made manifest to rule the entire world in justice and righteousness.

Yahweh the creator:[376] Yahweh as creator God presented in the Old Testament is not only limited to the context of Israel, but this idea of Yahweh is related to the universal history and Yahweh as he entire cosmos. The horizon of Yahweh as or God is much wider in its context. When people of Israel came in contact with the Canaanite and Babylonian religion, they had encountered their strong belief in their God as creator. This is also evident from the fact that Yahweh as creator I the OT was presented in different materials (Genesis, Psalms, Wisdom, and Prophetic literature), a sign of secondary development of the idea, God as creator. Also in the realm of salvation Yahweh as creator God is depicted in the OT. God as creator with omnipotence, who brings salvation not only to Israel but to all the nations as creator.[377]

Jones Muthunayagom is of the view that "the rule of Yahweh as king and creator of the entire world and protector of the human and earthly domain deabsolutizes or delegitimizies all other governances whether mythical or human which imagine that they are unfettered and absolute. This deabsolutisation and delegitimisation happened in the historical realm when Yahweh delegitimized the rule of Pharaoh (Ex. 15:1-18), Assyrians in Is.10:5-15, Nebuchadnezzar in Daniel 4."[378] In Daniel 4 the author writes as follows:

---

374 Walther Eichrodt, *Theology I*, p. 199.

375 J. Pedersen, *Israel: Its life and Culture*, Vol. III-IV (London: Geoffrey Cumberlege, 1959), pp. 524-534.

376 Some parts of this section are adapted with modifications from Muthunayagom, "The Image of God as King," pp. 35-37.

377 Th. C. Vriezen, *An Outline of OT Theology* (Oxford: Basil Blackwell, 1970), p. 337.

378 Muthunayagom, "The Image of God as King," p. 35.

> *The Most High is Sovereign over the Kingdom of mortals: He gives it to whom he will And sets over the lowliest of Human beings, (vs.17) All the inhabitants of the earth are accounted as nothing, and he does what he wills with the host of heaven and inhabitants of the earth. There is no one who can stay his hand or say to him, "what are you doing?" (vs. 5)*

As creator and owner of the created world (Ps. 24:1-2), Yahweh continues to uphold its security whenever any kind of demonic or chaotic powers threaten its existence and bring in chaotic conditions on it by suppressing God's justice and righteousness (Ps. 97:1-7). As the imperial ruler of all gods and nations, God's providential power is extended over all the peoples and nations. That means, as creator of the world, Yahweh allots to the nations their places in the world and continues to guide their destinies (Ps. 95: 5, 96:3-10).[379]

Psalm 65 is a hymn which describes Yahweh's universal dominion over the earth, for he has created the world and continues to provide his providential care offering fertility to the earth. Yahweh's providential care of the ecological realm is depicted as follows:

> *You visit the earth and water it, you greatly enrich it, the river of God is full of water; you provide the people with grain, for so you have prepared it. You water its furrows abundantly, settling its ridges, softening it with showers, and blessing its growth (Ps. 65:9-10).*

Yahweh's creative and providential function and care in favour of the world is fabulously picturized in Psalm 104 which is often designated as a nature hymn:

> *You cause the grass for the earth, and plants for people to use to bring forth food from the earth, and wine to gladden the human heart, oil to make the face shine, and bread to strengthen the human heart. The trees of the Lord are watered abundantly, the cedars of Lebanon that he planted (Ps. 104;14-16).*
>
> *O Lord, how manifold are your works! In wisdom you have made them all; the earth is full of your creatures; these all look to you to give them their food in due season (Ps.104;2-7).*

Yahweh's creative and re-creative power is magnificently exemplified in Jeremiah 10:12-16, a hymn that celebrates the creative power of Yahweh. Here Yahweh alone is understood to be the "maker of earth.... The establisher of the world, the unfolder of the heaven." In addition, the attributes of Yahweh are enumerated in this hymn as he creates by "means of his power, his wisdom and

---

379 Muthunayagom, "The Image of God as King," p. 36.

his understanding." The hymn illustrates creation as a continuing process in the world rather than a single completed action.[380]

In Deutero-Isaiah, Yahweh as creator God is depicted as not only the creator of the world, but also by his very creative action and intervention in the history, thus Yahweh as a creator God comes into the active form in the life of the people of Israel in a concrete way. As much as Israel knows the mane of Yahweh in their historical realms, they know the name of Yahweh much more concrete in the realms of creation where Yahweh's glory is fully revealed. Yahweh as creator God is confronted to the people of Israel by the very mystery of creation. In the wisdom literature, the very wisdom ideology is controlled by the realm of creation.[381]

Yahweh as Judge:[382] This metaphorical description of Yahweh as judge comes in the context of entire creation. This means that Yahweh not only judges human beings but the entire cosmos that includes non-human creation. Whenever a section of his created beings are unjustly treated or inequitable treatment is meted out to them, the divine king whose throne is crowned with justice *(mishpat)* and righteousness *(tsedeqah)* would intervene on behalf of them and restore justice to them. Yahweh stands against the so-called self-seeking and self-aggrandizing human justices. Thus, Yahweh is said to be "lover of justice" (Ps. 99:4, Is.61:8), one who cares about justice and one who is committed to this practice. The Hebrew word *shophet* attributes to God as 'Justice' is not restricted to judiciary and judicial activity. It includes the dimensions of "defending," "deliverance" and "punishing." Hence, God as Judge could be designated as a liberator of people who are under the dominant and oppressive power of the despots and tyrannical rulers.[383] The Psalmist describes the character of Yahweh as Justice as follows:

> *The world is firmly established; It shall never be moved, He will judge the peoples with equity for he is coming to judge the earth. He will judge the world with righteousness and the peoples with his truth (Ps. 96:10,13).*

As the creator-king of the world, Yahweh could even bring in 'litigation' against the gods who do not practice the justice of Yahweh:

> *How long will you judge unjustly, and show partiality to the wicked? Give justice to the weak and the orphan; Maintain the right of the lowly and the destitute, Rescue the weak and the needy;*
> *deliver them from the hand of the wicked" (Ps. 82:2-4).*[384]

380 Cf. Dominic Rudman ,"Creation and Fall in Jeremiah X 12-16", *VT* 48/1 (1998), p. 64.

381 Walther Zimmerli, *Old Testament Theology*, pp. 39- 40.

382 Some parts of this section are adapted with modifications from Muthunayagom, "The Image of God as King," pp. 37-38.

383 Cf. B. Anderson, *Understanding the Old Testament* (New Jersey: Prentice Hall, Englewood Cliffs, 1957), p. 105.

384 Erhard S. Gerstenberger rightly makes the following comment: "Polemics against others gods in a imperial context of hegemonistic economy, administration and military strategy required a

The right of the vulnerable segment of any society is the prime concern of Yahweh. In the psalms of individual laments, we find, in the context of the exploitative social situation, Yahweh-Judge is approached by the affected person for remedy and redressal. The psalmist espouses confidence in Yahweh as follows:

> *He judges the world with righteousness; he judges the peoples with equity. For the needy shall not always be forgotten, nor the hope of the poor perish forever (Ps. 9:8,18).*

The sphere of Yahweh's judicial administration is not limited to Israel; it is extended to all the nations as he is the creator and king of all the nations. In Psalm 94, the Psalmist makes a plea to Yahweh as follows:[385]

> *Rise up O judge of the earth; give to the proud what they deserve! O Lord, how long shall the wicked, How long shall wicked exult? They crush your people O Lord, and afflict your heritage They kill the widow and the stranger, they murder the orphan, Can wicked rulers be allied with you, those who contrive mischief by statute? (Ps 94:2-3, 5-6,20).*

Whenever justice is perverted and the poor and needy are deprived of their justice, (whereby the stability of created order in the world is threatened), the Yahweh-king pronounces judgement against that nation (Amos 1-2, Is. 2:12-17). As Amos puts it; "The eyes of my Lord God are against the sinful nation, and I will destroy it from upon the face of the earth" (Amos 9:8). From the perspective of the prophets, human injustice, whether Israelite or foreign, causes all of creation to suffer and threatens to return it to a state of primeval chaos (Hos. 4:3; Jer. 4:23-26). That is why all of creation rejoices at the announcement that God is coming to judge the world and the nations in righteousness (Ps. 96:10-13; 98:4-9). It is the divine king's maintenance of justice and righteousness that allows not only humans but the living creatures of the sea, the field and all the trees of the forest to thrive (Ps. 104).

In order to maintain a just order in the anthropological and ecological realm, Yahweh chose David and his house as his partners. The Davidic kings were meant to participate in the divine rule by establishing justice and righteousness that were the foundations of Yahweh's throne. We can recall the prayers of Psalmist in favor of the king in Psalm 72:1-2: "O God, your justice give to the king and your

---

comprehensive and absolute denial of obedience and an equally absolute allegiance to another power. Yahweh was the only possible alternative in downtrodden and despised Israel." Erhard S. Gerstenberger, *Psalms Part 2 and Lamentations* (Grand Rapids, MI: William B. Eerdmans Publishing Company, 2001), pp. 190-191.

385 Cf. David M. Howard, Jr., "Psalm 94 among the Kingship-of-Yhwh Psalms," *CBQ* 61, (1999) 667-85; C. Westermann, *Praise and Laments in the Psalms* (Atlanta: John Knox 1981), pp. 252-257.

righteousness to the king's son, that he may judge your people in righteousness, and your poor with justice." One of the king's primary roles according to this ideal was to deliver the poor and the oppressed from the hand of the powerful oppressors (Ps. 72:12-14). The king is committed to provide a just administration. He has to swear that he walks in integrity himself and will not put up with corrupt officials in his service (Ps. 101:2,6-8).

The prophets therefore condemned corrupt kings who did not live up to the ideal of the just kingship (Jer. 22; 13-19) and predicted the coming of the new king who would fulfill the role destined by God, the king-judge (Is. 8:23-9:6; 11;1-10, Mic. 5:1-5; Jer. 23:5-6).

Yahweh as shepherd:[386] Yahweh as a shepherd came out more strongly when Israelites experienced failure on the part of the earthly kings and the very monarchy itself. The pastoral image for Yahweh is also closely related to Yahweh's governance. It is a combination of the semi-nomadic pastoral image and the agrarian royal image. In the ancient West Asian cultures, human kings were designated as shepherds and the people were figuratively known as sheep or flock. The image signifies a wise, caring and attentive personality who watches over, guards, leads and protects a flock that is vulnerable, exposed, dependent and in need of such help.[387]

Although there is a certain reluctance on the part of the biblical writes to directly address the leadership (political or religious) as shepherds, the term shepherd *(ro'eh)* is frequently alluded to in several scriptural passages (Num. 27:15-23; 2 Sam 5:2; Jer. 23:4-5; Ez. 34:23-24, 37:24; Mic. 5:1-3; Ps. 78:70-72, Zech. 13:7-9).

Except in a few passages that originated in the pre-exilic era, invariably the shepherd imagery appears in the exile (Hos. 13:4-14 and Ps. 23). In Hosea 13:4-14 the prophet Hosea accuses Israel for having forsaken Yahweh who looked after them as the provident shepherd. Because of Israel's infidelity and forgetfulness, Yahweh shall suspend his saving and shepherding activity, threatening them that he would become a lurking wild beast bent on destroying the sheep.[388]

In Psalm 23, through the image of the good shepherd (vv. 1-4) and bountiful host (vv. 5-6), the Psalmist who happens to be a Davidic king testifies to the Lord that as king he has been caring, providing and mightily protecting.[389] The shepherd image of Yahweh continues to reverberate in the Psalter (Ps. 74:1; 77:20; 78:52; 79:13; 80:1). Psalm 104 portrays Yahweh as the creator-provider who

386 Some parts of this section are adapted with modifications from Muthunayagom, "The Image of God as King," pp. 40-41.

387 Walter Brueggemann, *Theology of Old Testament*, p. 259.

388 Shaji Joseph Puykunnal. "The Shepherd and the Beast: Pastoral Imagery for Yahweh in the Book of Hosea," *Mission Today*, Vol. VIII/3 (2006), pp. 227-36.

389 John Eaton, *The Psalms* (London: T & T Clark, 2003), 122; Michael Goulder, "David and Yahweh in Psalms 23 and 24," *JSOT* 30/4 (2006), pp. 467f.

satiates the earth with rain, trees with water, animals with their food (Ps. 104:13, 16:27-28). In the context of Exile, when the people of Israel were scattered and dispersed, the prophets express the hope that Yahweh will serve as a shepherd by gathering the sheep in safety. The image of a gathering shepherd is very powerful in the Bible. Deutero-Isaiah declares that the shepherd-king will feed his flock and he will gather his lambs in his arms, carry them in his arms and gently tend the mother sheep (Is. 40:11; cf. Jer. 31:10).

In Ezekiel 34, after having indicted the Davidic king for his irresponsible shepherdship, Yahweh promised that he will act as a proper and responsible shepherd to the feeble sheep. He will destroy the fat sheep who were the dominant and exploitative leadership in Jerusalem. The shepherd image has two fold functions: To the vulnerable people he will do the restorative and rehabilitative act as a soft shepherd, and to the exploitative sheep he will act as a harsh shepherd (cf. Zech.10:3-12).

As we discussed elsewhere in this book, king as shepherd is all that was expected to give providential care and concerns for the sheep in Israel. But when that failed the prophets took on the human kings and depicted Yahweh as the only good shepherd provided his care for the people despite their disloyalty to him.

The Uniqueness of Yahweh and the claims of monotheism: In the OT we often find the claims for uniqueness of Yahweh in the context of Israel's faith. The very polemics developed against Baal, the polemic against all idols, Yahweh will never tolerate the worship of other gods by the people of Israel. Perhaps it is due to this unique claim of Yahweh by Israel brought a focus of homogenous tradition among Israelite religion and faith in the midst of variety of traditions of gods she has.[390] The unique claims for Yahweh was more developed from the time of Moses, especially in the context of Israelite struggle in the Egyptian bondage. Moses time and again recalls that the people of Israel should not lose sight of this uniqueness of Yahweh in all their faith journey (Deut 4:35-39). This understanding of the uniqueness of Yahweh in Israel is developed in the context of many other gods. It is Yahweh and none other delivered the people from their Egyptian bondage.

The ideas of uniqueness of Yahweh also to be noticed in the overall growth of Yahwism, particularly during the time of Elijah and his confrontation with Jezebel and subsequent attack on Baalism. On Mount Carmel in an episode of encounter between Baal and Yahweh, Elijah emerged victorious (1 Kings 18). But Baalism could not be wiped out altogether from the land of Israel. Again the book of Deuteronomy, although not intended to teach monotheistic claims on Yahweh, nevertheless it stresses on the uniqueness of Yahweh as the God of Israel. It is the worship of one and only Yahweh Israelites express their utter loyalty to Yahweh. In the reformation of king Josiah the book of Deuteronomy is followed for

390 Ronald E. Clements, *OT Theology*, p. 74.

strengthening the idea that there is one God Yahweh, one sanctuary in Jerusalem and one land where Israel and Judah will be united as one God's people.

Evaluation on the theme and its relationship to the Revelation in and through Jesus Christ: The revelation of Yahweh in and through the history of Israel stays decisive in the human history. This becomes a standard by which the whole life of Israel and the universal connotation of Yahweh's sovereignty is manifested. On the basis of our foregoing discussion we now make the following observation so as to see their revelatory aspect in and through Jesus Christ.

First, throughout the OT, at every step in the life of Israel Yahweh was their guide in their faith journey. Israel was at the disposal of Yahweh and lived in utter dependence on him in all the departments of their life. Both in times of joy, celebration, victories in the war and at the same time in times of war, pestilence, danger and threats from their enemies Yahweh was the guide of the people of Israel.

Second, the very name Yahweh has become concrete and dynamic in the lives of the people of Israel. Israelites always felt the immediacy of God in this very name, as they experienced Yahweh's presence in realistic and concrete life situations.

Third, The divine name Yahweh and because of its unique claims always caused problems in the history of Israel by bringing into a tension between particular and universal. This name Yahweh always pushes for a particular people and particular nation, although at times this particularism transcends the national boundaries and projected Yahweh as the God of all nations.

Fourth, in the context of Baal and other gods among Israel, this very name Yahweh puts the people of Israel in a unique position. Despite the syncretistic religious tendencies that prevailed in the land of Israel, be it in Canaan or in Babylon, at all times Yahwism was preserved and thus the people's faith is sustained in this very name. Thus, it is no wonder to say that such a heterogeneous tribal groups among Israelites were perhaps unified in the name of Yahweh.

Fifth, Yahweh exercises his liberative and dynamic power for establishing rehabilitation and restoration. Yahweh as a king may be a threat and danger to the imperialistic and globalizing powers in the contemporary world that continue to oppress the marginalized segment of our communities, but not a threat to the vulnerable segment of our communities such as the poor, the subaltern and women. In fact, the royal imagery of God provides a hope for their emancipation and restoration of justice. Yahweh's image as king never advocates the continuance of a stratified and hierarchical social and political order that undermines social justice and wholeness of life to both the human and ecological domain.[391]

Sixth, revelation of God in and through Jesus Christ in the history of humankind is very decisive. Throughout the NT Christ is proclaimed as the savior of the world as we see for instance in Acts 4:12: *there is salvation in no one*

391 Muthunayagom, "The Image of God as King," pp. 42-43.

else It the saving God who acted in sending Christ and thus the salvation that has begun in the OT continues in the NT. Westermann rightly points out this process as follows:

> The proclamation of God as savior remains the same even though salvation in the Old and New Testaments may mean something different. The message of Christ as savior rests upon what the Old Testament says about God as savior. What is said in the New Testament about salvation from sin and death through the work of Christ would be incomprehensible without the experience of physical rescue from the danger of death. There would be no confession of Christ as savior from sin and death if there were no thanksgiving on the part of the person saved from the danger of death. Hence, even in the New Testament God remains the savior from the physical threat of death as the accounts of the Gospels show.[392]

Seventh, at the same time there is uniqueness in terms of the revelation and salvation of God in both the testaments. Again Westermann clarifies this when he writes:

> If, however, the history of the saved people, or the history which grew out of salvation process is compared with the New Testament, then a very great contrast appears. In the Old Testament God's saving act inaugurates the history of a nation which, from the possession of the land up to the collapse, is based on political-military power, as one nation among others. In the New Testament, God's act of salvation in Christ establishes a religious or cultic congregation without any political power, made up of followers from many peoples, and similar to other cult-congregations within the Roman Empire.[393]

Lastly, we may conclude that the revelation of God manifested in both the OT and the NT has definite continuity despite the difference in the way in which the events unfolded in terms of the demonstration of God's salivific and revelatory acts in both the testaments. Again, Westermann is right when he states:

> What is said in the Old Testament about God does not come to an end with the close of the historical books, and what is said in the New Testament about God cannot begin with the birth of Jesus. The working of the creator remains the same in both the Old and the New Testaments; God is just as much the creator for Christ or for Paul as

392 Claus Westermann, *What Does the Old Testament Say About God?* (Atlanta: John Knox Press, 1979), p. 82.

393 Ibid.

> he is for David or Isaiah. What is said in Genesis 1—11 about the relationship of God to the world and to humanity remains valid even after Christ's coming. The history of God's people in both the Old and New Testaments is related to the history of the world and of humanity. In the Old as well as in the New Covenant God works not only for his people but for the sake of *all* men.[394]

Thus, we conclude that God's acts in Yahweh and Christ continues even toady in different manifestations as God continues to reveal, save and liberate his people from all over the world. For that matter God's acts are manifested in the entire realm of God's creation in which human beings are only a small part.

4.4 God of Covenant, Blessing and Curse in the Old Testament and Implications for us in Today's Context

The people of Israel perceived themselves as a faith community of God and are always conscious of serving as an alternate community in covenant with God. It was a religious, political, social and economic reality that this covenant community existed in the history of the world. It was always perceived that this community called itself as an alternate community that lived in the midst of its neighboring cultures—Mesopotamian, Egyptian, and Canaanite—of the biblical period. However, there are influences from these cultures on Israel at various levels, even when the basic perspective of Israel remained different from her surrounding cultures. Whenever Israel tried to emulate and follow her surrounding cultures the prophets and the other messengers of God called the people of Israel back to covenant faithfulness.[395] While it is not so easy to resolve the actual historical[396] details involved in the covenant making ceremony it is not an easy matter to negate either the important turning point that context of Mosaic covenant made in the history of Israel. This was precisely the point of time that the people were reminded of their special responsibility and obligation towards God and towards their neighborhood. In that sense, Israel was expected to be an alternate covenant community with deeper commitment to her God and to her surrounding world.

Even though there are other covenants prior to Sinai Covenant and latter with David which are spoken as decisive in the history of the people it is in the Mosaic covenant God's revelation is actualized and articulated more decisively than in other covenants. Moreover, it is in this covenant all the fundamental traditions of Israel are strengthened. Even when the Hebrew term *berith* that

394 Claus Westermann, *What Does the Old Testament Say About God?* (Atlanta: John Knox Press, 1979), p. 83.

395 For some details on this point see Bruce Birch, *What Does the LORD Require?: The Old Testament Call to Social Witness* (Philadelphia: The Westminster Press, 1985), pp. 50ff.

396 It is beyond the scope this presentation to talk about the complexities involved in the historical discrepancies of the covenant ceremony and its related matters in the Mosaic covenant.

meant in some contexts as agreements between human partners (as in the case of Jacob-Laban stories in Genesis chapters 32-36) and also meant to promises given by God to the ancestors (Genesis 15, God's covenant with Abraham), from the time of Sinai Covenant it refers to God's concrete relationship with the people of Israel, especially the term *berith* is seen in the light of the Exodus event and God's liberating activity in and through the wilderness wanderings. Israel from the time of Sinai covenant was expected to be the alternate covenant community in comparison with the imperial power they encountered in their brutal oppression from the Egyptian super-power.

Egypt was built on its military prowess and all their might was also measured in terms of the power vested in their deities. It was believed by the Egyptians that when their deities are powerless their military might and superiority will also be reduced. Moreover the Egyptian greatness is also measured in terms of their cultural and economic power. In a similar manner, the power of Israel is measured in terms their God and mighty works of God they have already experienced. This was given a concrete and definite shape from the time of the Mosaic covenant. Israel from now on was clearly defined as an alternate community of covenant standing not only in loyalty to their God but also exhibiting as an inclusive community in every respect by having special concern towards aliens, orphans and widows that are living among them and in their surroundings. The laws that were codified later times and perhaps legislated during the time of monarchy are geared towards this concern of inclusive community where justice and equality will be executed at all levels in the community life. Thus, even the boundary marks of the property of any individual or community (may be tribal boundaries) have to be respected and honored.[397]

In the religious sphere, the understanding of covenant has three important elements: first, covenant is a gift which was given by Yahweh to his people; second, it is a bond of communion between Yahweh and his people; third, covenant is an obligation(both on the part of the one who initiates and the one who receives it)[398]

Covenant in the ancient West Asian texts: In the Hittite treaties, which are derived from the early Mesopotamian context are basically two kinds of treaties are noticed. They are parity and suzerain-vassal treaties. In the case of the parity treaty, it is a treaty made between two equal partners. For instance, there was a treaty made between a Hittite king Hattiusilis III and the Egyptian king Ramses II. In this treaty seven common elements are normally recognized. They are: i) mutual titulature; ii) history of the past relations; iii) affirmation of brotherhood; iv) stipulations; v) list of divine utterances; vi) curses and blessings; vii) addendum concerning the fugitives. This type of treaty normally fosters the mutual bond of

397 John Barton thinks that the property rights and regulations is one of the important ethical regulations that God insisted that the community of Israel should follow. For details on this point see John Barton, *Ethics and the Old Testament* (London: SCM Press, 1998), pp. 53 ff.

398 Edmond Jacob, *Theology of the OT* (London: Hodder and Stoughton, 1958), p. 211.

strengthening each other, and they always work for establishment of good and peace with each other. For instance we see this goodwill between the Hittites and Egyptians in the following text:

> "...And as for (the relationship of) the land of Egypt with Hatti land, they are at peace and brothers like us forever."[399]

In the case of Suzerain-vassal treaty, the suzerain always demands certain obligations from vassal and there are six common elements present in this type of treaty as follows: i) preamble: the message from the suzerain to the vassal; ii) historical prologue: a description of previous relations of both the parties; iii) stipulations: here vassal is bound to certain obligations stipulated by suzerain; iv) the deposit and public reading: the treaty documents are deposited in the sanctuary of vassal and read periodically; v) the list of witnesses: apart from the gods, mountains, rivers, springs, heaven and earth are called as witnesses. These witnesses are sought because gods will punish the vassal if there is any breach in the treaty or agreement; vi) the blessings and curses: if vassal is obedient he will be blessed with divine protection, continuity of the vassal's line, health, prosperity and peace; if disobedient the curses will be on the vassal such as destruction, sterility, misery, poverty, plague, famine etc.[400]

Covenant terminology in the OT: While the term *berit* is very complex in its origin the following meanings may be considered as follows: i) the word *berit* is translated as "covenant" and in Greek it is rendered as: διαθηκη and in Vulgate it is *Testamentum* or *pactum*; ii) the word *berit* comes from the root *brh* (noun form) means to eat, to dine (2 Sam 3:35; 12:17; 13:5; Ps 69:21; Lam 4:10 rec.). This refers to a festival time with a meal of fellowship; iii) *berit* is from the Akkadian root *birit* translated as between or among as the Hebrew word *ben*; iv) *berit* also means determining or fixing (see Isa 28:15, 18) which is also parallel to mean selecting or determining or even it amounts to pledging; v) this word also comes closer to another Akkadian root *biritu* means clasp, fetter, which is used in the context of a treaty between Akkadian and Hittite. On the basis of all these possible root meanings, it can be summarized that the word covenant may denote an agreement between two human beings (Gen 26:26-33). However, the semantic range of the word covenant is much wider such as oath, commitment, love, friendship and so on (see Deut 7:9; 1 Kings 3:6; Ps 89:25, 50; Isa 54:10, 55:3 etc.).

---

399 This is a treaty between king Hattiusilis III and Ramses II. The words are published in *ANET* p. 202.

400 G. E. Mendenhall, "Covenant," *Interpreter's Dictionary of the Bible*, Vol. 1 (New York: Abingdon Press, 1962), pp. 714-716. There are some parallels in the OT which might fall under this category of suzerain-vassal treaty. In 1 Sam 11:1, Jabesh-Gilead offers to serve Nahash in a covenant relationship. In Ezek 17:13f it was reported that there is a suzerain-vassal treaty executed between the Babylonian power and king Zedekiah.

Covenant during Abraham and David: Both the Abrahamic and Davidic covenants are combined here because of the reason that they belong to the category of promissory covenant. In the case of Abraham, it is God's promise of land and in David's case it is the promise of dynasty. In this type of covenant although the one who receives promise had to fulfill certain obligations, the conditions are not so rigid regulations like suzerain-vassal treaty. In the case of Abraham the covenant is explained in two different traditions: J (Gen 15) and P (Gen 17:1-14). Von Rad identifies that this promissory type of covenant is Abraham is the first stage of priestly understanding of covenant concept (Gen 17:1-14) in the three-tier system what he calls: Abraham became a people, then Yahweh's new relationship with people through Sinai covenant is initiated, and then finally the possession of the land by the people has taken place. In other words, through Abraham, God promised that his descendants will inherit the land as a gift from Yahweh, the people will be recognized as a people (hitherto not recognized as such). This covenant then assures a future promise of the people and the land as a gift. In J account (Gen 15), the ideas of election and covenant are intertwined. J's intention in presenting a series of patriarchal narratives as blessings of a nation in the form of future inheritance of the land is evident (see Gen 12:1ff; 25:23; 39:29; and chapter 49). The covenant with Abraham is a recollection of the covenant at Sinai (Gen 15:17; 26:24; 27:29a; 28:13ff etc.).

In the Davidic covenant God made a promise to David that his dynasty would continue on the throne of Judah and that promise is a divine gift to David (2 Sam 7:1-17 and 1 Chr 17:1-15) without imposing any specific obligations. This is also called a grant type of covenant because of the reason that "the grant par excellence is an act of royal benevolence arising from the king's desire to reward his royal servant."[401] Apart from the fact that both Abrahamic and Davidic covenants are promissory types of covenants, there is also a close relationship between them because of the reason that "2 Sam 7:18-29, with its notion of the Davidic covenant as humanity's character, provided for the future of the race under the leadership of Davidic house and thus foreshadowed the fulfillment of Abrahamic promises."[402] Even when the prophets talked about the downfall of Israel and Judah, they recalled the fall of the physical dynasty of king David, yet a remnant was promised in the midst of terrible downfall.[403]

Mosaic covenant: The covenant during Mosaic period is very crucial one since it is believed that through the Sinai covenant God entered into a special relationship with the people of Israel and also the people know Yahweh in a special way. Mosaic covenant is also understood in the context of commandments. Two

---

401 M. Wienfeld, *Deuteronomy and Deuteronomic School* (Oxford: Clarendon Press, 1972), p. 77.

402 W. J. Dumbrell, *Covenant and Creation* (Devon: The Paternoster Press, 1984), p. 163.

403 Some of the prophetic words which talked about the downfall of Israel and Judah in the context of the fall of Davidic dynasty can be found in Isa 29:1ff; 22:1ff, 16. The remnant and the saving of David's house is promised despite fall in Isa 11:1ff; Jer 32:14-18.

things can be stated on this point: first, Israel has encountered a unique experience with a holy God; second, the covenant or agreement however is made on the basis of Israel's total obedience and surrender to divine grace.[404]

In Exod 34: 10-28 we find the details regarding the covenant renewal ceremony. The renewal of the covenant with God is necessary for the Israelites because of their apostasy (Exod 32)and thus they need to restore their relationship with God once again. This passage has been subjected to many scholarly debates. Without getting into those details of the debate we may argue that this passage is from J source but a later point edited by Deuteronomic source where there is a strong emphasis on the cult in the context of God's theophanic manifestation. The role of mediator is also stressed here in this passage with the intention that the J writer wanted to communicate the will of Yahweh and his demand from the people of Israel for a total obedience in the whole covenant process.[405]

Covenant in the Deuteronomy and Deuteronomic texts: Deuteronomy reaffirms the idea of the covenant of patriarchs that is, Yahweh's covenant with the fathers in the context of election (Deut 7:9, 12b). The main idea of covenant in Deuteronomy is that it is not because of the merits of the people but because of Yahweh's grace God entered into a special relationship with the people of Israel. Moreover, this covenant is valid only in so far as the people's total obedience to Yahweh (Deut 7:7-18). Thus, Deuteronomy affirms the basic principle as Yahweh the God of Israel and Israel the people of Yahweh. On the one hand the Deuteronomic covenant affirms God's relationship with the people from the past, that is from the time of patriarchs, on the other hand it talks about the present and enduring relationship between Yahweh and the people in a new and renewed way (Deut 7:9ff; 1 Kings 8:23 etc).

One other significant aspect of covenant theology in Deuteronomy is to be understood in the context of the land. Deuteronomy derives this land theology from the older covenant traditions of Abraham and David, the land and dynasty as objects of the covenant respectively. In its original setting of Abrahamic and Davidic covenants of the land was not attached with any conditions (Gen 18:19ff; Ps 132:12), but Deuteronomy makes this unconditional grant of land, and dynasty as conditional and these will be granted according to Deuteronomy only when the law is observed (Deut 4:1, 25-26, 40; 6:17-18; 7:12 etc). Von Rad points out that the Deuteronomy's concern for the land has to be seen in the total perspective of Israel's redemption, that is God redeemed Israelites from the bondage and led them to a land of rest from all their enemies. "The life of a chosen people in the 'pleasant land' at rest from all enemies round about, the people owning their love for God and God blessing his people—this is the epitome of the state of the

404 Walther Zimmerli, *Old Testament Theology*, p. 53.

405 D. J. McCarthy, *Treaty and Covenant* (Rome: Pontifical Biblical Institute, 1963), pp. 165-166.

redeemed nation as Deuteronomy sees it."[406] Thus, the land theology is closely connected with the idea of covenant in Deuteronomy.

Covenant and prophets: Prophets are believed to be the people who basically used the covenant tradition within their preaching of emphasizing the relationship between Yahweh and the people of Israel. During late seventh century and early sixth century BCE Jeremiah makes no explicit reference to the use of covenant (chapters 2-6). In him however, there is clear contrast between old and new covenant (Jer 31:31ff), thereby Jeremiah wanted to affirm God's new creative action in the overall plan of God's redemption. In the message of Jeremiah it is made clear that as he offers a critique on the existing social order in order to bring a radical change. Ezekiel used the idea of covenant in an eschatological sense (Ezek 34:25; 37:26); according to the prophet God would give the guarantee of a new covenant for the returnees of destruction.[407]

In Deutero-Isaiah a profound theology of covenant is seen in a more vivid form. Deutero-Isaiah uses the idea of *berit* (Isa 54:10; 55:3) in order to link it with the past that is, with the election of Abraham (Isa 41:8f; 51:2). For Deutero Isaiah, the old covenant is totally overshadowed by the new covenant which Yahweh himself will initiate. However, this covenant is mediated through the servant who is the covenant mediator not only to Israel but to all the nations (see Isa 42:6; 49:8). This covenant mediated through the servant is also to be seen in the context of justice and righteousness (Isa 45:22; 51:5).[408] Furthermore, the servant's task is seen in the two-fold function in the context of the covenant that is, covenant of a people and light to the nations. Thus, the task of the servant is seen in the context of liberation and justice for the whole world (see also Micah 7:8ff; Hosea 6:5; Zeph 3:5). On the whole we can see that the prophets whenever announces the doom subsequently talk about restoration initiated by covenant Kerygma.[409]

Covenant in the post-exilic period: Priestly writer blends the earlier covenant ideas in a more vivid fashion, especially in the context of universal creative action

406 Gerhard von Rad, *The Problem of Hexateuch and Other Essays* (Edinburgh: Oliver & Boyd, 1966), p. 95. On this point the views of Patrick D. Miller Jr., "The gift of God: The Deuteronomic Theology of the Land," *Interpretation* 23 (1969), pp. 451-465 is worth considering. Miller argues that the land theology in Deuteronomy has to be seen in the context of God's gift to the people of Israel, the land (Deut 1:39; 3:18; 4:21, 38; 5:31; 12:1; 13:4; 19:2, 10, 14, 20; 21:21; 24:4; 26:1). Israel's very existence as people and nation is in their possession of land which is a gift from Yahweh. This also recalls the fact that the Lord alone is the giver of the land, and it is God alone who enables people to inherit it and also gives the opportunity to share this gifted land with poor and those who are deprived of their land.

407 Walther Eichrodt, *Theology* I, pp. 59-60.

408 Ibid., pp. 61-62.

409 E. Gerstenberger, "Covenant and Commandment," *Journal of Biblical Literature* 34 (1965), p. 38.

of God in the history. Until the time of Moses beginning from creation two universal covenants are presented (that is in Noah and Abraham) and then the Sinai covenant. Priestly writer views these two in different light. The former (Noah and Abraham) are like grant type without any obligations and the latter one (Sinai covenant) is seen as obligatory type. Priestly writer uses the phrase *nātan berit* translated as "establishing the covenant as referred in Gen 9:12; 17:2 and Numb 25:12. And this covenant for P comes only by the grace and mercy of God. For Priestly writer this covenant has universal implications, that is, Yahweh will establish his covenant for the entire world. By presenting this type of covenant with universal implications brings two poles together, that is, the poles of creation and eschatology are brought together in the sense that God has entered into covenant not only with Abraham, Noah, but to the entire world till the end.[410]

Chronicler talks about God's covenant in the post-exilic period in the light of God's grace. The covenant for Chronicler is that which purifies the religion of the people (2 Chr 15:12; 23:3, 16; 29:10; 34:31).

Covenant as a major theological concept in the Old Testament: In the above discussion we have made a general survey on the theological idea of covenant during various historical periods in the history of Israel. However, any discussion on the idea of covenant should not be simply limited to the history alone and thus we should not make it as static concept. Rather covenant is to be understood as "event in dialogue" between God and his people which is a continuous process of verbal action.[411] We shall now look at various aspects of covenant in its theological discussion in the Old Testament.

Covenant and Election: In the context of election covenant is made dynamic in the OT. In a way covenant is a visible and dynamic manifestation of election. It is because that the people of Israel are chosen for the specific task to perform, to begin with this task is confirmed in the intimate relationship between God and people of Israel. Three important concerns can be noted in talking about the relationship between covenant and election. Firstly, covenant is election that is, God chose only Israel from among many nations (Amos 3:2a). Secondly, since covenant is election it is also a bond that is, people will be united in Yahweh in a close relationship and thirdly, because Yahweh has chosen Israel and entered into a covenant with them, Israel in turn will be obedient to the will of Yahweh as the subjects are obedient to their king, the people of Israel shall follow the guidance and leadership of Yahweh (Exod 15:18; Numb 23:21; Deut 33:5; Judg 8:23).[412] There is a sense in which we say that the covenant and election are parallel and even they are identical, because both these concepts talk about the reciprocal relationship: Yahweh choosing Israel and Israel choosing Yahweh. In this reciprocal

410 C. D. Jathanna, 'The Covenant and Covenant Making in Pentateuch," *Bangalore Theological Forum* 3 (1969), p. 54.

411 Claus Westermann, *Elements of OT Theology* (Atlanta: John Knox Press, 1982), p. 45.

412 Edmond Jacob, *Theology of the OT*, pp. 209-212.

relationship Yahweh promises Israel that he will be their God (Exod 6:7) which means Yahweh intervenes in all situations of Israel whenever they are in need that is, Yahweh is their helper (1 Sam 7:12). In turn it is the duty of Israel to be faithful to Yahweh to Yahweh's covenant and election with them (Deut 4:1, 9, 15: 5:33; 6:2 etc).[413]

Looking at the understanding of covenant and election historically it is evident from the time when Israelites settled in the land of Canaan covenant was merely reduced to some cultic practices under the influence of Baalism. Although the prophets of eighth century did not explicitly made any reference to covenant, they affirmed that it is because Israel is chosen and in covenant with Yahweh they are in particular are subjected to punishment than all other nations (Amos 3:2). Thus, Israel has special obligation not to forego this covenant bond between them and God because they are the chosen ones of God.[414]

In Deutero-Isaiah we find that both covenant and election ideas are blended together. In Isa 44:1-2 the idea of election of patriarchs is emphasized and through this the prophet wanted to affirm the same election-covenant act of God continues even now and in fact the old act is foreshadowed by new creative act by which Yahweh will intervene and manifest in a dynamic way in the history of Israel (Isa 44: 3-5 and 34-38).[415]

Covenant and Law: As was noted earlier, law is bound up with the covenant in the Old Testament. Just as election and covenant are interwoven concepts, law is yet another visible expression of election and subsequently the covenant. The giving of law by God (Exod 19:1-20:21 and 24:1-11) is firmly rooted in the basic relationship of Israel with her God in the total realm of God's election.[416]

In the context of Israel's experience of divine blessings, it is possible for them to receive such blessings only if they keep God's commandments. In other words, the commandments given by God in Exod 20-23 reminds us that Israel needs to translate their faith in covenant God in their practical and concrete manifestation of day-to-day life situations of upholding and practice of the law given to them. The law will not have any force unless it is seen in the redemptive work of God in their daily lives.[417]

---

413 L. Köhler, *OT Theology*, pp. 68-69. Also see R. E. Clements, *OT Theology*, p. 103. Clements is of the view that "in every aspect of God's election of Israel, covenant is manifested in a particular way. Therefore, covenant and election are very much interlinked." (p. 103). See also Gen 12:1-3, 13, 15ff; 15:17-21 etc. In all these passages it is evident that whenever God enters into covenant, his election is specified.

414 Edmond Jacob, *Theology of the OT*, p. 214.

415 C. Stuhlmueller, *Creative Redemption in Deutero-Isaiah* (Rome: Biblical Institute Press, 1970), pp. 126-129.

416 H. J. Boecker, *Law and Administration of Justice in the OT and Ancient Near East* (Minneapolis: Augsburg Publishing house, 1980), p. 136.

417 W. J. Dumbrell, *Covenant and Creation*, p. 91. See also R. E. Clements, *OT Theology*, pp. 101-102. Clements is of the view that the stipulation found in the torah are binding upon

Covenant and Kingship: Some would think that covenant in the OT is linked with the office of kingship. The king in Israel is understood to be the custodian of the law (or the covenant law). It is because of this reason the king is understood to have the duty of proclaiming the law during the course of covenant cult.[418] The origin of royal ideology after the Babylonian exile is also a significant factor in understanding the relationship between covenant and kingship. After the exile, the people of Israel began to ask the question: is there any more covenant relationship existing between them and God? An answer to this question was somewhat partially answered in the promissory type of covenant when the dynasty of David continued on the throne of Judah. Two factors are particularly noted when we talk about covenant and its relationship with the kingship. First, kingship was part of the divine choice/election. Both Saul and David are carefully appointed by the prophet with the divine choice of election. This is a confirmation that Yahweh is in close covenantal relationship with the people of Israel. Second, by their appointment to kingship both Saul and David are anointed by the prophet, which is once again an affirmation of close relationship that can exist between Yahweh and king. Also, by this earthly king God's kingship and God's close and covenant relationship with Israel is confirmed.[419]

Covenant and divine revelation and divine protection: The God of covenant through whom Israel came to the definite and more concrete grips with his revelation more particularly through Sinai covenant and subsequently through his continuous protection of his people Israel. In fact, Yahweh's statement about himself (Exod 3:14) is the starting point of his concrete manifestation of covenant with the people.

Walther Eichrodt points out three specific theological principles in operation in the divine revelation that are significant for the faith of Israel. First, God's revelation is made factual through the covenant i.e., revelation is seen as not merely a speculative otherworldly principle, rather it is to be experienced in the very life of the people and in their every dealing God intervenes within their history (Exod 3:16 and see 6:2-9). By intervening and revealing himself in the history of the people and sharing their burdens God's revelation becomes very much real to the people. Second, through the covenant in the context of God's revelation God's will and purpose in the lives of the people is made strong and positive, i.e., "you shall become my people and I shall be your God"—as Eichrodt points out about this theological statement: "it provides (covenant) life with a goal and history with a meaning." Moreover this factual revelation of God to his people provides an atmosphere of trust in God and security from him, especially in the midst of

---

Israel because "to obey the law (torah) and to obey the covenant become virtually synonymous expression" (Jer 2:6,8).

418 G. Widengren, "King and Covenant,: *Journal of Semitic Studies* 2 (1957), pp. 2-9.

419 W. J. Dumbrell, *Covenant and Creation*, p. 139.

threats from their enemies.[420] Third, covenant in the context of revelation also makes the people to realize their unique position in God and their obligation to him alone.[421] Through this divine revelation the covenant relationship is to be actualized, the name Yahweh alone will be remembered and he alone will continue to protect them by his divine providence. This is further strengthened by the fact of giving the people the commandments and emphasizing that there shall be no other gods for the people of Israel except Yahweh whom they should worship (Exod 20:3).

Covenant and Creation: The understanding of covenant is more vividly present in the creation narratives in the book of Genesis, particularly after the flood narratives. In Gen 6:18 it is stated *And I will establish my covenant with you and you shall enter into the ark, you and your sons, your wife, and women of your sons (wives of your sons) with you.* This particular verse comes from priestly source which is a part of larger unit of Gen 6:5-8:22. The section Gen 6:9-22 is combination of P and J source. The use of the word covenant is expressed in the phrase: "And I will establish (set) my covenant" is to be understood in the context of God's saving acts. Furthermore, Gen 6:18 needs to be interpreted in the context of Gen 1:28, the blessing of God in the covenant relationship.[422]

The term used here is *hēqim berit* needs some explanation. The verbal form *hēqim* comes from the verbal root *qûm* which means 'to arise' or 'to stand', in the causative sense it means 'to cause to stand' which is also equivalent to 'erect' or to 'establish.' This causative usage also refers to the act of God's covenant to fulfill, to confirm (Deut 9:5; 1 Sam 1:23; Isa 44:26; Jer 28:6). In other contexts the phrase *hēqim berit* (Gen 6:18; 9:9, 11; 177, 19, 21; Exod 6:4; Lev 26:9; Deut 8:18; 2 Kings 23:3) is meant to refer not the institution of a covenant but its perpetuation. To sum up, the main stress of this text regarding the use of *berit* in the context of creation is that despite human failure and sinfulness God would continue to keep (establish) his covenant with Noah and to the whole humanity.[423]

In Gen 9:1-17 the theology of covenant and creation is more profound. The word *berit* is used in many place in these seventeen verses. Seven times the word *berit* is used very emphatically in this passage. The passage is divided into two parts: vv 1-7 – provision of food for humankind; vv 8-17 – God's promise in the form of covenant, and a sign of covenant. This passage also talks about God's covenant is initiated not only with the humankind but with the entire universe. If we further elaborate on the structure it looks as follows: v 13: God's covenant with the whole earth; v 15: covenant between God-humans-living beings; v 16: covenant between God and all living beings; v 17: covenant between

420 Walther Eichrodt, *Theology* I, p. 36.

421 Ibid., p. 36.

422 Claus Westermann, *Genesis 1-11*, pp. 422-423.

423 W. J. Dumbrell, *Covenant and Creation*, pp. 25-26.

God and all flesh on the earth.[424] In this passage P's description of on the 'sign of covenant' is simple and obvious natural phenomena through which God would bind the people in himself, even the whole creation is bound to God in this sign of covenant.[425]

The purpose of these two creation narratives is to present the covenant concept in a dynamic way. Two observations can be made in this regard: first, the affirmation of P that the whole creation is in the covenant relationship with God, that God is in control of human beings and the entire cosmos. Just because God is in covenant with the whole creation, God will continue to be faithful in preserving the creation; second, even in the midst of the threat and destruction, God will be faithful to keep his covenant, thereby once again he preserves the creation, that God recreates, and reaffirms his faithful commitment to the entire creation.

Thus, the covenant has its dynamism in all the realms of life of the people of Israel as we discussed in its various facets.

Blessing and Curse in the Old Testament and its theological significance: In a globalized world where the prosperity is measured in terms of materialism and mundane blessings, it is very hard to make a meaning out of it. So, also the word curse is very hard to measure as it implies many shades of meaning in different contexts in ancient Israel.

Etymologically the Hebrew root for blessing comes from the word *brk* meaning 'to bless.' Somewhat closely associated roots; *rsh* and *rason* means 'be favorably pleased' or 'favor.' Another root *sih* means 'to advance' or 'prosper.' He books of Psalms and Proverbs emphasizes the idea that 'happy' are those who experiences God's blessings. The state of wellbeing and security that emerges from blessing may be encompassed in the term shalom. The etymology for the word curse comes from the Hebrew root words: *'lh, 'rr, qll.* The word *'lh* reflects the meaning of vocal or written imprecation. The word *'rr* means a kind of banning of receiving any benefits.

Blessing in the Pentateuch: In Genesis 1-11 in the primeval story in the context of creation blessing is vividly presented. In the patriarchal narratives blessing functions in the family or clan and in Deuteronomy blessing functions in the entire nation. The priestly writer in Gen 1:28 communicates the idea of blessings in five verbal terms: fruitful, multiply, fill the earth, subdue and have dominion. These verbal imperatives convey the meaning that God intends to bless and prosper the humanity and given them wellbeing. Priestly writer in the Genesis stories also talks about the land that comes as a sign of blessing (Gen 17:20; 28:1-4). In all these accounts the writer wants to emphasize that blessing is universal that will be in effect through one or two individuals.

424 Claus Westermann, *Genesis 1-11,* pp. 461 & 472.

425 Ibid., p. 472.

Yahwist talks about blessing in a different light. In Gen 12:1-4 we can find that blessing is initiated through Abraham with the dominance of promise motif. Two aspects are noted here in this promise: promise of the land and promise of descendants and both are unconditionally granted. For J blessing is not simply associated with the grant of land but a land filled with fertility and abundance. The blessing is also simultaneously associated with curse in that o\if the land is not filled with fertility and prosperity then it will result in a complete degradation and infertility (Gen 12:39; 27:29; Numb 24:1-6). Elohist depicts the idea of blessing in yet another dimension. In Gen 12:20, the blessing on Abraham is conferred in the midst of foreigners. In Gen 21:17 we see that blessings are mediated through an angel of God to Hagar. In presenting the idea of blessing, Elohist is concerned with God's protection (Exod 14:24-25), the fear of God (Gen 22) which leads to obedience. Deuteronomy particularly deals with the idea of blessings in terms of God-given land as a gift and all the blessings are connected in terms of prosperity and peace in the land. Moreover it makes the gift of land as conditional that Israel has to be in total obedience to God's commandments (Deut 30:10).

Blessing and the prophets: The prophetic literature depicts blessing in terms of God's salvation that will be initiated in the lives of the people of Israel. Jeremiah communicates the blessings of God in terms of the wellbeing that will be seen in the lives of the exiles (Jer 29:4-7; 32:15). Deutero Isaiah proclaims the state of blessedness to the Babylonian exiles in the midst of their despondent and illusory hope that the people would returned to their own land and this deliverance communicated by the prophet is nothing but the blessings that will be showered upon them. The prophetic utterance of blessings is also connected with peace as a sign of blessing and promise (Micah 4:3-4 and Isaiah 11).

Prophets and curse: Prophets very often talk about curse in different contexts as a condition opposite of blessings. Jeremiah in 20:14-15 pronounces a double curse of the day when he was born and on the person who brought the news to his father about his birth. The main reason why Jeremiah pronounces this curse is to know the purpose of unknowable and inscrutable nature of God.[426] During the eighth and seventh centuries prophecy curse was pronounced as war threat, siege warfare, exile and imprisonment and destruction of basic source of subsistence. The curse imagery found in prophets (Jer 20:5-6; 31:45; Zeph 1:7-13; Amos 5:11) clearly project the socio-economic and political condition of the above mentioned centuries due to the growth of urbanization. The debased religious, moral and ethical standards of the time invited a condition of alienation between the people and God as the people's minds are perverted and even become corrupt.[427]

426 Jack R. Lundblom, 'The double curse in Jeremiah 20:14-18," *Journal of Biblical Literature* 104 (1985), pp. 589-600.

427 See Jeremy D. Smoak, "Building Houses and Planting Vineyards: The Early Inner-biblical Discourse on an Ancient Israelite War Time Curse," *Journal of Biblical Literature* 127 (2008), pp. 19-35.

Blessing and curse in the Psalms: Artur Weiser is of the view that "blessing and curse originate in the magic-dynamic sense of being alive; originally they are conceived to be magical charms capable of producing an effect by their own inherent power and had the purpose of increasing or decreasing the vitality of human beings, that is to say, of producing salvation (*heil)* or disaster (*unheil*) by the virtue of their own power."[428] While this may be the situation for the ancient poetic and Psalmic literature, the book of Psalms is freed from such a magical influence although the evocative power of the words were very much found in the psalms. The psalms basically affirm that Yahweh is the source and dispenser of blessing (Pss 24:5; 128:5 and 134:3). Blessing is pronounced who abides by the covenant commandments of Yahweh (Pss 2:11; 34:8; 40:4; 84:5; 112:1; 146:5). It must be noted that the curse and its formulaic expressions are also rooted in the realm of magic and probably some such influence of curse may be noted in Deut 27, 28 chapters and in Josh 5:23; 21:5. The curse is also associated with the stipulations of the covenant as found in the formula "cursed before the face of Yahweh" in Josh 6:26 and 1 Sam 26:19. In Pss 109 and 137 we find curse that is addressed towards the tormentors and the enemies. In psalms curse could also take the form of judgment (Ps 83:9f), adversaries (Pss 37:34; 149:7) and prayer of vengeance (Pss 17:13; 28:4; 54:5; 56:7; 58:6).

Curse in the book of Job: In the book of Job in 3:1-31, the pronouncement of curse is response to catastrophic suffering which calls for a radical reordering of life. In this text, it is to be noted that Job's crisis reflects human predicament and suffering that goes against traditional understanding of misery and suffering. Job's rhetoric in the above mentioned text shatters and dismantles all that is seen in order and without any disruption. The words of Job moves from disorientation and deconstruction to reconstruction and also from curse (discontinuity) to blessing.[429]

Blessing and creation: According to Claus Westermann God's activity in blessing is based on the blessing bestowed on humanity within the context of creation. This blessing is not simply confined to Israel but to all the creatures of God. Creation is basically understood within the framework of blessing. God created all living beings and then blessed them including human beings. More particularly the living creatures including human beings are blessed in the sense of giving them the ability to reproduce and multiply in number and thus the whole earth may be filled with living creatures and human population. Furthermore, God endows the creatures with his blessings so that they will be preserved and in the case of earth it will be renewed and the land becomes fertile and yields its fruit in due season.[430]

428 Artur Weiser, *The Psalms: A Commentary* (London; SCM Press, 1962), p. 86.

429 See Valerie Forstman Petty, "Let there be Darkness: Continuity and Discontinuity in the Course of Job 3," *Journal for the Study of the Old Testament* 24:4 (2002), pp. 89-104.

430 Claus Westermann, *Elements of OT Theology*, pp. 114-117.

Blessing and kingship: In the Old Testament the concept of blessing is concretely related to the institution of kingship. God's blessing is continued to be demonstrated in and through the kingship. Westermann is right in saying that God's continued activity of blessing is shown in three essential features of kingship. First, kingship is universal just as blessing is universal. God as the king rules over the people and bestows on them the blessings for their wellbeing and the whole creation. Second, the human king is understood as the one who mediates God's blessings to the people. The kings are appointed by Yahweh as his vicegerents so that they would lead the people in the path of blessing and prosperity. Third, just as the father leads and guides the family as its leader, the king is also the mediator of God's blessings upon the people. In times of danger and threat from their enemies king led the people of Israel by fighting on behalf of God and led them to victory which is a practical manifestation of God's blessings upon them.[431]

Blessing in the context of worship: Numbers 6:22-27 is considered to be a key text to invoke God's blessings upon the people by means of a priestly blessing mentioned. This passage talks about both act and word through which God's blessing is transferred to the people with the help of the priest as a mediator. This formula through which priestly blessings are pronounced is an advanced stage within the history of the people of Israel that God no longer speaks to the people directly but only through mediation. The liturgical elements including this priestly blessing in Numb 6 has become significant in this direction including the celebration of festivals and veneration of holy places. Thus, God's blessings are channelized in and through these liturgical elements in the context of worship.[432] It is firmly believed that in the context of cult God's blessings are experienced. God pours out his blessings on his devotees in order to bless them with prosperity and wellbeing.

Blessing and deliverance: In the Old Testament God's salvation is seen as his blessing and it is an act of God's liberation, rescue and redemption. God's saving activity on human beings is practically demonstrated through God's deliverance and blessing. Claus Westermann is of the view that blessing is a continuous act of God that is either visible or not visible. Thus, it is a constant act of God present in its different manifestations. The God who saves and delivers the people from all kinds of oppression is also the one who blesses then with wellbeing. Therefore we cannot separate the activity of God as the savior and as the one who blesses. Both are interlinked and operative in the lives of Israel.[433]

Blessing and the law: Law in the Old Testament is seen as that which builds character and results in a form of life under blessing (Ps 119:30-32). The commandments and the law as a whole given by God to the people of Israel

---

431 Claus Westermann, *Elements of OT Theology*, pp. 108-109.

432 Ibid., pp. 109-110.

433 Claus Westermann, *Blessing in the Bible and the Life of the Church* (Philadelphia: Fortress Press, 1978), pp. 1-14.

directs their path of life and shape their very personality not only in relation to God but with the other communities. Law also manifests the life under blessing that is lived by the people when they live in total obedience to God's law. George W. Coates is of the view that the blessing, the power of God to persuade creatures in anticipation of their choices, is the power of future. It is here that god's lure expresses its call for obedience to the creature. And indeed, it is here the lure takes on the form and shape of law. If law functions as an expression of god's power to persuade, it is blessing. If lapses into negative form, it becomes a burden, indeed it becomes coercive rather than persuasive.[434] Thus, the law functions in the realm of blessing as a way of life that people of Israel always lived under God's guidance and blessing even in the midst of threats and dangers that surrounded them.

Evaluation and conclusion on Covenant, Blessing and Curse: In the light of our foregoing discussion on the theological understanding of covenant, blessing and curse in the Old Testament we now make the following observations, comments and further reflections.

First, throughout the OT we notice that covenant is seen as dynamic concept that it is through this covenant God-human-creation dynamics are unfolded. Through a historical decisive moment God enters into covenant with the people and thereafter operates on how the human beings respond to what God has done in one decisive moment.

Second, covenant in the context of God's election of the people of Israel creates and opens up a wider possibility for them to be accommodative to other nations. In other words, God's elect should not be proud even one moment because God also elects other nations and they are well within the universal plan of God's covenant. Deutero-Isaiah particularly emphasizes this aspect of covenant in 42:1-9; 49:1-6; 53:1-10; 55:35.

Third, in the realm of creation covenant becomes a dynamic concept. Here, covenant in the context of creation is operative in a way that preserves human life on this earth. God creates human beings and other creatures and enters into covenant with them so that they will live in peace, prosperity and in well-being. It is not only human beings but the entire creation is brought under God's covenant in the realm of creation.

Fourth, blessing as a state of being that is to be experienced in the rhythmic flow of everyday life is something we should take note of in the present context of materialistic and consumerist world. If this is the case, then blessing cannot be measures in terms of goods and other possessions. It is the very fact of God's presence with his people that should be counted as blessing. In this sense, it can be stated that God creates, God enters into covenant with human and non-human creation and God constantly blesses them with prosperity, fertility and wellbeing.

434 George W. Coates, "The Way of Obedience – Traditio-Historical and Hermeneutical Reflections on the Balaam Story," *Semeia* 24 (1982), pp. 53-79.

Fifth, the same, God who blesses his people also initiates curse not out of his desire but out of human greed and disobedience. Curse come as an eventual possibility that God resorts in order to redress the skewed situation. In this sense, Lewis S. Ford is right in stating that "the curse of God as punishment could take the form of re-evaluation of the possibilities that people confront in such a way that they embrace."[435] In this sense, curse can open up a new possibility where once again a new blessing is experienced.

Thus, we can conclude that God's covenant, blessings and curse are integrally linked with one another and they need to be articulated together as God's way of grace and mercy on the people.

4.5. Election, Law and Justice in the Old Testament as God's Manifestation of Dealing with Israel and its Implications for us in Today's Context

Election and its significance: The concept of election although used in the key biblical texts, especially in the Old Testament, received less attention in the biblical scholarship. It looks as if there is scarcity in dealing with this topic or priority is not given to this topic like covenant, creation and others concerns. In the OT election is used in the context of the people of Israel, termed as the people of God because Yahweh has chosen them for a particular purpose. Sometimes. Election is used along with other themes like covenant, and law, the latter two as the visible manifestation of election.[436] This presentation concentrates on the theology of election and its related concepts in the Old Testament and before we shall also look briefly into various religious traditions including the some examples from ancient West Asian background.

Election ideas in the ancient West Asian texts: In the ancient West Asian creation theology, particularly in the accounts of the creation of human beings it is made very clear that they are chosen for a particular purpose, that is, to carry out the task of serving the gods.[437] It is argued by some scholars that the idea of election in the OT is borrowed from the ancient West Asian culture, especially in the idea that a particular tribe was chosen by a patron deity.[438]

In one of the Mesopotamian text of creation, it is evident that the human beings are created and chosen for the purpose of their service being rendered to gods. The text reads as follows: " ... create them Lullu (lu-lu-la-a: the savage, the first man) and let him bear the yoke, the yoke he shall bear ... the burden

435 Lewis S. Ford, "The Divine Curse Understood in Terms of Persuasion," *Semeia* 24 (1982), pp. 81-87.

436 Edmond Jacob, *Old Testament Theology*, p. 209.

437 H. H. Rowley, *The Biblical Doctrine of Election* (London: Lutterworth Press, 1952), p. 16.

438 F. M. Cross, *Canaanite Myth and Hebrew Epic*, p. 105.

of creation man shall bear."[439] Furthermore it is stated that the human beings are created and chosen to ease the burdens of gods. The text reads: "I will establish a savage, 'man' shall be his name, verily, savage-man will I create, he shall be charged with the service of the gods, that they might be at ease."[440] In another text it is made clear that human beings are created and chosen by gods in order that they might perform certain specific cultic functions. The reads: "The Anunaki, who fix destinies, both (groups) of them, made answer to Enlil: In uzumma, the bond of heaven ad earth, let us slay (two) lagma gods, with their blood let us create mankind. The service of gods be their portion, For all times ... To increase the abundance in the land, o celebrate the festivals of the gods, To pour out cold water in the great house of god, which is fit to be an exalted sanctuary."[441]

Election ideas in Hindu and Islamic religious traditions: In Hindu religious tradition, especially in the Vedic hymns of creation, particularly in the creation of human beings it is stated at several places that human beings are created and chosen by gods for the ultimate establishment of the law in the manifested world (Atharvaveda xix: 51:1).[442] Furthermore, in the creation hymns of Vedas it is mentioned that man has to participate in the splendor of god by realizing their function in the universal adventure of reality, that is, man has been created by a god for the purpose of definite action.[443] In Upanishads the doctrine of karma affirms that human beings are created and chosen for a cyclic process of karma samsāra. In Chāndogya Upanishad (v:10:17) it is stated that if one has pleasant conduct, they will be reborn either in the womb of Brahman, Kshatriya or Vaisya, but those who has bad conduct will enter into either a womb of a dog, a swine or an outcaste.[444] These texts reveal that human beings are created and chosen for the karma to which they are destined.

In Islam we don't find direct references to the idea of election. However, there indirect references in this regard. The word *'ahd* (injunction or command) convey the idea of covenantal relationship between Allah, his prophets and believers. Here Allah chooses the prophets and particular individuals like Noah, Abraham, Moses and so on (Surah 37:40).[445] Another word *'aqd* (contract) is used in Quran to signify the election bond between Allah and his people. In Surah 38:47 Muslims in general are addressed as "purified ones" or the "elect ones."[446]

---

439 S. G. F. Brandon, *Creation Legends of Ancient Near East* (London: Hodder & Stoughton, 1963), p. 110.

440 J. B. Pritchard, *ANET*, pp. 99-100.

441 S. G. F. Brandon, *Creation Legends*, p. 110.

442 Jeane Miller, *The Vision of Cosmic Order in the Vedas* (London: Routledge, 1985), p. 125.

443 Raimundo Panikkar, *The Vedic Experience* (London: Longman & Todd, 1985), p. 338.

444 Yakub Masih, *The Hindu Religious Thought* (Delhi: Motilal Banarsidas, 1983), p. 86.

445 Ellen, M. Umansky, "Election," in *The Encyclopedia of Religion*, Vol. V (New York: Macmillan Publishing Company, 1987), p. 80.

446 Ibid.

The idea of election is further developed in Sufism of Islam. In the words of Sufi saint Abū Yazid, human beings are created by God and they are chosen for the purpose that the creator's glory may reflect in them. All creatures may see that glory in human beings.[447]

The term "election" and its metaphorical usage in the OT: The most common word used for election in the OT is *bāchar* which refers to the sense of a careful choice, selection in the light of certain criterion. Further, this word is in the sense of Yahweh as the subject of election. It is Yahweh, not the Israel who chose his people out of many others on this earth. The term election is also widely used with variety of metaphors in the Old Testament. In the covenant theology the idea of election is explicitly presented. In Deut 26:17-18 election is explained in terms of covenant which is reciprocal, that is, God's choice of Israel and Israel's choice of God. Here in this context, election and covenant are used in synonymous terms. As a result of God's election Israel should be loyal to God's covenant and this loyalty is essential to the continuance of election.[448]

Election is explicated in the OT by means of two other metaphorical usages. In their metaphor of marriage union, prophets Hosea (2:1-7), Jeremiah (3:11-22) Ezekiel (chapters 16 and 23) and Isaiah (50:1; 54:5; 62:4-5) talks about God's election of Israel in greater significance. Just as in marriage the wife becomes the 'property' (as per the ancient Israelite understanding) of her husband who has purchased her for money, Yahweh has taken possession of the people of Israel. Like a faithful husband he assures them fertility and prosperity; the wife in turn owes obedience abd faithfulness, her infidelity would be a refusal to acknowledge the grace of election. Another image is borrowed from the realm of natural relations is that of a relationship between a father and a son is used in the context of election in the Old Testament. Yahweh calls Israel 'the first born son of Yahweh' (Exod 4:22) and gives as realistic s sense to the idea as to the Pharaoh's family relationships the idea to which this election is compared and contrasted. In biblical language, the son is the one who was created by the father and who consequently is in a relationship of dependence in regard to him, that is why the divine fatherhood is endowed with a sovereignty which was vainly sought for in human relationships (see Isa 63:16; 64:7).

Election and creation theme in Deutero-Isaiah: In a more convincing manner Deutero-Isaiah talks about the theme of election in the light of creation. Before taking on the discussion of some specific texts in this regard, let us discuss a brief historical background of the prophet in this regard. The prophetic message is primarily directed to the exilic situation of the people of Israel when Israel has confronted with the might of Babylonian power. Prophet wanted them to assure of a great comfort, and on the part of Israel, they were seeking God's abundant grace than ever before. It is at this point, Deutero-Isaiah combined two independent

447 R. C. Zaehner, *Hindu Muslim Mysticism* (London: Athlone Press, 1960), p. 94.

448 H. H. Rowley, *The Biblical Doctrine of Election*, p. 68.

traditions, i.e., creation and election. Keeping in mind a definite need of the people Deutero-Isaiah has an urge to talk about the creation tradition. At this time of history, Deutero-Isaiah makes particular use of the "literary category of the priestly oracle of response for his proclamation of salvation."[449] This fact is further substantiated by the use of certain vocabulary by the prophet. Words like 'fear not', 'I redeem', 'I strengthen you', 'I am with you', 'you are mine' (Isa 41:10, 13; 43:1, 5; 44:2ff) affirms the fact that Isaiah in a marvelous way blends together creation-election traditions, in the historical situation in which he was placed.[450] For Deutero-Isaiah it is the election that precedes creation in the sense that at the time of exile when people have thought about their situation as 'the elect' evokes them to reflect upon creation. Thus, both election and creation traditions are interlinked.

Some important texts in Deutero-Isaiah on election-creation theology: We shall now focus on few significant texts in Deutero-Isaiah for a more closer understanding of election in the light of creation.

<u>Isaiah 41:9</u> here the verb *bāchar* is used with the shade of meaning in tune with Deuteronomy. The idea of election in this text refers to God's choice of Israel out of many other people, and that Israel is chosen with a future hope.[451] Further, the prophet refers to the fact of election that was initiated with patriarchs, but it is actually intensified in the creative action of Yahweh by his special intervention in the history. Thereby, Isaiah once again brings out creation and election traditions blending them together in order to affirm to the people of Israel that they are chosen people and at all the points in the history and at all circumstances God was with them.[452]

<u>Isaiah 44:1-5</u> perhaps this is one of the most crucial passages of Deutero-Isaiah's theology of election-creation. In this passage the election tradition is understood more than the exodus event. The prophet affirms that it is in the election framework that the deliverance of Israel took place in the history of Israel. This fact is further strengthened by the prophet by referring to creation (as creative redemption of Yahweh).[453] This passage is generally considered to be an oracle of salvation[454] with the following structure: vv 1-2a: salvation or introduction; v 2b: expression of encouragement; vv 3-4: results of Yahweh's intervention; v 5: purpose and summary of Yahweh's intervention. Unlike any other oracle of judgment, one element is not noticed here i.e., the reasons for encouragement are not mentioned, but implicit reasons for encouragement are presented in the first

449 Gerhard von Rad, *Old Testament Theology*, Vol. II, 1965, p. 241.

450 Ibid., p. 241.

451 Claus Westermann, *Isaiah 40-66* (London: SCM Press, 1969), p. 70.

452 Ibid., p. 71.

453 Ibid., p. 135.

454 Carroll Stuhlmueller, *Creative Redemption*, p. 265.

two verses. The Sitz im Leben of this passage is explained as cultic plaint (see also Isa 43:23-28).

Vv 1-2 begins with a consequential note of the phrase "Israel whom I have chosen." This phrase occurs both in v 1a and v 2b in the Hebrew text. The main emphasis falls on the choice of Jacob here as Yahweh's servant in the past and the continuation of that choice in the present. Vv 3-5 combines the idea of election with creation that the result of Yahweh's choice of Israel is explained. The words used in this contest include: water, spirit and blessing are the words used in the sense of re-creation, purification and renewal and God's creative power. Yahweh provided a new dimension to the election to the chosen ones even in the helpless situation. Thus, the prophet theologically affirms the fact of Yahweh's creative redemption in election in that Yahweh controls, guides and provides in all areas of life and existence.[455]

Law and its significance: Law in the Old Testament is aimed at all levels in maintaining the community of Israel. It also enables the members of the Israelite community to live together peacefully. On the whole we can say that the law includes both the direction of life in the community and punishment if disobeyed to that direction. Law in the OT defines the fundamental existence of the people of Israel in all walks of their life. In this presentation, we shall briefly consider few important concerns of the theology of law in the OT that includes its terminology, law in the ancient West Asian and other Indian religious traditions, law in relation to election, covenant, creation, law as revelation and promise, law in the eschatological sense.

Law in the ancient West Asian religious traditions: Several laws have been identified and discussed from the ancient West Asian religious traditions. The ancient laws have been discovered from the Sumerian king Ur-Nammu of the city of Ur. It is dated that these laws belong to 2050 BCE. Same way another collection of were identified from Amorite king Bilalama of the city of Eshnunna dated in the last quarter of twentieth century BCE. Perhaps the most prominent collection is from the law collection of Hammurabi, king of Babylon, dated from the end of eighteenth century BCE. These laws in general are collection of daily regulations in the community, articulation of legal procedures and observances. Sometimes these law codes are very systematically organized with well developed structure. The code of Hammurabi has a prologue and an epilogue. King Hammurabi mentions all important gods of the country who had authorized him to write a code. The epilogue contains a brief blessings for the kings who applied the laws and extensive curses for those who did not observe the code. In the first part the code essentially deals with legal subjects that govern public order. We also find prescription on the ordered administration of justice, the protection of property, duties towards king and state. While the large section deals predominantly with the interest and concerns of the individual citizen, prescription about the family

455 Carroll Stuhlmueller, *Creative Redemption*, pp. 128-129.

and property law, inheritance, bodily integrity and problems that occur in the context of trade and agriculture. The code has been shaped for the purpose of establishing an ordered and just judicial process. The purpose of the legislation as expressed in the prologue and the epilogue is "to cause justice to prevail in the land" is incorporated into the code itself right from the beginning. Legislations of restitution were also strictly laid for the criminals and the theft of temple and palace property. Basically, death penalty was meant for the thefts and the criminals.[456] All these general concerns of the law from Hammurabi can be found in the Pentateuchal law codes in different places.

Law in some major religious traditions: In classical Hinduism we dot find any difference between law and religion. Both these are articulated in the concept of dharma. There are four sources of dharma in legal literatures. The primary one among them is Veda. All the things related to dharma can be traced in the utterances of Vedas. Smirti literatures attempt to each righteousness as reflected in the conduct of one's life. Puranas, a sub-category of Smirti consists of mythological stories related to establishing righteousness by the incarnation of various gods. In Mahabharata and Ramayana we find large portions of didactic teachings aiming at justice and righteousness in the society. In Dharmashastra, a popular and technical name for legal material in Hinduism we find a code of Manu called Manusmriti, we find a lot of legal materials and statements of the principles of righteousness, although some laws are clearly prejudiced against the Dalits in the Indian society.

In Islam we find Shariah, an Arabic term used to refer to Islamic law. It originally meant a path trodden by a camel to reach its water source. For a Muslim it is the way that leads a righteous to paradise in their afterlife. Shariah is not just religious law but it also covers daily affairs of human beings. The interpretation of Shariah depends on each Islamic school and their division.

Law in the Old Testament and its theological significance: The word for the law in the OT comes from the word *torah* which is translated as law but more importantly the word means to instruct, direct, aim or point out. Various other meanings are possible with this word: Torah refers to religious instructions by a priest (Jer 18:18). Torah also includes rules of cultic, ethical and hygienic realm.[457] Other terms apart from Torah used for Israelite law are: *mitzwah* (Gen 26:5); *dābar* (Exod 34:28), *chq* (Amos 2:4); *mishphat* (Exod 21:1) and *dāt* (Esther 1:8). These words are translated as commandment, word, decree, precepts, judgment, custom etc. In the next few paragraphs we shall look at the theological significance of law in relation to certain themes in the Old Testament.

Law as God's will: Yahweh's will is communicated to the people of Israel in and through the law that is given to them. In the OT the law is primarily associated with the divine name Yahweh. Further, the law giving and the theophanic

456 Hans Jochen Boecker, *Law and Administration of Justice*, pp. 79-86.

457 Ronald E. Clements, *OT Theology*, p. 106.

manifestation of God is associated with commandments is an indication that law and holiness are interconnected. In this regard both the chapters 19 and 20 of Exodus are inseparable. For Israel Yahweh is personal God who actively participates in their historical events. It is this that makes the life of the people of Israel a special one as they are under God's will. The law makes that God's will a possibility. Yahweh's will is clearly directed in every single word and commandment that is communicated to the people through Moses.

Law and Self-revelation of Yahweh: Israel has experienced a greatest moment in their lives and history when Yahweh revealed himself to Moses. It is a decisive moment in the entire history of the people of Israel. God has not withheld God's revelation from the people, but in varying measure, according to the capacity and willingness of the people to receive it, had been granted to them. The uniqueness of God's choice of Israel was the uniqueness of the degree in which God purposed to reveal God's character and will through the people of Israel. The media pf revelation was frequently manifestation in the theophanic realm. Most important element of the law in the Old Testament is the divine revelation through the word, the giving of the law at Sinai (Exod 31:18). In and through the events related to the Sinai episode Yahweh revealed the divine will and Yahweh's purpose for the life of the people of Israel. After the Sinai revelation the people of Israel are no more the same as before; they were transformed as a people of God renewed and rejuvenated than ever before.

Law and Election: Israel always believed that they are specially chosen people of Yahweh. But it is stated emphatically that Israel's election happened not because that they are special people than all other people in the world. But Israel is chosen completely out of God's love, chose Israel in her weakness and worthlessness (Deut 7:6, 7f; 9:5f). Alongside the talk of Israel's election in the event of deliverance from Egypt, which may be found evenly distributed throughout the Old Testament, there stands the instance that the election of Israel is grounded in the election of Israel's ancestors: Abraham, Isaac and Jacob. Israel was elected by God against the background of the total depravity of the whole human race, and thus in this election, before the law was given, the promise of salvation was already given. H. H. Rowley talks about the concept of election in the light of services demanded by the one who elected Israel. God chose Israel in order that God might choose Israel in order to serve him as a result of her gratitude towards God's election.[458] Those who claim that they are the heirs of ancestors of Israel have to faithfully follow God and be obedient to him in all respects and this should be clearly demonstrated in the covenantal laws and stipulations that they received from God. As an elect nation and people this is the fundamental duty of the people towards the one who chose them. The elect people are given various laws in order that they might be guided by those stipulations and laws.

---

458 H. H. Rowley, *The Biblical Doctrine of Election* (London: Lutterworth Press, 1950), p. 45.

Law and Covenant: The first mention of covenant in the Old Testament is found in Gen 9:9-12 wherein the covenant between God and Noah after the flood is mentioned. God now sets up eternal covenant with the humanity through Noah. Universal laws on the nature: day and night seasons of different kind are now set up once again after the initial creation act of God already mentioned in Genesis chapter 1. God gives laws to Israel because God redeemed them from the Egyptian slavery (Exod 20:1-2; Deut 5:6). The two law collections of Leviticus and Deuteronomy both conclude with lists of blessings and curses (Lev 26:3-45; Deut 27:12-28), and Moses summarizes the choice between them in a clear fashion as follows: "see I set before you today life and prosperity, death and destruction" (Deut 30:15). Israel's very participation in the covenant was dependent on their attitude towards the law. Continuous disobedience to the law would lead to the loss of all covenant privileges on the part of Israel. The Book of Covenant marked a decisive consequence for the Old Testament understanding of law and justice. The law is essentially understood as the divinely given law to the chosen people. The understanding of the law developed along with the desire to protect the distinctiveness of the covenant people over against the syncretististic and assimilationist religious influences surrounding Israel.

Looking the relationship between the law and covenant more closely, particularly in the context of the covenant, law could be understood as stipulations given by one partner to another, may be exemplified by the law given by a king to a vassal. During the eighth century BCE prophet Hosea and his contemporaries argued that the covenantal faithfulness expressed in the Sinai tradition. The narrative section of Hosea clearly depicts a contrast between the faithfulness of Yahweh and unfaithfulness of Israel towards God's covenant. Prophet Jeremiah is of the view that In the old covenant Israel failed to obey God's law and thus God would once again initiates a new covenant whereby a new law would be initiated in that God will put this new law in the hearts of the people and they would therefore obey the new law that God would write upon the hearts of the people.

Law and Creation: God's creation of the universe in six days and resting on the seventh day speaks of integral connection between law and creation. God has set the universal laws at the time of creation and thus those eternal laws and universal principles will stand and remain as long as God's creation continue to exist. The day and night, light and darkness, sun, moon and stars and other created beings as well as in animate things will never cease to exist as long as the universe continue to exist. Thus, God as lawgiver has set everything in perfect order that is good for the entire creation. Even the idea of human domination in the context of human 'superior' status in the creation is against God's policy of creation in the context of law. Human beings are not given any sanction to dominate the earth's rich resources created by God is the basic law that is given by God must be upheld by the human beings at all times. The institutions of sabbatical and jubilee years are the clear examples of this fact that land is to be cultivated and not to be exploited at any cost (Exod 23 and Lev. 25).

Thus, the multi-dimensionality of the understanding of the law as discussed above is a clear aspect that Israelites rested their faith in God. The law as noted above has also become the basic core of Israelite faith and existence in all the walks of their life.

Implications of the Old Testament understanding of the law in the Indian context: Law in the Indian context has some similarities with that of the Old Testament presentation of the law and various law codes. To cite one concrete example in this regard, we can cite Indian penal code as the case in point. It has lot of scope and similarity if we compare it with the Old Testament law in several aspects.

Justice in the Old Testament: The understanding of justice in the Old Testament is very complex and multi-faceted in its approach and content. For the want of space we shall concentrate on the very important dimensions of this theme found in the Old Testament and later show its general relevance in our contemporary Indian situation. Moreover justice is always a relational concept in the Old Testament and it is never understood as an abstract and isolated concept. Justice as a relational concept in the ancient Israelite society is the most important theme in that it pervades all walks of Israelite life and her existence on this earth.

The concepts of *mišpāt* and *sedāqā* used in the prophetic literature represent the highest value of human behavior and human condition.[459] Both these appear as spheres of power which already exist in advance of human actions. In Amos 6:12 they are compared with draught animals, productive powers which a person needs in order to live. Once they are misused they become poisons with a sinister effect. They also resemble like a fluid. They are expected like the ever flowing stream and river over the people (Amos 5:24). But, once they are misused they turn into a bitter liquid. This river comes from above as the source of it is Yahweh who indeed makes it rain *sedāqā* (Hos. 10:12; Joel 2:23).[460] Moreover, these concepts not only are related to the individual spheres of life but also radiate out to the whole land, creating harmony between *society and nature* (Ps. 72:1-3; Joel 2:21-23). The reversal which turns *mišpā*t into the bitterness of wormwood destroys environment, making fields unfruitful (Hos 10:4). Thus, both these concepts are not abstract principles but they are spheres of powerful activity and interaction between God and humans and between humans and humans. These concepts are also supported by linguistic parallels from the Canaanite background. In Canaanite religion the words *sedeq* and *mišōr* (also used for *mišpā*t in Isa. 11:4) were gods. But they were not self-contained, individual figures. They were active forces which a person adopted and made his own, and in which he realizes

459 Klaus Koch, *The Prophets,* Vol. 1. *The Assyrian Period* (Philadelphia: Fortress Press, 1983), p. 57.

460 Ibid., p. 58.

himself. When Israel took over this language from Canaan, it rejected the ritual veneration of forces of nature and other elements but gave them a new function as Yahweh's active powers. For a Hebrew what is more sensible and valuable is to express his or her solidarity with his or her brother even at the time when a festive celebration is carried out. This sense of solidarity created an awareness and consciousness of community, not only between God and humans but also humans and nature. Thus, both *mišpāt* and *sedāqā* are like active forces power that are permeating the entire realm of individual and community life in ancient Israel and to these prophets became the guiding light of the people.[461] In other words the Hebrew prophets envisaged a kind of created and established order in which a particular course of God's salvation history is established in the realm of society, particularly to those *dallim* who are marginalized in the society. This created order alone provides the conditions and possibilities for a successful and harmonious life in the society. If anything counters this established order it is the reversal of *mišpā*t and *sedāqā* and that condition is expressed in the term *Pesa'* which is a violent rebellion against Yahweh. It is at the same time a stupid demolition of the foundation of one's own life.[462] Thus, in very clear terms and conditions the Hebrew prophets communicated their uncompromising message of justice and righteousness to the people of ancient Israelite community.

The term *mišpāt* is often used as a breach of justice suffered by Israelites at the hands of their corrupt leaders (Isa 1:17, 21; 5:7; 10:2; 59:8-9; Hab 1:4). Due to this, Yahweh himself enters into judgment with his own people. The Lord's judgment is not only directed against corrupt leaders but towards the people for their sin (Isa 4:4; Jer 5:1; Ezek 5:6-7; 20:11; Hos 5:1; Mal 3:5).[463]

Concerning *sedāqā* and its dynamism James L. Mays states:

> *sedāqā* is the quality of life displayed by those who live up to the norms inherent in a given relationship and thereby do right by the other person or persons involved. The two most important spheres for righteousness were the relationship between Yahweh and Israel defined in the covenant and expressed in the cult, and the relationship of man in the social order of the folk ... In Amos *sedāqā* applies to the relational life of the social partners in the people of Israel. Of course Yahweh is regarded as the patron and enforcer of the social order, but what is in view is the righteousness of Israelites in relation to each other.[464]

---

461 Klaus Koch, *The Prophets: Vol. 1. The Assyrian Period* (Philadelphia: Fortress Press, 1983), pp. 59-60.

462 Ibid., p. 62.

463 Peter Enns, " *mišpāt*," in Willem A. VanGemeren (ed.), *New International Dictionary of Old Testament Theology and Exegesis*, Vol. 2 (UK: Patennoster Press, 1996), p. 1144.

464 James Luther Mays, Amos*: A Commentary* (London: SCM Press, 1969), pp. 92-93.

Amos and other prophets in the Hebrew Bible often relate the concept of *sedāqā* to the issues of social justice and it is talked in terms of maintenance of relationship between God and people.[465] There can be no future if the reversal of *mišpāt* and *sedāqā* takes place in the community of Israel. The well-being of the community very much depends on these two aspects and how they become operative on a day to day basis. There is no place for any individualism in this quest to establish justice and righteousness. On a similar concern Brueggemann writes:

> There can be no viable future of well-being for the Jerusalem establishment, except on the condition of the well-being of the entire community. This conviction is characteristically stated in the negative, as in the prophetic lawsuit speech. It is not, however, difficult to transpose the threat into a possibility. When strong and powerful mobilize their resources and energy for the weak and vulnerable, peace and prosperity are generated for all ... Prophetic mediation of Yahweh, rooted in deep covenantalism, strikes a profound blow against all individualism that assumes that private gifts from Yahweh can be had at the expense of the community. The community to which Yahweh attends is grounded in nothing less than Yahweh's summons to membership, a summons that cannot be evaded. For this reason the prophets stand against kings who characteristically imagined they were exceptional.[466]

The justice and righteousness thus talk about just dealing in the social sphere, particularly as they are related to *derek*, "way" of life as found in Gen. 18:19 "So that they keep the *derek* of Yahweh by dealing with righteousness and justice." In Isa 59:8-9 we find similar words: "They do not care for the *way* of integrity, there is no justice in their course. They make their *paths* crooked, no one who walks in them cares for integrity. That is why justice is far from us, and righteousness does not reach us."[467]

Theological significance of justice in the Old Testament: In the light of the above discussion we can note that justice in the Old Testament is always a relational concept and one cannot see it as an abstract entity. The justice and righteousness as noted above are the basic tenets of God's grace and love that they cannot be separated from the very being of God. In the above light we would

465 David J. Reimer, "sdq" in Willem A. VanGemeren (ed.), *New International Dictionary of Old Testament Theology and Exegesis,* Vol. 3 (UK: Patennoster Press, 1996), p. 763.

466 Walter Brueggemann, *Theology of the Old Testament*, pp. 645-46.

467 Moshe Weinfeld, *Social Justice in Ancient Israel and in the Ancient Near East* (Jerusalem: The Magnes Press, 1995), pp. 30-31. In the Code of Hammurabi and in the Mesopotamian account of kittum u mīšarum similar statements can be noticed: "He led the people in the way of truth." "The road/way of truth and equity."

like to discuss few aspects of justice that are theologically related and intertwined with one anoyjer. The overall affirmation is that when God comes to seek justice on this earth and when God comes to judge the earth the discrepancy between justice and injustice will be eliminated (Isa 2; Pss 96 and 98). This understanding of justice of God is inseparably linked to the social justice that is to be practiced in the everyday life of the people.

Justice and Torah: The laws concerning justice emerged since the time of ancient Israelite tribal society. However, there is another notion that the laws only emerged from the time of monarchy since that time necessitated the requirement of the laws to be promulgated for a just governance of the kingdom on the part of the monarch. Laws are enacted as the need in the social realm of the kingdom in the ancient Israel. For instance, the laws concerning just measure of both weight and quantity (Deut 25:13-15) has its addition by the Holiness Code as justice measure in both length and liquid quantity to be sure that all possibilities would be covered (Lev 19:35-36). Injunction against moving of landmark at the border of a neighbor's property (Deut 19:14 and 27:17). Deuteronomy also commanded that the poor, hired servants be paid their wages on the day that were earned (Deut 24:14-15)[468] The spirit of the law, justice and power are inseparably tied in the Old Testament. In general justice means an impartial system of administering justice by settling grievances under the purview of law. The three dimensions of the law and its integral relationship with the justice and vice versa can be noted as follows: first, justice is treated in magnitude with the law; second, justice is taken to be inherent in relation to the law and thirdly, justice is to be seen as an existential reality that is to be regarded as the law is operated in every decision making process. Thus, we can see an integral relationship between law and justice is always maintained and sustained for their health coexistence.

Justice and Shalom: In the Old Testament there exists a fundamental relationship between justice and peace. In other words, justice and peace are sometimes seen as virtual synonyms in the Old Testament. Justice, Shalom and righteousness are seen as parallel themes in the prophetic sayings in the Old Testament (Isa 48:18; 59:8; Zech 4: 11-14; 6:12-14; Mal 2:5-6). God's justice cannot be separated from God's peace, love and mercy since they together constitute God's nature and being. By preaching social justice the prophets of ancient Israel emphasized that the shalom or peace refers to the totality of life and God's shalom refers to living justly and rightly because God is just and righteous. Since peace comes from God, the human beings are expected to maintain justice and peace in everyday realm of their life. Moreover this peace is also integrally connected with God's covenant which calls for a right relationship between God and human beings and between humans and humans and between humans and the rest of creation. This may be called as God's covenantal peace that is manifested

468 Bruce V. Malchow, *Social Justice in the Hebrew Bible* (Collegeville: The Liturgical Press, 1996), pp. 22-24.

in Yahweh's blessings on human and non-human creation. Thus, those who are in this covenantal relationship with God are expected to live and practice shalom in their day to day living that is intrinsically bound up with the practice of justice. Thus, shalom and justice are the twin principles of God's justice and peace that are given to the human beings to be practiced in their day to day living.

Justice and the office of prophets/kingship: The understanding of justice in the everyday life of the individuals and the community is manifested in and through the offices of kingship and prophets. The prophets are regarded as social reformers, the spokespersons for the people on behalf of God. They preached law, future judgment in as much as they preached about the message of hope and salvation. By and large the prophets raised their voice against the social injustice perpetuated by the rich and the aristocrats of the then society (Micah 3:1-3; Hab 1:2-4; Jer 22:13-17; Isa 5:8 and Amos 2:1-2; 4:1; 5:7, 11, 24; 6:11). By this one can note the point that the Hebrew prophets were the champions of social justice Similarly the kings of Israel were also be seen as responsible persons for establishing and maintaining order in the society. The royal psalms in particular depict that king as a representative of the people before God is also seen as the ruler of Yahweh, the one responsible for maintaining justice in the day to day affairs of the society. The king in the ancient Israel is thus assured of Yahweh's support and guidance in the battle against the enemies of Israel (Pss 18:20; 21 and 144). Moreover it is affirmed that the chief concern of the king is to protect the poor and marginalized in the society against their oppressors and thus maintains justice and order in the society (Ps 72).

Justice and Power: Power as a relational term for the understanding of justice or justice in relation to power is yet another significant concern in the Old Testament. In God both justice and power are harmonized since God is God of justice and love. In the Old Testament power is always directed towards establishment of justice and peace among people. Since, God is the source of all power and authority that power is always directed towards establishing peace, justice and order in the society and not to act as ruthless authority. God appoints kings or other rulers and gives them power in order that they become accountable to God in their exercise of power (Prov 28:15-16). This accountability comes by not bossing over the people rather it comes by establishing order and justice and restoring the fortunes of the poor and vulnerable in the society.

On the basis of our foregoing discussion on the themes of election, law and justice and their various facets in the Old Testament we now make the following concluding observations:

First, election was always an important concept through which Yahweh manifested his guiding presence towards Israel in all their life. At the same time, election puts them under tremendous responsibility as the people who should abide and follow God's commandments more than other people. Yahweh deals with Israel more firmly than other nations because of this election bond between them and God. Also Israel is chosen to function as light to other nations. However, God's election is also extended to other nations apart from Israel.

Second, law as guiding principle of the ancient Israelite society is its basic core pervades in all walks of their daily lives. If at any time the community falters in any of the ordered principles law corrects that kind of aberration and puts the people back on a right path. Law as a guiding force also leads them against injustice and chaos in the society.

Third, just as law is the fundamental core of the ancient Israelite society, justice is the cardinal principle upon which the society is established. The order and peace is manifested and maintained by the just practices of the people, God's appointed prophets and kings and also judges are supposed to maintain. Thus, justice is viewed as something inherently found in all realms of Israelite society. Justice along with God's grant of power is integrally interconnected so that peace and wellbeing of the entire creation is envisaged. Justice in this sense is viewed as God's power manifested towards restoring the fortunes of marginalized and vulnerable in the society.

Fourth, election, law and justice in the present Indian context are perverted and misused for personal and selfish gains in the society. It becomes hard to get justice, especially the poor becomes further vulnerable and alienated since justice is totally denied and is sold like a commodity in the market. Sometimes, on the part of Christians there is an exclusive tendency to separate themselves from other people and faiths because of the idea of election. But, nowhere in the Old Testament this sort of exclusive tendency is envisaged on account of God's election of Israel. Thus, one can see the Old Testament models of election, law and justice as appropriate principles to be followed and practiced in today's Indian context for a just and healthy society. Thus, the law and justice if properly viewed will serve the purpose of serving all sections of the society, particularly the poor and marginalized in the society. Eventually the principles of election, law and justice articulated in the Old Testament will have lasting effect in today's fragmented Indian society that craves for social justice and proper implementation of the legal procedures.

4.6 Israelite Monarchy, Prophecy and the Kingship of God in the Old Testament and their Significance in India Today

Ancient Israelite society had gone through tremendous transformation with the adoption of monarchy. As a tribal social system Israel had some distinctive marks and ethos that were radically altered soon after her choosing of monarchy. However, it is not so simple as it sounds. There are some crucial and significant concerns that needs to be considered in understanding the theological significance of monarchy in ancient Israel. While it is common to think that Israelites just adopted monarchic system of governance like any other ancient West Asian country, there are certain crucial indicators that one needs to look into when

Israelites adopted monarchy that is radically different from what was their tribal system.

Israelite Monarchy and Ancient West Asian Monarchy: In general it may be stated that in most of the ancient West Asian monarchial system the administrative system was a centralized one with the power centred in and around the king. Even before the Israelites adopted monarchy The Egyptian, Mesopotamian and Canaanite city-states were living under monarchic form of government. For Egyptians, monarchy was a central institution and the Pharaohs as kings had absolute power as the heads of the state. Moreover, in Egypt the Pharaohs were accorded with divine status and they are none other than the gods themselves. This idea is quite contrary to the Israelite monarchy where the kings are only representatives of God and at no time they were accorded with any divine status. The conception of monarchy in Mesopotamia has some similarities with the ancient Israelite system of monarchy. Both in Israel and in Mesopotamia one of the elders was elected as the king will be in charge of battles or of similar important occasion. The real king was identified with the god of the city who is also regarded as the real owner of the land and tribe. The elder as the king acted on behalf of the god and the people and so Mesopotamian kingship was also sacral in nature like the Israelite kingship.[469] Although these peripheral similarities exist between ancient Israelite monarchy with that of Babylonian system of monarchy we need to probe deeper into some theological issues of monarchy in ancient Israel and prior to that some individual kings need to be considered in the overall significance of Israelite monarchy.

Saul, David and Solomon as Kings of United Monarchy: Saul, a Benjamite tribe was the first chosen king soon after Israelites launched into monarchic system of administration. When Philistines became a threat to Israelites Saul's appointment assumes significance. According to Martin Noth, the achievements of Saul in the war-front not only restrained the Ammonites from further aggression but it produced a great psychological effect on the further progression of Israelites.[470] The result of this act of Saul elevated him to be appointed as king over Israel at Gilgal before all the people (1 Samuel 10:6). However, monarchy under Saul was still like chiefdom and only during the time of David it took the full form of state.

Saul's debacle ion other fronts helped David to consolidate his position as the king over all the tribes of Israel. David was appointed as a king by divine choice. With David the kingdom of Israel entered into a decisive phase as a political power that had tremendous influence in the ancient West Asian context. During this time, there was no option left for the elders of Israel so that they had

469 Sigmund Mowinckel, *He that Cometh: The Messiah Concept in the Old Testament and Later Judaism,* trans. G. W. Anderson (Grand Rapids, MI: William B. Eerdmans Publishing Company, 2005), p. 35.

470 Martin Noth, *The History of Israel* (New York: Harper & Brothers, 1958), p. 170.

to affirm the monarchy under the leadership of David. David was very shrewd to win the favor of all the tribes and that made him to rule Israel with considerable success. Additionally, by defeating the Philistines David brought about the change in the equation of power in the Palestinian region since it elevated the kingdom of Israel as one of the foremost nation. From now on Israel was no longer a national kingdom became an empire by bringing other kingdoms like Philistines, Edomites, Moabites and other non-Israelite population under her. Israel Finkelstein is of the view that the reign of David was a full blown state as it was characterized by territorial expansion with heterogeneous and multi ethnic state, creation of a developed administration and the foundation of Jerusalem as the real capital.[471]

Solomon's succession to the throne of David was marked by bitter dynastic fight and only by eliminating his opponents he was able to sit on the throne. Solomon carried forward the kingdom of David to the road of further development with his ambitious plans. His reign however was not only marked by splendid external achievements but he was known for his ruthless and cruel behaviour to eliminate his opponents. In order to make Israel a booming economic empire, he upgraded the military with better equipments, undertook massive construction projects in the form of the temple and royal palaces in Jerusalem and brought change in the administrative system to meet the demands of the time.[472] He also changed the old tribal administrative districts of his father by dividing the entire nation into twelve districts and centralized the command structure. Lemche thinks that this move of Solomon was an attempt to reduce the political influence of the tribes by replacing their local forms of leadership and also an administrative apparatus to exact revenues and labour.[473]

The Impact of Monarchy: during the Israelite monarchy, power came to be concentrated under few aristocrats and bureaucratic machinery dominated the voice of the common people. The economic system has been totally changed from subsistence to market economy. The land tenure system has also changed because in the tribal confederacy land was very much owned by the family, but now due to the land grabbing policy land was accumulated in the hands of few rich landlords. The production of staple crops was replaced by commercial crops which caters only the need of the rich. A situation came into being where the poor has no other way but to depend on the rich for survival which worsen their conditions they fell into debts. The result was that many of the Israelites lost their land and became tenant farmers, debt servants and landless wage laborers. Religion also came to

471 Israel Finkelstein, "The Emergence of the Monarchy in Israel: The Environment and Socio-Economic Aspect," *Journal for the Study of the Old Testament* 44 (1989), pp. 43-74.

472 Norman K. Gottwald, *The Hebrew Bible: A Socio-Literary Introduction* (Philadelphia: Fortress Press, 1985), p. 322.

473 Niels Peter Lemche, *Ancient Israel: A New History of Israelite Society* (England: JSOT Press, 1988), p. 139.

be more organized with professional priestly class, musicians, scribes who were responsible to compose, sing and write ritual texts. More significantly, Yahweh became the patron deity of the state with royal shrine located in the capital and under the control and protection of the king.

The Theology of Monarchy: With Yahweh as the king firmly established the formation or establishment of human kingship was bound to be a difficult and consider it as a challenge to Yahweh's kingship. The existence of two kings: divine and human raised the legitimacy of monarchy. It was thought that by accepting a human king it dilutes the idea of Yahweh as the king and subsequently and gradually the human king was accepted and thus we see tow traditions: pro and anti monarchic traditions was existing side by side (1 Sam 8-12). It is clear that in the beginning there was a strong resistance to monarch as it was seen as rejection of Yahweh but subsequently we also see it accepted but not without a warning (1 Sam 8:11-18). The anti-monarchic group regarded the history of monarchy in Israel as human history and far from expressing always God's will. The antimonarchic strain would be better understood if we understand the importance of the amphictyonic institution which was regarded being against the Canaanite city-states in terms of society, politics and theology. Israelites believed that Yahweh was experienced in the institution of tribal confederacy that led them to think that they could not experience Yahweh in the monarchic institution. The pro-monarchic group, in order to validate the establishment of monarchy came up with various theological reasons as discussed in the paragraphs that follow.

Monarch as the chosen one of Yahweh: The idea of the king as the chosen one of Yahweh and consequently by the people find its emphatic expression in 2 Sam 16:18: *I will belong to him who has been chosen by Yahweh, by his people and by all men of Israel.* The people were not to appoint anyone who was not chosen by God and the king was not to do his own will and pleasure. In other words, in the kingdom of Israel, the king is chosen by Yahweh is also approved by the people is endowed with the spirit of Yahweh and at no time the king can function on his own but will be guided by the spirit of Yahweh, In the case of Saul this was explicitly made clear when Samuel announced Yahweh's approval of the king (1 Sam 9:16).

Monarch as blessing: Once the king is chosen in the way that was described above then he occupies the most important place as the head of the entire kingdom. The king then becomes a channel of divine blessings. Then the king is a guarantor for all the people of the nation and becomes their defender in the event of any disaster, thus he is depicted as the lamp of Israel (2 Sam 21:17), he is also responsible for the nation's prosperity. He is thus depicted as people's shield (Psalm 84:10). Moreover at times the king functions as a priest in the absence of that office and acts as a mediator between God and the people and communicates God's blessings to the people.

Monarch as the anointed one: The choice of an Israelite king is based on the fact that he is not only chosen by God but also anointed by Yahweh. Although the ritual of anointing is done by the priest it represents the wish of the entire people In regal consecration, anointing marks God's gift of God's spirit to aid the king of Israel in administering God's rule. Anointing was a theological and ritual undergirding of kingship and therefore the anti-monarchic narrative in 1 Samuel 10:17-27 omits anointing clearly to indicate that Yahweh is not involved. However, the duration of the effect of transformation that are seen when the gift of the spirit falls upon the charismatic leader and when the king is anointed marks the difference between the two. While the transformation of the charismatic leaders relates to the momentary ecstasy which indicates a temporary commission from God and a gift of power, the anointing bestows something like an indelible character, a permanent commission and authorization. How important the spirit of gift can be seen from the reason given for the failure and rejection of Saul. It is said that the spirit departed Saul and as a result lost the ability to govern the people.

The King and the Torah: The king as a chosen one of Yahweh was not allowed to do his own will and act according to his pleasure but rule according to the law of God. The king is expected to be absolutely obedient to the law of God and thus required to study the words of Torah (Deut 17:20) The king is expected to be obedient and submissive to Yahweh by observing the commandments of Yahweh. The Torah gives guidance to the king and reminded him of his responsibilities and any deviation by the king on this matter was taken seriously and the prophets took the kings to the task if kings failed to observe the law. On the part of the king observing Torah will bring peace and prosperity in the entire land. Just because someone is king does not give him any special status, but king is made very much subjected to his observance of the stipulations prescribed by the law. On the basis pf the law the kings performance is evaluated and either they are accepted or rejected on that basis only.

The King and the Cult: Monarchy in Israel is understood not as a political but sacred institution. This is evident from the fact that that anointment of the king took place in a cultic setting and place and therefore anointment was also considered as a sacral act. According to John Bright, monarchy was accorded accorded a place in Yahwistic theology and an official notion of kingship was reaffirmed regularly in the cult on festal occasion where the king played a leading role.[474] The relationship between the king and the cult shows that the state has a divine sanction and thereby also the king has become the guarantor of the state's peace and prosperity.

The King as Son of God: The title son of God was used for the king in the ancient West Asia is also found expressed in the Old Testament. The title is used to describe the mutual relationship between God and king as described in

474 John Bright, *History of Israel* (London: SCM Press, 1980), p. 225.

2 Sam 7:14: "I will be his father and he will by my son." The notion of king as son of God does not concern any ontological claim or metaphysical status but is a powerful political claim of peculiar legitimacy. According to Mowinckel, the king as the son of Yahweh, the God of all earth, he has a rightful claim to dominion over the whole earth. However, the sonship does not exist by birth but is declared at certain point. It is declared not by begetting but by adoption or accession. The king is not to be understood in terms of god or heavenly incarnate but is designated heir by appointment. In this sense the king is differentiated between God and human.

The King as Messiah: The king is considered as messiah in ancient Israel. The term messiah is also related to the act of anointing. The anointing as part of the coronation ceremony of the king indicates that the king is the one chosen by Yahweh. Moreover, the anointing and choosing of the king is also metaphorically understood by the Israelites as the messiah is the one who has the particular task of liberating and saving the oppressed community of the people. Again we need to see the king as messiah in the light of the fact that despite optimistic expectations were built on the figure of king, due to the practical failure of this office, the idea of messianic figure was developed in due course. Thus, the coming of messiah is associated with an outbreak of peace. Messiah is not only seen a peaceful ruler, but his coming achieves a definite position, which is peace without ends (Isaiah 9:6). The messianic mission is also seen in terms of establishing justice and restoration of order upon this earth.

The King as Mediator: The king is seen a figure that is endowed with the gifts of leadership and imparting instruction to the people. Among the people who govern the king is expected to govern the people with equity and justice. The king is guided and governed by Yahweh's righteousness thereby he is endowed with the ability to maintain the customs, rights and prosperity of the community under the covenant obligations to judge, to rule rightly, maintain right order in the society. This more specifically involves the task of the king to save the people from the enemies, judge them with equity and justice, to particularly relive the oppressed from their burdens, to show favor towards the unprotected, helpless, the widows, fatherless and aliens. (Pss 45:5, 8; 72:1-4; 122:2-4, 12-14). The king as a mediator between Yahweh and the people bestows blessings in the land by means of rain, good harvest, safety, peace, fertility, sunshine, good season, good relationships between human beings, loyalty and contentment among the people under covenant etc. Thus, the king by being endowed with the spirit of Yahweh performs the will of Yahweh and transmits Yahweh's blessings in the land and thus represents as a mediator between people and Yahweh. At the same time, the king is not endowed with any divine status, rather he is only elevated as above the people by virtue of his being elected to that office.

Prophecy and its theological significance in ancient Israel: The term prophecy as important religious and theological phenomena in the Old Testament is very complex in its origin, history and scope. Prophecy in all different forms contributes to the dynamic process of the faith of Israel in the Old Testament. While it is not possible to explain and include all the important aspects of prophecy in this place, we shall focus on the overall theological significance of prophecy in its theological and religious terms and see how the phenomena of prophecy is relevant in a contemporary setting in the Indian context. This we shall do after few preliminary remarks on the prophecy in the ancient Israel.

The Words Prophecy and Prophets: Both these words are used in the Old Testament interchangeably. In general it is said that a prophecy is an utterance by a prophet about the future. However, it is not only the future, but rather a prophet is the one who derives the message from the present, In this sense the role of the prophets and prophecy may be understood "as the reflexive search for the future is generally bound up with a longing that form now as things will be better: in personal life, in society and in the world."[475] The major goal and of the Old Testament prophecy may be summed up as follows: prophets preserved the faith of Israel before, during and after the exile, and the new attitude or changed attitude in the very faith of Israel expressed in their actions is perhaps the major contribution made by the prophecy to the life of Israel. Moreover the terms prophets and prophecy is also a clear indication that God would intervene in the concrete socio-political and historical realms and affairs of the people of Israel through his servants prophets.

Prophecy in the Ancient West Asian Context - Some glimpses: In the ancient West Asian context the prophecy was a common phenomena. In the Arabian context the name *kaahin* is associated particularly with the one who speaks prophetically to the king about the catastrophe that might take place in the near future. *Kaahin* is consulted when certain important decision needs to be taken, then he is said to have been interceded with the divine in an ecstatic exclamation.[476]

In the context of Mesopotamia prophecy is basically understood in terms of divination. In the Mari texts the word *aapilu* (fem: *aapiltu*) which is translated as "to answer" and they have the function as messengers who might deliver rational message related to the future.

In the Akkadian context prophecies are directed towards the prediction of the past as well as the future events and in this sense it may be closer to Old Testament apocalypticism than the prophecy. For example in one of the texts this idea is seen:

> A ruler will arise, he will rule for thirteen years. There will be an attack of Elam against Akkad and the booty of the Akkad will be carried off

475 Klaus Koch, *Prophets* I (Philadelphia: Fortress Press, 1983), pp. 1-2.

476 J. Pedersen, "The Role Played by Inspired Persons among Israelites and the Arabs," *Studies in OT Prophecy,* ed. H. H. Rowley (Edinburgh: 1950), p. 134.

> ... There will be confusing disturbance, and unhappy events in the land ... another man whose name is not mentioned will arise ... [477]

In Ugarit, in a Baal epic the pronouncement of oracle by artisan god Kothar War-Hasis is addressed as follows:

> I tell you, O Prince Baal, ... Behold your enemy, O Baal ... Behold you shall destroy your foes, you shall take your eternal kingdom, your dominion for generation after generation.[478]

The above oracle is understood as prophecy in the sense that it refers to the future event. One aspect must be borne in mind that the prophetic phenomena in the ancient West Asia is not homogenous rather it is a mixture and combination of several aspects and same may be said in the case of ancient Israelite prophecy.

Theological Significance of Prophecy during various Historical Periods: Before venturing into the aspect of various historical periods let us make some brief comments on the origin of prophecy itself. In order to understand the origins of prophecy as such several questions are to be taken into account. First of all some scholars are of the view that it was due to the semi-nomadic life that was brought forward by the Israelites on their entry into Palestine that had tremendous influence in prophecy. It was also possible that prophecy in Israel was influenced by the Canaanite background, especially when Israelites came down to settle in the land of Canaan syncretistic elements were influential in their religious realm. The phenomena of prophecy according to Walther Eichrodt emerged precisely from the point when there was a revival in the religiou of Yahwism. In other words Eichrodt calls this early part of Israelite prophecy as nabism, arose as a new movement against the process of Canaanization, perhaps not occurred from before the time of Moses onwards[479] Moreover it is argued that the entire prophetism at its early stages might have influenced for the end of the veneration of sacred objects. Also in the context of priestly domination (in their function), who tried to control the entire act of divine to the mere mediation (rather priests were made as mediators between the people and the divine). In this context, prophecy asserts the fact that there can be divine power experienced quite outside the human control or monopoly.

Prophecy before the time of Amos: There are certain distinct features that can be found in the prophecy and the prophets before the time of Amos. Prophetic figures like Samuel, Nathan, Elijah, Elisha, Ahijah and Micaiah ben Imlah are

---

477 James B. Pritchard, *Ancient Near Eastern Texts* (Princeton: Princeton University Press, 1955), p. 606f.

478 Helmer Ringgren, "Prophecy in the Ancient Near East," in *Israel's Prophetic Tradition,* ed. J. R. Porter (Cambridge: Cambridge University Press, 1982), p. 11ff Ringgren cites this text from Halder A, *Association of Cult Prophets among the Ancient Semites* (Uppsala, 1945), p. 81.

479 Walther Eichrodt, *Theology of the Old Testament* I (London: SCM Press, 1960), p. 328.

some of the known figures of this period. The prophets of this period displayed an extraordinary charisma despite other dominant offices like the priest and the king. Perhaps prophecy as an innovative principle of charisma was beginning to mark its impact from this period. The whole activity of prophets during this period may be summed up in the words of Norman K. Gottwald as follows: "The prophets were consistently pre-monarchic or anti-monarchic. They championed the strict interest of national God, and in the very military operations which they supported they could find reason to condemn a king who failed to follow out their wishes in all matters."[480] Among the prophetic figures mentioned during this period notable is the contribution made by Elijah during the ninth century BCE. His role was significant at the time of Ahab when he was involved in his strong condemnation against the religious syncretism involving the worship of Baal. Elijah championed Yahwistic religion and anything that went contrary was challenged by the prophet and thus challenged the very house of Ahab and the entire royal dynasty. In this sense along with Elijah other prophets of the ninth century or before the time of Amos are the innovators of the political set up that was built upon the strict practice of Yahwism in the midst of complex religious situation.

Eighth century prophecy: Eighth century prophecy was unique in the sense that the entire nation rather than the individuals were brought under the ambit of prophecy. Moreover these prophets proclaimed the theme of justice in all their oracles than ever before. They condemned the disparity that was existing between the rich and the poor in all their oracles (Amos 5:7; Isa 5:23; Micah 3:1). Associated with this factor was that throughout eighth century prophets in Israel reminded them that they have forgotten Yahweh their God, who in his saving acts wonderfully led them at every stage (Isa 1:2-3). However, a cautious note must be added that not all the eighth century prophets were operating on the same level with same message. For instance, prophet Hosea was basically concerned with the cultic irregularities; Isaiah was operating from royal tradition even explains the political developments and changes as part of God's plan and purpose. Amos goes even beyond Isaiah and he was not interested in political alliances rather he was concerned with the very deeds of the people. Despite this specific concern of each of the eighth century prophets, there was also a common thread that was running in all the prophets of the eighth century as they were operating on the schema of sin-judgment-salvation. For these prophets salvation of Yahweh comes only when Yahweh begins to perform his acts among the people.

Exilic and Post-exilic prophecy: At the very close to the exile prophecy took some important turn, especially from the catastrophe that began in 701 BCE. When the Assyrian king Sennacherib made his impact through his invasions in the north Israelite kingdom and brought its end. Prophecy was almost silent at this time. There was also a general feeling that persisted all over Israel that the history came to an end especially in the light of large threat still looming the southern

480 Norman K. Gottwald, *All Kingdoms of the Earth* (New York: Harper & Row, 1964), p. 67.

kingdom of Judah. The word from the prophets at this juncture was hardly pronounced. But sooner with the breakdown of Assyrian power and the emergence of Babylonian power once again prophetic activity took a center stage. Prophets like Zephaniah, Nahum and Habakkuk and also two great literary prophets like Jeremiah and Ezekiel played a significant role in delivering the oracles of God's message. Gerhard von Rad notes that there are at least two significant elements that can be noted regarding the prophecy of this time: firstly, the message of the prophets at this time was broader theologically and also more deeper. Yahweh and his dealings in this world are mde clear to the people of Israel (Ezek 16:23; 18; Jer 29; Isa 41:26; 43:9f). These prophets for example, talk a message that in the midst of everything that seems to be a failure, the word of Yahweh stands an authority (Jer 23:28 ff), which brings into life creative action of Yahweh and his presence in this world (Isa 40:6-8; 45:10f). This word of Yahweh not only gives restoration to the people, but also a bold confirmation of the hope to the prophets themselves.[481] Secondly, the future of God was another central element. That is, God's covenant and his faithfulness to make this covenant effective in the lives of the people. However, each prophet of this presented this idea in a profound and distinct way. In the case of Ezekiel, he wanted to stress that each individual is taken into account in what they will be judged according to their individual actions (Ezek 18). Jeremiah too answers the question of making father's sin to be borne by the son, for which the prophet was condemning (Jer 31:29ff). To sum up, von Rad thinks that these prophets, strongly pointed out the deep gulf found in the saving acts of Yahweh and this gulf even led the people ultimately to death (Ezek 37) and it cannot be restored by the past events that is the saving events of the old time.[482] Jeremiah and Ezekiel totally reject the false and illusory visions and signs and thereby call the people to uphold truth and practice justice... Moreover these prophets radically affirmed that only the downfall of the people might bring restoration and the re-constitution of the very life and existence of the people. This message of the prophets is seen as a new vision and creative action of God towards his people. In the case of Deutero-Isaiah the universalistic ideas are very much prevalent in his message. Deutero-Isaiah proclaims in particular the universal mission of Israel; especially in the figure of suffering servant this mission is envisaged.

The post-exilic prophets like Trito-Isaiah, Haggai, Zechariah and Malachi reaffirm the message of the classical prophets, and immediately after the exile kept the idea of restoration of God alive, which is founded upon God in Jerusalem. The message of Trito-Isaiah is seen in this light: to bind up the broken hearted, to proclaim liberty to the captives Isa 61:1. Unlike the earlier prophets, Trito-Isaiah was dealing with a group that was considered as people of little-faith and thus calls them to accept Yahweh as their God (Isa 59:1) The message of Haggai and

481 Gerhard von Rad, *Message of the Prophets* (New York: Harper & Row, 1965), pp. 231-232.

482 Ibid., pp. 232, 238ff.

Zechariah is directed towards the advent of Yahweh and imminent establishment of his kingdom. Furthermore, this message is linked up with the rebuilding of the temple which was already destroyed by thc Babylonians during the exile (Hag 1:1; Zech 8:3). In the book of Malachi we find that an eschatological trend (perhaps the imminent restoration by the love of Yahweh Mal 1:2ff). There is also a message of cultic legalistic tendencies that are to be set right, perhaps as a process of restoration (Mal 1:6-2:9).

The book of Joel and Jonah perhaps stand at the last stage of the Old Testament prophecy before the fully developed apocalyptic thought. We can even see the dawn of apocalyptic thought in the book of Joel and it may be a transition period between prophecy and apocalyptic. The day of the Lord is the dominant idea that is interpreted in this book (Joel 1:15-16). The book of Jonah, whose date is disputed particularly, calls our attention to the condemnation of Jewish particularism instead the book affirms God's plan of universal salvation.

Prophecy and Apocalyptic thought: The post-exilic prophets were unique in the sense that they stressed the need of the ritual, in line of the development of Judaism, in terms of eschatological restoration of the temple in Jerusalem. Perhaps from this point onwards the prophecy was dissociated with the reality of the day. Moreover, after the exile when the nation Israel was no longer stood as a nation, the prophets failed to translate that reality into the universal message of Yahweh. At this juncture, prophecy precisely turned into an apocalyptic thinking. The book of Daniel is seen as overwhelmingly apocalyptic where it is mostly dominated with the reports of vision and dreams in a concealed message. The book so much places its emphasis on the visions and dreams in that God's in the long course of history are interpreted. Ultimately in the end (which is given in terms of calculation of precise years or periods) the sovereignty of God will be a dominant principle. Moreover, the message of the apocalyptic thinkers is universalistic in its outlook in that they emphasize on two aeons, an old aeon which is in sharp contrast with the new aeon and this new aeon will bring salvation. It was argued by Walther Zimmerli that during the Maccabean crisis the apocalyptic thought dominated (almost replaced the role of prophecy) in the pseudonym called Daniel who was in exile during neo-Babylonian period cannot be actually identified as Daniel (Ezek 14:14; 20; 28:3).[483] Perhaps the main theological emphasis of apocalyptic thought may be that in the final analysis the sovereignty of God and the establishment of God's rule will be done. Gerhard von Rad makes a helpful distinction between prophetic and apocalyptic eschatology. The former is about God's action within the realm of history and the latter one may be God's action at the end of history.[484] Moreover it is argued that the apocalyptic eschatology is limited to a particular

483 Walther Zimmerli, *Old Testament Theology in Outline* (Atlanta: John Knox Press, 1978), p. 230.

484 Gerhard von Rad, *Old Testament Theology* Vol II (Edinburgh; Oliver & Boyd, 1965), pp. 303-304.

group (could be religious group), totally separated itself from the national and religious life of the people and refers to a future cosmic transformation.[485]

Some Theological Categories of Prophecy in the Old Testament: In order to be more precise on this area and to be very brief to the point we shall consider some of the important theological categories of prophecy in the ancient Israel so as to see their overall and general implications for our Asian and Indian context.

Prophecy and Tradition: It is generally argued that prophets were totally dependent on different traditions in order to articulate their concerns. One of the basic traditions used by the prophets in general may be the covenant tradition that is stressing the relationship between Yahweh and Israel. Prophets also widely used election tradition and an innovative interpretation was given by the prophets in their interpretation in this regard. Prophets explained clearly that Israel cannot be in any way boast about their unique position as an elect nation since God's election should be viewed more in terms of universal dimension and Israel as an elected nation has more responsibility to be obedient to God's command. Even God's covenant is not to be taken for granted by the people as the prophets time and again remind the people that they need be in constant fear of their God in maintaining their right relationship and in this was did not give a blanket approval for people claim or being proud of their unique traditions. This could also be seen as prophets' unique or radical review of existing tradition in ancient Israel.

Prophecy and History: According to Gerhard von Rad, who looks at the entire material of the Old Testament in the light of historical traditions, not in one single tradition but a variety of traditions within the ambit of salvation history that begins with a little historical creed (Deut 26:5 ff) and through this creed Israel had come out freely from the concept of linear history. There by realizing in the saving acts of Yahweh who has a definite plan for them. Further von Rad argues that the history is related to the eschatology in the message of the prophets. But the word eschatology in this context cannot mean far way event rather every saving act of God is to be seen within the history[486] during the post-exilic prophecy in particular, prophetic view on history is particularly widened. Yahweh as God of Israel hitherto was interpreted as in history as God of universe, is now moved beyond by the prophetic stress of cosmological dimension of the history stressed in an eschatological sense.[487]

Salvation and judgment pattern in the OT prophecy: The entire prophetic corpus may be placed under this pattern in the Old Testament. While some would like to make a clear distinction between prophecy of judgment before exile and prophecy of salvation after exile that clear distinction may not be viable all the time. It is argued that the theological principle involved in the prophetic announcement of repentance may serve as a bridge between the oracle of judgment

485 Paul D. Hanson, *The Dawn of the Apocalyptic* (Philadelphia: Fortress Press, 1975), p. 11.

486 Gerhard von Rad, *Message of the Prophets*, pp. 83 & 91.

487 J. Lindblom, *Prophecy in Ancient Israel* (Oxford: Basil Blackwell, 1963), p. 421.

and oracle of salvation (Jer 26:2 ff). According to Claus Westermann, the prophecy of judgment occupies a very central place in the entire history of Israel and he further recognizes two stages of this happening: firstly, until the time of Amos, we hear about the judgment that was pronounced to the individuals particularly to the king. Secondly, from the time of Amos until 587 BCE which is again divided into two further stages: (i) the prophecy up to the fall of northern kingdom in 722 BCE and (ii) their further involvement in the southern kingdom.[488] The threats of the judgment can be noticed not in the concern of the prophets about their individual sins but the prophets were concerned about the sins of Israel as a whole that drastically threaten the very life and existence of the nation as a whole. These accusations covered a wide range of the issues related to the nation like: social, political, economic, cultic and religious. Prophets also uttered oracles of hope that convey the salivific acts of God for the Israelite nation. This has been done by the Israelite prophets in different ways and means. For instance, the motif of land as a central aspect of promise and hope was preached by the prophets. Prophets preach the message of hope through land theology in that the people are supposed to regain their land and their original status is restored and they will be gathered in their own land under a single ruler. (Ezek 37:15-23). Moreover Israel is restored and united under a king in Davidic line (Amos 9:11-12; Hosea 2:5; Isaiah 9:2-7; 11:1-9; 32:1; Jer 33:13-26 and Ezek 37: 24-28) and this idea is further extended to the coming of a saviour as heavenly figure, the future messianic hope.

Prophecy and the Cult: In general, the Hebrew prophets are called as prophets of cult. It is wrong assumption to think that prophets are against cult, rather it is to be clarified that the prophets only denounced the outward expression of cult without the practice of matters related to justice and righteousness. For instance Ezekiel's theology was directed towards cult, which is centered around the key phrase: "I am Yahweh," that is, Ezekiel declares that everything that is done in the name of cult in Israel should be in line with the obedience to the will of Yahweh. During the post-exilic times the prophecy of salvation was deeply rooted in the eschatological restoration of the temple and the city of God (cf. Zech 12 and Haggai 2) and the prophets of this period particularly prophets like Haggai and Zechariah are often called as cultic prophets. The basic theological implication of the cult for the prophets is not simply the more institutions like temple, priesthood, sacrifice; prophets did not out rightly rejected these institutions as such, rather people's false assumption that these institutions are indispensible factors of God's favour irrespective of their behaviour was sharply condemned by the prophets. People begin to feel secure because of the cult by thinking "no evil will come upon us" (Jer 5:12). Prophets emphasize that the ceremonial purification ultimately should lead to moral purification and concern

488 Claus Westermann, *Elements of Old Testament Theology* (Atlanta: John Knox Press, 1978), pp. 127-128.

for justice and righteousness should be the priority of the people along with the cultic practices 9 Isa 1:16ff and Amos 5:23-24).

Prophecy and Law: At every stage of their ministry prophets were concerned about teaching the people through the instructions of the law. Prophet Amos at several points makes use of legal background as a basic premise of his teaching (Amos 2:6-8; 3:9-10; 4:1; 5:11-12; 6:12 etc.). However, it is very difficult to determine with precision what kind of laws Amos used in his preaching. Prophets also referred to certain legal institutions such as the failure of judicial system, misuse of the power those who are in the legal circles, especially at the court, gate etc 9 Amos 5:10, 12, 15; Isa 1:23, 26; 3:2; Micah 3:9-11). Connected with the law and prophecy, prophets used a Rib-pattern in their messages as a kind of threat used to restore the relationship between Yahweh and the people (see Micah 1:2-9; 6:1-8; Hosea 12:13-18; Isa 1:1-29; Jer 2:9, 12-13 etc). In this rib-pattern, God enters as a contender by calling the people to repentance when things are not maintained in order. To sum up, the role of law in prophets is not to mean that they introduced anything new law, but they radically interpreted the demand of the law in terms of justice and righteousness.

Prophecy and the concerns of justice: The concerns of justice are of particular importance in the teachings of the prophets. It is here the prophets in ancient Israel had made a strong connection between Israel's faith and their contemporary life situation. The prophets call on the people to behave in a proper way in maintaining their right relationship with their neighbors. The prophets always attacked the rich in the society since they are careless towards the poor and are enjoying at the expense of the poor by grabbing all their rights and privileges. In order to talk about the right relation between God and the people, prophets always measured rich people's attitude towards their poor neighbors. In this light the prophets always attacked the rich and affluent call of leaders, kings, princes and others who are responsible for administration for their acts of injustice (see Amos 5:7; 6:12; Isaiah 3:14-15). In general, the Israelite prophetic concern for justice may be seen in three major areas: first, justice as an important theological term in the very language and vocabulary; second, justice as a moral value, a sinuous term with righteousness; and third, justice in relation to love. To seek justice means to hate evil and love good, in this sense justice is part of the total existence of the life of Israel. This justice concern expressed by the prophets should be viewed in the overall concern of economic development in Israel in their society; more particularly this is seen in the area of land ownership and land-grabbing policy followed by the high class landlords in Israelite society. The accumulation of wealth by the rich landlords resulted in accumulation of large wealth and estates and thus the poor are left with landless situation and this resulted in a wide disparity between rich and the poor (see Amos 2: 6-7 and Micah 2:10). Some would call this development in Israel as early capitalism: the reasons for this development is due to "the shift of the primary social goods, the land, from the function of support to that of capital; the reorientation of social goods from personal values and economic profit ..."[489] This is a long process but institutionalized with the coming of monarchy with the emergence of a system of government. The redistribution of land in an unfavorable manner to the poor and the oppressed is one of the major accusations of the prophets to those who are responsible for it (Isa 5:8-10 and Micah 2:1-2). In the context of the court of law, the term justice in the message of the prophets takes a definite and concrete shape. In the name of the law heavy fines and taxes are collected from the common people. The entire legal administration was corrupt that only rich and wealthy could afford to have justice in the court. In other words there was a legal and commercialized situation to which prophets address in particular: Amos 5:7, 10; Isa 1:21-26; Micah 3:1-3. Micah speaks about corruption, Amos speaks about bribes in the legal court, Isaiah speaks about the officials who desire bribe. In this way concerns for justice became the very crucial matter of prophetic message. The prophets in their overall framework of justice call for the change in the entire society and that change is very radical expectation of flow of justice in their daily walks of life as the chosen people of Yahweh.

Prophecy and Eschatology: While the prophets emphasized the daily walk of life and their relationship with their neighbors and God is seen as concrete, there remains an open-ended question towards the end of prophecy that what will be the outcome of all these in the near and distant future? But Israel was sure of Yahweh's power and his intervention in a miraculous ways (Zech 8:8 ff). The relationship between prophecy and the world history is the real crux of the prophetic message of eschatology, the change that was experienced by the prophets themselves in and through their utterances. For example, Amos and Isaiah working in the Assyrian context of threat, Jeremiah in the context of the impending disaster from the north, Deutero-Isaiah in the context of Persian Emperor Cyrus taking a central stage of Israel's politics, all of them talk about eschatological hope not as a distant future but as imminent event that will happen right in the history of the nation itself. These prophets talk about the intervention of Yahweh in the very history of the people in a decisive manner (Isa 2:12; 13:6,9; Jer 46:10; Ezek 7:16; 13:5; Joel 1:15; 2:1-2; 4:14; Amos 5:18-20; Obad 15; Zeph 1:7-8; 14-18; Zech 14:1). In all these cases the prophets talk about the Day of the Lord concept not as an abstract principle rather the unfolding of the events in the light of concrete realities of the history of Israelite nation. Thus, the prophetic eschatology takes into account the history of Israel in particular and the history of the world in general and operates ultimately in some definite and concrete events in which Yahweh would act.[490]

Kingship of God and its theological significance in ancient Israel: The kingship of God and its importance in ancient Israel has to seen in the overall

489 Lames Luther Mays, "Justice Perspectives from the Prophetic Tradition," *Interpretation* 37 (1983), p. 9.

490 For more details on this point see Paul D. Hanson, *The Dawn of the Apocalyptic*, p. 11ff.

development of the theme not only in Israelite background but in the light of ancient West Asian setting. The essential elements of the ideology of the kingship of God comprise of conflict with the forces of chaos in nature, history and the moral order. The significance of the theme need not be exaggerated as it assumes importance in the context of Israelites choosing a king at the time of prophet Samuel and further consequences of that choice. The word *mlk* occurs as verb thirteen times to mean Yahweh's being or becoming as king and as noun it occurs around forty times as a divine title. Thus, it is imperative for us to study this theme briefly and see how it is integrated with monarchy and prophecy as a thematic component.

The idea of kingship of God in the ancient West Asia: The metaphor of God as king or ruler is found in Mesopotamia. An/Anu, the god of heaven regarded as the highest god and head of the pantheon of the Sumerian gods is addressed as king in the story of Adapa, the myth of Enki and Sumer and the hymn to Ishtar. Other god like Enlil also have been spoken of in kingship language when he is said to have a crown and thrown and considered as lord of heaven and earth.[491] However, the most significant presence of the concept of kingship is found in the *Enuma Elish* in the form of Marduk who was proclaimed the king and lord and was given the kingship of the universe. The overall recognition of Marduk is seen in the declaration of Marduk as king in the prologue and epilogue of the Hammurabi Code where Marduk is seen as the supreme king and also from the confession of Nebuchadnezzar, Nabonidus and Cyrus who called Marduk as "king of gods and lord or lords."

In Egypt according to the Turin Papyrus and in the history of Manetho, Re the sun-god, figures as the first king of Egypt. According to Smith, the kingship of Re who is also known as Khepri, Atum and various dual names, goes back to the time of creation which signifies the creator assuming kingship over his creation.[492] According to Frankfort, creation to the eastern mind does not mean bringing forth out of nothing but has the idea of regulation of cosmos. The kingship of Re is frequently expressed in the formula "king of the gods." Mention can also be made of other god kings like Ptah, Seth and Horus. Ptah, the ehthonic god of Memphis was considered as creator of the universe and was given the kingly title "Lord of two Lands" while Horus has been called the "great kings of Egypt."[493]

In Ugaritic text, Baal's kingship is the central theme of Baal-myth. Baal's kingship is established through his fight against Yam which implies that god struggle is expressed in terms of kingship. According to Smith, the struggle is to have dominion and kingship over all other powers and the king as the figure of

491 Gary V. Smith, "The concept of God/Gods as king in the Ancient Near East and the Bible," *Trinity Journal,* Vol 3, NS (1982), p. 20.

492 Ibid., p. 30.

493 Henri Frankfort, *Kingship and the Gods: A Study of Ancient Near Eastern Religion as the Integration of Society and Nature* (Chicago: The University of Chicago Press, 1948), p. 151

power provided the most ideal analogy to symbolize a dominant force in nature.[494] A god by definition was not necessarily a king, but when a god held a dominion, he sat on the throne of his kingship and ruled the world. El also appears in the Ugaritic text as king of the gods who has the power of creation. The graphic representation of El on a limestone stela as a majestic figure on an ornate throne, wearing a crown supports the kingly view of the god El.[495]

The kingship of God in Israel – An Overview: With the advent of monarchy in Israel, the vocabulary of kingship came to be supplied to Yahweh. From this point on Yahweh was called as *melek*, king and by other titles like *melukah* and *mamlakah* denoting royal power, kingship, reign and kingdom to describe God. A survey of the passages that speak about Yahweh's kingship vividly describe the characters of his kingship that includes that also includes timelessness (the Lord will reign forever and ever – Exod 15:18; The Lord is king forever and ever – Ps 10:16), universal kingship (1 Kings 22:19; Isaiah 6:3) and as an eschatological hope (Micah 2:13; 4:7 and Zeph 3:15). According to Eichrodt, it is difficult to establish the exact time-frame of the development of the idea of kingship in Israel. He argues that the conception and the designation of the deity as king are primitive Semitic practice and so Israel must have had acquaintance with it but the absence of mention of worship of a god as *melek* in the Old Testament makes it difficult to establish any distinctive character. He goes on to say that the title king was applied to Yahweh in the pre-monarchic period as shown by the divine throne of the sacred Ark and the idea of heavenly court.[496] Ficker echoes Eichrodt when he suggested that the concept was developed in the later pre-monarchic period as in the sanctuary of Shiloh, Yahweh was worshipped as 'Yahweh Sebaoth' (1 Sam 1:3) where the Ark was also kept for sometime.[497] But, Ficker is of the view that the idea of Kingship of God might have been known in Israel prior to the establishment of monarchy, the concept of kingship was not known during the nomadic period but only after Israel had adopted a sedentary life which Indicates probably after their settlement in Palestine. The geographic situation in Palestine also made it practically impossible that the theme of kingship of God with its elements like conflict, establishment of order and judgment not being applied to the contemporary political situation. Gray is of the view that it was in the concept of the kingship of God that the Israelites derived their message in times of crisis. The rise and fall of empires were seen as judgment of the divine king. By borrowing from Canaan the particularistic faith in a militant God of a tribal confederacy was

494 Smith, "The concept of God/Gods, p. 27.

495 Frankfort, *Kingship and the Gods*, p. 26.

496 Walther Eichrodt, *Theology of the Old Testament,* Vol. 1. trans J. A. Baker (Philadelphia: The Westminster Press, 1961), pp. 4-5.

497 Rodolf Ficker, "The Kingship of God in Psalms," *Bangalore Theological Forum* 12:1 (1980), p. 56.

related to plane of universal and so when Israel was politically submerged in great world empires she maintained her faith in her God and preserved her identity.[498]

Theology of the Kingship of God: The concept of kingship of God enabled Israel to confess Yahweh's supreme and universal rule first and foremost over the nation and then to the gods and creation. They adopted the alien category 'king' which stem from a polytheistic background as a theological category in order to express its own faith in Yahweh. In the encounter with other religions, Israel was forced to express its faith through theological categories which were meaningful and known in the surrounding religions to maintain their religious identity as well as to express the belief in Yahweh's universal significance for the nations and for the world as a whole. Israel's confession and proclamation of Yahweh as the universal king was to describe a theological expression to establish Yahweh's relationship to the nations and the whole earth are under his dominion. Another ground for the assertion that God's universal dominion as the king is derived from being the creator. The idea here is that since God created everything it is acclaim made over against all other gods.

According to Patrick D. Miller the assertion and affirmation of God's kingship is articulated in the context and in the face of all human questions and fears. He substantiates his point by pointing out that just as in Psalm 72 the claim of the king's rule is found in his deliverance of the needy and the afflicted, Psalms 9-10 also answer the cry of the poor for help with the conviction that God is ruler and therefore he will hear and answer.[499] This implies that the manifestation of God's rule is to deliver the weak and the afflicted from the oppressors, from the wicked and the evil ones (Pss 9:12-13; 10:16-18). God performs the above acts as a judge and warrior who fight on behalf of his people. According to Koehler, since God is the king, he also acts as judge in his people's dispute and helps to make things right, as a champion of justice he takes the side of the just against the unjust and the battle of Yahweh is also to be seen as an action of God securing the right for his people. Thus, God's reign is marked with justice and peace.[500]

Integral link between the themes: Monarchy, prophecy and kingship of God – an evaluatory conclusion: On the basis of our foregoing discussion on the three above mentioned themes we now make the following remarks to see how they arte integrally connected and what are some of the implications we can draw from such a thematic integration:

First, monarchy was an inevitable institution that Israelites adopted during 10th century BCE as the time demanded taking into account several

498 John Gray, "The Kingship of God in the Prophets and Psalms," *Vetus Testamentum* 11:1 (1961), p. 28.

499 Patrick D. Miller, *The Way of the Lord: Essays in Old Testament Theology* (Grand Rapids, MI: William B. Eerdmans Publishing Company, 2004), p. 173.

500 Ludwig Koehler, *Old Testament Theology,* trans A. R. Todd (Philadelphia: The Westminster Press, 1957), pp. 32-33.

factors surrounding the nation. Even through there remain conflicting views on monarchy both for and against its approval, the fact that monarch was appointed by the prophet Samuel initially had a definite divine sanction. Whether or not an individual king performed well in the process the institution of monarchy served well the purpose of nation and the figure of king itself served the interests of the nation despite its ups and down.

Second, the prophecy served its purpose very well from its beginning (no one can exactly say when it all began) when the monarchy seems to have either failed or disappointed God's purpose. The prophets either directly or in a diplomatic way addressed the problems of the nation by intervening as God's spokespersons. They either upheld or even helped in dethroning the kings and their rule depending upon their response. At times the prophets became thorn in the flesh of monarchy and thus fulfilled God's purpose for the entire nation. The prophets never coaxed with the rulers even if it matters their suffering and excommunication from the kingdom. In this way we may see the institution of prophecy served very well for not confirming with the self-serving interests of the monarchs. Their hunch was that in so far as the monarchs do not serve people and God's purpose they have no right to continue on their throne and thus they are either dethroned or adjudged as 'wicked' in God's sight including the chosen king David who lost favor in the sight of God. With such openness prophets worked and fulfilled God's purpose in order to strengthen the hands of the oppressed and demolish the wicked schemes of the so-called monarchs and other rulers responsible for the suffering of the people.

Third, in the light of the failure or insufficiency of the office of monarchy, it is the prophets once again pressed the importance of the idea of kingship of God in their articulations among the nation Israel. Prophets time and again reminded the people that despite earthly powers and structures, it is God's conflict with the powers of chaos and his victory over those chaotic powers that bring salvation to the people. Prophet Isaiah talks about God's triumph over the powers of chaos and God's condemnation and judgment of those. Here, the power of chaos is identified with all that is incompatible with God in his essentially moral nature. The emphasis that Amos lays upon the judgment and Yahweh's providence in the moral order implies the belief in the kingship of God. For Deutero-Isaiah the kingship of God is seen in his idea of God as 'King of Israel' (Isa 41: 21; 44:6), emphasize Yahweh as supreme and the only God, the creator of the world and the controller of history and thereby the God above all gods. Another significant feature of prophets' view on the kingship God was its eschatological character by looking forward to the day when God's kingship will be more effectively established. For instance, in Zephaniah 'that day' is associated with the revelation of Yahweh as king in Zion (3:15, 17) when Israel will be vindicated and her enemies will be judged.

Fourth, in the present Indian context where the church and its leadership has thoroughly failed to live up to the expectation of God's reign, the Old Testament themes of monarchy, prophecy and kingship of God has something to teach us to follow. When our rulers fail to perform and act in accordance with God's will there should be multiple prophetic voices that should correct the corrupt leaders and affirm the reign of God as an eventuality that should sustain the church and society at all levels. When all institutions fail thoroughly the only possibility is to look up to God who already conquered the anemic and self-serving forces of chaos and restore God's own reign on this earth, even when that seems to be an eschatological hope. In this direction all the above mentioned themes are helpful to be articulated in the despondent situation of the Indian church or any other such situation all over the world.

4.7 Shalom in the Biblical Context and its Implication for Today's World

The term shalom expresses as one of the very important ideas articulated in the theology of the Old Testament. While the term itself is very comprehensive in its meaning, it simply denotes the overall meaning as 'complete and sound.' While an amount abstraction can surround the term shalom it is possible to understand the fine nuances of the term in different contexts and the way in which it is used in those specific contexts. It is with this brief note we shall now look into the term and its various theological facets of shalom so as to see its relevance and what implications it can bring in today's fractured world.

The term shalom in Hebrew denotes the general idea of peace. The root word for this is found in its equivalents in many Semitic languages. The Akkadian word *salamu* gives a closest meaning to the root which means "to be whole and complete." It is also related to the act or state of well being and also acts of repayment, reward and retribution. Etymologically shalom is a multi-faceted term since its root gives various meanings like: to be whole, uninjured or even undivided. The term is also used for describing everyday things of domestic life to the most profound religious expectations. In one form or another, the notions of wholeness, health and completeness notify all the derivations of the word in its full sense of the term. The Greek word *eirene* (peace) means an international calm and a relationship of goodwill between God and human beings. But most frequently it describes a social reality, a state of reconciliation and wholeness among a group of people. It is generally argued that peace is absence of war and that notion delimits the understanding of shalom as it implies more than the absence of war.

Shalom in the ancient West Asian Culture: We cannot directly find the ideas of shalom in any ancient West Asian religious thought and culture but the opposite situation is described to that of peace and wholeness. In most of the mythological stories there is always a situation of chaos and struggle between gods out of which some order was established and that situation may be called as equivalent to what we mean by peace or shalom in ancient Israel. The struggle between the pantheons of gods for establishing their supremacy was always presented as non-peaceful situation. In Enuma Elish for instance, Marduk emerged as victorious god after slaughtering Tiamat, a symbol of chaotic power and thus brought order in the entire creation.

Shalom in the Old Testament: As was already stated the Old Testament understanding of shalom varies in different historical contexts, It employs the word shalom in relation to the ritual acts, reconciliation, welfare of society, wholeness etc. In the Pentateuch, shalom is understood as the sacrificial law as a means of making peace with God. Peace offerings are intended to bring peaceful relations between human beings. The book of Exodus and Numbers talk about several references to peace offerings (Exod 20:24; 24:5; 29:28; Numb 6:7; 15:29) and in Leviticus we see the idea of peace is institutionalized (Lev chapters 3, 4, 6, 7, 9, 10, 17 and 19). These references indicate a situation what is required of maintaining peace with God. The essential elements of peace offering have to do with the sacrifice of animals and pouring out of their blood. Porter is of the view that "the actions of peace offering with the blood may strike the modern reader an almost monstrous, but they serve several useful purposes, including that of drawing attention to the costliness of peace. Peace is not simply an empty wish; it is the result of a process that, in the instance, exacts the high cost of life."[501] But at the same time shalom is attributed in the sense of blessing, the Aaronic blessing uses shalom as a benediction seeking from God. In the period of Judges, shalom had been mentioned in relation to the victory against the enemies in the war (Jud 8:9). During the time of king Solomon as it is mentioned in 1 Kings 9:25 peace offerings (shalamim) in the temple was offered to indicate completeness (Shallem). A debt is made good (Shallem) through payment of money and vows are completed (Shallem) through sacrificial offerings. We can notice a drastic change in the understanding of shalom during pre-exilic and post-exilic period. Prophets introduced a new sphere of shalom according to the socio-political and economic changes in the ancient West Asia as per the times. In the wisdom literature the theology of creation reflects that the world is intended by God for peaceful coexistence, fruitful and productive life.

Understanding of Shalom in the prophetic apocalyptic literature: In the apocalyptic literature the understanding of shalom is very significantly presented. We shall make a brief survey of this literature for more significant thought on the subject in the following paragraphs.

For the Israelite community living under the shadow of foreign rulers shalom means nothing more than how to organize itself, particularly in political and religious terms. This question in complicated since Israel understood the previous

---

501 S. F. Porter, "Peace," *New Dictionary of Biblical Theology* (2000), p. 682.

polity, monarchy as given by God. Series of questions[502] are raised by them in this regards to appropriate the understanding of shalom in this context: Must Israel remain a political entity under Persian Empire? Must the civil authority be a Yahwist? What role should the priests have in a new polity? What import did the promises for an everlasting covenant with David as king offer in such circumstances? What was the relationship of those Yahwists living outside the land to those who resided in or around Jerusalem? All these questions are political as well as religious in nature. Prophet Ezekiel in chapters 40-48 deal with the above mentioned questions by means of a dense but provocative description of life after the temple has been rebuilt. In this vision the prophet envisions a rebuilt temple as God's return to it. The vision also offers a description of the land and of priestly responsibilities and prerogatives. There is no place for a king, only for a price or a leader. This vision of Ezekiel puts emphasis on hierocracy, a nation ruled by priests.

Prophet Haggai as a political strategist advocates for the rebuilding of the temple as a means of achieving shalom of the entire community. He believes the importance of restoring Davidic monarchy (Hag 2:20-23). In order to achieve the lost shalom the community must not only have the temple but also a king of the Davidic line.

Prophet Zechariah gives a third option to build up the shalom community that he proposes a dyarchic model of leadership where the responsibilities are shared by a political and a religious leader by suggesting "the two anointed ones" who are identified as Zerubbabel, the governor and Joshua, the high priest (Zech 4:14).

All the above three visions envisaged by the prophets indicate the conflicted situation that the Yahwists were confronting at the end of the sixth century BCE where there was so much of desire was present to go back to the days of shalom community as of Davidic kingdom. Although in the ensuing centuries none of these options saw their development in pure form the so called prophetic apocalyptic visions made their impact upon the exilic community.

Shalom in the Book of Daniel: Issues of identity that were crept and solidified in the community of Judaism during the Persian period were raised again as the cultural force of Hellenism impinged upon Jews, both in diaspora and in homeland. The book of Daniel is widely influenced by this trend apart from other complex issues. We shall point out few crucial issues in this regard as factors that are responsible for building up a community of shalom in the midst of their complex socio-religious and political situation.

The Role of God: In the book of Daniel, the designations for God (the Lord, God of heaven, Most high God) are chosen to reinforce the ambiguous relationship between God, Jews and Gentile king. It is often stated that paganism

502 For details on this discussion see, Bruce C. Birch, et. al, *A Theological Introduction to the Old Testament* 2nd Edition (Nashville: Abingdon Press, 2005), 431-32.

is a major target of the book of Daniel. While the heroes bear Babylonian names compounded with Bel, Nebo and Marduk, these gods themselves play no part in the action. As many have suggested that idolatry is the main theme of the book, but it is doubtful whether it is true. The incompetence of the Babylonian wise men in chapter 2 is said to be a symptom, not of the impotence of their gods, but of their inaccessibility to the wise men (2:11). In chapter 6 we find that there are no pagan gods mentioned. The Jew is victimized as disobedient subject of the king, not as one who impiously rejects the local deities. The Jews' God, and his power, are being opposed not to other gods, but to political powers, be they kings or courtiers.

The sober view of God of Israel is present throughout the book. God is represented as showing to the king that "there is a God in heaven who reveals mysteries, and he has made known to King Nebuchadnezzar what will be in the latter days" (2:28). God also reveals, for the benefit of the king, the interpretation in 2:30: "not because of any wisdom that I have than all the living has this mystery been revealed to me, but in order that the interpretation may be made known to the king, and that you may know the thoughts of your mind."

In the vision stories, the Jewish-Gentile relationship has undergone a drastic transformation. In the midst of the conflicting situation there is a positive affirmation that God would heal and establish this relationship as sign of his shalom in the future kingdom. There is an emphasis on the Jewish people as a nation. In chapter 7 they are the 'holy ones of the Most High' who will succeed all other earthly kingdoms; in chapters 10-12 we find constant reference to the 'people' (10:14; 11:14, 32, 33 and 12:1) and to the prince who 'stands for them', Michael (10:13, 21; 12:1). In these stories the idea of exemplary Jew in the stories is replaced in the visions by the suffering, but soon to be vindicated, nation. Correspondingly, the Gentile kings and kingdoms are destined for destruction. In chapter 2 we are given a picture of successively degenerate kingdoms; in chapter 7 they are successively more brutal, and instead of the Gentile king who needs enlightenment and correction, as in the stories, we are shown a procession of beasts whose destiny is perdition. To sum up the stories in the book in chapters 1-6 are about the harmony between Jew and Gentile, overseen by a providential God, whereas the visions are about a definitive confrontation between Gentile and Jew, or, more accurately, Gentile king and God. Here, God is the final destroyer of all Gentile kingdoms, and the only immediate resolution to the present crisis is the advent of a Jewish kingdom. The challenge to God comes not from other gods, but from human kings.

God of history: Not only does God acts as defender of his people and nation, the book of Daniel also present God as God of history. God *knows* all, he *controls* all, and he *rescues* as 2:21 and 6:27 affirms: "He changes times and seasons; he removes kings and sets up kings; he gives wisdom to the wise and knowledge to those who have understanding." "He delivers and rescues, he works signs and wonders in heaven and on earth." In this chapter the issue is omniscience of God. It is not simply what God has provided to Nebuchadnezzar the interpretation of his dream but *what has been revealed is the future, and only the God who controls the future can reveal it. The God who has revealed the dream is the same God who will fulfill it* (v. 44). In other words, what this leads is to the claim that the succession of the kingdoms is in control of this God, and the interpretation is a demonstration *not so much of the mantic power derived from God, but of his control over history.* This control of God is made very clear in a more concrete manner in chapter 4:17 as follows: "The sentence is by the decree of the watchers, the decision by the word of the holy ones, to the end that the living may know that the Most High rules in the kingdom of men, and gives it to whom he will, and sets over it the lowest of men."

In the visions, the sequence of world events is at a greater remove from the time of Daniel than in the stories, and in chapters 10-12 we see that the course of history has been ordained in the minutest degree. This gives an assurance to those suffering persecution. Even their own misery has been foreseen, yet its end will not be delayed, for it can be measured in days. This is exemplified in some verses as follows: 10:19: "He said, do not fear, greatly beloved, you are safe. Be strong and courageous! When he spoke to me, I was strengthened and said, let my lord speak, for you have strengthened me." 11:43: "He shall become ruler of the treasures of gold and silver, and all the riches of Egypt; and the Libyans and the Ethiopians shall follow in his train." 12:1-2: "There shall be a time of anguish, such as has never occurred since nation first came into existence. But at that time your people shall be delivered, everyone who is found written in the book. Many of those who sleep in the dust of the earth shall awake, some to everlasting life, and some to shame and everlasting contempt."

Unlike the stories in 1-6 chapters we do not find in the visions that there is a little or no place for divine intervention in history. The historical process unfolds as planned, and the God behind it all becomes visible only at the last. Providence consists in God's foreknowledge from the beginning and at his final intervention, but between these two extremes of history there is no room for divine action. God as God of history is demonstrated in the culmination of the royal confessional statement in 3:29 as follows: "There is no other god who is able to deliver in this way … His dominion shall be to the end. He delivers and rescues, he works signs and wonders in heaven and on earth." This statement indicates that the Jew looks for his God to rescue him 'on earth', here and now. The idea of shalom in the book remains in the Jewish belief that God *will* deliver, because he is the God of the Jews, he is just, and he is the lord of history.

Shalom in the Book of Revelation: The New Testament gospel is all about the coming of the new age in the Kingdom of God. The book of Revelation is not only filled with symbolic-poetic descriptions but it does talk about the visionary experiences that breaks forth in dawning the new shalom and new age. This message of newness is unfolded in the descriptions of the poet's understanding of new temple, new covenant, new Israel and new Jerusalem. We shall discuss each of this briefly.

New Temple: The paradisal city-temple of Revelation 21:1-22:5 encompass the entirety of the newly created earth. Earlier prophet Deutero-Isaiah compares new Jerusalem with former Jerusalem (54:2-3). Now the poet of Revelation describes the world-encompassing nature of paradisal temple lies in the ancient notion that the Old Testament temple was microcosmic model of the entire heaven and earth. Ancient Near Eastern literature also reflects the notion that temples of the gods were microcosmic models of heavenly temples or of the universe. Since the Old Testament understanding of the temple localized dwelling of God's presence on earth, the understanding of cosmic temple in the book of revelation points to the eschatological goal of God's presence tabernaceling throughout the earth, thus results in out breaking of God's new rule and shalom upon the earth (21:3).

New Covenant: Revelation 21:3-4 affirms that because of God's dwelling is confirmed in the manifestation of his new temple and this confirms his new covenant with his people: "They will be his people, and God himself will be with them and be their God." This covenant is an indication that the history is moving towards new creation. As already promised by prophet Jeremiah this new covenant is inaugurated by Jesus Christ. In the case of Sinai covenant there is a limitation for the people to approach God directly but is possible through the high priest once in a year. These limitations will not exist in the new covenant because all those "whose names are written in the Lamb's book of life will see God's face and take delight in being in his presence. This experience is nothing but an out breaking of shalom.

New Israel: The new creation unveiled in Revelation 21-22 is presented in images which clearly indicate that its inhabitants are to be viewed as a new Israel. This picture is created by an interesting 'fusion of tribal and apostolic imagery' (12:12; 21:14). The continuity between tribal 'Israel' and apostolic 'Israel' builds on God's desire to create for himself a special shalom people as we may see similar ideas in Exod. 19:6; I Pet. 2:9; Gal 3:29; Rev. 21:2.

New Jerusalem: John's vision of a 'new heaven and new earth' centers on the descent from heaven of the 'Holy city, the new Jerusalem.' The new city, radiant with God's glory and constructed from the most precious of minerals, dominates the landscape. To this new Jerusalem the nations will bring their glory and honor in worship of the Lord God Almighty and the Lamb. This entire situation is understood as a condition of shalom in which the righteous will have their dwelling place. This new Jerusalem city image is drawn based on Jerusalem/Zion model, the city of David and the city of God's dwelling place. While the earthly Jerusalem is doomed to destruction, believers are encouraged to come 'to Mount Zion, to the heavenly Jerusalem, the city of the living God' (Hebrews 12:22).

The book of revelation thus portrays the condition of shalom in the midst of perils and persecution and it powerfully communicates the point that the sovereignty of God and Christ is redeeming and judging brings the believers glory, which is intended to motivate saints to worship God and reflect his glorious attributes through obedience to his word. This situation of Shalom is the end result of the long struggle and conflict of the persecuted against the evil forces in this world.

Contemporary relevance of the apocalyptic understanding of peace: The understanding of the message of peace or shalom in the apocalyptic thinking of the biblical books like earlier apocalyptic prophets, Daniel and revelation has the following hallmarks of its theological implications:

The apocalyptic message provides a template by means of which people in many periods can understand what is going on around them. It allows individuals, particularly if they are part of a group that suffers, or thinks they have been marginalized, to comprehend the source of their plight. Moreover, they understand that God is in control of their fates and that, ultimately, they will be victorious. The dualistic elements will enable them to distinguish their own situation from that of others, whom they may perceive as their oppressors, creating an "us/them" mentality.

The apocalyptic thought creates an opportunity of thinking newness even when such a possibility seems beyond the present life. For instance the Dalit Christians in India to *embrace cross as the central symbol of shalom*. This becomes for Dalit Christians a major identifying symbol, an ugly embodiment of rejection and hostility. Walter Brueggemann[503] explains how cross expresses old age/new age imagery:

The cross is about the abandonment of the old and it is about embrace of the new, in all its terror and precariousness. The cross is about repentance, of departing from the old but entering into a new experience of shalom. In the cross all the life negating forces that thwart the establishment of shalom is to be abandoned. This abandonment is articulated in terms of building walls that secure our own existence, to control our neighbors, and to be filled with greed that we should posses at the expense of others. At the same time the cross leads us to embrace the gift of life and security that is freely given to those who affirm life renewing realities. It leads us to work towards a society where equality and justice reign as marks of shalom society. The books of Daniel and Revelation talks about the new age where the life is handed back to us, after it is broken and after it is established under God's rule. This kind of thinking of newness requires hope that the prophetic verses of Daniel proclaims and the vitality of the poet of Revelation to know that everything has happened. These writings arose in contexts of great spiritual crisis, when God's people were tempted to despair and wonder who was

503 See chapter 11 in Walter Brueggemann, *Living Toward a Vision: Biblical Reflections on Shalom* (Philadelphia: United Church Press, 1976).

in control of history or if they would survive the present distress. The apocalyptic message thus reiterates the fundamental assertion that life has been given up and it has been received again. The intention of apocalyptic is not to chart out God's plan for the future so future generations may draw up calendars but to assure the present generation that—perhaps contrary to appearance—God is still on the throne (cf. Dan. 7:18,21-22, 27; 8:25; 12:1-4), and that the future is firmly in his hands. All things are envisaged under God's rule towards building of shalom society in which all things are new. the temple localized dwelling of God's presence on earth, the understanding of cosmic temple in the book of revelation points to the eschatological goal of God's presence tabernaceling throughout the earth, thus results in out breaking of God's new rule and shalom upon the earth (21:3).

Theological significance of Shalom in the Old Testament: Although we have discussed above some specific relevance of apocalyptic literature in relation to the understanding of peace, we shall now focus on the overall implications on the theological significance of shalom in the Old Testament. Shalom in the Old Testament was always viewed as something positive. It always was manifested in the life of the community. It brings a total harmony within the community. It is in this sense understood as relational term rather than abstract concept. It is also connected with the covenant (Numb 25:12; Deut 29:19; Isa 54:10; Ezek 34:25; 37:26). Shalom in the Old Testament is also spoken in terms of restoration of justice and righteousness of God. In Psalm 34: 14 it is stated: "Do good, seek peace and pursue it." Here the peace is seen in terms of its practical and concrete manifestation of everyday life and this it is not simply a means but an end in itself.

Shalom is not simply absence of war in general terms. According Paul D. Hanson, one can recognize shalom where chaos is not allowed to enter. Hanson relates shalom to war concept in the Old Testament. He argues that the Yahwistic religion has provided little abstractions regarding the concept of shalom. But at the same time counter to the early Yahwistic notion the later Yahwistic ideology attributed the absolute power to the earthly king. But in numerous passages, peace is negotiated at the end that precludes hostilities and conflicts (Deut 20: 10-12; Josh 9:15).[504] Roland de Vaux is of the view that the peace in a political sense is not only the absence of war in a purely negative sense, but it includes the ideas of friendly relationship between two people (Judg 4:17; Isa 7:14; 1 Kings 5:4; 22:45).[505] In some cases peace and prosperity are discussed as paired and relational concepts (Micah 3:5; Zech 8:12 and Mal 2:5) in the sense that peace is seen as economic freedom. Quite contrary to this idea prophet Jeremiah talk about peace only if the nation Israel surrenders to its enemy Babylonians. It is clearly argued

504 Paul D. Hanson, "War and Peace in the Hebrew Bible," *Interpretation* 38:4 (1984), pp. 342-362.

505 Roland de Vaux, *Ancient Israel: Its Life and Institutions* (New York: McGraw Hill, 1961), p. 254.

that what Jeremiah meant peace here is to be seen in the context of false prophets existing at his time who preached the false peace even though Babylonian threat was imminent and that was seen as universal plan of God in the history of Israel. It is in consonance with God's plan prophet Jeremiah was proclaiming real peace for the nation that can come only if they surrender themselves to the Babylonian power at this point of time in history or else they will perish if they simply believe in false prophets' teaching.[506]

On the basis of our foregoing discussion on the concept of shalom in the Old Testament with specific reference to the apocalyptic literature we now make the following observations and draw some implications for our contemporary Indian situation.

First, God's creation itself can be described as shalom when everything was complete and set forth in order out of chaos. This order was intended to create peace, justice, completeness and harmony that encompasses the idea of shalom in the Old Testament. However, this harmony was destroyed by human hubris right at the beginning in different ways. By murder and hatred within the community relationship of Cain and Abel story the idea of shalom was shattered. Human arrogance always dominated despite God's order in everything that he created. Nevertheless in the final analysis peace is always negotiated and advocated for healthy human relationships. The Deuteronomic theology affirms that in all walks of people's community life even when the southern royal ideology insisted on the power of few on the top thus made a disruptive presentation of peace that infringed upon the freedom of the poor and marginalized in the society. But the prophets really worked hard to bring the false notions of peace of the rulers in Israel and confronted them with reality of Yahweh's will for the nation.

Second, the ancient Israel then struggled as a minority nation always tossed between the big nations. She was shattered by wars and other socio-political struggles all the time. In such a situation Yahweh's shalom was the only hope to her to pull on with her existence amidst all her existential struggles. The prophetic vision of shalom (new heaven and new earth (as stated in Isaiah 11 and 65) time and again encouraged the community of Israel who were given the promise of God's redemption and restoration in their lives. The vision of Davidic and Zion traditions hoped for an eschatological redemption in the future. This shalom ideology not only prevented Israelites from worshipping other gods but also regenerated hope in the life of worship as a chosen community of God (Isa 2:2-4; 9:3 f; 11:1-9 and Micah 4:3).

Third, talking about shalom in our present context is very important. In India and elsewhere the desperate look for shalom is very much present. The church and society is filled with violence and thus there seems to be a situation of anarchy prevailing in every place. The church which is supposed to be an

506 P. J. Sisson, "Jeremiah and the Jerusalem and the Conception of Peace," *Journal of Biblical Literature* 105:3 (1986), pp. 429-442.

agent of peace often perpetuates hatred and violence among communities for parochial and vested interest political gains. Marginalized communities like Dalits in India are treated in a very menial way and they are not made as part of any important decision making process. They are kept out of the frame of mainline decision making. How can we call that shalom is prevailing in the land when such deliberate marginalization takes place? Even if sometimes Dalits are co-opted into the mainline decision making process, they are expected only to serve the interests of the dominant class and caste people. Thus, shalom is all the more necessary in such a subtle situations.

Fourth, the biblical idea of shalom has still be the hope of many millions of the down-trodden in India that one day God's reign will break in their lives and that they will plant their own gardens and eat their own fruits and that there shall be a situation of shalom where all are treated with equal dignity and human worth.

4.8 The Land as God's Gift and People's Identity in Ancient Israel and its Implications for the Land Struggles in Today's World

Land is an important theological topic in the Old Testament due the way in which Israelites existence and identity was totally dependent on the land in which they lived. It has argued that the theme land is a central one if not the central in the Old Testament theology. This topic is also very significant because of the in the preset world land has become an important issue of both struggle and identity for many people. The land in ancient Israel is all the more important as a mark of their identity since it had been promised, possessed, lost and longed for by the people all the time in different contexts during various historical periods. In this presentation we shall present focus our attention mainly on the importance of land in its terminology, its other theological nuances and with particular focus on the land struggles and rights of the Dalits in the contemporary Indian scenario as a way of drawing implications of land theology from an Indian perspective.

Three Hebrew words are employed in the Old Testament to refer to the word land as follows: *'eretz* often used to mean and represent a geographical or political territory. The word *adamah* refers to agricultural qualities of land that is connected with the dust or the land of fertility or non-fertility. The word *'sadeh* refers to imply cultivated land or the open country side or a particular country side (Gen 14:7). Among these words the first one is used most commonly. It can be translated as land, earth, ground and country. At the same time other two words are also used frequently in different contexts to mean the land in the was we described above.

Theology of Land in the Old Testament: The biblical understanding on the importance of the land begins with the creation narratives in the book of Genesis as land assumes its significance because it is created and evaluated as good land by God. The people of Israel from the time of their Egyptian bondage value the land with a great expectation as they remained landless for several hundred years and thus struggled with their identity problems. But God's promise was very firm in their lives as they moved out of their Egyptian oppression and as promised they were made to posses the good land and settle there. In the light of this overall view of the land we need to look at the theology of the land in the Old Testament and see how certain features described about God-given land is important for our implications of landlessness in the contemporary situation.

God as the creator and owner of the land: The Bible in Gen 1:1 clearly affirms that the land is created by God The heaven and earth is created by God as foundational for all other things and things to exist and survive. Human beings are created as crown of creation and given a great responsibility to take care of the earth and its rich resources created by God as stewards of the land. The book of Deuteronomy affirms that God is the owner of the land that he created. Yahweh is the owner of the land and Israelites are only aliens and tenants of this land created by God. Moreover Yahweh is portrayed as God and ruler of all lands, the ne who is controlling the world from on high (Deut 4:39; 10:14, 17). All the richness and resources of the land belong to God being the owner of the land (Ps 24:1). It is because of this idea of God's ownership of the land no human has any right either to exploit or to plunder the rich resources of the land. Instead human beings have to take care and preserve the resources of the earth in a responsible manner.

Land and Covenant: The promise of the good land by God to the people of the Old Testament is clearly depicted in the migration narratives. In this sense the idea of land is closely connected with covenant. After God's covenant and promise with Abraham the land giving to his inheritance is again and again reiterated. This is made clear in Genesis 17:8-9 as it reads: "And I will give to you and to your offspring after you, the land where you are now an alien, all the land of Canaan, for a perpetual holding, and I will be their God .., As for you, you shall keep my covenant, you and your offspring after you throughout their generations." Thus, we can see the land theology is closely connected with the idea of God's covenant and promise he made to the ancestors of Israel. While it is an unconditional nature of promise that is reflected here in Genesis 17, Leviticus and Deuteronomy makes this promise of God as conditional. In Lev 18:24-30 we see that the people of Israel were sternly warned not to defile themselves by mixing with the Canaanites (also see Numb 35:34). It is clearly depicted that during the time of Joshua people rededicated themselves at Mount Ebal (Joshua 8:30-35) and the conditional promise of land associated with the covenant is found here. Thus, both the covenant of God and land-giving are inseparably connected.

Human beings as land related beings: Right from the creation of human beings in the Yahwistic account of creation, human beings are viewed as soil-land related beings. Because *adam* was created from *adamah* he will eventually return to the ground and the same process is applicable to all human beings as they finally returned to the dust or ground soon after their death. This also shows the facility of human nature, the perishable nature of human life and thus they are at the mercy of the Lord for all purposes. After Adam was expelled from the garden he is sent back to the land where he should make his living closely associated with agricultural life-setting. All the human beings are destined to return to the ground after their life span in this world is something that God had fixed right at the beginning of creation (Gen 3:19 and Psalm 146:4). One may also look at the land-relatedness of human beings as very positive in that land as a place of human rest and enjoyment and also a place of safety (Deut 12:9-10; 25:19). In this way, we may say that land is necessary for each human being for home, bread, survival and for burial. In this sense without land a person can easily get an idea of being rootless, homeless and lost.

Land Economy: The land in the pre-industrial age like the time of Israelites not gives them identity but also was a source of sustenance, wealth and even prestige. The absence of land implies loss of occupation and space for living. When Israelites possessed the land of Canaan they were allocated different portions of the land as per their tribes that indicate their survival and existence for the centuries to follow. At that time onwards, they had their national identity as they continued to exist in the midst of giant nations surrounding them. Israelites as a political nation and reckoned force in the region was mainly because of the land they possessed and occupied. Otherwise they would have lived as an insignificant nation and perished without any identity.

Land as Nahalah: The word *Nahalah* is translated as inheritance in the Old Testament (Deut 4:31; 12:9 etc). It is clear once again from this concept that in order to talk about the intimate relationship between God and the people of Israel this concept is employed metaphorically. Land comes as a term that unites the people and God to one another. The description of land as Israel's inheritance underlines the status of Israel as Yahweh's "firstborn son" (Exod 4:22). Nahalah can also mean not simply the land handed down from generation to generation, but the entitlement or rightful property of a party that is legitimated by a recognized social custom, legal process or divine character.[507] In this sense giving of Nahalah means giving a legal a legal grant of land or property. In the case of Naboth vineyard story in 1 Kings 21 this was the issue as the right to his land Naboth resisted to his legal right and claim to anyone, which is in accordance with the right legal procedure. It is argued that the Naboth's story in 1 Kings 21 is an important reference point of the interface between a social reality and biblical text. We shall dwell on this issue with more details in the paragraphs that follow and see how the issues of biblical text interconnect with the issues of Dalit land rights and struggles.[508]

507 Norman C. Habel, *The Land is Mine: Six Biblical Land Ideologies* (Minneapolis: Fortress Press, 1995), p. 35.

508 We must note the point that when we talk about land and Dalits we cannot assume that Dalits have their own land. Dalits are alienated from their own land and their rightful claim of their

Land Ownership and Tenure in Ancient Israel: As was stated earlier the issues related to land tenure are crucial in our narrative of 1 Kings 21 to evaluate the role and actions of each character, particularly, the three non-prophetic figures. In principle, Yahweh is the real owner of the land. Land tenure and ownership are related issues in our story. As opposed to modern understanding of private ownership of land, ancient Israel apparently understood land to be held by a kinship group, a clan based in a village or villages. Individual extended families of the clan were granted the holding of plots of land for their use, but ultimately the land belonged to the clan-wide or family-wide inheritance and could not be given or "sold" out from inheritance. If a particular individual family ran into economic difficulty, incurred debts beyond their ability to pay, lost family members to debt slavery, or had debts foreclosed and lost their land, other family members were responsible for redeeming the family and land from creditors. This social "safety net" protected not only family members but also the land for the "inheritance."[509] The primary pressures against such democratic land tenure and ownership and its related and supportive social structures were the intrusive activities of the elite classes of the society. In this process the king and his royal administration in agrarian monarchies had an active interest in acquiring and controlling land for their own uses. Whenever a king and his officers obtain a land either by legal or illegal means, it is always done with lot of enthusiasm because it would allow the king and his royal court to obtain economic surplus directly. These acquired lands also serve as grants given by the king to his loyal followers, officials, and military officers. In the similar way those who possessed land increase their power, status, and pride in the society by accumulating more and more lands. Because of this highly stratified social systems developed in agrarian societies. This also resulted in little or no middle class between the vast majority of peasant producers and the very minority of elite families who own and control majority of lands.[510]

Jezebel's response in verses 5-7 indicates two important factors that are interrelated to one another. One is the issue of Canaanite kingship as an institution that can rule and manipulate; the other is a mercantile view of land in which land is a commodity to be secured by whatever means. Jezebel has no appreciation for the inalienable quality of a family inheritance. Walter Brueggemann points out the contradicting views of land ownership and tenure in this story:

> "Inheritance" as a land notion directly contradicts royal notions of land management that know no limitation and that sanction confiscation and royal prerogatives generally. The idea of inheritance affirms that there are enduring and resilient networks of meaning and relationship into which one is placed, and these are fundamental to the shape of

own land is denied to them from several centuries.

509 Paula M. McNutt, *Reconstructing the Society of Ancient Israel*, pp. 158-62.

510 Marvin L. Chaney, "Systemic Study of the Israelite Monarchy, *Semeia* 37 (1986), pp. 53-76.

> society. The queen believes ... that persons and property are replaceable parts, each a component in a grand royal design that can be shuffled and rearranged at the whim of the managers.[511]

Jezebel misunderstood the whole land tenure and ownership and its dynamic relationship between God and the people. Her response "I will give you the vineyard" in verse 7 is a sheer misunderstanding of inheritance because she proposes what cannot be given. Inheritances are not given by the royal authority. But in her view land is a negotiable, which is entirely a false conception on the part of Jezebel. Jezebel miscalculated the whole deal in simple terms that some impediments in the deal can be overcome by the manipulation of legal procedures. But her confiscation of Naboth's land not only thwarts the highly valued social custom of the day, but it goes against Yahweh's dictum on the land. The very perception of land ownership and tenure are wrongly perceived by Jezebel. It is Yahweh who assigned the land, and when it is given by Yahweh it is a gift-land and no one has the right to pervert its particular character set by Yahweh. Thus, Naboth is no longer the owner of his land but it is his responsibility to protect the gift land he received from his God, Yahweh.[512]

Dalits and Land Issues: Dalits are the most socially vulnerable class of people exploited on the basis of their land and the violation of human rights in relation to Dalits is a common feature in the post independent India. It is often argued that when an elephant walks in the forest stampede is to be expected and several insects and small organisms are the victims of this stampede. So Dalits are oppressed and discriminated against in the name of caste and particularly on the land issues. As we pointed out at the beginning of this essay several Dalits are uprooted and displaced in their very land. Their rights are not protected and the confiscation of the poor Dalit farmers' land is a common phenomenon in several parts of our land. The dominant caste controls the Dalits as long as they are without land of their own. Thus, they adopt all means and ways to see that Dalit become landless and only remain tenant farmers and even if they progress and move up in the social ladder they are made dependent on the dominant castes all the time.

While the plight of Dalits is getting pathetic as ever before due to the lack of strict enforcement of land ceiling and reforms acts, the alienation and exploitation of Dalit populations continue in modern India with the latest onslaught on their lives being brought about by the implementation of the SEZ act. It was envisaged due to the SEZ policy more employment would be generated and marginalized classes like Dalits would be part of such benefit. But in reality it is far from what is expected. Apart from the displacement and land acquisition, non-existence of the implementation of land ceiling laws had always led to serious plight for

511 Walter Brueggemann, *The Land*, pp. 88-89.

512 Ibid., p. 90.

Dalits. The biggest farmers and politicians of India have a lot of land, illegally held and almost impossible to acquire by the state. The state governments in conjunction misuse the Supreme Court's orders with the rural power elite. Dalits as victims of caste structure have hardly any scope to claim land unless land ceiling act is implemented. Accessible land is concentrated in the hands of powerful farmer communities, who are politically very mobile and violent. It would be almost impossible to take the land from certain dominant caste groups. To address the issue of displacement a new relief and rehabilitation policy has been tabled in Parliament recently. It promises a 'Social Impact Assessment' of development projects, which displace human populations involuntarily. It also promises 'compensation, rehabilitation and resettlement ahead of displacement.' These assurances encompass landless families who are to be trained to be 'self-employed' and/or given jobs in construction projects. The experience of Singur runs counter to this claim where private enterprise to set up a car factory has clearly said that it needs specialized workers on its firm. Also, landed families losing land to development projects are to be allotted land elsewhere. There are also special rehabilitation measures for displaces SC/ST groups. But these are yet to be employed. Additionally, these promised measures are almost paradoxical to the existent SEZ measures and which measures gain priority is really up to the government to decide. Apart from all this there are legal violations made in the course of SEZ policies which should have significant negative influence on the Dalit community: Relaxation/inapplicability of many labor laws like industrial disputes act, violation of Panchayat Raj Act (1996) for local self-government. With no laws of the Indian state being applicable to SEZs, there will be no question of jobs being reserved in the SEZs for SC/ST candidates.

A Jesuit priest, Fr. Anchanikal T. Thomas, aged 46, was murdered in the Hazaribagh district in Bihar. He was working with the Dalits in the villages for their land rights. Fr. Thomas was killed for questioning the exploitation by the landlords, violations perpetrated by people working for the landlords and supported by the corrupt police force. He was killed for questioning the very practice of bonded labor system in the surrounding villages of Hazaribagh district. In all this Fr. Thomas was fighting for the cause of Dalits and their land rights.

Dalits account for a sixth of India's population, but not of its land. Dalits are mainly landless and where they own land at all, it is marginal and usually of low quality. As much as 77 percent of Dalit workforce is in the primary or agricultural sector of economy. But very few of them own land. They form, instead, a bulk of agricultural laborers in India. (Historically, they have been major victims of land grab). Of the Indian poor, 40 percent are landless agricultural laborers; 45 per cent are small or marginal farmers. 60 per cent of the Indian farmers own less than an acre of land. This means that 85 per cent of the poor are either landless or marginal farmers. It's in the first category that we will find Dalits in large numbers. Of the 15 percent, 7.5 per cent are rural artisans and those who labor in the other non-farm occupations. Again we will find Dalits in this group, particularly those who work on leather. Lastly, all the remaining categories of poor, including diverse segments of urban poor, constitute "others" who live in poverty. Here, too, we find Dalits; in construction labor, in road laying crews and very prominently in scavenging and other sanitation work. All Dalits in these 15 per cent are again, landless people.[513]

Honor and Shame in Ancient Israel and Dalit Cultures: In our biblical story of 1 Kings 21 we learn something important about the threat of Elijah to the kingdom of Ahab. Besides the devastating loss of power for the ruling house or dynasty, the loss of a "house" in ancient Israel also signifies the loss of status as a family or patrimony in a social structure that is based on family. The threat that every male will be destroyed aims exactly at this sense of patrimony because the execution of that threat will kill every male capable of carrying on the family name and inheritance. There is no clearer way to communicate that what God is doing is wiping out the name, family, and heritage of the entire family of Ahab.

The death sentence proclaimed by Elijah on the king and queen can also be viewed in terms of honor and shame in the culture of ancient Israel. Their gruesome deaths, when dogs lick up their blood and eat their corpses, as well as deaths of members of their family, are a clear and devastating shaming of them as persons. The lack of a burial and the ignominious end of their bodies signals a disastrous fall in status from the highest to the lowest station in society. All these events will happen in the most public of ways, visible to all in the society. The utterly public loss of honor adds to the disgrace in the already grisly death scenes.[514]

In Dalit culture, the idea of shame and honor carries tremendous weight in the overall culture of Dalit identity. Despite several measures that are taken up to fight against the caste system it prevails in different forms that calls us to examine our poor enforcement of laws and their practice in reality. The following statement by a scavenger in Ahamedabad reveals that the instances of honor and shame experience of Dalits in India:

> When we are working, they ask us not to come near them. At canteens, we have separate tea glasses and they make us clean them ourselves and make us put in dishes away. We cannot enter temples. We cannot

513 The content for this section is modified and adapted from Asian Human Rights Commission – Urgent appeals from http://www.ahrchk.net/ua/mainfile.php/1997/7/

514 Lyn M. Bechtel, "Shame as a Sanction of Social Control in Biblical Israel: Judicial, Political and Social Shaming," in David J. Chalcraft, ed., *Social Scientific Old Testament Criticism* (Sheffield: Sheffield Academic Press, 1997), pp. 238-50. Also see, Saul M. Olyan, 'Honor, Shame, and Covenant Relations in Ancient Israel and Its Environment," *JBL* 115(1996), pp. 201-218.

> use upper caste water taps. Our children in schools are not treated as children of others. We live in colonies of our own.[515]

When such instances are repeated in several parts of the post-independent India how can we talk about an envisioned world of equality and justice? When the dignity and honor of Dalits is radically put in question and to understand the instance of honor and shame Fr. Samuel's Rayan's words are useful:

> Dalitness is a human creation. Its first victim was God; its most remarkable historical victim was Jesus of Nazareth ... Dalitness then invades the human world. One cannot make others untouchable without becoming an untouchable oneself. Having dalitised God, woman and man found themselves naked; their sense of self-worth declined; they began to shift blame. And finally brother killed brother, the stronger destroyed the weaker because the latter was perceived as a friend of God ... It is from within this situation that God would fight dalitness. He would subvert oppression by exploding it from within its own structures. He acts as the God of the oppressed who smashes the chains of the peoples dalitised in the Empires of Egypt, of Assyria, of Babylon, of Persia, of Greece, of Rome.[516]

Converging points of Biblical and Dalit World: As noted above we can find certain common factors that are found both in the biblical and Dalit world. From the biblical narrative we can draw certain interesting parallels can be drawn for our world today. The unjust economic system prevalent in the biblical times is also very much present in our times. Certain marginalized communities like Dalits are the worst victims of land grab, land confiscation and accumulation of large estates of land by the dominant caste communities directly impacts the growth and development of economic base of the Dalit communities. As our story in 1 Kings 21 and the prophetic response reveals that the socio-economic injustices and land issues are not happening in accident. Elijah's status as a peripheral prophet explains both his authority and message. In an agrarian social context, only the representatives of the divine (priests, prophets, and the like) had a source of authority "independent" of the elite governing classes. Here Elijah had come back as the one whose reauthorization from God brought him back to the central stage to offer critique to the royal house. Elijah represents the interests of the marginalized in society and the divine power who stands on their side.

515 This quotation is taken from Maria Goretti, F. S. "Purity and Pollution," in Leonard Fernando and James Massey (eds.), *Dalit World – Biblical World: An Encounter* (New Delhi: Centre for Dalit/Subaltern Studies and Vidyajyoti College of Theology, 2007), p. 116.

516 Samuel Rayan, "The Challenge of the Dalit Issues: Some Theological Perspectives," in V. Devasahayam (ed.), *Dalit Women: Quest for Humanity* (Madras: Gurukul, 1992), pp. 127-28.

Clearly, Jezebel's actions have warranted the attention and condemnation of a God who has been all along represented as demanding righteousness and justice. And Ahab is included in the condemnation since everything was done in his name and by his authority. Elijah threatens with the warning to the royal house that the kingdom of Ahab would be brought to an end by ending the dynasty of Omri. The prophetic response to the injustice meted out to an ordinary citizen is something caused by human geed and the structures created to fulfill the desires of the dominant and privileged socio-economic groups. The dynamic relationship between the religious and covenantal symbols on the one hand and the values of socio-economic institutions created by the rulers on the other hand is at the root of the story of Naboth's vineyard in 1 Kings 21. This link is very powerful as it determines our value system in our day. How do we define the unending discrimination and marginalization based on different castes that divides the Church and the very core of the gospel message? How can we justify the rampant violence that is meted out to Dalits day in and day out because they were born as Dalits? How can we justify the idea that Dalits have to suffer because it is their fate to suffer in this world and that they cannot even question their oppressors? How can we just ignore many honor killings in the name of caste where Dalits are the worst victims of such a killing?

The prophetic vision and message in our story of Naboth's vineyard challenges us to think of an alternate vision for Dalit liberation and emancipation just as the prophets in the biblical world worked with the same goal. A situation however may appear hopeless and completely dis-oriented and dis-juncted in the worldly standards. Out of the crisis situation comes the bold vision and message of the prophet that seeks to address the irreparable loss created by the violation of sincere laws created for the common good of all the human beings. In the Dalit world there are sincere attempts towards such a universal vision of God to articulate God's freedom and justice for all. "While having the on-going memory of imposed segregation, Dalits keep on projecting their horizons in new direction of new hopes."[517]

4.9 Cult and the Presence of God: Temple, Sacrifice and Priesthood in the Biblical World and its Relevance for Today's World

It is not an exaggeration to say that cult is one of the major topics in the Old Testament through which many other themes can be understood and articulated. Hans Joachim Kraus by citing Sigmund Mowinckel rightly captured the meaning of cult in the Old Testament as follows: "the cult is not only by its origin, but in all places and at all times it is sacred reality, not merely an acted drama or a play, but a

517 A. Maria Arul Raja, "A Casteless World is Possible: Building Dalit Horizons from Apocalyptic Ethos," in Leonard Fernando and James Massey (eds.), *Dalit World – Biblical World: An Encounter* (New Delhi: Centre for Dalit/Subaltern Studies and Vidyajyoti College of Theology, 2007), p. 171.

real drama and one that manifest reality, a drama which realizes the dramatic event with real power, a reality from which real forces emanate. In other words, it is a sacrament. The cult of primitive man is this and nothing less ... The basic idea is this: that through the dramatic symbolic presentation, realization and reanimation of the particular events, this event is actually and really repeated; it repeats itself, happens all over again and exercises afresh the same mighty, redemptive effect that is exercised for our salvation on the first occasion at the dawn of time or in the distant past."[518] We cannot bifurcate between cult and worship in the Old Testament since both these aspects are integrally interconnected. Yet we can argue that there are cultic elements from their neighbors that have been integrated into Israelite worship practices. It is proper for us at this point that we make a theological evaluation of cult during various historical periods and its significance in the light of their worship practices so as to derive the theology of cult and its implication for our contemporary situation.

Cult in the Patriarchal narratives: During the patriarchal era cult was characterized by the presence of God. Patriarchs or ancestors worshipped God where God appeared to them or met them. It was discovered that "sanctuaries were erected when nature manifested the presence of God of Abraham, Isaac, and Jacob—near a tree for example, or a natural height, or by a water source, but they were erected perfectly in places where God had shown himself in a theophany."[519] It is firmly argued by A. S. Kapelrud for the following elements present in the cult of Israel in general: first, mythical features, God's marching as the head of his people; second, historical element wherein Israel's march through the wilderness; third, theophany in the ancient style of rain and storm God; and fourth, the presence of God of Israel at Sinai and later at Zion was always significant in the history of Israel.[520]

It was argued that the thought, life and culture of Israel was destined and shaped by the cult. The above mentioned elements of the cult were always present in the Israelite cult in as much as they were shaped by the cult in the traditions that were described above. Moreover all the above mentioned elements of the cult were found in the preaching of the prophets. In fact cult was the foundation of all the traditions, as the fertile soil out of which all existing traditions were born and developed... It was believed that cult was central in the lives of ancient Israel in all their different aspects.[521] With all this discussion it is difficult to identify the cultic God whom the ancestors worshipped, because of "the two traditions in the

518 Hans Joachim Kraus, *Worship in Israel* (Richmond, Virginia: John Knox Press, 1962), p. 9.

519 Roland de Vaux, *Ancient Israel: Its Life and Institutions* (London: Darton, Longman & Todd, 1980), p. 289.

520 A. S. Kapelrud, "Tradition and Worship: The Role of the Cult in Tradition Formation and Transmission," in *Tradition and Theology in the Old Testament,* ed. Douglas A. Knight (London: SPCK, 1977), pp. 101-102.

521 Ibid., pp. 102-103.

Bible, one of which attributes the introduction of the worship of Yahweh in Israel to Moses and denies that the patriarchs knew God by that name Ex 6:2; and the other of which traces the worship of Yahweh back to the beginning of human race and freely brings Yahweh into the association of the patriarchs, Gen 4:1, 26."[522]

It is well known that patriarchs worshipped God under different names like in Exod 6:3 God is identified with El-Shaddai, and in Gen 14:22 God is identified with God of Melchizedek El-Elyon, whereas El seems to be prominent in non-biblical texts which correspond to the ancient Semitic deity El. El is also found in other titles such as El-olam and El-roi. Occurrence of these different names of God, which were worshipped by the patriarchs suggests for the polytheistic nature of the patriarchal religion. It is also possible that the patriarchs worshipped the local gods of Canaanite origin, since god El was the high god of the entire Ugaritic pantheon. This name is also used by the ancient Israelite religion, but the Israelite religion never accepted Baal as God who was widely worshipped in Canaan. On the other hand Baal and his worshippers were cursed and condemned throughout the Old Testament.

One cannot for sure say who was the God of Patriarchs, to whom they attributed their success and failure and were always aware of his mythical guidance and presence with them. They acknowledged his presence by performing acts of worship such as sacrifices, individually on the altars erected by them. We read of such altars in Bethel in Gen 12:8, Shechem in Gen 12:7, Mamre in Gen 13:18, Beersheba in Gen 26:25, Moriah in Gen 22:9 and Mizpah in Gen 31:54.

In the above light we can say that the patriarchal was not an established cult but was an expression of an individual towards the deity. Theophany of God compelled the patriarchs to build an altar and offer sacrifice to celebrate his presence.

Cult from Exodus till the Temple: In the book of Exodus Yahweh reveals to Moses and claims that slaves in Egypt are his people, by identifying himself as God of Abraham, Isaac and Jacob. Exodus also marks the event of deliverance from Egypt which became the central theme of worship for later Israel. In Sinai declaration and afterwards people of Israel were repeatedly reminded that they were slaves in Egypt and it was Yahweh who delivered them. The Sinai episode represents a shift from Individual worship of the patriarchs to the corporate worship of all the people. Because Yahweh delivered the people of Israel, he became their king and the people of Israel his vassals, who entered into covenant with Yahweh. One can say that the covenant relationship between Yahweh and the people of Israel began at Sinai al guided and determined their theology. Here the Sinai event is to be reckoned as of great value because through the event of Exodus the slaves in Egypt came to know Yahweh as their God. Further the cult in this period is particularly seen in several stages with each stage demonstrating its particular form and character.

522 H. H. Rowley, *Worship in Ancient Israelin Forms and Meaning* (London: SPCK, 1967), p. 8.

Cult during Wilderness Wanderings: During the wilderness wandering period of Israelites, the central place of cult was the tent of re-union or of meeting or of rendezvous when Yahweh spoke with Moses face to face. Tent was the place where Yahweh came and dwelt among the people and everyone who wanted to consult Yahweh went to the ten when Moses acted as his spokesperson before God. Roland de Vaux comments that these kind of portable sanctuaries which were believed to have supernatural power were quite common in Bedouin tribes, which were called "utfa, merkab" or "abu-Dhur". Thus, it is quite possible that the Israelites adopted the tent cult from the existing religious belief of the contemporary Bedouin tribes.[523] However, a special feature of Israelite tent cult was that it was considered as a holy place, the dwelling place of Yahweh who protected and guided the people of Israel during their desert journey.

Ark of the Covenant: The Ark of the Covenant occupied a central and very important place in the tent which contained the two tablets on which the law was inscribed. The ark was directly connected with the presence of Yahweh. According to Numb 10:33-36, when the Israelites set out from the mount of the Lord the ark of covenant of the Lord went before them. Whenever the ark set out, Moses would say "Arise O Lord let your enemies be scattered and your foes flee before you" and whenever it came to rest Moses would say "Return O Lord of the ten thousand of Israel." While priestly traditions mention about the ark, the Deuteronomic traditions do not give any description of the ark and also do not connect it with the tent. Yet we cannot say that it was a cultic object adopted by the people of Israel from the Canaanites because, "the ark then like the tent was part and parcel of the worship in the desert, but it had a longer history than the tenth. The ark without the tent stood in the camp at Gilgal (Josh 7:6). The ark was also said to be kept at Shilah and was taken to the battle at Apheq (1 Sam 3:3 and 4:3).

The ark was considered to have supernatural powers of Yahweh who gave victory to the people of Israel. We also have stories in 1 Sam 5 concerning the destruction brought about by the ark on the Philistines who captured it and took it to Ashdod. The ark was also considered as the throne of God and was the visible sign of God's presence and power. We can say that the ark was the most important of honor and reverence before the temple was built. When the ark arrives at the Israelite camp the Philistines say: "God has come into their camp" (1 Sam 4:7) and the capture of the ark is taken as the loss of God's presence when it is considered that the glory has been taken away from Israel (1 Sam 4:22). In 1 Chr 28:2 the ark is called the footstool of God and it is the ark of which Pss 99:5, 132:7 and 1 Sam 2:2 speak.

Cult during Tribal Confederacy: During this period, the assembly of people or tribes at certain sanctuaries or regular occasions or on special times symbolized the presence of God as the people recited wonderful deeds of Yahweh and affirmed

523 Roland de Vaux, *Ancient Israel*, p. 295.

their covenant with him. Since was supposed to be present during such an assembly there was a recital of creed and the people's affirmation of loyalty towards the divine law which formed the basis of their tribal union.[524] Deut 31:10f mentions one such gatherings where Moses commands the people to assemble after every seven years before God in the place which he will choose. In another passage in Deut 27:11-26 where the laws are proclaimed in a different way. It tells how the tribes gathered in Shechem and were divided into two groups one standing on Mount Gerizim for the pronouncing of blessing and another on Mount Ebal for the pronouncement of curses. It is also presumed that the offerings and sacrifices must have played an important role both on ordinary occasions and at local shrines and at the formal gathering of the confederacy. But, what is distinctive during this period is the recital of the law and God's mighty deeds by the people, which was not seen as an act of the past but the recitation became realistic for the present generation. In Deut 5:2f the proclamation of the divine law by the chosen representative of God would have been heard by the people as the word actually coming from the mouth of God. The worshipper in the cult actually would have felt participating in the event.

Cult during the Temple and Monarchic Period: Biblical tradition attributes the bringing and establishment of the ark of the covenant in Jerusalem to David. Obviously David's purpose to transfer the ark to his new capital was to make it more important from the point of view of religion as well as a political strategy. It was Solomon who built the temple which remained as a religious centre of Israel even after the separation of the United Kingdom of Israel.

During the monarchy the city of Jerusalem was regarded as the place which Yahweh had chosen (1 Kings 11:32). Temple at Jerusalem occupied a very important place in the life and worship of all Israel and Judah. "The faithful in the northern kingdom never ceased to look toward Jerusalem—even after the fall of the city, pilgrims from Shechem from Shiloh and from Samaria brought their offerings to the ruined temple (Jer 41:5)."[525] The temple was considered to be the divine seat of Yahweh, it was the house of God; the cloud in the stories of the desert symbolized the presence of Yahweh filled the temple (1 Kings 8:10). "This belief in Yahweh's presence in the temple was the whole reason for the worship celebrated there and for the pious customs of the faithful."[526] For this reason Amos says: Yahweh roars from Zion and utters his voice from Jerusalem (Amos 1:2), therefore Jerusalem was believed to be protected by Yahweh himself. While Isaiah gave Zion a religious meaning (2:2-3 and 6:1-4), for Jeremiah too the throne of Yahweh's glory was in Zion (7:1-15 and 14:21). Ezekiel also saw God's glory leaving the temple due to the sin of Israel (8-10 chapters). Yet he believed that Yahweh

524 Robert C. Dentan, *The Knowledge of God in Ancient Israel* (New York: Seabury Press, 1968), p. 81.

525 Roland de Vaux, *Worship*, p. 325.

526 Ibid., p. 326.

will come again and dwell in Zion, among his people forever. The passages like: Ezek 43:1-12; 48:35; Amos 1:2; Isa 2:3; Micah 4:2; Pss 20:3; 134:3, all confined the dwelling and presence of Yahweh in the temple who is considered to the God of universe. The Deuteronomic redactor asks the question can God really dwell with people on earth (1 Kings 8:27)? The answer is found in 1 Kings 8:30-40, that when faithful prays in the temple God hears their prayer from heaven.

We also find the theme of election that Yahweh chose Jerusalem as the site of the temple, his dwelling place (2 Sam 24:16; 2 Chr 3:1). Psalms 132:3 and 68:17 and Deut 12:5 stresses the election of Jerusalem even more by saying that Yahweh chose Jerusalem among all the other tribes to make his name known there, while Davidic dynasty claimed that Yahweh chose David and promised that his descendants shall rule and endure in Jerusalem. Zion as the house of Yahweh theme became more strong when Jerusalem was mysteriously delivered from Sennacherib's siege (2 Kings 19:34; Isa 34:35).

The temple was also believed to be the centre of the whole world, but we do not have any text that supports the cosmic significance of the city of Jerusalem. Yet we can say the belief that Yahweh chose Jerusalem as his dwelling place might have given way to the idea that Jerusalem is the centre of the world from where Yahweh rules over it.

We can say without any reservation that the major theological contribution to the faith of Israel comes from the temple cult where Zion theology originated and gave rise to many psalms and laments. The faith of Israel was shaken when the temple was destroyed in 587 BCE. It was the time when prophets proclaimed that the election of Zion will be renewed once again, after the return from exile.

The Temple Cult and the Sacrifice: Sacrifice was the main act of worship in the Israelite cult. While it was a freewill offering to God out of gratitude during the patriarchal era, it became a highly ritualistic act of worship during the temple cult. The book of Leviticus gives details concerning various kinds of sacrifices and makes it more legal and obligatory.

There was a shift "from the recitation of saving history and the proclamation of law to three other features as the main centres of interest."[527]

i) A new importance was given to the regular offering of sacrifice.
ii) The temple was regarded as the visible sign of Yahweh's dwelling place among the people from where his power works for his people.
iii) An importance was given to the king as the mediator of Yahweh's saving power.[528]

Sacrifices became the regular feature of the temple cult, which seems to be originated in other Semitic religions. Yet Israelite sacrifice had a distinctive feature

527 Robert C. Dentan, *The Knowledge of God*, p. 81.

528 Ibid., p. 87.

that "when an animal was sacrificed, the victim or at least a part of it was burnt upon the altar. Broadly speaking we find two kinds of sacrifices beside Passover (before the temple period) and later on in the temple cult. First is the whole 'burnt offering' (olah) and second is the 'peace offering'. The purpose of the whole burnt offering was to express homage to God and too gain his favour. It was a pleasing odour to the Lord during patriarchal period, but the priestly code with its emphasis on sin gave the whole burnt offering an expiatory value. The peace offering on the other hand was for maintenance or restoration of good relations with God based on the recognition that wellbeing of all humans rested on the relationship with God.[529]

Fat and blood were the important elements in the whole burnt offering since they belong to God and must be offered on the altar, yet they were not food for God. Roland de Vaux comments that fat and blood were considered sacred and thus must not be eaten by human beings. This offering symbolizes human beings' communion with God but it was not sharing a meal with God.[530] But it was certainly considered to have expiatory value given by the priests. Since blood was believed to have expiating value, it can expiate sin because it is the means of life. "Before the exile communion sacrifices were more frequent than holocausts but after the exile the holocausts became more frequent and important kind of sacrifices."[531]

Cult and the Prophets: Gerhard von Rad recognized that there were various kinds of prophets and prophecy. It was a general assumption that prophets denounced cult. But they often performed priestly function. For instance, Samuel presided over the sacred meal at Ramah. Elijah presided over the sacrifice on Mount Carmel to challenge the prophets of Baal. It was believed that Jeremiah and Ezekiel were both priests and prophets. However, it a debatable issue that prophets has any official and full status as cult functionaries. At the same time they seem to have not denounced the cult and its importance per se. What they emphasized was the right kind of cultic practices that should enhance the life of the poor and the oppressed so that cult along with the principles of justice ought to go hand in hand (see Isa 1:10-17; Amos 5, Jeremiah 7 and Micah 6). If people were more focusing on the cultic embellishment in order to capture the divine attention at the expense of poor and oppressed communities, that kind of cult was totally denied by the prophets. Their cult criticism was drawn in line with their social critique. Thus, the prophets upheld and affirmed the right kind of cultic life accompanied by the quality of the life of the people by practicing justice and righteousness.

Cult and the Psalms: Psalms give a multi-colored picture of Israel's cult and traditions. Worship in Israel, in tribes and then during monarchy and kingdoms

529 H. H. Rowley, *Worship in Ancient Israel*, pp. 120-121.

530 Roland de Vaux, *Ancient Israel*, pp. 418-419.

531 Ibid., pp. 124-126.

was based on Yahweh's meeting with his people in a theophanic manifestation. Psalms 47, 95, 97-100 and 104 reflect the great annual festival, may be the new year feast when the Israelites greeted Yahweh and worshipped him as creator and king. In fact the kingship of God is widely and firmly manifested in and through all these psalms. There is also a mythical element involved in al these psalm descriptions because Yahweh is portrayed as the king and God who brought victory to the people by defeating the chaotic forces. Sigmund Mowinckel calls these psalms as the psalms of Yahweh's enthronement. But this theory cannot be proved since tow problems arose out of this proposition of Mowinckel: if Yahweh was enthroned at a particular time who made him so? Second, if Yahweh was made as a king, then was there a time that he was not a king? Moreover, the expression 'Yahweh has become king' seems to be a little away from the understanding of God of the people of Israel. Since for them Yahweh is eternal king, the Lord of history (Ps 93:2). Psalm 29 pays homage to the voice of Yahweh as it reads: "The voice of the Lord is powerful ... The voice of the Lord breaks cedars of Lebanon." When the presence of God is celebrated Pss 94 and 99:1-2 and 8 reflects Zion theology by describing theophany of Yahweh. According to Kapelrud, this psalm shows three theological view points: First, Yahweh is more than than the ancient rain storm god and he is the God of history. Second, he is the God who chose his people like Moses, Aaron and Samuel and third, he is the God who gave them the law.[532] In addition we see that this psalm depicts Yahweh as forgiving, avenging and holy God (vv 8-9). Thus, on the whole we can notice that Israelite cult gave rise to many psalms or many psalms use cult as medium through which they talk about the deep relationship between God and the people.

Cult and Priesthood: Just a small note about the role of priests in the cult is in order at this point. One cannot really separate the role of priesthood in the overall cult of the Israelites. What has been discussed above so far on the cult is inevitably linked with the role and function of the priests in the cult. But it was obvious that the cultic embellishment became complex and more significant during the time of second temple period than all other times. The role of priesthood no doubt at this time became extremely complex in the midst of several theological and religious currents. To capture such a situation of complexity and plurality the analysis made by Otto Plöger is appropriate at this point. Plöger[533] maintains that based on several theological currents of post exilic community we may come down to talk about two great currents that captures the overall religious situation of the community. The one is the theocratic tradition and the other is the eschatological tradition. In the former case we can find the priestly tradition and Chronicles which is handed down by the official circles of the restored community in the post exilic times. The latter contains of late prophetic texts like Joel 3f, Zech. 12-14,

532 Kapelrud, "Tradition," p. 118.

533 O. Plöger, *Theocracy and Eschatology* (Atlanta: John Knox Press, 1968), pp. 106ff cited in Albertz, *A History of Israelite Religion*, pp. 438-39.

Isa. 24-27 which can be seen in the form of small coventicles. Plöger notes that these may be seen as forerunners of Hasidim mentioned in some places in the books of Maccabees in 1 Macc. 2:42; 7:13 and 2 Maccabees 14:6, and perhaps these are handed down to apocalyptic book of Daniel.[534] While there are others who did an extensive research on this area it would suffice to say that priests had definitely played very significant role despite they being branded as aristocratic ruling party in traditional ways. Their influence on bringing back the rigor of the cult like the first temple period cannot be denied.

In the light of the foregoing discussion on various theological aspects of cult in the Old Testament we now draw the following implications and conclusions for our contemporary situation in India.

First, cult was a medium through which all other traditions both religious and others have been demonstrated in the lives of the ancient Israel. The relationship between God and the people was always judged and measured in and through their special allegiance to Yahweh. Even when others look at Israelites as exclusive religious community the cult and worship practices were inevitably liked to such exclusiveness, it was the necessity of their day for their own survival and existence in the midst of their surrounding nations. The identity of the people of Israel has been mapped and tucked in the light of their cultic observances. So, in India today many religious minorities go through the same identity issues. In the name of globalization our world is dangerously moving towards the creation of monolithic culture that destroys the local cultures and value systems. The danger of syncretism creped into our religion and theology is guiding us towards an unknown land of desertion. In such a situation Ezra and Nehemiah reminds us of how to be intact as a covenant community although they appear to be a close-knit community.

In the present Indian scenario, the forces of Hindutva still dominate as a threat to the minorities like Christian and others. This ideology still lives and reigns supreme. It serves as a cultural hegemony that threatens and undermines the freedom of the marginalized communities in India. It tends to denigrate the cultural and religious other and to reinforce the marginalization of the victims of the traditional caste system through its patronizing attitudes and programs. Hence Hindutva as a force of cultural hegemony endangers the values of equality for all.[535]

---

534 Albertz commenting on this proposal of Plöger maintains that in view of the complexities of Israelite religion of the post exilic times it is very simplistic estimation of the situation by just merely reducing the whole religious current into two trends. See, Albertz, *A History of Israelite Religion*, pp. 438-39.

535 Prasad Lankapalli, "Revisiting Hindutva: An Indian Christian Theological Response," *Vidyajyoti Journal of Theological Research* 71:6 (2007), pp. 447-61. For more details of discussion on this point see, M. T. Cherian, *Hindutva Agenda and Minority Rights: A Christian Response* (Bangalore: Center for Contemporary Christianity, 2007).

Second, the question of identity crisis of the cultic community of Israel was the major problem during the post-exilic community. For instance, the community of Ezra and Nehemiah all along had to struggle with the issue of identity crisis in the midst of plurality of currents and groups that were prominent at their own time.[536] In the present scenario in India the dalit Christians and other minorities are living under the constant threat of expressing their religio-cultural diversity and to work towards their social emancipation. This is because of the fact that "Hindutva nationalism tends on the one hand to denigrate the cultural and religious other, and on the other hand to reinforce the marginalisation of the victims of the traditional caste system through its patronising attitudes and programmes, it endangers these goals."[537] Thus, when identity of any minority community is threatened like that of Ezra and Nehemiah and Dalit Christians it is natural for such a community to take strict measures towards protecting its boundaries. These boundaries were cultic regulations in the then Ezra-Nehemiah community and caste and other narrow conceptions in the present Dalit community and such other marginalized groups.

Third, the cult defined by the Israelite community gave them an opportunity to live in close relationship with Yahweh their God despite some failures on the part of the people in maintaining and sustaining that relationship in a consistent manner. Cult was rather a correcting medium through which the relationship between God and the people is always measured. When that relationship is fractured time and again the prophets and priests in Israel called the people back to their fundamentals of practice in their faith. In any community today in India, particularly, the marginalized communities like Dalit Christians their only hopes and aspirations are rested in their God who made them to live in dignity and self-respect. Thus, the cultic background in Israel and its various lessons and nuances of faith are very much applicable to the faith and life of marginalized communities in India.

Fourth, cult in the name of fractured denominationalism has also caused serious damage to the Christian minorities in India. Many Christian groups preach and practice a very narrow conception of cult and worship practices. Instead of witnessing community of faith it has become a stumbling block to those who want to sincerely follow the steps of Christ. This must be checked otherwise Christianity will never be able to impact in India in the coming years except that which was accomplished by the Christian missionaries in the 19th and 20th centuries it still lives like a reminiscence. God's presence in the cult is more important than all other external elements involved in the cult. Christians in India must highlight and emphasize that aspect.

---

536 This was already noted that through their wholesale ban on the mixed marriages Ezra and Nehemiah maintained strict boundaries of community identity even at times of crises.

537 Prasad Lankapalli, "Revisiting Hindutva." p. 452.

4.10 Salvation History and the Idea of Messiah in Ancient Israel and its Significance in the Contemporary Indian Situation

Today the understanding of salvation history has a wider impact in the theological debate than ever before. God revealed and continue to reveal in and through different acts both in the history and beyond is the popular notion. The Old Testament shares such a notion in general. Scholars claim that the word *Heilsgeschichte* (salvation history) was coined in the middle of the eighteenth century in Pietistic circles in Germany. Toward the middle of nineteenth century there appeared an opposition to the historical positivism of the *Religionsgeschichte Schule* (history of religion school), and the so called *Heilsgeschichte Schule*, which flourished especially in Germany. Its main representatives were Tobias Beck (1804-1878) and Johann Christian Konrad von Hofmann (1810-1877). It was Hofmann who introduced the word *Heilsgeschichte* which was later translated as "Salvation History" or "Redemptive History" or 'Saving History."[538] Richardson refers *Heilsgeschichte* to the saving acts of God in human history which are recorded in the scriptures of the Old and New Testaments.[539] The concept of *Heilsgeschichte* came into existence in order to counteract a static view of scripture. It talks about the scripture where there are series of divine acts which are originally connected and grew gradually until they are fulfilled in Jesus Christ. Thus, Jesus Christ is seen as the climax of the developing process of divine revelation in history. The school of *heilsgeschichte* depicts the history as revelation. It is further stressed that God had made Godself known in and through the historical process in historical acts. This is further accentuated by the idea that the Bible contain and is the redemptive history through which the salvation history of God is demonstrated.

The Oldest View of Salvation History in the Bible: Yahweh who brought Israel out of Egypt is probably the earliest and at the same time the most widely used confessional formula of salvation history. There are others such as designate Yahweh as the one who called the patriarchs and promised them the land, etc. Along these formulae are the confessional summaries of the saving history, covering an extensive span of the divine action in history. Among these the most important is the creed in Deut 26:5b-9 which is the earliest form of an Israelite confession of faith in which the most important stages of the salvation history are mentioned, from the time of patriarchs down to the time of conquest. In the historical creed, von Rad saw a confession of saving facts which grateful Israelites recited in connection with the feast of weeks at Gilgal.[540] The words in Deut 26 recapitulate the main events in the saving history of from the time of patriarchs down to the conquest, and they do this with the close concentration on the

538 Arlis John Ehlen, 'Old Testament Theology as Heilsgeschichte," *Concordia Theological Monthly* 35:9 (1964), p. 517.

539 Alan Richardson, *The Bible in the Age of Science* (London: SCM Press, 1961), p. 122.

540 Gerhard von Rad, *Old Testament Theology* I, p. 297.

objection historical facts. The greater presentation of saving history closely allied with Deut 26:5b-9 is found in Josh 24:2b-13 where unlike Deuteronomy narrates many details concerning the saving history. The ancient confession of faith which centers on a recitation of Yahweh's saving deeds on Israel's behalf was fundamental in the faith of the community of Israel. This creed represents the earlier example of Israel's saving history.[541]

The Concept of Heilsgeschichte According to Hofmann and von Rad: The work of Hofmann was defined in terms of a divinely guided history of redemption, a heilsgeschichte, which has as its ultimate goal the establishment of the kingdom of God. Hofmann is of the view that history recorded in the Old Testament is the history of salvation. For him the Old Testament theology describes the history of proclamation of salvation implied in that history and at the same time teaches the divine revelation by word.[542] Hofmann recognized the impact of historical studies on biblical interpretation and seized upon heilsgeschichte as the clue to understanding both divine revelation and the scripture. The focal point of Hofmann's conception of history is the eternal God becoming historical by emptying God self into Jesus in order to reconcile the whole world to God. According to Hofmann the world history can only be understood properly within the historical self-giving to the triune God who is love. Salvation history is the special relationship that God, who is first Lord of the whole creation, has established as direct communication and partnership by choosing particular people. This communication is first established with the patriarchs and run its course through the life of Israel and the church in Jesus Christ: because the heilsgeschichte is first and last, at its centre and its origin, the history of Jesus Christ.[543]

Heilsgeschichte is the word which von Rad used for Israel's view of history. According to him history was recounting of heilsgeschichte (saving or salvation history) that witnessed to God's continuing redemptive actions for Israel and the world. Von Rad was concerned to trace the social and historical development of Israel's traditions for it was in these that Israel's faith was embodied.[544] In his salvation history description von Rad refers to the series of events which Israel used to explain her arrival in Canaan, the saving history, from the patriarchs down to the Israelite entry into Canaan, the divine history with Israel, the revelation of Yahweh, events between Israel and Yahweh or the history of Israel's dealings with Yahweh. Von Rad argues that in the saving history, Yahweh made the truth of the promise good in the face of all the failure of Israel, and he did not let any part of

541 E. W. Nicholson, *Growing Points in Theology: Exodus and Sinai in History and Tradition* (Oxford: Basil Blackwell, 1973), p. 2.

542 J. C. K. von Hofmann, *Interpreting the Bible,* trans Christian Preus (Minneapolis: Augsburg, 1959), pp. 134-135.

543 Henning Graf Reventlow, *Problems of Old Testament Theology in the Twentieth Century* (Philadelphia: Fortress Press, 1985), pp. 94-95.

544 Gerhard von Rad, *Old Testament Theology* I, p. 357.

his great plan in history be taken out of his own hand.[545] Heilsgeschichte become one of the central and purpose of von Rad's theology as it served the unique feature of Israel's faith. For von Rad, Old Testament tells of God's history with Israel, with the nations, and with the world, from the creation of the world down to the last things, that is to say, down to the time when dominion over the world is given to the Son of Man. This history can be described as the saving history as God's will to save, in spite of many acts of judgment, to achieve its goal. This saving history has its beginning in Israel; it is characterized by the revelation that God is at work in acts of election and in the making of covenants which long precede any action of human will.[546]

Heilsgeschichte and the Prophets: In their prophetic message the Hebrew prophets proclaimed the saving history of God. Gerhard von Rad thinks that the overall prophetic message is rooted in saving history. The prophets like Jeremiah, Ezekiel, Zechariah, and more than anyone else, Deutero-Isaiah, placed a very different interpretation upon the breaking-off the history with God upon them. The tenor of their message is: "the old is done away with; now Yahweh will bring about something completely new, a new exodus, a new covenant, a new Moses." Israel's old confession of faith is presented now only as something which is done away with, since Yahweh is about to act along the line of his earlier saving acts in an even more splendid way.[547] Ezekiel sees Zion as the centre of a restored nation and pictures a healing stream which flows from the new Temple and brings life to the nation and the land, including the Dead Sea, which shall be cleansed of its salt that fish may live again in its water (Ezek 47:1-12). He depicts that God's glory will return to dwell in the Temple and the name of the city in that day shall be "the Lord is there" (Ezek 48:35; 37:27).

Deutero-Isaiah in the foreign land consoled and encouraged the people not to fear as Yahweh is going to deliver them from the Babylonian captivity. Just as Yahweh enabled the people of Israel in their first exodus to miraculously pass through the sea and the river, so he will lead them now to their homeland. Deutero Isaiah further depicts that servant song portraying the servant of Yahweh, through whose undeserved suffering others shall be redeemed. In a similar fashion Jeremiah brings the picture of the promise of new covenant offered hope that the past with its sins and the present with its despair could be overcome by God who would reunite the people, re-establish the relationship of God and Israel, write the divine law on people's hearts and be present to people with forgiveness and mercy. Thus, the picture of redemption through the messianic suffering emerged. The savant will gather up the suffering of Israel in him, identify himself with its judgment which even Israel does not deserve. Through Yahweh's servant, Israel

545 Gerhard von Rad, *Old Testament Theology* I, p. 126.

546 Ibid., pp. 357-358.

547 Ibid., p. 127.

will be the light to the Gentiles and proclaims Yahweh's salvation to the ends of the earth (Isa 49:6).

Heilsgeschichte and Typology: it is through the concept of salvation history for the first time the connection is established between the revelation of God in Israel and in Jesus Christ in the scripture of the Old and New Testaments. For von Rad the tension between the promise and fulfillment is fully consummated in the Christ event. Von Rad arrives at the crowning consummation of salvation history in the Christ event as a result of the combination of three conceptions: the centre of Deuteronomistic history, the predominance of event over word, and the interpretation of history from the movement along the line of tension between promise and fulfillment.[548] He further depicts that the heilsgeschichte and typology can be seen God's history with Israel from creation of the world down to the time when dominion over the world is given to the Son of Man. Thus, the saving history has its beginning in Israel continue in the New Testament. The Old Testament saving events, God's promises and their temporary fulfillment points to the future fulfillment in Jesus Christ.[549]

Von Rad insists that the proper relationship between the two testaments is understood in saving history. For him the New Testament repeats and continues the saving history of what is already going on in the Old Testament. He speaks of a typological relationship, implying that there is an immediate correspondence between the Old Testament text and the Gospel of Christ. He affirms that: the writers of the Gospel saw even the details of Jesus' life on earth, his passion, his death and resurrection as the fulfillment of Old Testament prediction."[550] The Hebrews, for instance, is one of the strongest testimonies to the fact that the old saving history was full of predictions of the Christ event of the New Testament. Von Rad further suggests that Paul too thinks in terms of **saving history and typology** for Paul sees in Abraham's faith a prefiguration of Christian faith, and he equates the rock from which the Israelites drank in the wilderness with Christ himself (1 Cor 10:4). Therefore, the above discussion reflect the New Testament saving event appear as the extension and conclusion of Israel's history with God which the Old Testament records.[551]

The problem with the above discussion is that if we take this kind of linear historical and developmental approach to link between the Old and New Testaments, does it mean that there is nothing original in the God's revelation in the Old Testament? Does it also mean that the OT has to necessarily wait until the fulfillment is seen in the NT? These problems cannot be resolved so easily and thus it would be better to take the message of God's redemptive history found

548 Gerhard F. Hasel, *Old Testament Theology: Basic Issues in the Current Debate* (Grand Rapids, MI: William B. Eerdmans Publishing Company, 1972), pp. 88-89.

549 Gerhard von Rad, *Old Testament Theology* II, p. 357-374.

550 Ibid., p. 327.

551 Ibid., p. 383.

in the OT in its own right and where possible we can see the continuity of such God's redemptive act in the NT rather than making two Testaments inevitably depending on each other.

Messiah and its Theological Significance in the Old Testament

The understanding of messiah in the Old Testament is always intriguing and aroused so much of discussion because it has been understood by the Christians now as applicable to Jesus Christ. Precisely because of this lot of misunderstanding also occurred in the debates related to messiah till today. In this brief presentation we shall talk about the theological understanding of messiah in the Old Testament and its relationship to the New Testament after a brief discussion on the terminology.

The term Messiah: The word messiah is transliteration of the Greek word: *Messias* (John 1:14; 4:25) or the Aramaic word *Meshiha* or the Hebrew word *Masiah*. The word means "the anointed one." In the Old Testament, objects as well as people could be anointed. Jacob anointed a pillar at Bethel (Gen 31:13). The tabernacle was anointed (Exod 30:26) as well as altar and vessels (Lev 8:11). Persons anointed in the Old Testament include the priests (Exod 29:7), some prophets (1 Kings 19:16; Ps 105:16; Isa 61:1) and the patriarchs (Ps 105:15) and the kings (Saul, David Solomon etc.). On the basis of this terminological discussion it has been argued that messiah means a political present and future figure or a religious leader, could be a priest, king and even a prophetic figure. W. H. Rose defines the term messiah as follows: "a future royal figure sent by God who will bring salvation to God's people and the world and establish a kingdom characterized by features like peace and justice."[552]

The Messiah as a Political Figure: In the ancient world, both persons and things were anointed by sweet-smelling oil poured or smeared over them. The original idea was that the oil possessed an abnormal holy power. In the act of anointing, this power and holiness were transmitted to the person anointed. Among all the anointed things or persons, the one who is called Yahweh's anointed is a special case. He could be the earthly king who at any given time is reigning over Yahweh's people. In most practical terms the Yahweh's anointed king was later on understood as reigning king of David's line, the king of Jerusalem, designated, installed and anointed by Yahweh by a priest or even a prophet.

Sigmund Mowinckel is of the view that the word Messiah as such does not appear in the Old Testament but it is an abbreviation of the fuller expression 'Yahweh's Anointed'. This shows that the eschatological Messiah derived his name from the sacral title of the ancient kings of Israel. Moreover Messiah was not only seen as an eschatological figure, but always had a measure of political significance. The messiah is he who shall restore Israel as a people, free her from her enemies,

552 W. H. Rose, *Zemah and Zerubbabel: Messianic Expectations in the Early Postexilic Period* (Sheffield: Sheffield Academic Press, 2000), p. 23.

rule over her as king, and bring other nations under her political and religious sway. Thus, the word Messiah has the political sense from the beginning.[553]

Understanding of Messiah by Judaism: Throughout their existence the Jews never forget that they were special people chosen by God among all others in the world. They always hoped that they will have their saviour coming one day in the line of David who would politically conquer all the nations of the earth to establish justice and righteousness on this earth. Further they regarded the messiah, an earthly king, who would restore Israel from the grave misfortune which had befallen her; bring about national and political deliverance of the people from oppression and distress, and for a moral and religious purification and consummation.[554] This concept of another earthly king from the Davidic line emerged when the chosen people of God were carried to Assyria and when Babylonians conquered and captured Jerusalem and carried the Jews away as captives from their homeland. One after another they experienced rulers over them and when they came to the Roman period they anticipated that the messiah will come as a political king or ruler to deliver them from the oppressive Roman Empire.

During the intertestamental period the messianic movement got strengthened against the Roman ruling system and its attitude towards Jewish religion and culture. Though this period brings out the idea of violent and warrior messiah, it was due to the disastrous situation of the context in which Jews were pushed at that time. The period of Persian and Hellenistic domination also gave scope for the idea of messianic hope among Jews. The promise to David and the prophecies of a future Davidic king were known during this period (Sir 47:11, 22; 1 Macc 2:57). During the Hasmonean period the hope of an anointing royal figure who would deliver Israel became more prominent.[555] After the death of Herod in 4 BCE the Jews pressed Herod's son and heir apparent, Archelaus, for a number of reforms. What followed after that was a violent resistance movement one after another and they clearly demonstrate the Jewish messianism deeply rooted as political movements.

Theology of Messiah: In order to focus more on the significant features of the understanding of Messiah in the Old Testament we shall now move on talk about the theology of messiah and draw some relations ship between salvation history and messiah and see their overall implication for Indian context.

The Messiah as King: Jacob the patriarch was the first one to foretell the messiah's role as a ruler in Gen 49:10 to whom the nation would obey. The

553 Sigmund Mowinckel, *He that Cometh: The Messiah Concept in the Old Testament and Later Judaism,* trans. G. W. Anderson (Grand Rapids, MI: William B. Eerdmans Publishing Company, 2005), p. 7.

554 Ibid, p. 285.

555 Kenneth Atkinson, "On the Herodian Origin in Militant Davidic Messianism at Qumran" New Light from Psalm of Solomon 17." *Journal of Biblical Literature* 118:3 (1999), p. 435.

messiah's sovereignty would extend over the whole world. He shall rule from sea to sea and from river to the ends of the earth. All kings shall pay him homage, all nations shall serve him (Ps 72:8-11; Zech 9:10) Balaam prophesied in Numb 24:17 as follows: "I see him, but not near; I behold him, but not close at hand. A star shall rise out of Jacob, a scepter shall come forth from Israel. The coming ruler shall crush the temples of Moab, shall dash to the earth all the sons of warmongers." These words points to the distant future and the star symbolizes a ruler and the scepter royal power. Though kings and people rise against this ruler, Yahweh will install him as a king (Pss 2:6; 110:1). The kingship of the messiah will bear little resemblance to earthly kingship. His governance shall establish peace, justice and righteousness forever. With justice he will judge the lowly and with fairness arbitrate in favor of the poor in the land. He will smite the oppressor and the evildoers shall be slain by the breath of his mouth (Isa 11:4). Furthermore the characteristic virtues of the messianic king will be meekness and love. As a good shepherd he will be deeply attached to all his sheep, particularly those standing in greatest need of help.[556]

The Messiah as Prophet: In Deut 18:15-18 the writer clearly explains that God would raise an ideal prophet and his features are explained. Moses further explained that God would raise a prophet in the future after his death who would teach people concerning God and God's holy will and proclaim revelations more profound that those taught of old. The messiah as a prophet would be favored with the fullness of the spirit, "upon him shall rest the spirit of Yahweh, the spirit of wisdom and understanding, the spirit of counsel and fortitude, the spirit of knowledge and the fear of Yahweh," (Isa 11:2). God's spirit would illuminate and strengthen the messiah as he went about his prophetic mission of bringing salvation to the world. "It would equip him with wisdom to select the best means to attain his purpose; with understanding to apply them properly; with counsel to make the proper judgments and to give prudent advice; with fortitude to execute his decisions; with knowledge of divine secrets far surpassing all other prophets; with fear of Yahweh spurring him on to communicate sanctity."[557] Moreover, Yahweh does not send this prophetic messiah only to Israel, for his mission as a prophet is to lead all human beings back to their creator as it is stated in Isa 42:6-7: "I am making you a covenant with the people of (i.e., Israel), a light to the Gentiles ..."

The Messiah as Servant: Four poems in Deutero-Isaiah speak of a servant figure of Yahweh. The first poem in Isa 42:1-9 describes God's choice of the servant who will bring justice to the nations. His task is to establish a just order among Israel and nations. The purpose of his commission is to restore the land of the chosen people and to rebuild the desolated places in Jerusalem. He is given

556 Paul Heinisch, *The Theology of the Old Testament,* trans. William D. Heidt (Collegeville: The Liturgical Press, 1955), pp. 348-349.

557 Ibid., p. 351.

the task to be the mediator not only between Yahweh and the people of Israel alone but even with other nations. The second poem in Isa 49:1-6 describes in the servant's own words his experience of having been called by God to be a light to the nations. In verse 6, by calling the servant "saving help" of the nations, Yahweh has made it possible for his salvation to reach the ends of the earth.[558]

The third poem in Isa 50:4-9 describes Yahweh has opened his ear, and he has responded with implicit obedience. In the course of his mission, the servant has been subjected to physical violence, scourging, pulled out of bread and insult. Despite the attacks and insults on him, the servant has not rebelled against receiving the word from God and has not refrained from coming forward with it to those for whom it was designed. The last poem found in Isa 52:13-53:12 which is called the song of the suffering servant, describe the transference from atonement by animal sacrifice, the traditional ritual means of atonement in Israel, to atonement by a human being's suffering. By his suffering, the servant of Yahweh receives God's punishment for the sins of the group. The suffering and the death of the servant viciously for many has opened up a new possibility that many from the nations come into the fold of Yahweh's community. Because of the servant's mission as a sufferer, Yahweh will reward him and his kingship will be extended to the whole world. [559]

The anointing of the servant found in Isa 61:1-3 is considered to be the servant song of Trito-Isaiah, parallel to those in Deutero-Isaiah. Some would even call it as the fifth servant song. The anointed prophet (messiah) will comfort the broken hearted, proclaim liberty to captives and free the prisoners. The prophet looks at his age as a time of liberation as proclaimed in jubilee years. So when the days come, all people will respond to it. The days will be a time of peace and concord in which Yahweh's presence will provide all needed light. The Gentile will also receive the good news. Jesus saw this as a messianic prophecy to be fulfilled in him. He identified himself as the anointed one mentioned in the poem and declared that his mission was spelled out in this prophecy and that the messianic era had arrived (Luke 4:18-19).

The Messiah as Divine: Isaiah in 9:6 prophesized that "a child is born to us, a son is given to us, upon his shoulders rest the sovereignty, and his name shall be called wonderful counselor, mighty God, eternal father, prince pf peace." Yahweh is called "mighty God," *'el gibbor* (Isa 10:21). Now if the messiah too is called "mighty God" *'el gibbor*, it follows that Yahweh is appearing in him. Isaiah's other titles likewise have a ring of divinity in them and become more profound in the light of the "mighty God," and "wonderful counselor," neither Moses nor any other prophet who by God's power performed miracles and showed men the way of God received this name. The child in Isaiah's vision is greater than all who

558 Daniel Jones Muthunayagom, *The Relationship Between Election and Israel's Attitude the Nations in the Book of Isaiah* (Delhi: ISPCK, 2000), p. 125.

559 Ibid., p. 138.

preceded him, for only God is full of wonders (Isa 25:1; 28:29). The redeemer "has his origin from the beginning, from the days of eternity" (Micah 5:1). In this sense the messiah is understood as son of God. In Psalm 110:1 we see the writer is describing this messiah who shares in Yahweh's divine power and is described to govern the world and Yahweh humbles his enemies to make them acknowledge as highest Lord.

The Messiah as the Future Hope: The notion of messiah as the future hope originated and developed after the fall of the state. According to the messianic hope in the strict sense arose at the same time as the hope of restoration. Hope was sustained by a faith in Yahweh which looked for the prince whom Yahweh had appointed to realize the ideal, to be the king after Yahweh's heart and the bearer of the promise to the dynasty and the nation. The hope of messiah who was yet to appear originated in the situation when Israel was facing the worst of all the afflictions and punishment which had befallen the nation throughout its fatal history, namely the destruction of the state, the degradation of the royal house, the dispersion of the people and their subjugation of foreign ruler: the exile and diaspora. That the messiah belongs to the future means that he is part of the Israelite hope for the future. The messianic hope is the hope in the restoration of the state, nation and monarchy. Thus, the messiah is the ideal king of David's line, who will reign in the restored kingdom of his ancestor when the nation has been raised from degradation and freed from foreign dominion, when justice has been established and godliness and virtue prevail in the land.[560]

The Messiah as the Son of Man: In two passages in the Apocalypse of Enoch the title "the Messiah" or "the Anointed" is applied to the Son of Man. The same identification is found in the Apocalypse of Ezra. Here too it is 'the man,' 'one like a man,' who is the deliverer in the end time and who will overthrow the heathen world power and carry out the judgment. Of him it is explicitly said that he 'shall spring from the seed of David' (4 Ezra 12:32 cf, 7:29). 4 Ezra 13 speaks of the deliverer of the world, the Son of Man, but gives the Jewish messianic title "My (i.e. the Lord's) servant," and represents him as the one who will be revealed on Zion, and will deliver first the Jews, and then the dispersed ten tribes. In other words, he is the Jewish messiah. The same is true of Syriac Apocalypse of Baruch. The eschatological deliverer, who is described there, has the cosmic, supernatural features of the Son of Man; but he is called 'My messiah,' 'My servant, messiah.' All this discussion indicates that the son of man is highly nuanced in various ways in the extra-canonical literature which is a later development in the understanding of messiah.

The Messiah as Eschatological Figure: The messiah of the Psalms of Solomon is explicitly Davidic (17:4, 21). The awaited Davidic king of Israel "shall be the Lord messiah" (17:32), who will appear in the appointed day" (18:5). He will drive out the wicked (17:27), purge Jerusalem of sinners (17:30, 32, 36)

560 Sigmund Mowinckel, *He that Cometh*, p. 155.

and will lead Israel (17:26), judging the tribes of the people (17:26), who will be distributed upon the land according to their tribes (17:28). In the later Judaism the messiah denotes an eschatological figure. He belongs to 'the last time'; his advent lies in the future. To use the word 'messiah' is to imply eschatology, the last things. The word 'messiah' by itself, as a title and a name, originated in later Judaism as the designation of an eschatological figure. In Christian eschatology too the messiah (Christ) became the central figure in the expectation of the last time.

The Day of Messiah (Yahweh): 'The day of grace' (Ps. Sol 14:10), when messiah will come, is also called 'the day of Messiah' (4 Ezra13:52). This term reappears in the New Testament as the day of Christ (1 Cor 5:5; Phil 1:6, 10; 2:16). The expression is formed by analogy with the earlier 'day of Yahweh.' It means when Yahweh or the messiah will appear as king, assume the royal title, and he is acclaimed as king. The day of Yahweh will be a day on which he has accomplished his messianic work, crushed his enemy, save his people, and restore the kingdom of Israel. The day when the messiah appears and accomplishes his messianic work of salvation is the day when he 'is revealed' as what he is destined to be, as the messiah. By performing messianic works he 'reveal his glory' (his dignity as messiah), as the fourth Gospel puts it (John 2:17).[561]

The Immanuel Prophecy and Messiah: The Immanuel prophecy in Isaiah 7 sheds clearer light on the wonderful royal child. The situation is the threatened assault on Judah by Ephraim and Damascus. King Ahaz does not dare to trust in Yahweh's help, but wants to appeal to the king of Assyria, which, to Isaiah is synonymous with unbelief for Yahweh, setting the power of man above the power of God. But Isaiah does not give up hope of turning Ahaz to the right way. Then come the sign: "Behold the young woman has conceived, and she will bear a son and she will call him Immanuel ... For before he has discerning to refuse what is bad and choose what is good, the land whose two kings you dread will be desolate." However, there has been serious debate about the identity of woman and the child mentioned here. The passage in Isaiah 7 does not inform that he will reign as king over Israel, or indeed that he will be of royal rank, or that he will deliver the people from distress. On the contrary, it is stated that before the child is old enough to distinguish between what is useful and what is harmful (in a few years time) the enemy will be destroyed by Yahweh.[562]

The sign of Immanuel is to make Ahaz believe absolutely in Yahweh, surrender himself to God in complete trust and obedience, and in virtue of this choice decide to adopt the right attitude in the contemporary situation. It also means that the sign must come to pass soon and it should not happen after the event, but simply to confirm the divine intervention as it was done elsewhere in Exodus 3:12. This also means a direct Christological interpretation is out of

561 Sigmund Mowinckel, *He that Cometh*, pp. 302-303.

562 Ibid., p. 110.

question. Isaiah cannot here be referring to the birth of Jesus more than seven hundred years later. He foretells that since king Ahaz has not had sufficient courage and fear of God to make him ask for a sign from Yahweh, Yahweh himself will give him a sign without delay. 'The young woman,' already with a child, will bear a son and give him a name expressing absolute trust that Yahweh protects his people.[563]

On the basis of our foregoing discussion on the themes of the salvation history and the messiah we now draw some implications of both the themes for our contemporary Indian context in the paragraphs that follow.

First, salvation history was a common factor that united all the traditions in ancient Israel in a novel and variety of ways. It functions like a thread that runs throughout the Old and New Testaments demonstrating how God's dealing with his people is in effect undertaken in God's own redemptive plan. All the individual traditions like cult, creation, history, blessing, elections, covenant, land, revelation etc are unfolded in and through salvation history. The integral theological and historical link between the Old and New Testaments is better articulated in the theme of salvation history. It is not an exaggeration to say that salvation history is the centrals of both the testaments to understand God's dealing with his people.

Second, messiah is a particular theme of salvation history how God addressed their needs of redemption at the time of crises and hopelessness. When crisis surrounded them after they lost temple, kingdom and all other traditions associated with their faith and life the promise of messiah was the only hope in which they sustained their faith in their God. The prophets continuously warned the Israelites to pay attention to their arrogance and reckless attitude towards their God and they tried to make things better for the people. But the people were not interested to pay attention to such warnings of the prophets, instead they relied on their pride and the invincibility of royal traditions, particularly the royal Zion and Davidic traditions that God would never bring any disaster upon them on account of God's promise of perpetual line of inheritance in the line of David. No matter any amount of caution given by the prophets it hardly went into their hearing. However, God was gracious on the part of the people and thus messianic hope was given to them in order to continue God's promise of salvation even at the brink of their history.

Third, both the themes of messiah and salvation history is relevant for the marginalized communities like Dalits, tribals, women and children in India today. Many attempts were made to bring down the lives of these marginalized communities in India. Time again they were targeted in order that they may be wiped out or mellowed down when they tried to raise their voice against the oppressor. Dalits and other marginalized communities in India live in a messianic hope and that hope is deeply rooted in their future that all their suffering will

563 Sigmund Mowinckel, *He that Cometh*, p. 111.

one day will end. The following words of Namdev Dhasal will tell the future aspirations of Dalits in a metaphorical way as follows:

> Our blood was spilled for this glorious city and what we got was the right to eat stones. Now, now, we must explode the building which kisses the sky. After a thousand years we were blessed with a sunflower. Now, now we must, like sunflowers, turn our faces to the sun.[564]

As we noted above the voices of Dalits echo very strongly in their socio-political and economic milieu. Even though they faced severe opposition and reprisal at times they never lost their vigor for voicing out their strong concerns. 'You can kill everything but not the voice' says Gaddar as he extols the virtues of the songs and music that are capable of bringing on revolution. His prophetic voice is geared towards emancipating the millions of Dalits who are crushed under the feet of oppressor in the name of caste system. His attire and costume reminds the audience that unquenching thirst for revolution. His voice is like the voices of Bhimrao Ambedkar and Jyotirao Phule who fought against the oppression of caste and untouchability. His voice also reminds us the voices of several Dalit martyrs whose sweat and blood brought the Dalit cause thus far. Such is the voice of messianic hope of Dalits to proclaim God's redemptive history and plan of salvation in their own lives. They therefore, live in such unshakable hope that is sustaining them even today amidst all kinds of odd situations they face.

4.11 Hope and Eschatology in the Biblical World and its Relevance in Today's Indian Context

The theme of hope and eschatology was always sidelined in the theological discussions of the Old and New Testament as it would be difficult to pin down exactly those themes in the light of other overwhelming themes in the Bible. That trend need not delimit the importance of both the above said themes and their overall significance in the Old and New Testament theologies. In this short presentation we shall endeavor not only to integrate both the themes in order to draw some implications for our context in India, we shall also note few remarkable potentials that both the themes carry in the light of their overall significance of Old Testament theology in particular and New Testament Theology in general. There is certain amount of overlap in the discussion of these themes as they might cross over into the areas of salvation, deliverance, apocalyptic thinking etc in the Old Testament.

In the Old Testament hope is expressed in several words. We shall consider few of them while just mentioning all the words. The word *betakh, khasah, yakhal, and qauneah,* among these the first word has connotations that are both positive

564 Namdev Dhasal, *An Anthology of Dalit Literature,* ed. Mulkraj Anand and Eleanor Zelliot (New Delhi: Gyan Publishing House, 1992), p. 60.

(to rely on someone), and negative (to have false security), is reflected in LXX translation of Ps 115 (LXX 113). *Khasah* connotes shelter and the LXX generally renders it as "confidence." It is often found in laments (Ps 57:2, Heb 57:3) and in other eschatological texts (Isa 4:6).[565]

Hope in the Pentateuchal and Historical Books: Hope in the Old Testament is found in the religious narratives of Israelite history. These narratives are underlined by the promise of Yahweh expressed in terms of God's covenants with creation and Israel as people of God. They affirm as the creator, preserver, liberator and benefactor of Israel, desiring their prosperity and shalom (welfare, completeness, peace). The creation narratives (Gen 1-2) express Yahweh's fundamental relationship to humanity, offering prosperity and shalom (Gen 1:28, 31). The flood narrative also (Gen 6:5-9:17) demonstrates Yahweh's willingness and ability to intervene within history to bring an end to an intolerable situation (Gen 6:11). The history of hope continues when Israelites were enslaved in the land of Egypt. The story of hope is initiated by Yahweh through Moses and Aaron by sending them to the people in bondage to deliver them from the oppressor. Despite several turns and twists in the story eventually the hope of the people is confirmed by Yahweh by leading and guiding them to the promised land of Canaan.

Throughout its history Israel struggled with the covenantal requirement of monotheism. Yet the hope can be derived from the Deuteronomistic presentation of cyclical pattern that is intensely discussed in the case of Judges as follows: apostasy, oppression by a foreign nation, arrival of a judge, and deliverance from oppression (Judg 2:1-9). This pattern demonstrates the conditional/unconditional nature of Yahweh's covenant with Israel; the actualization of shalom requires covenantal fidelity of Israel and Yahweh's faithfulness to preserve Israel even in spite of their apostasy. After the time of judges, David becomes a prototype of righteous king, and Yahweh makes an unconditional covenant with hi (2 Sam 7). The promise that Davidic king will always occupy the throne of Judah will become significant after the Babylonian exile, for it provides a nationalistic hope for dispossessed Israel. Further, it was essential in the post-exilic development of messianic hope, eventually becoming a component of Christian message.

Hope in the Psalter and Job: Hope is manifested in the Psalter and in other wisdom book in different ways. The belief that Yahweh will intervene to end the suffering of the present crisis is strongly present in the lament psalms. One third of the psalms are in the language of grievance designed to summon Yahweh to action, which is an expression of the incongruity of the memory of Yahweh's faithfulness in light of current crises. These expressions are hopeful because they are a rejection of the current crisis and an expectation that Yahweh can, should, and will rectify the situation. The psalms of lament can be seen as demanding for

565 Seung Al Yang, "Hope," in *The New Interpreter's Dictionary of the Bible D-H*, Vol. 2, ed. Katherine Doob Sakenfeld, et al. (Nashville: Abingdon Press, 2007), pp. 885-887.

salvation from enemies (Ps 7:6; Heb 7:7), a complaint against the personal neglect by Yahweh (Ps 44:9-16), a desire for resting place (Ps 27:4,5) or the preemptive praise for what one expects to be accomplished (Ps 35:9). In many psalms the image of Yahweh as warrior and monarchical supporter provided hopeful language (Ps 24:8).

The book of Job presents a complex hope for a "redeemer" (Job 19:21-29) which is open to several interpretations. Christians have interpreted this passage for a nascent hope of resurrection in the book Job and they even found a prophetic messianic hope in the statement: "For I know that my redeemer lives," (Job 19:25). For Jews Yahweh is the redeemer who lives to bless the children of Job and his property (Job 42:10, 13) and longevity (42:16-17). However, Job himself may not have envisaged resurrection here as he is of the view that a tree has more hope than a person of life being cut down (Job 14:7).[566]

Hope in the message of the Prophets: From the very beginning the prophets talked about trusting God in the midst of the hopelessness of the people of Israel. They looked at this hope as found in the distant future because of the continuing sin of the people and their reckless attitude towards God. Thus, the prophetic view on hope rests on the other side of the judgment. It is seen in two ways: First, the prophets viewed hope in the picture of God's kingdom. Second, the prophets talked about a definite hope only after God's judgment. We shall clarify these two trends of the prophets briefly.

Hope in God's Kingdom: The prophetic depiction of God's kingdom is that God's kingdom will come in the end in the future. Thus, one must look to God with hope for a proper understanding of future. That is to say, on the one hand, that the kingdom will come about for the sake of God. This idea is articulated by Ezekiel (36:22) as follows: "It is not for your sake, O house of Israel, that I am about to act, but for the sake of my holy name, which you have profaned among the nations." Thus, the kingdom is to vindicate, to express, and to demonstrate the holiness of God. God's people had forgotten the majesty of God who would not share his glory with another (Isa 48:11). On the other hand, the kingdom will come about by God's strength alone. God's word will not return empty and it a word which accomplishes for which it is purposed (Isa 55:11). This doesn't mean that human beings have no place in God's promises. In this context we need to remember what happened in the case of Jonah. When people repented, God changed his earlier decision to punish the people of Nineveh. So Jeremiah proclaims to the people in 7:5, 7 "If you truly amend your ways and doings ... then I will let you dwell in this place. The real hope that the prophets captured and proclaimed to the people is God's new creation. God would initiate every action to see that a new creation will result at the end as a sign of concrete hope in the midst of the people. Isaiah (52:8) proclaims that this will be a reality when he

566 Seung Al Yang, "Hope," in *The New Interpreter's Dictionary of the Bible D-H*, Vol. 2, ed. Katherine Doob Sakenfeld, et al. (Nashville: Abingdon Press, 2007), pp. 885-887.

says: "For eye to eye they see the return of the Lord to Zion." Many other images are employed to capture this idea of new creation by the prophets: It is called the mountain of the Lord (Isa 2:2-4 and Micah 4:1-3), Zion in Isa 51:11and Mount Zion in Obad 17. In all these references the prophets talked about earthly and bodily content of the hope. This is a remaking of God's creation in a new way. The creation will answer God's creative word with grain, wine and oil (Hosea 2:21-22). God's people will be planted on their land and never plucked up (Amos 9:14-15). Through the idea of remnant this hope is made very concrete in the prophetic preaching. For instance, in Zephaniah God pleads for those who are humble to seek righteousness so that on the day of wrath they will be protected. He goes on to declare in 3:12-13: "For I will leave in the midst of you a people humble and lowly. They shall seek refuge in the name of the Lord ... For they shall pasture and lie down, and none shall make them afraid." It is God who will preserve this remnant, he will carry and save them (Isa 46:3-4). Later the servant will become a mediator between God and people to carry on this hope. The servant (variously identified as different individuals and community figures) will lead the people to the hope they longed for and bring them near to God. And finally, as discussed above elsewhere in another topic, the idea of Messiah is proclaimed by the prophets in order to sustain the hope among God's people. This hope is talked in terms of deliverance like that of Moses from Egypt (Hosea 2:14-23), and it proclaims a better kingdom than that of David. In fact the imagery of the shoot from the stump of Jesse (Isa 11:1, 10), that is, the remnant of the house of David, is the most familiar image of the Messiah. The messiah is the son of David (Ps 2:7), seated at the Lord's right hand (Ps 110:1) and is himself divine (Ps 45:6).

The goal of God's redemptive work through which hope is articulated by the prophets is present at several places in the Old Testament. Jeremiah 31:31-34 talks about this hope that God is going to realize in the midst of his covenant people God's people will dwell securely in the lad God will give them and exhibit the righteousness of their Lord. Everyone will know the Lord from the least to the greatest. Hosea in 2:19 speaks of God's people being married to the Lord, betrothed in righteousness. This involves a change so radical that it can only be described as a resurrection of dry bones (Ezek 37:4-10), the giving of a new heart (Ezek 36:26), which is explained as the placing of God's own spirit within them. It is in this context a grand vision of hope is proclaimed by the writer of the book of Lamentations (3:21-23) as follows: "But this I call to mind, and therefore I have hope: The steadfast love of the Lord never ceases, his mercies never come to an end, they are new every morning, great is thy faithfulness."

Hope in the prophetic idea of Judgment: God intervenes in the lives of the people in order to put them in the right path and this happens in his judgment. While there are several nuances of the prophetic idea of judgment are found in the Old Testament, the main idea of the prophetic idea of judgment in the context of hope can be seen that the aggressor is punished and the victim is compensated. Looking in this way then judgment is part of God's redeeming activity. It is God's activity of restoring the fallen created order by punishment on the one hand, and deliverance on the other. There is affirming hope that manifests itself in God's judgment. Since judgment is God's (Deut 1:17), those who wait for God's judgment are blessed (Isa 30:18). All God's judgments are true and righteous (Ps 19:9). Judgment is a dynamic work of God involving discrimination and action together. Since God knows the human intentions and their heart God delivers the weak and fatherless (Deut 10:18 and Ps 82:3-4) and God punishes the wicked (Ezek 7:3; 25:11). It is because of this uncompromising nature of God's judgment and God's righteousness God is also the ultimate hope of the people who struggle to deal with situations of injustice and oppression in their daily lives. This character of God as the righteous judge is proclaimed by the psalmist with the firm hope in Psalm 96: 10, 12-13 as follows: "Say among the nations, 'The Lord reigns! Yea, the world is established, it shall never be moved; He will judge the people with equity … "Then shall all the trees of the wood sing for joy before the LORD, for he comes, for he comes to judge the earth. He will judge the world with righteousness, and the peoples with truth." That is why prophet like Amos talks about righteous judgment of God comes like a fire that cleanses the people. It is this idea of God that the prophets are proclaiming and it is in this God, the creator of heaven and earth whom the psalmist is in firm hope (Ps 121). It is because of this grand and sure purpose of God who acts in the history of the people by intervening in their lives there is a firm hope expressed in all the prophetic oracles through the centuries.[567]

Eschatological Hope: The unfulfilled expectations of the post-exilic prophets provided the basis of various forms of eschatology that are found in the apocalyptic literature surrounding the Maccabean period. The disappointments in the history raised doubts whether Yahweh's promises could be realized within history; therefore, hope began to be expressed as the expectation of the end of history. These writings produced hope literature in the context of Jewish conflict with the Hellenistic life and culture. These writings used heavenly visions and angelic mediators. They sought to assure the readers of the coming eschaton of a post-modern judgment and the reward of a transcendent world. Moreover these writings stand at the apex of the growing eschatological character of Old Testament hope and provide the immediate context for the first century Judaism, out of which the New Testament was produced. Unlike the nationalistic hope that the prophets proclaimed the apocalyptic literature mainly focused in individualistic piety and hope. The book of Daniel encouraged personal piety in times of trouble, through the example of young exiles in Babylon who are successful through their living (Dan 1:20). Because these young people refuse to defile themselves for the sake of assimilation

567 William Dyrness, *Themes in Old Testament Theology* (Downers Grove InterVarsity Press, 1977), pp. 230-237.

they are blessed (Dan 1:8). The righteous will resurrect and those who endure persecution will be rewarded at the end and those who may lose their lives will have the hope of eternal life, while their oppressors will be raised for eternal shame (Dan 12:1-2 and 2 Macc 7).[568]

Eschatology and its various nuances in the Old Testament Theology

Like hope in the Old Testament eschatology carries several nuanced meanings in different places. There is general feeling of lack of organic coherence in the theme of Old Testament eschatology because of this reason. Several expressions are use to denote eschatology in the Old Testament. Some of those expressions include: "in that day," "in the latter days," "the day of the Lord," "in those days," "behold, days are coming," and "the end." Some of these or one of these may refer to anything that is closer to what we may call eschatological in the Old Testament.[569] There are various opinions on the definition of eschatology in the Old Testament. P. R. Davies defines eschatology as a "dimension of belief that history moves in a direction, that this direction is set by God, and that God acts within history to insure this direction."[570] Gerhard von Rad talks only about "eschatological element" found in some of the prophetic writings in so far he talks about the message of the prophets as eschatological wherever it regards the old historical bases of salvation as null and void.[571] Claus Westermann talks about eschatology in the Old Testament as a "new saving act/coming of God."[572] G. A. F. Knight observed that Israel, unlike her neighbors, looked forward and backward and in this sense understood and defined eschatology.[573] Brevard S. Childs is of the view that the end time referred in eschatology in the Old Testament is not merely a return to paradise, Eden, or the primeval age. It is new. Something vital has occurred between the beginning and the end.[574]

While it would be unending and a long list can be furnished on a variety of definitions concerning eschatology, we shall now focus on various theological

568 Seung Al Yang, "Hope," p. 882.

569 Ralph L. Smith, *Old Testament Theology: its Method and Message* (Nashville: Broadman & Holman Publishers, 1993), p. 398.

570 P. R. Davies, "Eschatology in the Book of Daniel" *Journal for the Study of the Old Testament* 17 (1980), p. 33.

571 Gerhard von Rad, *Old Testament Theology* II, p. 118.

572 Claus Westermann, *Elements of Old Testament Theology* (Atlanta, John Knox Press, 1978), p. 60.

573 G. A. F. Knight, *A Christian Theology of the Old Testament* (London: SCM Press, 1959), p. 294.

574 Brevard S. Childs, *Myth and Reality in the Old Testament* (Naperville: Alec R. Allenson, 1960), pp. 73-81.

strands[575] on OT eschatology before drawing some implications for our contemporary situation.

Eschatology as the end or culmination of history: Israelites expected the end or culmination of events in their history and longed for such end times even when everything else seems to have failed in the course of history. God never permitted security in the present. Israel never found their "rest." No present was ever intended consummation. Every present is stamped with the seal "not yet." Israel's existence was always tentative and preliminary to what was still to come. Even the act of piety by the people which is supposed to generate hope was seen as acts of corruption and deception by the prophets. People were utterly shocked when they heard the words of Micah 3:12: "Therefore because of you corrupt leaders Zion shall be plowed as a field ... and the mountain of the house a wooded height." Haggai proclaimed that the latter splendor of the temple will be greater than the present even at the time when the temple was laid in ruins (Hag 2:9). Gerhard von Rad is of the view that Old Testament can only be read as a book of ever-increasing anticipation. It began with the hope of expectations of Promised Land to the patriarchs continued through the conquest, the promise to David and Zion traditions. Israel, unlike their surrounding neighbors always moved on a pilgrimage journey with the future hope of salvation. Israel's faith journey continued to the future into the New Testament.[576] In this regard Rylaarsdam argues that the Christian community in the New Testament interpreted Christ event eschatologically. Jesus Christ is viewed as the end of history, rather an eschatological end of history.[577]

Creation and Eschatology: In the Old Testament creation has a beginning, a continuous history and an end. There are every kinds of calculations on the longevity of creation presents in some places I the Bible which is to be seen as a contextual matter to be reckoned with (Dan 9:27; 11:40 and 12:13). At the same time the land is cursed because of human sin entered into this world (Gen 3:14-19; Hosea 4:1-3). The earth dries up and withers because the people "have transgressed laws, violated the statutes, broken the everlasting covenant" (Isa 24:4-5). Jeremiah goes on to say that earth is in desolation and waste and it lies as nothing but desert and the cities are laid in ruins before the fierce anger of the Lord (Jer 4:23-26). The destruction of the land was time and again announced by the prophets by means of earthquakes, droughts, and darkness (Isa 24:4-6; Jer 4:23-26; Hos 8:7; 10:8). These may be the signs of the day of the Lord like prophets are talking about (Amos 5:18; 8:9-10; Zeph 1:14-18). However,

575 For more details of these various strands see Ralph L. Smith, *Old Testament Theology*, pp. 401 435.

576 Gerhard von Rad, *Old Testament Theology* II, pp. 321, 332.

577 J. C. Rylaarsdam, "Jewish Christian Relationships: The Two covenants and the Dilemma of Christology," *Grace Upon Grace* (Grand Rapids, MI: William B. Eerdmans Publishing Company, 1975), pp. 70-84.

the dawn of the new age will be characterized by renewal, transformation, the cleansing of the world, and peace among the people and animals (Isa 11:6-9; 65:25; Joel 2:18-19, 24; 3:18; Amos 9:13-14; Zech 8:4-5, 12). The Israelite idea of difference between the world of creation and that which can be realized in history has continuously being made aware of. Therefore the period of salvation was postponed into an ever-receding future and eventually was expected to be the outbreak of a new age. This sort of understanding kept the Israelites to always live anticipation for the future redemption of God as an eschatological hope.[578] Thus, we can see a dynamic relationship between creation faith and eschatology is always sustained among ancient Israel.

Eschatology as the restoration of the nation and God's Universal reign: In the Old Testament much of the future hope and expectation are tied to the national and political fortunes of the nation. Israelites always hoped for the restoration of freedom from foreign domination and the recovery of her land and prosperity lost in battles with Assyria and Babylon. The prophets once again admonished the people for their gross sin of losing the land while they still anticipate their future fortunes. Amos (5:6) stated: "Seek the Lord and live." Hosea (14:1) articulated: "Return, O Israel, to the LORD your God." Isaiah and Micah spoke of the saving of the remnant. Moreover, they also spoke of a time in the latter days when the mountain of the house of the Lord would be established as the highest of the mountains and people would flow into it (Isa 2:2; Micah 4:1). The prophets also talked about the hope for national and political restoration of Israel included the defeat of the oppressors (Isa 9:3; 10:27; 52:2; Jer 30:8; Ezek 34:27); the restoration of the dynasty and kingdom of David (Isa 9:7; Jer 3:18; Ezek 37:15-28; Hosea 2:20; Amos 9:8; Obad 19; Micah 5:1-4; Zech 9:9-10); the reunion of two kingdoms (Isa 11:13-14; Jer 31:27; Ezek 37:15-22; Hosea 1:11; Zech 8:13; 10:6-12); the return from the exile (Isa 27:12-13; 48:20; 52:8; 57:13; 66:20; Jer 23:3; 30:3; 32:37; Ezek 11:17; 34:11-12; Hosea 11:10-11; Micah 2:12-13; Zeph 3:19-20; Zech 8:7-8; 9:11-12); the rebuilding of the temple and a cleansed priesthood (Ezek 40-48; Hag 1:7; Zech1:16; 3:4-5; 4:6-9; Mal 2:10-13); universal knowledge of God (Isa 11:9; Jer 31:34; Joel 2:28-29; Hab 2:14) and the universal peace (Ps 46:10; Isa 2:4; 9:4-7; Micah 5:9; Zech 10:10). Perhaps all these are expectations far beyond history apart from them being anticipated within the near future or history.

At the same time, Israelites depicted that God is their king and also the king of the universe. The idea of God as king was prevalent among Israelites even before they adopted monarchy (1 Sam 8:6). The idea of the kingdom of God was tied up to David's kingdom. David's throne is called God's throne (1 Chron 28:5; 29:3). The Lord chose David and anointed him (1 Sam 13:14; 16:12-13; Ps 89:3-4, 19-21, 26-29). The king is expected to rule according to the decree and

578 Hans Heinrich Schmid, "Creation, Righteousness, and Salvation," *Creation in the Old Testament,* ed. B. W. Anderson (Philadelphia: Fortress Press, 1984), p. 110.

authority of Yahweh (Ps 2:6-9). In the due course the earthly king failed to deliver the goods by means of executing justice and to protect the oppressed as expected (Ps 72:1-4). However, there were occasions that kings did perform well and lived up to the expectations of God as in the case of king Josiah of Judah.

Eventually the anointing of the kings opened the door for the idea of Messiah, who would perform the ideal function of a king chosen by God. This turning point of king to Messiah was presented by Isaiah in 7:10-17 when God rejected the reigning house of David, perhaps God would now choose the future ideal king and perhaps what Micah states in 5:2-4 a reference to Ephrathah provides a broad framework for the origin of Messiah and we shall now turn our attention to that theme briefly.

Eschatology and the Messiah: Although we have already discussed elaborately on the theme of messiah above, we shall present brief idea of messiah here in relation to eschatology. Originally the anointing of the kings was referred to the ruling kings in Israel at any given time. The kings were anointed in Israel until the last one before the destruction of Jerusalem. The messianic hope in the Old Testament is usually associated with the king in Jerusalem because of the reason that he was anointed by Yahweh. Several royal psalms depict the hope in the coming of messiah without any reference to the then ruling kings in Israel. Psalm 2 reflects the joint kingship between the Lord, the enthroned one (v.4) as a universal king, and the earthly king as his "son," or a representative (v.7). Psalm 72 is a prayer for a new Davidic king on his coronation day. The king here is highly idealized and some suggested that he is a messianic figure when all the ruling kings failed to meet the standards set in the psalms. Psalm 110 is mostly favored as it is frequently quoted in the New Testament. Probably here we see how the messianic figure shares even to the extent of a full representative of God's coming reign and kingdom. Again an idea situation is depicted in the psalm that no ruling king among Israel would suit this position.

The prophets in Israel envisaged an ideal situation in the messianic figure and their views on such an ideal figure certainly went beyond the ruling kings of Israel. The Immanuel prophecy of Isaiah (Isa 7) and other words of Micah and Zechariah certainly moved and predicted a messianic figure in the distant future although it is not very certain to confirm it. Because none of the ruling kings met their set standards of a messianic kingly figure we cannot help but to think in this way. That is the reason we see in Isa 11:1-9 the idealized figure of Messiah and the messianic age is pictures and without any hesitation we can assume that it went far beyond the then ruling regimes.

Eschatology and the Suffering Servant: In the first servant song (Isa 42:1-4) we notice that God empowers him (or the community) by his charisma to bring forth justice to the nations. Justice is the key to the mission of the servant in this song. The servant was to perform his mission of bringing justice without 5 fanfare, noise or street demonstration (42:2). His approach was soft, tender and caring. A bruised reed he will not break, and a dimly burning wick he will not quench (42:3). He will gently save that which could easily be snuffed out. He is interminably patient and faithful. He will not give up until justice is established in the remotest corner of the earth.

In the second song (Isa 49:1-6) the servant speaks addresses the coastlands and peoples of the world. He tells them that the Lord called him and named him before he was born (49:1). The word of his mouth was supposed to be a sharp sword and a polished arrow to penetrate the hearts and the ears of his hearers. Even before the beginning of his ministry, the Lord confided him of his plan: "You are my servant, Israel, in whom I will be glorified" (49:3). In addition to the mission to Israel, the servant is now given a new mission to be a light to the Gentiles, so that God's salvation might reach the ends of the earth (49:6).

In the third song (Isa 50:4-9) the servant says that God gave him the tongue of a teacher so that he could sustain the weary with a word of encouragement (Isa 50:4). He was obedient, not rebellious, even though his obedience brought suffering, humiliation, insult, disgrace and shame (50:6-7). Still he did not give up. He set his face like flint because he knew that God, who would vindicate him, was near (50:7-8a). The servant challenges his abusers: "Who will contend with me? Who are my adversaries?" This is courtroom language, and not the language of battlefield.

The last song (Isa 52:13-53:12) of the servant has been describes as the most influential poem in any literature. It is the longest and stands as the apex song of the series. It is made up of five equal stanzas of three verses each. The first stanza (52:13-15) announces the servant's surprising victory over suffering and death. He will surprise and startle many nations. Kings will shut their mouths at him. They will be speechless, for they will see and hear that which has never happened. The second stanza (53:1-3) says people will not believe that which ahs been revealed and heard (v 1). The servant grew up in an unpretentious place, with nothing in his form or appearance that would attract people. Actually, he was despised and rejected by others. His suffering and infirmities were repulsive, and people turned their eyes away from looking at him (53:2-3). The third stanza informs that the speaker and those who despised the servant and possibly contributed to his suffering realized and confessed that the servant was not suffering for his own sins. He was suffering voluntarily and vicariously for others (53:6). The fourth stanza (53:7-9) describes how the servant suffered submissively, unresistingly, deliberately. By a perversion of justice (53:8) he was taken away to prison, executed, and given a degrading burial, even though he did no violence or spoke any deceit. Finally in the fifth stanza (53:10-12) we are told that it was the plan of God to bruise the servant so that his life and death could become an offering for sin.

With all the above qualities are to be identified in a person, who is this servant? Gerhard von Rad is of the view that this poem "goes far beyond the description of anyone who might have existed in the past or the present. The picture of the servant of Jahweh, of his mission to Israel and to the world, and of his expiatory suffering, is prophecy of the future, and ... belongs to the realm of pure miracle which Yahweh reserved for Himself."[579] No one kingly figure of Israel could and will fit such a description of the servant and obviously we need to conclude that it is an eschatological prediction related to the future.

Eschatology and the New Testament: The question where and when does the Old Testament end is very complex to answer. The mainstreams of Christianity and Judaism add to the Old Testament. Judaism adds the Mishnah and the Talmud as aids in interpretation and application of the Hebrew Scriptures. Christianity adds the New Testament as the definitive and authoritative interpretation of the Old Testament. For Christians the New Testament is more than an interpretation of the Old Testament. It is the record of the last great saving act of God in human history as seen in the life, death, resurrection, and ascension of Jesus Christ (Heb 1:1-3).[580]

The Old Testament was only the scripture of the early church. It was natural for the first Jewish Christians to consider the Old Testament as their own. They began to search the Old Testament for passages which they believed referred to or were "fulfilled" in the life, death, and resurrection of Jesus (1 Cor 15:3-5). Evidently early Christians had a list of Old Testament passages which served as "messianic proof texts" before any part of the New Testament was written.

While there are tendencies to undermine the importance the Old Testament by some quarters in the early church and Christianity, by and large was accepted as the scripture for their life and faith. The New Testament regards the Old Testament as Holy Scripture, and its validity is by no means regarded as limited. Hartmut Gese asserted that God's revelation of himself is neither timeless nor restricted to one point in time. It begins in a historical time (kairos) and travels a historical path. The path has a goal, and revelation reaches its end, telos. The starting point is the revelation at Sinai, where God reveals himself by saying "I am Yahweh." and the end of Old Testament took place in grandiose manner. The three great streams of traditions—Torah, Prophets and Wisdom—came together to present in terms of content the many-sided Christology of the New Testament, "which is no less than the theology of the Old Testament."[581]

In the fullness of time Jesus of Nazareth entered into that historical realm which had been prepared by the history of revelation. In his life Jesus accomplished the messianic establishment of the kingdom of God. "Through this death (of Christ) of the Son of God the light of a new creation shines forth. According to the New Testament then the *telos* is reached, the path of revelation is at an end. The so-called Old Testament is completed by the events of the New Testament;

579 Gerhard von Rad, *Old Testament Theology* II, p. 260.

580 Ralph L. Smith, *Old Testament Theology*, p. 427.

581 Hartmut Gese, *Essays on Biblical Theology* (Minneapolis: Augsburg, 1981), pp. 25, 29.

it is brought to its goal."[582] In this way the eschatological fulfillment of the Old Testament is fulfilled in the New Testament and in Jesus Christ.

In the light of our discussion on the theological importance of hope and eschatology we now make the following observations and implications for our contemporary Indian context.

First, eschatology is the horizon that Dalit Christians and other marginalized communities work with in order to live in their life and struggle in their socio-political context. What if the casteist forces succeed and take over the marginal communities and their rights altogether? The protest literature of the Hindu Bhakti of medieval times is powerfully presented that in the end all that is considered impure comes from ones thinking and heart. Kabir's one poetic piece affirms the same. Kabir is famous for his iconoclastic outpours. Kabir is the best-known voice for equality of caste and religions divisions in poetic, picturesque, fiercely strong terms. He questions the concept of purity so-obsessively peddled by the twice-born Brahmins.

> He asks:[583] Tell me, O pandit, what place is pure where I can sit and eat my meal? (Trans., Dharwadkar, 124).
>
> And then he goes on to enlist practically every site of life that are dismissed by the brahmins as impure: Cowdung's impure,
>
> The bathing-square's impure – Its very curbs are nothing but impure. Kabir says. Only they are pure who've completely cleansed their thinking. (Trans., Dharwadkar, 125)

Kabir's poem articulates the poet's resistance to the caste structure in the form of an argument by questioning the Pandit, on what basis one can distinguish one place is the pure and the other is impure. He continues to argue and define the purity concept in a new way. He says that one can attain the ultimate purity only when he/she completely cleans and changes his/her thought pattern. Unless one changes this thought pattern it remains impure forever. Thus, Kabir out rightly argues that it is the Brahmins rather than the Dalits who are impure because of their unchanging attitude towards the Dalits. While it is a resistance mode of poetry that Kabir articulated as an eschatological hope that will sway in the end of history either in the near of distant future, there are voices that subvert any undermining of Dalit hope and aspiration even to the extent of their death.

Dalits are very optimistic about their future hope and this is once again symbolically expressed in the heart and soul of Dalit poetry in the following words:

582 Hartmut Gese, *Essays on Biblical Theology* (Minneapolis: Augsburg, 1981), p. 29.

583 Aman Deep, "Dalit Aesthetics: A Study of Bhakti Period," 2/4 (2010), 5.

> These clouds must be vanished. These walls must be ruined. This silence must be bursted. This gum must be dried up. O man, I want real citizenship, Will you give? What do I want, I want you, I want a place in your heart. I must wash my hands at your home. You must come to my hut and ask our girl for marriage. We must become relative's friend! This country becomes ours as we walk hand in hand this uneven earth become smooth will you come?[584]

The following words of Namdev Dhasal will tell the future aspirations of Dalits in a metaphorical way as follows:

> Our blood was spilled for this glorious city and what we got was the right to eat stones. Now, now, we must explode the building which kisses the sky. After a thousand years we were blessed with a sunflower. Now, now we must, like sunflowers, turn our faces to the sun.[585]

Second, Hope and faith in the deliverance of God in and through Jesus Christ is something that the underprivileged communities long for. For instance the Dalits even go to the extent of improvising the biblical text in their own terms and conditions in order to express their faith in Jesus Christ and the ability of God in Jesus Christ has given them identity and recognition. One such sharp writing comes from Jose D. Maliekal when he writes:

> When Ebenezer, the village elder and the Madiga ideologue ... boasted that St.Thomas, the Apostle, was a Madiga, because he had dared to place his fingers into the wounded flesh of Jesus, he was presenting the software-chip of a potential Madiga identity theology. He was trying to assert his pride in his traditional trade, the identity-marker of his caste, by tracing aetiology for it and taking the stigma attached to it.[586]

Here we can note the point that the interpretation of a Dalit in a village context is very fluid and with due respect (in the sense of hermeneutics of respect) to the Bible.[587] Although this interpretation of Ebenezer is overdone, nevertheless

584 Madduri Nagesh Babu, "What is Your Caste," in *What is Your Caste* (Narsarao Peta: Sreeja Publications, 1998), pp. 60-61.

585 Namdev Dhasal, *An Anthology of Dalit Literature,* ed. Mulkraj Anand and Eleanor Zelliot (New Delhi: Gyan Publishing House, 1992), p. 60.

586 Jose D. Maliekal, "Identity-Consciousness of the Christian Madigas: Story of a People in Emergence," *Jeevadhara* 31: 181 (2001), p. 25.

587 See Sathianathan Clarke, "Viewing the Bible." p. 260. Clarke notes that "The Bible is a fluid referent for Subalterns (Dalits Inclusive). It holds together a novel dialectic that does not easily end in closure: The dynamic of a correction which itself is a contextual assertion in need of further rectification."

suits for his purpose, to interpret the Bible in his own community context. This group of mādiga Christians are proud to talk about their God-given vocation and that the very wounds of Jesus Christ are helpful to them to assert their strong caste identity with the hope that Jesus as a Dalit God is their partner in their suffering and oppression. The resurrected Christ has made it possible for them to turn their derogatory labels of occupation as an identity marker and that they can now find their solidarity in the resurrected Christ.

4.12 Old Testament Theology and its Hermeneutical Task in the Present Indian Context

The rise of OT theology as a discipline distinct from dogmatic theology did not occur until eighteenth century C.E. Prior to this all theology was considered to be biblical, or, the distinction between dogmatic theology and biblical theology was not grasped. The Bible was understood as the repository of the very truth the theologians sought to delineate in a systematic manner. The Bible was thus seen as the basis for the theological enterprise, and no tension was perceived between biblical faith and contemporary faith and doctrinal formulations. In the light of the above discussion and debate how to separate or even liberate OT theology from the clutches of dogmatic theology, a proper definition of OT theology was attempted by scholars that will address the issue in a comprehensive manner. Along with this concern was also raised by scholars how to define the task, function and scope of OT theology? Put it differently, what is Old Testament Theology? It has been a difficult task to answer this question to a satisfactory level. But some attempts were made to define OT theology as follows:

For Walther Eichrodt the task of OT theology is descriptive, by which he means that OT theology has to present the material of the OT in a coherent and systematic manner. Thus, he states, OT theology is to "construct a complete picture of the Old Testament realm of belief."[588] What Eichrodt wanted to suggest is that OT theology is subjected to scientific and systematic study and thus it needs to a historical discipline. Contrary to Eichrodt, Gerhard von Rad[589] is of the view that the task of OT theology is constructive, systematic, apologetic and normative. By this von Rad wanted to make the Old Testament as normative for the faith and practice of the church. This definition of von Rad also takes into consideration of reading the OT along with NT as a whole scripture.[590] Thus, this definition seeks

588 Walther Eichrodt, *Theology of the Old Testament,* Vol. 1, trans. J. A. Baker (London: SCM Press, 1960), p. 25.

589 Gerhard von Rad, *Theology of the Old Testament: The Theology of Israel's Historical Traditions* Vol. 1, trans. D. M. G. Stalker (London: SCM Press, 1965), pp.105-106.

590 Rolf Knierim, *The Task of Old Testament Theology: Substance, Method, and Cases* (Grand Rapids, MI: William B. Eerdmans Publishing Company, 1995), pp. 1-2. Knierim discusses the question of where and how the OT theology should begin. He argues that OT should be studies in its own right and that study will not lead to any exclusivity. The basic question

to validate both the testaments are to be read as a whole and thus the normative value of the OT is addressed or fulfilled. Another group of scholars define OT theology having pluriform witnesses within the OT itself and thus it has to be seen in the light of semantic homogeneity of that plurality.[591] Rolf Knierim is of the view that the task of Old Testament theology is to interpret "the relationship between Yahweh/God and reality." This means that Knierim wanted to talk about both quantitatively and qualitatively how Yahweh and reality are related, and with whom and what is Yahweh related.[592] This is further strengthened by the universal dominion of Yahweh as the God of justice and righteousness who cuts across three essential realms that are related to one another: the natural world, human corporate existence (including that of Israel), and individual human existence. Moreover, Knierim's basic premise is that there exists a plurality of theologies in the Old Testament. He argued the inadequacy any principle or concept to address this plurality. Thus, any amount of systematization of the material of the Old Testament is inadequate.[593] While Knierim saw the plurality of theologies in the OT is a theological problem, responding to Knierim Walter Harrelson rightly asks: "What is wrong with a rich pluralism, a lush variety, a many-faceted picture of the relation of God to the world, to Israel, to the individual? What demands the relating of these, the ordering of them into some hierarchy, the discovery of

---

whether OT should be read on its own or it should be read together with the NT does not arise as long as both the testaments are read together eventually. Additionally Knierim states, the general claim that the OT's message may be significant only if it is read in the light of the NT, or in the light of Christ's message is imperialistic and counterproductive. It is imperialistic because "it censures the Old Testament's theological validity by external criteria, and it is counterproductive because the theological significance of Christ of the New Testament, is as much as the Old Testament has something to do with them, cannot be substantiated with reference to the Old Testament's theological insignificance." (p. 1). In the course of this presentation we shall take up the task of OT theology in the light of the NT with more details.

591 Ibid., p. 3.

592 Rolf Knierim, *The Task of Old Testament Theology: Substance, Method, and Cases* (Grand Rapids, MI: William B. Eerdmans Publishing Company, 1995), pp. 1-2. Knierim discusses the question of where and how the OT theology should begin. He argues that OT should be studies in its own right and that study will not lead to any exclusivity. The basic question whether OT should be read on its own or it should be read together with the NT does not arise as long as both the testaments are read together eventually. Additionally Knierim states, the general claim that the OT's message may be significant only if it is read in the light of the NT, or in the light of Christ's message is imperialistic and counterproductive. It is imperialistic because "it censures the Old Testament's theological validity by external criteria, and it is counterproductive because the theological significance of Christ of the New Testament, is as much as the Old Testament has something to do with them, cannot be substantiated with reference to the Old Testament's theological insignificance." (p. 1). In the course of this presentation we shall take up the task of OT theology in the light of the NT with more details, pp. 10-11.

593 Ibid., pp. 10-14.

what is central and what is subordinate?"[594] Looking at the proposal made by Walter Brueggemann with regard to the definition of OT theology, he notes the Jewish picture, the diverse and polyphonic character of the OT itself to argue against "reductionistic" approaches that subject the text to categories outside it. Brueggemann resisted both the hegemony of historical criticism and attempts made by scholars to find a theological center within the OT, at the same time insisted on the normative witness of the OT. Additionally, the testimonies in the OT are plural in nature with theological diversity and variety that is to be recognized by all those who do OT theology in a postmodern setting. For Brueggemann this approach in doing OT theology will be of immense help for two reasons: First, it breaks the hegemony of the so-called dominant and 'privileged' interpretations of the Old Testament that were in operation from several decades and centuries. Second, the plurality of testimonies in the OT enables the contemporary readers of the OT to look at the so-called marginal interpretations as equally important and responsible.[595]

Setting the Task: In the light of the above discussion and definitions for the OT theology this presentation intends to do the following:

(i) To affirm along with the other OT theologians (a brief description of the theological method of selected OT theologians)[596] that OT theology has the task of interpreting the plurality of testimonies/confessions/ traditions embedded within the Old Testament.

(ii) To look afresh the question of the task of the OT theology: whether it is descriptive or normative?

594 Rolf Knierim, *The Task of Old Testament Theology: Substance, Method, and Cases* (Grand Rapids, MI: William B. Eerdmans Publishing Company, 1995), pp. 1-2. Knierim discusses the question of where and how the OT theology should begin. He argues that OT should be studies in its own right and that study will not lead to any exclusivity. The basic question whether OT should be read on its own or it should be read together with the NT does not arise as long as both the testaments are read together eventually. Additionally Knierim states, the general claim that the OT's message may be significant only if it is read in the light of the NT, or in the light of Christ's message is imperialistic and counterproductive. It is imperialistic because "it censures the Old Testament's theological validity by external criteria, and it is counterproductive because the theological significance of Christ of the New Testament, is as much as the Old Testament has something to do with them, cannot be substantiated with reference to the Old Testament's theological insignificance." (p. 1). In the course of this presentation we shall take up the task of OT theology in the light of the NT with more details, p. 22.

595 For a more detailed discussion on this and related issues read Walter Brueggemann, *Theology of the Old Testament: Testimony, Dispute, Advocacy* (Minneapolis: Fortress Press, 1997), pp. 98-114 & 707-720.

596 OT theologians are selected at random. Walther Eichrodt and Gerhard von Rad are chosen since their works are considered as foundational even in today's OT theological discourse. Apart from these two, Rolf Knierim and Walter Brueggemann are chosen to suit our theological argument.

(iii) To explore different models of systematization of OT materials or interpreting the pluriform nature of OT in a particular format.
(iv) To look at the possible options of the Old Testament's theological interpretations in the light of Indian contextual realities.
(iv) To look at some proposals made by Indian biblical scholars and theologians[597] to see where the Indian biblical interpretation stands as on today.
(vi) To make some proposal for the future of OT theological enterprise in India.

Theological methodology (task of OT theology) of Select OT Theologians: In this section we shall consider few methodological discourses offered by the prominent OT theologians in order to see how their details demonstration of the task of OT theology will be of immense help for our purpose of doing OT theology in the Indian context.

Walther Eichrodt (1890-1978): Eichrodt's magisterial and monumental work on OT theology comes at a time when the history of Israelite religion dominated Old Testament studies for about a century or more. Eichrodt was a native German but later taught at Basel in Switzerland, was concerned over OT theology and the revelatory character of the Bible long before his magisterial three volume work began to appear. In the opening chapter of his study he described two approaches to the theology or religion (the term seems to be used synonymously on that occasion) of the OT which he repudiated as legitimate theological approaches: the first was the attempt to organize biblical material according to the outlines of dogmatic theology. The second was the historical treatment of the religious thought which he argued "fostered the idea that once the historical problems were clarified everything has been done."[598] For the second approach he had harsh words declaring that it "was high time that the tyranny of historicism in OT studies was broken and the proper approach to our task re-discovered." He further suggests that the real issue as he saw it, "this is no new problem, certainly, but it is one that needs be solved anew in every epoch of knowledge the problem of how to understand the realm of OT belief in its structural unity and how, by examining on the one hand its religious environment and on the other its essential coherence with the NT, to illuminate its profoundest meaning. Only so shall we succeed in winning back for OT studies in general and OT theology in particular that place in Christian theology which at present has been surrendered to the comparative study of religions."[599]

597 To balance our view point both Protestant and Roman Catholic biblical scholars and theologians are chosen.

598 Eichrodt, *Theology of the Old Testament*, p. 25.

599 Ibid., p. 30.

Eichrodt's program thus called for an exposition of OT belief in its structural unity but an exposition that was sensitive both to the ancient Near Eastern religious environment and to the later New Testament as well. Throughout his methodological statements, frequent references are mode to the New Testament, its revelation, and an expression of Old Testament faith that is analogous to it. For example, "the OT religion, ineffaceably individual though it may be, can yet be grasped in its essential uniqueness only when it is seen as completed in Christ."[600]

The hallmark of Eichrodt's program was to present a comprehensive survey and a systematic ordering of the material. He was confident that it was possible "to present the religion of which the records are to be found in the OT as a self contained entity exhibiting, despite every changing historical conditions, a constant basic tendency and character."[601] Eichrodt argued that this had to be done by a "cross-cut" (*querschnitt*) rather than chronologically, by a "long-cut" (*langsschnitt*). In order to present a cross-section of this constant self-contained entity, Eichrodt chose the idea of covenant which he felt could be shown to cut across all the various divisions and strata of the OT and which is a concept expressive of the divine-human relationship in Israel from the time of Moses onwards. Eichrodt elaborates on this as follows:

> In the face of all objections, the 'covenant' has been retained as the central concept, by which to illuminate the structural unity and the unchanging basic tendency, of the message of the OT. For it is in this concept, that Israel's fundamental conviction of its special relationship with God is concentrated. The decisive consideration on this point is neither the presence nor absence of the actual term *berit*, as certain all too näive critics seem to imagine, but the fact that every expression of the OT which is determinative for its faith rests on the explicit or implicit assumption that a free act of God, consummated in history, has raised Israel to the rank of the people of God, in whom the nature and will of God are to be revealed. The word 'covenant' therefore, is so to speak a convenient symbol for an assurance much wider in scope and controlling the formation of the national faith at its deepest level, without which Israel would not be Israel. As an epitome of the dealings of God in history the 'covenant' is not a doctrinal concept, with the help of which a complete corpus of dogma can be worked out, but the characteristic description of a living process, which was begun at a particular time and at a particular place in order to reveal a divine reality unique in the whole history of religion. Reference to this

600 Eichrodt, *Theology of the Old Testament*, p. 33.

601 Ibid., p. 39.

> living process in every single paragraph of this work will not escape the attentive reader.[602]

Thus, for Eichrodt the main concern or the task of Old Testament theology is to "construct a complete picture of the Old Testament realm of belief." In order to achieve this task, Eichrodt thinks that only a cross-section of the realm of OT thought will be appropriate. In his opinion, this approach will make possible both a "comprehensive survey" and a "shifting of what is essential from what is not." This step, according to Eichrodt, will enable both the "total structure" and the "basic principle" of Israel's religion to be exposed. In other words, Eichrodt says that "we have to undertake a systematic examination with objective classification and rational arrangement of the varied material." For instance, in treating the individual religious concepts, Eichrodt takes into account the major elements of their historical background and describes at length the major elements of the religion, but they are put under s systematic method of description. According to Eichrodt, we can see here two principles are in operation: "the historical principle operating side by side with the systematic in a complementary way."[603]

According to Eichrodt, there is a subjective element in every science including historical research. He maintains that "the historian will always be guided by the principle of selection and by goal which gives perspective to his work."[604] Both the principle of selection and the goal are subjective. The principle of selection in Eichrodt's theology is the idea of covenant and the goal that provides perspective is Christ of the New Testament.

Eichrodt is of the view that to arrange the material of the OT, one should not follow the system which is outside the OT theology. Eichrodt states: "it is impossible to use a system which has been developed on the basis of quite different from that of the realm of Old Testament thought to arrive at the Old Testament belief about God."[605] This he thinks would bring in alien ideas. The dogmatic theologian follows this scheme. Eichrodt proves them wrong by pointing out that the OT does not contain any formal "instructions" about being of God or his attributes and an Israelite knowledge of God comes to her from the realities of her own life, and not from any abstract concepts. Therefore, the procedure for the treatment of OT thought must be from within OT itself, along the lines of the OT's dialectic. In order to do this Eichrodt follows Otto Procksch's outline and presents the material of the OT under three main categories: God and the people, God and the world, God and man.

For Eichrodt Sinai covenant is most important in defining the integral relationship of God with Israel. For him Abrahamic covenant (Gen 15:17) and

---

602 Eichrodt, *Theology of the Old Testament*, p. 40.

603 Ibid., p. 41.

604 Ibid., p. 42.

605 Ibid., p. 43.

Davidic covenant (2 Sam 7) are not so significant because the former one is a remarkable retrojection of the covenant concept into the earlier period of the nation's life presented by Yahwist and Elohist. The latter one is considered to be a postscript to Sinai covenant, which was given too much importance by the Chronicler in the post-exilic period. Additionally Eichrodt chooses Sinai covenant over Abrahamic and Davidic covenants because the latter lack conditions and eternal validity. These can be proved wrong once (Psalm 89:2-30). Moreover these two are covenants with individuals but not with Israel as a whole nation as in the case of Sinai covenant. Furthermore, these two covenants are ahistorical, whereas Sinai covenant as clearly rooted in history.[606]

Apart from criticism from many quarters on Eichrodt's proposals we make the following critical comments on Eichrodt, particularly in his description on the task of OT theology:

First, Eichrodt's proposal on the cross-section, although convincingly presented by him, there could be many cross-sections and it is to be noted that the concept of covenant is far from its universal presence in the entire material of the OT.

Second, if Eichrodt or others who support his proposal think that covenant is an appropriate symbol of concept or an organizing principle under which the entire material of the OT can be organized they are mistaken. Even by its very conceptual presence it is absent in the prophetic literature, at least in the eighth century prophecy. Ludwig Köhler points out that there is no place where the "covenant is called, with the clarity of the definite programme, the fundamental pattern of Old Testament understanding of God."[607]

Third, the covenant was a symbol of special tie between Yahweh and Israel and as such, also represents particularism. But there are many places where OT transcends this nationalistic framework and began to consider religion in more universalistic terms as a relationship between God and the world or between God and humanity. The covenant had either no bearing whatsoever (especially in Wisdom Literature) or was expected to be superseded by a new covenant (Jer 31:31).

Covenant in the above light can also be seen as an inward-looking rather than opening a possibility for a wider mission God's covenant with other nations as well.

Gerhard von Rad (1901-1971): In his theology, with its challenges of previous methodologies and with its new proposals von Rad inaugurated a new epoch in the study of OT theology. Contrary to Eichrodt, von Rad is not for any organization of OT theology along the lines of central concepts, pervasive topics, assumed structures of Israelite thought or world of faith, or systematic theological categories, which had been characteristic, in one way or another, of all the OT theologies of the twentieth century wince this was to impose an alien structure on

606 Eichrodt, *Theology of the Old Testament*, **pp. 42-48.**

607 Ludwig Köhler, *Old Testament Theology*, p. 12.

the material. As an alternative, von Rad proposed that "the subject matter which concern the theologian is ... not the spiritual and religious world of Israel and the conditions of her soul in general nor is it her world of her faith, all of which can only be reconstructed by means of conclusions drawn from the documents; instead, it is simply Israel's own explicit assertions about Jahweh."[608]

For defining the task of OT theology both in a historical and theological fashion, following principles underlie his methodology:

1. The fundamental principles which he was asserting is that the OT itself must set the agenda for writing a theology not some scheme or ideas imposed from outside.
2. The OT is primarily a book of history concerned with the divine activity in history. "The Old Testament writings confine themselves to representing Jahweh's relationship to Israel and the world in one aspect only, namely as continuing divine activity in history. This implies that in principle Israel's faith is grounded in a theology of history."[609]
3. Von Rad wants to affirm that the traditions about Israel's sacred history or God's acts in history were formulated as testimonies or creedal confessions which were the products of Israel's thinking about herself and thus were used in differing ways and contexts since "Israel constantly fell back on the old traditions connected with the great saving appointments, and in each specific case she actualized them in a very arbitrary, and often novel way." Thus, the same traditions could be "actualized in different ways, at different times and probably also at different places."[610]
4. Von Rad wants to recognize that the OT does not contain a single, unified theology; "the unity of the Old Testament is even more open to question than before, for traditio-historical analysis has disclosed a number of theologies which differ widely both in their conception of the fundamental events of the saving history and in the way they understand the theology of history, the divine action."[611] Again von Rad states: "unlike the revelation in Christ, the revelation of Jahweh in the Old Testament is divided up over a long course of separate acts of revelation which are very different in content. It seems to be without a centre which determines everything and which could give the separate acts both an interpretation and their proper theological connection with one another."[612]

608 Gerhard von Rad, *Theology of the Old Testament*, pp. 105-106.

609 Ibid.

610 Ibid., pp. 105-106.

611 Ibid.

612 Ibid.

5. The relationship and tension between promise and fulfillment provided von Rad with perspective for viewing the way in which actualization of older traditions in the life of Israel. Von Rad writes thus:

    If we seek to extract from the bewildering number of these actualizations some characteristic, common, and continuing features, it is this in one way or another (the specific tradition determines the way) Israel was always placed in the vacuum between an election made manifest in her history, and which had a definite promise attached to it, and a fulfillment of this promise which was looked for in the future. Each successive generation had the task of understanding itself as Israel in Jahweh's eyes. Israel had many possible ways of understanding her position before Jahweh as an elect nation; for she had different election traditions which she actualized. The common element in all these was that Israel was poised between promise and fulfillment and that she saw herself as walking along a road which led from a particular promise to a particular fulfillment ... this continual actualization of the data of the saving history, with its consequence that every generation saw itself anew on the march towards a fulfillment, occupied such a prominent position in the Old Testament that a theology of the Old Testament must accommodate itself to it.[613]

6. Since the basic content of the OT is the sacred history or *heilsgeschichte* "re-telling remains the most legitimate form of theological discourse on the Old Testament." That is, since Israel made its confession in the form of historical statement, the rehearsal of these should form the basic content of the Old Testament theology which in its own way becomes a contemporary actualization of the biblical traditions.

In the light of the above discussion von Rad employs diachronic method by which he describes the longitudinal sections of the OT via each successive epoch in the canon with special attention to the chronological sequence of the various traditions and books. The organizing framework is a single confessional statement concerning God's marvelous deeds on Israel's behalf which was recited cultic settings and underwent constant revision according to the experience through which people passed. As the time passed, the cultic setting gave way and confessional statements were freed for use in many different contexts. Since the confessions constitute the crystallization of religious belief and are inextricably tied up with history they must be elucidated to arrive at a theology.

613 Gerhard von Rad, *Theology of the Old Testament*, p. 110.

The above being a form-critical assumption, von Rad rigorously uses the tool to interrogate each document about its specific kerygmatic intent. However, besides understanding the text in the light of its original intention, he also felt that attention should be given to every distinct stage of the tradition as well. And so by employing the history of the transmission of tradition method he trisects his presentation of God's history with Israel into the three gigantic works of the Hexateuch, the Deuteronomistic History and the Chronicler's History from the perspective of God's interventions and the differences of these interventions in every age. The retelling and re-structuring of Jahweh's former deeds is coupled with the proclamation of his anticipated action in the future.[614]

In other words, for von Rad, OT the task of OT theology is basically retelling of the traditions of Israel. How does these traditions unfolded in the Old Testament? It happened for instance, in the little historical creed (Deut 26) that is, Israel recited these words as part of their retelling traditions. In this little historical creed, two fundamental traditions are to be noted: the tradition of deliverance plus conquest and the tradition of settlement. Thus, two key events are to be noted in this direction: first, exodus and wilderness and second, settlement. Furthermore, von Rad says that two independent traditions such as Patriarchal and Exodus traditions are brought together at a later stage. Yahwist (J) brought all these independent traditions together in the following manner: first settlement and Patriarchal stories are combined with prefix of primeval stories, and patriarchal stories are further expanded and finally Sinai tradition is inserted.[615]

Von Rad postulated the above thesis on the grounds that a single confessional statement concerning God's intervention in the life of Israel was recited in different cultic contexts and was constantly revised depending on the experiences the people underwent. Therefore the Hexateuch is crystallized into a miniature historical credo. This is found in Deut 26:9, 6:20-24 and Joshua 24:2-13. This tradition was freely adapted in various cult lyrics (1 Sam 12:8, Pss 105, 135, 136 and Exod 15) until it was finally embellished with the elements of the Sinai tradition (Neh 9:6ff, Ps 106). The separate traditions, settlement and Sinai, testify to redemptive history and divine justice respectively, the creeds that recited Jahweh's saving acts were characteristic forms of theological expression in the OT.[616]

Applying the above framework to the entire OT von Rad argues that *heilsgeschichte* (salvation history) in the history of traditions is history of Israel's effort of understanding herself; Israel have done this by retelling the traditions in the light of her context. In this process, Hexateuch was present with the addition of two major blocks of material namely, Deuteronomistic History and Chronicler's History. Yahweh continued to act in the history by raising charismatic leaders, judges, divine election of Zion, by choosing David as king,

614 Gerhard von Rad, *Theology of the Old Testament*, p. 115.

615 Ibid., p. 116.

616 Ibid., p. 117.

by raising prophets and even by sending people to exile because von Rad thinks that exile is a time for reflection, and the Deuteronomic History is the product of this time, and during post-exilic reflection the material basically produced was Ezra-Nehemiah and Chronicler. In all these events Israel saw God's hand. All this von Rad calls an unfolding of traditions, that is, Israel's testimony to what God has done. But all these traditions are unfolded in their own way, not in a very systematic order of events rather the growth and formation of tradition itself is theological achievement, thus in von Rad the history of growth of tradition takes precedence over systematization. Therefore for von Rad, the task of OT theology is the unfolding of the testimony of Israel captured in retelling of traditions, thus OT theology should follow the sequence of events, not any systematic order.

Concerning the relationship between OT and NT von Rad demonstrates how a descriptive analysis of OT traditions contains within themselves an irrepressible eschatological expectation which demands fulfillment. Von Rad says the OT is a theological torso without the NT. By saying so von Rad wanted to make the OT relevant to the ongoing life of the community of faith. For von Rad it is only in the NT that the OT pattern of recital and hope which is kaleidoscopic, protean, shifting and elusive is impregnated with changeless content and its ultimate relevance is lucidly manifested.[617]

Von Rad attempts to reinstate a guarded and circumspect use of typology as a relevant paradigm for OT interpretation and its relationship to the NT. For him, typology is a historical and theological category to unite the OT to the NT. This method is based on the conviction that the OT bears witness to succession of new beginnings in which the religious and theological inheritance from the past is at once is interpreted and transcended when it is related to successive situations to which the new saving acts of God are experienced and the divine promises are heard. In other words, for von Rad, the principle of typological exegesis is the prefiguration of the Christ event in concrete OT revelation events. This typology is not traditional but concerned with 'the events between Israel and her God' ... events which place Israel in the great area of tension constituted by promise and fulfillment which is so characteristic of Israel's whole existence before God. Such typology rests on the recognition that the church, which lives between the 'already' and the 'not yet', portrays its existence in terms of analogies and images drawn in the events of Israel's salvation history. And so the OT looks forward the moment when all of Israel's traditions were radically reinterpreted and at the same time given their definite center in Jesus Christ. Anticipating the charge of a Christian rereading, von Rad clarifies that the actualization of the OT in the NT is a logical process commenced by the OT and culminating in the NT.[618]

In the light of the above comprehensive proposals made by von Rad for the task of OT theology we make the following critical observations and comments:

617 Gerhard von Rad, *Theology of the Old Testament*, p. 125.

618 Ibid., p. 136.

First, von Rad's proposition of Israelite history as retelling of the traditions is very innovative and allows the biblical interpreter to look at the OT material with creative look. Given the possible nature of the OT material the above proposition seems to be more reasonable and plausible.

Second, however, the above proposal may lead to a violent separation between factual and confessional history and in von Rad; the latter seems to be taking upper hand all along. Can the historical facts be reconstructed, even if it is done in plausible terms based on the recitals and traditions? Eichrodt accuses von Rad for violently wrenching apart the picture of history reconstructed by higher criticism and the salvation history portrayed in the utterances of OT faith. This leads to confession of 'spurious factuality' with historical truth. Thereby the link between the testimony of faith and the faith of history is seriously threatened.[619]

Third, von Rad's description of salvation history model applied to his retelling of traditions though reasonable has some problem as well. It looks as if everything in the OT will have logical conclusion only in the NT. B. S. Childs[620] criticizes von Rad on this point at three levels: i) von Rad's *heilsgeschichte* scheme tends to hinder the dialectic which is central to genuine biblical theology of going back from NT to the OT; ii) von Rad, Childs feels, has not taken into consideration sufficiently the immense diversity of witness with the NT. Von Rad allows harmonization's that he would methodologically refrain from in the OT; iii) von Rad raises the question of the Christian interpretation of the OT without dealing with the problem of Judaism.

Rolf P. Knierim (1928): Knierim finds inadequacy of employing a criterion based on a single concept, or topic and so on set by OT theologians, although their contributions are important. Following his predecessors like Gabler, Wrede, Stendahl and others Knierim believes that biblical theology must be based on a description of 'what the text meant.' Thus, right at the outset Knierim states: "As soon as we ask the legitimate question of its meaning 'for our time,' we are no longer dealing with Old Testament Theology but with Old Testament hermeneutic."[621]

Regarding the task of the OT theology, Knierim observes that there is a presence of plurality of theologies in the OT but they are also related to one another. Since these theologies coexist with one another, the task of OT theology is "to establish the criteria for the arbitration of the coexisted distinctive theologies and to interpret their relationship or correspondence. Moreover, one has to find whether there is one aspect or notion that governs or dominates all others, or which is relative to, dependent on, or governed by others."[622] On account of this, Knierim claims that the task of OT theology is to interpret "the relationship between Yahweh and reality" in the quantitative and qualitative aspects and deal

619 Eichrodt, *Theology of the Old Testament*, p. 45.

620 B. S. Childs, *Biblical Theology in a Crisis*, p. 12.

621 Knierim, *The Task of Old Testament Theology*, p. 38.

622 Ibid., p. 20.

with the issue "how Yahweh and reality" are related.[623] Knierim clarifies that quantitative means to see how Yahweh is related to the entire cosmos or to the totality of creation and this happens qualitatively by means of the demonstration of how Yahweh is related to the reality in the realms of justice and righteousness.[624]

Knierim talks about relativization by means of which he sets up the task of OT theology. For this he selects universal dominion of Yahweh in justice and righteousness as a criterion and principle which guides systematization. By this relativization the diverse and plurality of theologies n the OT are related to one another. Two main objectives are stated in this process: First, it provides the basis for our evaluation of the truth claims of the biblical texts. This belongs to the task of exegesis. Second, it also aims at the inclusion of all biblical texts. This can only be achieved through the comparison of different biblical texts.[625]

Knierim is of the view that OT theology not only speaks on basics of history, it also speaks of the world and of creation and the world order in general. In this sense OT does not speak about God alone but about God in relation to a reality that that consists of cosmos and reality, history and society, and the individual or existentiality. In this way the task of OT theology or theologian is to relate the above three spheres to the sovereignty of God.[626]

Compared to other OT theologians of his time Knierim's proposals seem to be different and creative. However, there are some problems in his methodology.

First, Elmer Martens is of the view that Knierim, on account of his proposal of descriptive method looks pessimistic about the current theological situation of the biblical theology. Martens opines that this pessimism can be encountered by a biblical theologian is to deal with the application of the text to a contemporary situation which is an optimistic view.[627] However, Martens misunderstood Knierim because in talking about the implications of OT theology Knierim clearly distinguishes between OT theology and OT hermeneutic having different tasks yet they are related one another.

Second, speaking about the plurality of theologies present within the Old Testament which is not only to be expected but also to be affirmed. And yet we need to seek some unity in the form of systematization. But this is a problem as well in Knierim's proposal of the task of OT theology. Roland Murphy objects to this proposal of Knierim and states that scholars are creating a synthesis which the Bible did not create and which cannot be expected to be a satisfactory conceptual expression of OT theology. Therefore, Murphy may be right in saying that there is no problem in having theological diversities (pluralism) even without any

623 Knierim, *The Task of Old Testament Theology*, p. 29.

624 Ibid., p. 23.

625 Ibid. , pp. 71-72.

626 Ibid., pp. 23-25.

627 Elmer A. Martens, *The Shape of an Old Testament Theology for Post Modern Culture*, Fall 1996, 25:2, pp. 5-15 in http://www. directionjournal.org/article/?921 (12th April 2013)

hierarchical systematization.[628] In this we feel that both Knierim and Murphy are justified in their own viewpoint.

Third, relativization as a method of study in Knierim's proposal is to be appreciated, because of this method one tries to see a conceptual unity within the plurality of theologies found in the Old Testament. Thus, a synthetic approach may be better in approaching the diverse material of the OT in line with Knierim's proposal.[629]

Walter Brueggemann (1933): Brueggemann found the mid 20th century's variances in theological exposition not as a disagreement. He found that "this conflict is rooted in the nature of the text itself."[630] This reflects "multilayered pluralism" in the OT text. In this light he considers and recognizes three following entities from the OT as follows: a) a pluralism of faith affirmation and articulation of Yahweh in the text itself (as was presented by Gerhard von Rad and Rainer Albertz); b) a pluralism of methods; and c) a pluralism of interpretive communities.[631]

Further elaborating on the above point Brueggemann suggests that postmodern interpretive situation (a pluralism of interpretive communities) cannot hold onto one theological essentialist tradition, hegemonic speech to articulate the faith of Israel as was done by Brevard S. Childs.[632] Brueggemann in agreement with Alasdair MacIntyre, he questions, "whose justice, which rationality?" These questions need to be taken into account in adjudicating pluralism of the Old Testament. Thus, the OT can make assumption and claims to what is real and concrete without silencing the countervoices.[633] In view of this and in order to make a coherent theological statement he suggests the following:

> Grouping of theological substance or themes in the OT broadly and inclusively as to be useless, a significant focus on the processes, procedures and interactionist potential of community present in the text and an interpretative context that allows assertions and counter assertions to constitute theological substance would lead to make coherent OT theological statement.[634]

---

628 Roland E. Murphy, "A Response to 'the Task of Old Testament Theology'" in Knierim, *The Task of Old Testament Theology*, pp. 28-32.

629 See also Richard J. Coggins, review of "Problems in Biblical Theology. Essays in Honor of Rolf Knierim.: eds. Henry T. C. Sun and Keith. Eades, *Journal of Theological Studies* 49:1 (1998), pp. 167-68.

630 Walter Brueggemann, *Theology of the Old Testament,* p. xv.

631 Ibid., p. xv.

632 Ibid., p. 65.

633 Ibid., p. 62.

634 Ibid., p. xvi.

Brueggemann maintains that speech leads to reality and thereby it constitutes the latter. Hence, God of Israel depends on the "utterance" of Israelites or the text. An intensive observation, treatment of pluralism and its interactions within pluralism enables us to make coherent statement in the OT theology.[635] Therefore Brueggemann proposes court room trial method.

Brueggemann uses the method of testimony, dispute and advocacy for the truth statement. He suggests that a court room trial mechanism would be adequate to discern the truth in the OT. According to him testimony is the character and mode of theological claim in the OT, i.e., "utterance of Israel." It neither points to history nor ontology. It needs to be understood in the realities of power, the securing of power, its maintenance and legitimatization. For instance, Brueggemann proposes how the Marxian program of reading the text reveals us a political and economic character embedded in the utterance of text.[636] Therefore, an attention to both power and powerlessness is the need. Israel's testimony offers 'core testimony' which focuses on the mediators between Yahweh and Israel, hence plurality of testimonies is required for courtroom appeal.[637]

Dispute is cross-examination over plurality of witnesses. Therefore, "truth is at issue and at risk." For God talk in the OT, God in Israel depends on the utterance of the Israelites/text. Therefore, both hegemonic utterances and counter-voices are "bids" for truth statement (this was suggested by Rowan Williams). Thereby, a plurality of witnesses is at hand. Brueggemann identifies the imagination as an ingredient in the verbal sentences that turns world's impossibilities" or Yahweh's to participants' to delight or disappointment in the narrative.[638]

Advocacy is the adjudicating witness with reference to Yahweh over against the witness with reference to Yahweh free. For theological interest Brueggemann suggests "a dramatic mode." In this drama, "YHWH is not subject to norms if inquiry but YHWH is subject only to the rules of the drama i.e., player/one of the character in the drama and hearers of the text are also participants at second hand."[639] Therefore, any particular utterance bids for Israel's allegiance over against the givens of either foreign lord or perhaps established power in its own community. Yahweh is played in the life of Israel as long as Yahweh is "played" in the drama of Israel.[640] In this connection Brueggemann talks about the use of metaphors in that they can represent what it is and at the same time what it is not, that is, Yahweh is a shepherd and at the same time Yahweh is not a shepherd. This kind of understanding also prevents Israelite monotheistic faith to be idolatrous.

---

635 Walter Brueggemann, *Theology of the Old Testament,* xvi,

636 Ibid., p. 51.

637 David J. Reimer, Review of *Theology of the Old Testament. Testimony, Dispute, Advocacy* by Walter Brueggemann. *Book List 7: Law, Religion and Theology*, pp. 142-143.

638 Ibid., p. 68.

639 Ibid., p. 69.

640 Ibid., p. 70.

Brueggemann takes this position in order to discard any established account of conventions of Yahweh in theological enterprise. Instead he suggests that Yahweh is always ready for new, outrageous self-disclosure, depending on the courage and freedom of Israel's speakers.[641]

Brueggemann, while presenting the major trends in the Old Testament theological enterprise in relation to the twentieth century antecedents, also draws our attention towards the interpretations of the OT by marginal readings that was not present before and also it poses a direct challenge to the "hegemonic interpretation that was once taken for granted can no longer be assumed or sustained."[642] Three examples are cited in this regard viz, Feminist interpretation of Phyllis Trible, Liberation reading of George Pixley and Black Theology of Itumeleng Mosala. After having listed out the merits of these marginal biblical readings Brueggemann talks about the interface between the so-called centrist and marginal readings of the biblical text. Here he presents the task of OT theology in the present interpretative context as something important. Brueggemann states:

> In any case, a student of Old Testament theology in our present interpretive context must attend to the centrist voices that represent a long established consensus in ecclesial and academic communities. Such a student must also attend to the insistent voices of those at the margin who are able to see things in the text that centrist interpretation, either by doctrinal conviction or Enlightenment restraint, is not able to discern.[643]

Brueggemann is of the view such an interface will have to address new methodological questions and face vital interpretive issues. What he argues is that there is no interest-free interpretation even in the centrist approaches or there cannot be any claim of objective interpretation by any one. Thus, no one interpretation is conclusive on the text.

Brueggemann talks about the polyphonic character of the Bible. There are two listenings of the Old Testament. The first is the original listening and the second is the listening that is beyond Jewishness. With regard to the second listening community Brueggemann quotes the following statement from Mark Coleridge:

> The Bible insists upon a common narrative, but one which includes a diversity of voices; many stories comprise *the* story. God's story is both single and several. It also insists upon a narrative which at times is

641 David J. Reimer, Review of *Theology of the Old Testament. Testimony, Dispute, Advocacy* by Walter Brueggemann. *Book List 7: Law, Religion and Theology*, p. 66.

642 Ibid., p. 98.

643 Ibid., p. 102.

> most disjointed and connectedness of which is perceived only by way of struggle. The Bible is no easy read.[644]

Brueggemann concludes that in a world of self-serving, hegemonic, and dominant metanarratives, Israel's testimony opens up a possibility of sharing and caring, nurturing and upholding metanarratives about her relationship with Yahweh and with their neighbors defines an alternative model that we need to capture in our theological interpretation of the Old Testament

Review on the Current Indian Biblical Interpretation: In this section we shall focus on the important trends the Indian biblical interpretation has taken in the present interpretive context. For the want of space we shall only focus on the important works, while there may be other works that are significant that this presentation has not cited. While it is beyond the scope of this presentation to define what 'Indian' is, we shall clarify some details in this regard.[645] Our attempt to define what 'Indian' is or what is truly 'Indian' is limited in so far it is connected with the biblical interpretation.

Twenty five years ago M. V. Abraham[646] has made an attempt to define the Indian context in relation to the developing and teaching of biblical theology in India. He talks about two such contexts: the religio-cultural contexts and the socio-economic context.

The *religio-cultural context* in India is marked by at least six major religions and overwhelming majority of Indians are adherents of Hinduism. In this sense one may even equate Indian religio-cultural ethos with the Hindu ethos, though this is an over-simplification. Christians in India cannot help but to confront Hinduism in different forms as they live their day to day life. In India Christianity is often considered (though erroneously) as a western religion, more so by the people of other faiths in India. Though Christianity was originated in Palestine (West Asia), Christ was not limited to the messianic categories of Palestinian Judaism. Christ was interpreted to the Graeco-Roman world by St Paul, St John and others, and later to the larger world by Alexandrians and Antiochenes, and the Latin and Greek Fathers. In the process both the Gospel and Christ was

---

644 Mark Coleridge, "Life in the Crypt or Why Bother with Biblical Studies,' *Biblical Interpretation* 2 (July 1994), pp. 139-151, see especially p. 148 for this quotation. Cited in Brueggemann, *Theology of the Old Testament,* p. 89.

645 For a brief clarification what is "Indian" in relation to Indian Christian Theology see, Joseph Prabhakar Dayam, "From (on) the Banks of Ganges through the Dusty Soil to (in) the Beat of the Drum: Indian (Ecumenical) Christian Theology in Our Times," An Unpublished paper presented at the United Theological College Faculty Research Seminar on 30 January, 2013.

646 M. V. Abraham, "The Teaching of Biblical Theology in India Today," in *The Indian Journal of Theology* 29:3, 4 (July-Dec 1980), pp. 124-132.

culturally conditioned and adapted. Therefore such a process of adaptation was the requirement in the Indian context.[647]

There is an undeniable fact that India is not only known for pluralism but filled with *multiple aspects of pluralism*, a pluralism of religion, of race, of caste, of class, of culture etc. Hinduism with its various sects, Buddhism and its branches, Jainism and its nuances, Islam with its hundreds of sects and sub-sects, Sikhism and its variations, Christianity with all its denominations, and Parsee religion, though numerically small, constitute the religious pluralism in India.[648] In addition to this religious pluralism Mariaselvam points out to the other aspects of pluralism: "India swarms with very many racial groups each claiming superiority. To make things worse, the caste-system has taken roots in our society, and each caste tries to establish its power over the others, or to assert itself and gain freedom or hegemony. There is also the class-struggle that is gaining ground and control in our developmental process. Pluralism of cultures in India is more and more felt, projected, protected and propagated."[649]

The *socio-economic context* in India has to be taken into account seriously in an attempt to talk about the Bible and its relationship to the Indian context. In Latin American context, liberation theology made a tremendous impact on the people on the basis of its biblical interpretation. Unlike Latin America and South Africa, In India we have a broad spectrum of religious and cultural diversity which influences socio-economic aspects of life.

Marginalization is another serious problem in the present Indian social setting in the Indian context. Two groups can be mentioned in particular, although others like tribal and adivasi communities can also be brought under this problem. Dalits are discriminated against all kinds of situations in the caste-ridden Indian social system. In many towns and villages the plight of the Dalit men and women

647 Ibid, p. 129. Though, it is not new the process of inculturation in the Bible was a hot-topic in the Indian Church from several decades. Several articles and works appeared on this topic. For the want of space we shall mention one important article: Abraham Pezhumkattil, "Inculturation in the Bible," *Bible Bhashyam* 30:2 (2004), pp. 83-103. In this work Pezhumkattil brings to the light how in the Old Testament and in the entire Bible the process of inculturation has taken place. In trying to establish relationship with other nations, Israel was at the crossroads of fixing her identity on the one hand and making compromises with the people of other faiths and cultures in adapting syncretistic religious practices. In this process they were advised by her prophets to separate themselves from other nations and upholding the values of covenant based on the Torah ideology. The cultural and religious influences have become more forceful in the post-exilic Judaism as Jews encountered Greek and Persian religio-cultural nuances in their socio-political life. This part of the history of the Jews experiences more a kind of resistance and apathy towards other cultures. The process continued in the time Jesus as well. Jesus became more than a symbol of unity and openness in breaking the walls of exclusivist tendencies among the Jewish community in the New Testament period (Eph 2:11-22).

648 A. Mariaselvam, "Biblical Interpretation for India Today," *Bible Bhashyam* 28:3 (2002), pp. 505-520.

649 Ibid., pp. 505-520.

is worse than that of animals. The official estimate reveals that every six hours a Dalit woman is raped and one Dalit is killed every three days. It was noted in the Durban conference that among many social evils that exist in the world and make communities marginal, "caste discrimination is a kind of 'hidden apartheid' and a 'systemic cultural Dalitocide.'"[650]

Marginalization is still more subtly perpetrated on women in India. Gender inequality is taken for granted in all walks of life all over the world. Starting from the household realm, this inequality is spread all the way in professional circles, land ownership, basic provision of human needs and in many other areas women are discriminated against the male members of the society.[651]

There are other global and local problems that affect the religio-cultural and socio-economic-political context in India that include: issues related to religious fundamentalism and terrorism, globalization, ecological crisis and poverty etc need not be elaborated. In the light of the above discussion ad multiple issues addressed, the biblical interpretation both in the past and in the present attempted to articulate several of the above issues in their exegetical and hermeneutical enterprise.[652]

While there are number of attempts from the Indian biblical scholars to address the contextual problems in the light of the Bible before the year 2000, the post 2000 has also produced number of significant works on the Indian interpretation of the Bible. In the year 2000 two major works appeared one by

---

650 Prakash Louis, "Globalising Caste or Nationalising Hypocrisy?", *Subalterns* 9:4 (2001), p. 4.

651 For more details on this topic see, Amarthya Sen, 'Many Faces of Gender Inequality," *Frontline* 18:22 (Oct 27 - Nov 9, 2001), pp. 4-14.

652 There many attempts at the interpretation of the Bible in the Indian context. Space will not allow us to mention all of them. Apart from the works already cited, a few important works can be mentioned here at this point: James A. Bergquist, "Critical Exegesis in the Life of the Indian Churches: Some Professional Perplexities," *Indian Journal of Theology* 18:2,3 (1969), pp. 101-111; R. H. S. Boyd, "The use of the Bible in Indian Christian Theology," *Indian Journal of Theology* 22:4 (1973), pp. 15-20; George Soraes-Prabhu, "Towards an Indian Interpretation of the Bible," *Bible Bhashyam* 6 (1980), pp. 151-165; George Soraes-Prabhu, "Interpreting the Bible in India Today," *The Way, Supplement* 72 (1991), pp. 70-80; S. J. Anthonysamy, "Christian Mission in the Context of Many Religions Today: A Biblical Perspective," *Indian Theological Studies* 30:2 (1993), pp. 93-107; K. V. Mathew, "Prophetic Witness to Mission in a Pluralistic Context," *Bible Bhashyam* 21:2 (1995), pp. 105-114; M. Mani Chacko, "Crisis and Hope in the Exodus Story," *Bible Bhashyam* 24:4 (1998), pp. 223-252; P. A. Sampathkumar, "Current Trends in Indian Biblical Studies," *Bible Bhashyam* 25:1 (1999), pp. 64-77; Joseph G. Muthuraj, "Rereading NT in the India: Some Hermeneutical Explorations," *Asia Journal of Theology* 13:1 (1999), pp. 14-30; Paddy Meagher, "Biblical Hermeneutics in India: The New Testament," *Bible Bhashyam* 30:4 (2004), pp. 260-279; Mathew Vellanickal, "Church: The Interpreter of the Bible," *Bible Bhashyam* 31:4 (2005), pp. 224-240; Prema Vakayil, "Biblical Pluralism: Its Expressions," *Bible Bhashyam* 32:4 (2006), pp. 257-271.

Dharmaram Publications[653] and other by UTC/ISPCK publications.[654] Both these publications were the *Festschrift* publications in honor of two eminent Indian biblical scholars. The Dharmaram publication covers wide range of issues based on Indian socio-religious-economic-political issues and their biblical relationship. These were the stimulating and creative exegetical and hermeneutical essays written by eminent OT and NT scholars. Some essays are particularly covered on the methodological concerns in the biblical interpretation. The UTC/ISPCK publication also covers wide range of topics from the Indian socio-economic and politico-religious context, Part I in this book covers the issues that are related to the biblical interpretative context. While some essays in this section are historical, exegetical and theological in nature, one essay by Renthy Keitzar talks about "studying Old Testament in India." In this essay Keitzar presents a wide spectrum of methods and new approaches available in the OT studies and their appropriate use in the Indian context.

In the year 2005 another joint publication by Asian Trading Corporation and United Theological College, Bangalore came out with another *Festschrift* publication in honor of O. V. Jathanna.[655] In the first section of this book, some essays were written by biblical and other scholars on biblical and hermeneutical explorations of grace. The first essay written by E. C. John on the title : "The Reception of Old Testament in India," is a fine essay on the reception of the OT by Indian Christians and a couple of examples are shown how the OT was either positively or negatively received by Indian leaders of Hindu religion.

In the year 2008 Board of Theological Education of Senate of Serampore College/South Asia Theological Research Institute (BTESSC/SATHRI) came up with a publication is yet another *Festschrift* in honor of Dhyanchand Carr.[656] In this volume several important biblical essays were written based on the Indian contextual realities. Among nineteen biblical essays in the first part of the book, two essays have covered the biblical interpretation in the Indian context in particular. Mani Chacko reviews the Indian biblical interpretation based on new development in the overall biblical hermeneutics. J. G. Muthuraj charts out clearly how to read the New Testament in a pluralistic Indian context.

The Society of Biblical Studies in India (SBSI) released a Golden Jubilee volume in December 2012 is another innovative attempt at the recent trends in

653 Augustine Thottakara (ed), *Indian Interpretation of the Bible: Festschrift in honour of Prof. Dr. Joseph Pathrapankal* (Bangalore: Dharmaram Publications, 2000).

654 Daniel Jones Muthunayagom (ed), *Bible Speaks Today: Essays in honour of Gnana Robinson* (Bangalore/Delhi: UTC/ISPCK, 2000).

655 Joseph George (ed), *God of all Grace; Essays in honour of Origen Vasantha Jathanna* (Bangalore: ATC/UTC, 2005).

656 Israel Selvanayagam (ed), *Light on Our Dusty Path: Essays for a Bible Lover* (Bangalore: BTESSC/SATHRI, 2008).

the Indian interpretation of the Bible.[657] Among several innovative essays in this book few significant ones can be noted as follows: Joshua Samuel talks about the re-contextualizing Dalit hermeneutics[658] where he suggests new models for Indian Christian Dalit interpretation of the Bible. Shobana talks about the biblical jubilee in the light of Ecofeminist critique of redistribution of land in ancient Israel and its relevance to Indian context. Dexter Maben talks about the paradigm of jubilee ethic for Christian witness in India in the light of Pauline communities in the New Testament. V. J. John argues for ecological biblical hermeneutics in the light some Indian contributions.

The above discussion reveals the fact that serious attempts have been made and are still in the process of making the biblical interpretation in the Indian context both at the exegetical as well as hermeneutical levels. A strong Indian contextual implications are drawn from the biblical texts in order to articulate Indian interpretation of the Bible.

Use/reception of the OT in the Indian context: A brief review: In this section we shall briefly review how in particular Old Testament was received and used in the Indian context. As noted earlier E. C. John, the former Old Testament Professor at the United Theological College in Bangalore talks about the reception of the OT in India.[659] In this article John argues how the OT has been received in India from the beginning of the modern Protestant Missionary movement. The Hindu authors viewed the OT both in the positive as well as in the negative light. They admired the prophetic ethic of the OT while at the same time, they were highly critical of monotheistic claims of OT religion. Indian Christians like Vengal Chakkarai and S. K. George received the OT with great admiration. The ready reception of the OT having the subaltern and Dalit hermeneutics was

657 Kondasingu Jesurathnam, Abraham Saggu and Hrangthan Chhungi (eds), *Liberation Hermeneutics in the Indian Interpretation of the Bible* (Bangalore/Tiruvalla: SBSI/Christava Sahitya Samithi, 2012).

658 Several articles and books have appeared in the last two decades on the issue of Dalit Hermeneutics. This approach takes several biblical texts and books from the OT and the NT and argued for the Indian liberative hermeneutical engagement for Dalit liberation and emancipation. Space will not allow us to mention all the works here. For some details on this subject see K. Jesurathnam, "Towards a Dalit Liberative Hermeneutics: Rereading the Psalms of Lament," *Bangalore Theological Forum* 34:1 (2002), pp. 1-34. Also see several commentaries on the biblical books (Dalit Bible Commentary Series of both the OT and the NT) are produced by Center for Dalit and Subaltern Studies (CDSS) in New Delhi.

659 E. C. John, "The Reception of Old Testament in India," in Joseph George (ed), *God of all Grace; Essays in honour of Origen Vasantha Jathanna* (Bangalore: ATC/UTC, 2005), pp. 1-10. See also his earlier article on the same subject entitled: "Theological Research and the Churches in India: Old Testament," *Bangalore Theological Forum* 10:1 (1978), pp. 6-11. In this article, E. C. John describes briefly how the OT is neglected or at the most seen as the proof-text for certain NT messianic interpretations.

welcome sign to show how the OT contains a potential message for liberative hermeneutical engagement in the Indian context.[660]

Long before the above article M. H. Harrison wrote an article in 1956 on the place of OT in Indian theological education.[661] In this work Harrison reports how the apathy towards the OT as the Jewish Scripture continues in India and often the OT was replaced by other Hindu Scriptures like Upanishads and Bhagvadgita. At the same time the OT was accepted, it was gradually accepted in the Indian theological curriculum as an important part of the Christian Scripture, and instructional courses were introduced at the BD level. However, the general trend of receiving the OT was in the following light of ambivalent nature of the OT with the Indian religious thinking. Harrison writes:

> It may be that we shall dispute some of the interpretations of historic events to which the Old Testament witness came. But the contrast with the typical thought of India is clear and should be made plain by detailed study. The monotheism to which the Hebrew prophets came is a very different thing from the philosophical monism of India, and it should be one of the tasks of Old Testament teaching to make this so evident in the Christian church that it will never for a moment yield to the temptation to consider all forms of religious life of equal value for the world today. There are other characteristic emphases of the Old Testament which may be stressed in teaching, its insistence on the holiness of God, its long struggle to deal satisfactorily with the problem of the existence of evil in the world which set it off from the typical thought of India, but perhaps what has been said will give some indication of the interests with which the student and teacher in India will approach his tasks.[662]

In 1969, James A. Bergquist made some remarks on the importance of the OT in the light of a critical and reflective exegesis in Indian churches.[663] He notes that the Church in India (during his time) needs to be more open to the critical thinking and preach exegetical sermons with an open mind and attitude so that

---

660 E. C. John, "The Reception of Old Testament in India," in Joseph George (ed), *God of all Grace; Essays in honour of Origen Vasantha Jathanna* (Bangalore: ATC/UTC, 2005), pp. 1-10. See also his earlier article on the same subject entitled: "Theological Research and the Churches in India: Old Testament," *Bangalore Theological Forum* 10:1 (1978), pp. 6-11. In this article, E. C. John describes briefly how the OT is neglected or at the most seen as the proof-text for certain NT messianic interpretations.

661 M. H. Harrison, "The Place of Old Testament Studies in Indian Theological Education," *Indian Journal of Theology* 5:1 (1956), pp. 1-8.

662 Ibid, p. 8.

663 James A. Bergquist, "Critical Exegesis in the Life of the Indian Churches: Some Professional Perplexities," *Indian Journal of Theology* 18:2,3 (1969), pp. 101-111.

the prophetic and other critical dimensions of the text becomes more clear to us as well as to the members who receive biblical interpretation. Pointing to the wide gulf between the theological teaching in the Seminaries and the preaching in the Church, Bergquist further suggests that both the OT and the NT have the critical potential inherent in them, and Indian preaching should recapture this aspect.[664]

In 1985, Paul Kalluveettil talked about the marginal dialectics in the OT and beyond to show how God's preferential option for the poor and the underprivileged is vital for biblical theology in the Indian context.[665] Drawing texts from all over the OT, the author of this article shows how consistently the OT's message is constructed around the dialectic of marginalization in and through God's action in the concrete historical realms of the Israelite society and thus the OT must be interpreted in the same manner in our day in the Indian context.

D. N. Premnath in 1988 and in 1995 through his presentations underlines the message of liberation from the OT applicable for today's Indian context.[666] Talking about the methodological shifts and new trends in the recent OT studies, Premnath is of the view that an interdisciplinary approach with multiple disciplinary tools has to be applied in each context for a better and creative understanding of the biblical text, especially in a context like India. The author also draws implications from the context of biblical eighth century prophecy, and its then sociological implications are seen as relevant for the modern society of India.

In the year 2000, Renthy Keitzar while talking about the studying OT in India makes a few important observations on its interpretation.[667] Presenting various methods and trends available in the OT interpretation, Keitzar proposes a potential possibility for a creative OT interpretation in the Indian context.[668]

---

664 James A. Bergquist, "Critical Exegesis in the Life of the Indian Churches: Some Professional Perplexities," *Indian Journal of Theology* 18:2,3 (1969), pp. 101-111.

665 Paul Kalluveettil, "The Marginalizing Dialectics of the Bible," *Bible Bhashyam* 11:4 (1985), pp. 201-214.

666 D. N. Premnath, "Recent Developments in Biblical Studies," *Bangalore Theological Forum* 20:3 (1988), pp. 1-7. Also see by the same author, "Biblical Interpretation in India: History and Issues," Unpublished paper presented at the Society of Biblical Literature Convention, Philadelphia, 1995.

667 Renthy Keitzar, "Studying Old Testament in India," in Daniel Jones Muthunayagom (ed), *Bible Speaks Today: Essays in honour of Gnana Robinson* (Bangalore/Delhi: UTC/ISPCK, 2000), pp. 21-32.

668 Other major works published that covers a part of the Hebrew Bible and yet a comprehensive interpretation of the OT in the Indian context: J. Susaimanickam, *Commitment to the Oppressed: A Dalit Reading of the Book of Job* (Unpublished doctoral dissertation; Rome: Gregorian University, 1996); Kondasingu Jesurathnam, *Dalit Liberative Hermeneutics: Indian Christian Dalit Interpretation of Psalm 22* (Delhi: ISPCK, 2010); Naveen Rao, *The Formulation of Scripture: Liberative Hebrew Paradigm for Dalit Scripture* (Delhi: ISPCK, 2010).

In the light of the above discussion it is clear that the use and reception of the OT in the Indian context is a mixed baggage of positive as well as negative attitude towards it. Though there are attempts like Marcion to discredit or even reject the OT over against the NT, by and large the issue has not taken deeper roots and the OT has survived in the academia and in the Church and has continued to make its strongest impact ever on the community of believers.[669]

The task of OT and OT theology in the Indian context: A few methodological issues and proposals: In the opening section of our essay, we stated a few definitions of the OT theologians on the task and function of OT theology. Those definitions emerged in contrast to the history of Israelite religion which was the dominant subject discipline during the late nineteenth and early twentieth century. In the light of the works of Walther Eichrodt, Gerhard von Rad and Walter Brueggemann, let me suggest a few methodological options available for setting up the task of OT theology in the Indian context:

First, ***the emergence of marginal interpretations of the OT is a sign of hope.*** In the 1970s and 1980s, there was a paradigm shift in the rethinking of biblical interpretation mostly under the influence of Latin American Liberation theology. During the last three decades or more, biblical interpretation in India has focused more on the marginal interpretations. Unlike the historical critical methodology, the Indian interpretation of the Bible is focused on the dialogue between the text and the reader, to enable the emergence of new meanings. Reading the Bible in the light of Indian socio-economic and religio-cultural concerns has thus yielded much fruit in the last few decades.[670] As was pointed out earlier a number of Dalit and tribal interpretations and also by way of interfaces between them, have appeared during this time focusing on the OT texts. The centrist readings have been challenged by the emergence of these marginal readings. The basis for such a meaning derived from the text and in conversation with the reader, for instance, is like a new born baby, where the text will continue to live on its own and go on communicating new meanings for the new readers.[671] These marginal readings from the OT texts thus enhance the life-giving and liberative scriptural meaning for their meaningful existence and relationship with the deity. Eichrodt's model of the covenant as a pervasive theological theme of the OT can be a model for us today in India for a marginal reading. For marginal communities like Dalits, tribals and women in India, the covenant as God's revelation is thus made factual that

669 Theological curricula in India make it mandatory to the study of the Old Testament; for instance in the Senate of Serampore BD curriculum, on par with the New Testament, more credits are allocated for the OT studies.

670 See for more details George M. Soares-Prabhu, "Editorial," *Jeevadhara* 25:146 (1995), pp. 100-104.

671 See the interpretation of Psalm 22 by the readers of the text differently in different ages including the contemporary Dalit Christian readers. For details see, Jesurathnam, *Dalit Liberative Hermeneutics* and Naveen Rao, *The Formulation of Scripture.*

is, it is not merely a speculative other-worldly principle, rather as an experience in the very life of the people. It is presented in a real and concrete way in which God intervenes in the lives of the people and thus it "provides life with a goal and history with a meaning."[672]

The above reading context as purported by Walter Brueggemann opens up a possibility that the Bible is polyphonic or even multiphonic so that all centrist voices as well as marginal voices in its reading can be heard. As rightly pointed out by Brueggemann, in the midst of establishment voices that seem to have supported the centrist readings of the OT, in the midst of self-serving, hegemonic, and dominant metanarratives, Israel's testimony opens up a possibility of sharing and caring, nurturing and upholding metanarratives, and in the midst of hegemonic and dominant establishment voices the marginal readings of the OT presents the very nature of Yahweh, who at times was marginalized when the vision of new earth and new heaven seems to have failed.[673] The theological task of the OT in India will have this privileged position and opportunities abound in this direction.

Second, ***the integral link between the OT and the NT, has to proceed from the OT to the NT and not from the NT to the OT.*** There has always been a serious debate from the beginning either in the formulation of OT theology or biblical theology on the issue of relationship between OT and NT. At times one or the other testament is dominantly emphasized in the process of the debate. Some scholars see the importance of the OT until as far as the NT and once the NT comes into the picture, the OT becomes either redundant or it becomes unimportant. Gerhard von Rad is right in stating that OT's eventual scheme of *heilsgeschichte* comes to a fulfillment in the NT. By this von Rad is not suggesting that OT is null and void once the fulfillment schema is taken up in the NT. For von Rad, the comprehensive and integral relationship between the NT and the OT is important. B. S. Childs only misunderstood OT-NT dialectic of von Rad without considering the above point. In other words, what von Rad is suggesting is that, overemphasis of any one of the testaments is not healthy for an authentic biblical theology. While it can be agreed that the OT is a theological torso without NT, NT without OT can lead to unauthentic interpretation of the Christ-event and God's revelation to the entire creation. As was stated earlier, Knierim is right to state that the OT has to be seen in its own right (see note 3) and that right should not be determined by the NT's message.[674] Thus, the interpretation of the OT and NT as one integral whole of the

672 Eichrodt's expression. Also see George Koonthanam, "Yahweh the Defender of the Dalits: A Reflection on Isaiah 3:12-15," *Jeevadhara* 22:128 (1992), pp. 112-123.

673 For more details see Paul Kalluveettil, "The Marginalizing Dialectics of the Bible."

674 In this regard Walter Brueggemann is of the view that "the task of Old Testament theology, as a Christian enterprise, is to articulate, explicate, mobilize, and make accessible and available the testimony of the Old Testament as all its polyphonic, elusive, imaginative power and to offer it to the church for its continuing work of construal toward Jesus. That is, Old Testament theology in my judgment, must prepare the material and fully respect the important connections made

biblical message is the task of OT theology in India since at the popular level NT seems to be prioritized over against the OT.

Third, ***pluralistic tendencies within the OT are an affirmation of the future of OT Indian interpretation.*** As was noted above, in the theology of Gerhard von Rad and in the proposals made by Walter Brueggemann there cannot be any central concept or an organizing pattern into which OT can be systematized. While von Rad is clear in stating that the Israelites had always and in a novel way understood Yahweh's deeds in the history and these deeds are affirmed, recaptured, retold in the form of liturgical and other traditions, however wherever, this retelling happened it happened in a variety and in a creative way. The entire OT is the product of such a retelling process. Thus, von Rad looks at the OT as an actualization of the plurality of traditions at various times and at various places. For him, this process of actualization itself is a theological achievement.

For Walter Brueggemann, the OT consists of the plurality of texts, methods and interpretive communities. If this is the case then OT is not to be seen as a monolithic text as if there is one linear message present all over it. Yahweh is always ready for change, newness, in ways that are unknown and startling and it is that freshness Israel encountered in her God-experience. This is how the text becomes dynamic and bold in presenting to its readers in ways that are ever known before.[675]

In the light of the above discussion the task of OT theology in the Indian context can be very challenging as it needs to take into consideration the multivalent pluralism: pluralism of the texts, methods and communities. In such a methodological posture, the outcome will also be rich and rewarding. This pluralism also scuttles the attempts to maintain hegemonic and dominant interpretations and opens up more and more marginal readings of the Bible as a real possibility.

Fourth, ***the task of OT theology can be both descriptive as well as normative in the future biblical interpretation in India.*** In the formative years of the OT theology, the main debate was to see whether OT theology should be descriptive or normative? For Eichrodt, OT theology is descriptive in the sense that it should present the materials of the OT in a comprehensive and systematic manner. As was already noted for von Rad, OT theology is for the normative function of the ongoing life of the church. Brueggemann is of the view that the text of the Old Testament is descriptive as well as normative in the sense that "these materials are deliberately evocative, and what they evoke is an interpretive practice always draws the ancient testimony into contemporaneity

in the New Testament and the subsequent church; but it must not make those connections, precisely because the connections are not to be found in the testimony of ancient Israel, but in the subsequent work of imaginative construal that lies beyond the text of the Old Testament." Brueggemann, *Theology of the Old Testament*, p. 732.

675 Ibid., p. 66.

is characteristically concerned with Jesus as a historical agent, or Jesus as an undoubted and enduring power, presence, and authority in the church."[676]

In the light of the above discussion it is clear that, in the Indian context the task of OT theology is to interpret the OT as it should be relevant for the church, but that relevance should come from the evocative meaning of the text that the church should be willing to receive rather than controlling the text on the basis of her doctrines and traditions. Both the descriptive as well as normative tasks are to be undertaken in OT theological enterprise in India. The descriptive task is required as Indian reading cannot afford to replace historical criticism but will complement it. This happens only when both the descriptive as well as normative tasks are combined or complemented. In this context George Soares-Prabhu rightly affirms: "if the interpretation is not to remain barren, with a hermeneutical reading which will determine the significance of the text for the reader here and now, by engaging text and reader in a critical conversation, that respects not only the meaning trajectory of the text but the new Indian context in which the text is now placed."[677]

Fifth, ***OT interpretation in future in India is not only done by the majority in the academia and in the Church, but also done among the common masses who hold the key to the interpretation of the text.*** By now it is clear that the interpretation of the OT in India is done by a majority of theologically trained elite, although they are numerically very small in number. Brueggemann rightly talks about a radical shift in the interpretive communities in the postmodern biblical interpretation. He writes: "the great new fact of interpretation is that we live in a pluralistic context, in which many different interpreters in many different specific contexts representing many different interests are at work on textual (theological) interpretation. The old consensus about limits and possibilities of interpretation no longer holds. Thus, interpretation is no longer done by a small, tenured elite, but interpretive voices and their very different readings of the texts come from many cultures in all parts of the globe, and from many subcultures even in Western culture."[678] Thus, reading along with the many diverse voices

676 In this regard Walter Brueggemann is of the view that "the task of Old Testament theology, as a Christian enterprise, is to articulate, explicate, mobilize, and make accessible and available the testimony of the Old Testament as all its polyphonic, elusive, imaginative power and to offer it to the church for its continuing work of construal toward Jesus. That is, Old Testament theology in my judgment, must prepare the material and fully respect the important connections made in the New Testament and the subsequent church; but it must not make those connections, precisely because the connections are not to be found in the testimony of ancient Israel, but in the subsequent work of imaginative construal that lies beyond the text of the Old Testament." Brueggemann, *Theology of the Old Testament*, p. 733.

677 George Soares-Prabhu, "Interpreting the Bible in India Today," *The Way, Supplement* 72 (1991), p. 75.

678 Brueggemann, *Theology of the Old Testament*, pp. 61-62. For more details on the conversation between the Dalit and 'non-Dalit' interpretations see, Jesurathnam, *Dalit Liberative*

in the public as well as in private spaces would yield the creative, evocative and even emotive meanings from the text and our perspectives are constantly in the process of transformation for the liberative and emancipatory purposes of the communities in and around us.

Therefore the task of the OT theology is to foster such groups, and biblical interpretations where possible and from whichever side the initiative comes, they must be ready to use it for a creative biblical interpretation.

Concluding remarks: On the basis of our foregoing discussion we now make the following concluding remarks .

First, OT theology as a historical discipline has seen several phases of growth as well as decline in the midst of changing historical and contextual circumstances in the period of last few centuries. This trajectory is also applicable to the biblical interpretation in India and more specifically to the reception and interpretation of the Old Testament.

Second, on the basis of our review of the history of biblical and OT interpretation in the Indian context, OT theology has a polyvalent and even multivalent task in the Indian context in the midst of its pluralistic or even multi-pluralistic context. There is thus no one theological essentialist tradition and there is no hegemonic speech in the biblical interpretation in the Indian context. It is the task of OT theologians in India to always look for innovative and creative methodologies that will address the needs of the communities from all levels and for all people and move towards just and egalitarian society. This does not come as easy as we might expect, but the biblical interpreters have to find new ways and means and struggle to achieve this end.

Third, in view of the above Old Testament theological interpretative task in India, it has to be a combination of both historical criticism and other text-centered and reader-centered methods in complement to each other to interpret the 'truth' in the text in a more reasonable and meaningful manner. This comprehensive and complementary approach will be helpful for both the academia and the church in India.

Fourth, as was realized in our discussion the Bible is not easy to read, more so it is to be realized in the Indian context. In the midst of its complexities and life-struggling contextual realities the Bible therefore has to be read amidst joy, pain, and struggle and hence the task of OT theology is to make a transformative application of the biblical text to all those whose lives are being transformed and guided by the word of God with all its evocative, emotive and transformative potential.

Hermeneutics; Naveen Rao, *The Formulation of Scripture* and Monica Jyotsna Melanchthon, "Research, Methodologies, the Bible and the Marginal Communities in India," in Joseph Prabhakar Dayam and P. Mohan Larbeer (eds), *Margins in Conversations: Methodological Discourses in Theological Disciplines* (Bangalore: BTESSC, 2012), pp. 1-16.

Epilogue

The Old Testament Theology has many trajectories of articulation and application as we have gone through in the above pages of this text-book presentation. Despite all the odds and complexities to stop the Old Testament from being used or even permitted to be used in the Christian communities in India it emerged as important part of the Bible in the faith and practice of Christian Church in India today. All kinds of Marcionic attempts to discredit Old Testament as Christian scripture have not succeeded. Instead the Old Testament has emerged as more significant in the life, faith and witness of the church in India today. Therefore the author of this volume hopes and believes that the vast amount of material presented here for reading and appropriating for an academic degree will not simply end with academic pursuit rather this material will manifest in the faith, life and witness of several Christian communities in India today. If that goal is achieved then the hermeneutical task of Old Testament will move forward much faster than the previous centuries of biblical interpretation and appropriation in India.

Selected Bibliography

Abraham, M. V. "The Teaching of Biblical Theology in India Today," in *The Indian Journal of Theology* 29:3, 4 (July-Dec 1980), pp. 124-132.

Achtemeier, Paul J., *The Interpretation of Scripture: Problems and Proposals.* Philadelphia: Westminster Press, 1980.

Agrawal, Girish and Colin Gonsalves., *Dalits and the Law.* New Delhi: Human Rights Law Network, 2005.

Anderson, B. W. (ed), *Creation in the Old Testament.* Philadelphia: Fortress Press, 1984.

Anderson, G. W., "Hebrew Religion," in *The Old Testament and Modern Study: A Generation of Discovery and Research,* ed. H. H. Rowley. London: Oxford University Press, 1951, pp. 283-310.

Anthonysamy, S. J.,"Christian Mission in the Context of Many Religions Today: A Biblical Perspective," *Indian Theological Studies* 30:2 (1993), pp. 93-107.

Baker, D. L.,*Two Testaments. One Bible: The Theological Relationship Between the Old and New Testaments.* Downers Grove, IL: InterVarsity Press, 1977.

Barr, James., *Old and New in Biblical Interpretation.* London: SCM Press: 1966.

Bergant, Dianne., *Israel's Wisdom Literature: A Liberation-Critical Reading.* Minneapolis: Fortress Press, 1997.

Birch, Bruce C., et al., *A Theological Introduction to the Old Testament.* Nashville: Abingdon Press, 1999.

___________., "Old Testament Foundations for Peacemaking in the Nuclear Era," *The Christian Century*, December 4, (1985), pp. 1115-1119.

___________., *What Does the LORD Require?: The Old Testament Call to Social Witness.* Philadelphia: The Westminster Press, 1985.

Blenkinsopp, Joseph., *Wisdom and Law in the Old Testament: The Ordering of Life in Israel and Early Judaism.* Oxford: Oxford University Press, 1995.

Boecker, H. J., *Law and Administration of Justice in the OT and Ancient Near East.* Minneapolis: Augsburg Publishing House, 1980.

Boyd, R. H. S., "The Use of the Bible in Indian Christian Theology," *Indian Journal of Theology* 22:4 (1973), pp. 15-20.

Brandon, S. G. F., *Creation Legends of Ancient Near East.* London: Hodder and Stoughton, 1963.

Brueggemann, Walter., *Theology of the Old Testament: Testimony, Dispute, Advocacy.* Minneapolis: Fortress Press, 1997.

___________., *Living Toward a Vision: Biblical reflections on Shalom.* Philadelphia: United Church Press, 1976.

___________., *The Prophetic Imagination*. Philadelphia: Fortress Press, 1978.

Bultmann, Rudolph., "The Significance of the Old Testament for the Christian Faith." in *The Old Testament and Christian Faith: A Theological Discussion,* ed. Bernard W. Anderson. London: SCM Press, 1964, pp. 8-35.

Camp, Claudia., *Wisdom and the Feminine in the Book of Proverbs.* Sheffield: JSOT Press, 1985.

Childs, Brevard S., *Old Testament Theology in a Canonical Context.* Philadelphia: Fortress Press, 1986.

___________., *Introduction to the Old Testament as Scripture.* London: SCM Press, 1979.

Clements, Ronald E., *Old Testament Theology.* England: Marshall, Morgan and Scott, 1978.

Crenshaw, James L., *Old Testament Wisdom: An Introduction.* Atlanta: John Knox Press, 1981.

Crüsemann, Frank., *The Torah: Theology and Social History of Old Testament Law,* trans. Allan W. Mahnke. Minneapolis: Fortress Press, 1996.

Dawkin, Richard., *The Blind Watchmaker: Why the Evidence of Evolution Reveals a Universe without Design.* New York: W. W. Norton & Company, 1961.

Dentan, Robert C., *Preface to Old Testament Theology.* New York: Seabury Press, 1963.

DeSmet, R., "Job's 'Insufferable Comforters' and the Law of Karma," *Vidyajyoti Journal of Theological Reflection* 58 (1994), pp. 308-318.

Devasahayam, V., "Job: Demythologization of Karma Theory," in V. Devasahayam (ed), *Dalits and Women: Quest for Humanity.* Madras: Gurukul, 1992, pp. 227-31.

de Vaux, Roland., *Ancient Israel: Its Life and Institutions.* New York: McGraw Hill, 1961.

Dumbrell, William J., *The Faith of Israel: A Theological Survey of the Old Testament.* Grand Rapids: Baker Academic, 2002, Second Edition.

___________., *Covenant and Creation.* Devon: The Paternoster Press, 1984.

Dyrness, William., *Themes in Old Testament Theology.* Downers Grove InterVarsity Press, 1977.

Eichrodt, Walther., *Old Testament Theology,* Vol. 1, trans J. A. Baker. Philadelphia: The Westminster Press, 1960.

Fishbane, Michael., *Biblical Interpretation in Ancient Israel.* 0xford: The Clarendon Press, 1985.

George, Joseph (ed)., *God of all Grace; Essays in honour of Origen Vasantha Jathanna.* Bangalore: ATC/UTC, 2005.

Gerstenberger, Gerhard., *Theologies in the Old Testament.* Minneapolis: Fortress Press, 2002.

Gese, Hartmut., "Tradition and Biblical Theology," in Douglas A. Knight (ed), *Tradition and Theology in the Old Testament.* Philadelphia: Fortress Press 1977, pp. 301-326.

Goldingay, John., *Old Testament Theology: Israel's Gospel/ Faith,* 3 Vols. Downers Grove, IL: InterVarsity Press, 2003-2009.

Gottwald, Norman K., *The Hebrew Bible: A Socio-literary Introduction.* Philadelphia: Fortress Press, 1985.

Habel, Norman C., *The Land is Mine: Six Biblical Land Ideologies.* Minneapolis: Fortress Press, 1995.

Hanson, Paul D., *The Dawn of the Apocalyptic.* Philadelphia: Fortress Press, 1975.

___________., "War and Peace in the Hebrew Bible," *Interpretation* 38:4 (1984), pp. 342-362.

Harrison, M. H., "The Place of Old Testament Studies in Indian Theological Education," *Indian Journal of Theology* 5:1 (1956), pp. 1-8.

Hasel, Gerhard F., *Old Testament Theology: Basic Issues in the Current Debate.* Grand Rapids: Wm. B. Eerdmans, 1991. Fourth Edition.

Hayes, John H., and Fredrick C. Prussner., *Old Testament Theology: Its History and Development.* Atlanta: John Knox Press, 1985.

Høgenhaven, Jesper., *Problems and Prospects of Old Testament Theology.* Sheffield: Sheffield Academic Press, 1992.

Henry, Sarojini., *Science Meets Faith: An Interdisciplinary Conversation.* Mumbai: St. Paul's Publication, 2009.

Hyers, Conrad., *The Meaning of Creation: Genesis and Modern Science.* Atlanta: John Knox Press, 1984.

Jacob, Edmond., *Theology of the OT.* London: Hodder and Stoughton, 1958.

Jesurathnam, K., "Towards a Dalit Liberative Hermeneutics: Rereading the Psalms of Lament," *Bangalore Theological Forum* 34:1 (2002), pp. 1-34.

___________., "Is there not a prophet of the LORD among you?: Micaiah ben Imlah, Ahab and Jehoshaphat," in Israel Selvanayagam (ed), *Light on Our Dusty Path: Essays for a Bible Lover.* Bangalore: BTESSC/SATHRI, 2008, pp. 156-166.

Jesurathnam, Kondasingu, Abraham Saggu and Hrangthan Chhungi (eds), *Liberation Hermeneutics in the Indian Interpretation of the Bible.* Bangalore/ Thiruvalla: SBSI/Christava Sahitya Samithi, 2012.

Jesurathnam, Kondasingu., *Dalit Liberative Hermeneutics: Indian Christian Dalit Interpretation of Psalm 22.* Delhi: ISPCK, 2010.

Kaiser, Walter C., *Toward an Old Testament Theology.* Grand Rapids: Zondervan Publishing House, 1978.

Kalluveettil, Paul., "The Marginalizing Dialectics of the Bible," *Bible Bhashyam* 11:4 (1985), pp. 201-214.

Knierim, Rolf. P., *The Task of Old Testament Theology: Substance, Method, and Cases.* Grand Rapids: Wm. B. Eerdmans, 1995.

Knight, G. A. F., *A Christian Theology of the Old Testament.* London: SCM Press, 1959.

Koch, Klaus., *The Prophets. Vol. 1. The Assyrian Period.* Philadelphia: Fortress Press, 1983.

Köhler, Ludwig., *Old Testament Theology,* trans. A. R. Todd Philadelphia: The Westminster Press, 1957.

Legaspi, Michael C., *The Death of Scripture and the Rise of Biblical Studies.* Oxford: Oxford University Press, 2010.

Lind, M. C., *Yahweh is a Warrior.* Scottsdale: Herald Press, 1980.

Livingstone, David N., *Darwin's Forgotten Defenders: The Encounter Between Evangelical Theology and Evolutionary Thought.* Grand Rapids: Wm. B. Eerdmans, 1953.

Madanu, Francis., *Understanding of the Poor in Job: In the Context of Biblical Wisdom Literature.* Hyderabad: St. John's Regional Seminary, 1997.

Malchow, Bruce V., *Social Justice in the Hebrew Bible.* Collegeville: The Liturgical Press, 1996.

Mariaselvam, A., "Biblical Interpretation for India Today," *Bible Bhashyam* 28:3 (2002), pp. 505-520.

Melanchthon, Monica Jyotsna., "Research, Methodologies, the Bible and the Marginal Communities in India," in Joseph Prabhakar Dayam and P. Mohan Larbeer (eds), *Margins in Conversations: Methodological Discourses in Theological Disciplines.* Bangalore: BTESSC, 2012, pp. 1-16.

Miller, Patrick, D., *The Way of the Lord: Essays in Old Testament Theology.* Grand Rapids: Wm Eerdmans, 2004.

Mowinckel, Sigmund., *He that Cometh: The Messiah Concept in the Old Testament and Later Judaism,* trans. G. W. Anderson Grand Rapids: Wm. B. Eerdmans, 2005.

Muthunayagom, Daniel Jones., "Contemporary Approaches to Old Testament Interpretation," in Indukuri John Mohan Razu (ed), *Interweaving*

Methodology and Praxis-Exploring Disciplinary Options in Today's World. Bangalore: BTESSC/SATHRI, 2007, pp. 172-173.

___________ (ed)., *Bible Speaks Today: Essays in honour of Gnana Robinson.* Bangalore/Delhi: UTC/ISPCK, 2000.

Muthuraj, Joseph G., "Rereading NT in the India: Some Hermeneutical Explorations," *Asia Journal of Theology* 13:1 (1999), pp. 14-30.

Narasaiah, G. Lakshṃi., *The Essence of Dalit Poetry: A Socio-Philosophic Study of Telugu Dalit Poetry.* Hyderabad: Dalit Sana Publications, 1999.

Ollenburger, Ben C., *The Flowering of Old Testament Theology.* Indiana: Eisenbrauns, 1992.

Overmann, Richard H., *Evolution and Christian Doctrine of Creation.* Philadelphia: Westminster Press, 1952.

Prasad, Suraj Nandan., *Ambedkar and Indian Code of Laws.* Jaipur: ABD Publishers, 2010.

Premnath, D. N., "Recent Developments in Biblical Studies," *Bangalore Theological Forum* 20:3 (1988), pp. 1-7.

Rao, Naveen., *The Formulation of Scripture: Liberative Hebrew Paradigm for Dalit Scripture.* Delhi: ISPCK, 2010.

Rendtorff, Rolf., Canon *and Theology.* Minneapolis: Fortress Press, 1993.

Reventlow, Henning Graf., *Problems of Old Testament Theology in the Twentieth Century.* Philadelphia: Fortress Press, 1985.

Rowley, H. H., *The Biblical Doctrine of Election.* London: Lutterworth Press, 1950.

Sampathkumar, P. A., "Current Trends in Indian Biblical Studies," *Bible Bhashyam* 25:1 (1999), pp. 64-77.

Smith, Ralph, L., *Old Testament Theology: Its Method and Message.* Nashville: Broadman & Holman Publishers, 1993.

Soraes-Prabhu, George., "Interpreting the Bible in India Today," *The Way, Supplement* 72 (1991), pp. 70-80.

Spener, Philipp Jacob., *Pia Desideria,* trans. Theodore G. Tappert. Philadelphia: Fortress Press, 1964.

Steck, Odil Hannes., *World and Environment.* Nashville: Abingdon, 1980.

Terrien, Samuel., *The Elusive presence: Toward a New Biblical Theology* San Francisco: Harper & Row, 1978.

Thottakara, Augustine (ed)., *Indian Interpretation of the Bible: Festschrift in honour of Prof. Dr. Joseph Pathrapankal.* Bangalore: Dharmaram Publications, 2000.

von Rad, Gerhard., *Old Testament Theology,* 2 Vols. trans. D. M. G. Stalker. London: SCM Press and Oliver & Boyd, 1962-1965.

___________., *Wisdom in Israel.* London: SCM Press, 1972.

Vriezen, Th. C., *An Outline of OT Theology.* Oxford: Basil Blackwell, 1970.

Watson, Francis., "Enlightenment," in R. J. Coggins and J. L. Houlden. eds. *Dictionary of Biblical Interpretation.* London: SCM Press, 1990, pp. 191-194.

Weinfeld, Moshe., *Social Justice in Ancient Israel and in the Ancient Near East.* Jerusalem: The Magnes Press, 1995.

Westermann, Claus., *Elements of Old Testament Theology.* Atlanta: John Knox Press, 1978.

____________., *Roots of Wisdom: The Oldest Proverbs of Israel and Other Peoples,* trans. J. Daryl Charles. Louisville: Westminster John Knox Press, 1995.

Wilson, Robert R., *Prophecy and Society in Ancient Israel.* Philadelphia: Fortress Press, 1988.

Yang, Seung Al., "Hope," in *The New Interpreter's Dictionary of the Bible,* Vol. 2. D-H. ed. Katherine Doob Sakenfeld, et al. Nashville: Abingdon Press, 2007, pp. 885-887.

Zimmerli, Walther., *Old Testament Theology in Outline.* Atlanta: John Knox Press, 1978.

Index of Authors